SO OBSTINATELY LOYAL

James Moody, in the dress uniform of an officer in the Loyalist provincial regiment, the New Jersey Volunteers. Oil on canvas, London, circa 1784, artist unknown. Courtesy of John Wentworth Moody, Ottawa

Obstinately Loyal

So

Loyal

James Moody
1744-1809

Susan Burgess Shenstone

PUBLISHED FOR CARLETON UNIVERSITY
BY McGILL-QUEEN'S UNIVERSITY PRESS,
MONTREAL & KINGSTON, LONDON, ITHACA

Printed and bound in Canada

Canadian Cataloguing-in-Publication Data

Shenstone, Susan Burgess, 1927-
    So obstinately loyal : James Moody, 1744-1809

Includes bibliographical references and index.
ISBN 0-88629-355-3

    1. Moody, James, 1744-1809. 2. United Empire loyalists—
Nova Scotia—Biography. 3. American loyalists—New Jersey—
Biography. 4. United States—History—Revolution, 1775-1783ˉ
Biography. I. Title.

FC2321.41.M66 54 1999   971.6 02 092   C99-901441-2
E278.M8 54 1999

Cover: BCumming Designs
Interior: Mayhew & Associates Graphic Communications, Richmond, Ont.
in association with Marie Tappin

McGill-Queen's University Press acknowledges the financial support of the
Government of Canada through the Book Publishing Industry Development
Program (BPIDP) for our publishing activities. We also acknowledge the support
of the Canada Council for the Arts for our publishing program.

To Michael

CONTENTS

ILLUSTRATIONS

MAPS

PREFACE

THIS IS THE STORY OF JAMES MOODY, an American Loyalist hero from New Jersey who later settled, and became a prominent figure, in Nova Scotia. Famous in his own day, he deserves new recognition today. His life gives us a picture of the Loyalist experience, from the turbulent times of the American Revolution through to the subsequent refashioning of a British colony to the north.

James Moody was a New Jersey farmer who believed that rebellion was constitutional anarchy. He enlisted in a Loyalist provincial corps and was sent out on special, often dangerous, missions behind the Patriot lines. Suffering from what would later be called battle fatigue, he went to England in 1782, just as the war was ending. There he wrote and published his *Narrative of his Exertions and Sufferings in the Cause of Government since the Year 1776*, a compelling story that explained the convictions that had made him a Loyalist and chronicled his exploits during the Revolution. Settling in Nova Scotia after the war, he threw his energies into the new community, building ships, working toward the establishment of an Anglican parish, representing his county in the House of Assembly, enlisting again in the wars with France, and more.

He was one of nearly sixty thousand Loyalist refugees from the American Revolutionary War who settled in what is now Canada. As Americans, they knew the land and understood its challenges. They brought with them their political and civil institutions and worked to remake a society that furthered the ideals for which they had been fighting: a better society, they hoped, than the one they had left, a society where there would be no need to rebel.

The story of James Moody gives us a glimpse of the American Revolution from the other side. Through his *Narrative*, we gain an insight into the issues that made this colonial war a civil war. Finally, James Moody's experience in Nova Scotia provides a personal account of the vision this second, transplanted, American society had of themselves and their attempts to make that vision a reality. Men like Moody brought to the province new money and skills, a spirit of entrepreneurship, but also a sense of public service and political responsibility that helped the province to grow and prosper on a sound institutional base. Their legacy remains important to Canada today.

*

Gathering material for the story of an American Loyalist presents special problems. There is, to begin with, the scholarly border of 1783. What happened before the close of the revolutionary war is considered American history; what happened after, for the Loyalists, is Canadian history. One reads in American county histories that So-and-So after the war "removed" to Nova Scotia only to die "ignominiously," and often obscurely. In the Canadian account, one learns that So-and-So came from New York — the point of evacuation, though he may have really been a native of New Jersey or Pennsylvania or wherever — lived a worthy life in his new land, and died regretted by all who knew him. One hardly recognizes the same human being. The two sides of one life have become separated, and must be uncovered in quite different locations.

The second difficulty is that much of the Loyalist material is held in bits and pieces in scattered and little-known collections. The fact that the Loyalists were refugees, dislocated, and forced to abandon most of their effects, including personal papers, makes the task of reconstructing their lives both more arduous and more fun. It is not simply an issue of finding needles in a haystack: one must first discover which haystacks, in which fields, contain the needles.

The starting point of this biography was James Moody's *Narrative*. My chance discovery of a rich collection of Moody family papers in the possession of a direct descendant of James Moody in Ottawa, where I live, gave me copious additional primary material.

For the American section of James Moody's life, the sources are both English and American. The Loyalist claims are the greatest single repository of material for Loyalist studies; the originals are held in the Public Record Office in England with microfilm copies in the National Archives of Canada and in a few major American libraries. In addition, the papers of British commanders in chief contain valuable information. So also do the letters of Anglican clergymen reporting back to the Society for the Propagation of the Gospel. There is, of course, contemporary material in the form of diaries, letters, petitions, court records, newspaper accounts, and so forth. Local nineteenth century county histories provide some clues, though these are not always reliable. There is also much to be found on Loyalists in the papers of Patriots, material that is often omitted, perhaps for lack of interest, when these papers are published under the direction of American scholars, so that it is often necessary to go back to the original manuscripts. This was so even for the Washington papers.

For the Nova Scotia end of the story, the material is scattered between England and our eastern seaboard. Shipping registries, vestry records, journals of the House of Assembly, letter books, the long confidential correspondence between the governor and the undersecretary of state in England are just some of the sources. Unfortunately, the Nova Scotia letters in the Moody papers are, with one minor exception, all to James, so that what he wrote to his correspondents has had to be extrapolated from their replies. Some of the Nova Scotia material has been drawn on for two articles in the *Nova Scotia Historical Review*, cited in the bibliography.

All this is to say that there are a great many people without whose kindness and generosity of time and thought, this book would never have been written. I would first like to thank John Wentworth Moody of Ottawa, who allowed me free access to his collection of James Moody papers and who, with his late wife, Betty, welcomed me into their house several afternoons each week over several years while I studied documents and talked about James Moody. Professor Willard Randall, historian and biographer of William Franklin, Benedict Arnold, Thomas Jefferson, and George Washington, generously guided my reading in the Loyalist literature, indicated where I might find original material, added vital rare books to my collection, and continued to be a stimulating scholar with whom I could discuss the project. I must also thank Mrs. Pauline Miller, of Tom's River, New Jersey, Director of the Ocean County Cultural and Heritage Commission, historian and author, who accepted me into her house and drove me around the New Jersey shore. She also found extensive information about the Little Egg Harbour region, including maps and sources, and arranged for photographs of rare portraits and prints. Brian Cuthbertson, historian, archivist, and heritage officer, gave me invaluable help in sharing and locating material on the Nova Scotia part of the book and in providing useful criticism. Charles Armour, archivist and author, lent me his own tapes and other shipping information from the British Trade Office, essential to discovering the full extent of James Moody's shipbuilding. Professors Carl E. Prince and Mary Lou Lustig, editors of *The Papers of William Livingston*, allowed me a preview of volumes 3 and 4; this gave me valuable material about Moody and Livingston, some of which for reasons of space was eliminated from the published volumes. David Fowler of the David Library of the American Revolution, helped me find obscure but significant documents.

I must also mention the kindness of William Mead Stapler, businessman and local historian, for help, and his wife, Mary, for hospitality, in Sussex County; Thomas Wilson, historical researcher and publisher, for rare New Jersey material; Brereton Greenhous, military historian, for Loyalist military material; Ambassador Joseph Small of Ireland for documentary publications; James Burant for prints from the National Print Collection of the National Archives of Canada; Bernard Pothier, historian, formerly of the Canadian War Museum, for material concerning Father Sigogne; Mrs. Francis E. MacNeill for access to Weymouth vestry records; Margaret McKelvey for advice on publishing; H. Basil Robinson for wise counsel; Helen Small for the use of her copying machine; Professor Antonio Gualtieri for continued support; and the late Theodore Brush, whom I never met but whose articles on James Moody led me to John Wentworth Moody in Ottawa, which in turn made this biography possible.

I would also like to thank for their unfailing help, the staffs of the National Archives of Canada, the National Library of Canada, the libraries of the University of Ottawa, Carleton University, and the Canadian War Museum, and the Library of Parliament, Ottawa; the Robarts Library and the Thomas Fisher Rare Books Library at the University of Toronto, and the Metropolitan Toronto Reference Library; the Public Archives of Nova Scotia, the Killam Library of Dalhousie University, and the Legislative Library of the House of Assembly, Halifax; the Land Registry Office, and St. Peter's Anglican Church, Weymouth; the library at Fort Anne and the Court Records Office for Annapolis County in Annapolis Royal, Nova Scotia; the New Brunswick Archives, Saint John; the Library of Congress and the National Archives, Washington, DC; the State Archives of New Jersey, Trenton; the New Jersey Historical Society, Newark; the library of Princeton University; the Sussex County Public Library, the Sussex County Court Records Office, and the Sussex County Historical Society, in Newton, New Jersey; the David Library of the Revolution, Washington's Crossing, Pennsylvania; the New York Historical Society and the New York Public Library, in New York City; the William L. Clements Library, University of Michigan at Ann Arbor; the Public Record Office at Kew; the Guildhall Library, London; and the Royal Archives at Windsor Castle.

I must also thank Doctor Naomi Griffiths of Carleton University, for her unwavering critical support of this book in manuscript; Professor Barry Moody of Acadia University, for his patient and tactful historical editing; David Raymond, for his elegant adaptation of the two Moody maps and the discovery of the unpublished 1816 John Harris map; Rosemary Shipton and Mary McDougall Maude for their early invaluable advice; Jennie Strickland, the cheery and devoted production manager of Carleton University Press, as well as Heather Sherratt, my copyeditor, and all those who so kindly saw this manuscript through its final stages.

Finally, I would like to thank my family: my cousins Felicity Leung and Edward and Jean Harrington, my children, and my patient, supportive, and untiringly helpful husband, Michael.

NEW JERSEY (1744-82)

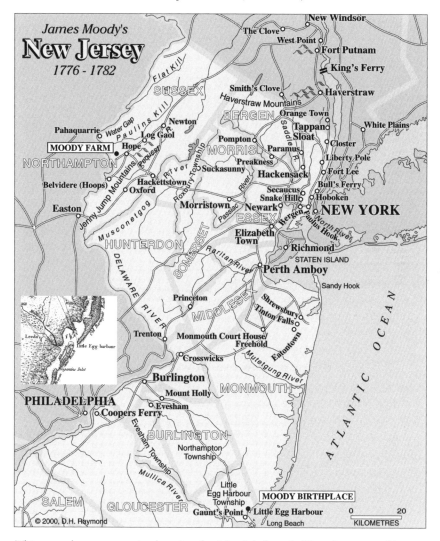

This map shows a tentative location for Moody's farm in Knowlton township, Sussex County, NJ. The exact location has never been determined.
Cartography by David Raymond

I

THE EARLY YEARS

ON SUNDAY, MARCH 28, 1777, on a country road in a remote corner of northwest New Jersey, the peace of the Sabbath was suddenly broken. Patriot militia men were marching up to the house of a suspected Tory. The owner had not sworn allegiance to the new American revolutionary government. He must comply. The soldiers looked up beyond the house and glimpsing a tall man walking with a companion, recognized the "traitor" they were seeking. Three shots rang out, but the villain had already vanished into the dark forest behind.

The man they had come to seize was James Moody. For some months he had been harassed and threatened. But now he knew that there could be no more compromises. He must leave his family, his farm, his land, and flee to the shelter of the British lines. Only from there could he fight to maintain legitimate government, the only kind of government that in his eyes could defend freedom in his country. A few weeks later he had gone, taking 73 of his neighbours with him.

This incident is recounted in *Lieut. James Moody's Narrative of his Exertions and Sufferings in the Cause of Government since the Year 1776*, a slim volume first published in London in 1782.[1] A second edition appeared a few months later. Told with laconic self-deprecation, it was a narrative of bold events lived through the American Revolution, the freeing of Loyalist prisoners, the capturing of rebel mails, the outsmarting of the enemy, repeated near-brushes with death. It also presented the ugly side of guerilla warfare, imprisonment, the heartache of losing a brother to the Revolutionary gallows, a father demented from grief. In the book, the author explained the thinking that had made him a Loyalist and showed the British public the sacrifices he and tens of thousands of other Loyalist Americans had made fighting for the British cause, not for the government, but for the rights and freedoms they believed it represented.

James Moody's little book appeared just at the time that the articles of peace between Great Britain and the new American nation were being debated in the British Parliament, when English public opinion was sympathetic to the rebels and rather contemptuous of the Loyalists. It helped to turn the British government from indifference to the fate of these nearly eighty thousand dispossessed persons, to accepting responsibility for their plight and awarding them one of the most generous compensations of modern times. The generosity was not unlike that eventually accorded by the Canadian government to the veterans of the Second World War, moved by the testimony of paraplegics and other young disabled soldiers just after the peace. The help given to Loyalists like James Moody enabled them to rebuild their lives and, in the process, develop what remained of British North America. James Moody went to Nova Scotia. There, many years after the Revolutionary War had ended, people were still reading his book.[2]

Who was this James Moody? Where did he come from? Why was he so at odds with the new American authority when he could have, with honour, remained in peace and comfort on his land? What happened to him during his struggle? What happened to him in defeat? How did he rebuild his life in Nova Scotia? Why did so many believe and suffer as he did, in a cause that 200 years later seems to have been doomed from the start? His story gives some of the answers to these questions.

When his world crashed around him in 1777, James Moody was 32, married with a young family, and established on five hundred acres of newly settled land.[3] Exceptionally tall for the period — six feet two inches in his stocking feet — and heavily built, he was an impressive figure. His portrait painted some eight years later shows a man of strong features, clean shaven, with a large English nose, a wide mouth, and a solid jaw. Under thick black eyebrows, his pale green gaze reflects an almost truculent intelligence. He is more aware than you think but not very convinced by your argument. One senses in this person a physical energy not to be confined to the drawingroom or the park, that marks him as an American, rather than an English, gentleman.[4]

There was nothing in his background to indicate that James Moody would become what the Revolutionaries would regard as one of the more notorious Loyalists. He was born in Little Egg Harbour, a small village on the southeast coast of New Jersey on January 1, 1744. His ancestors, like those of Washington and many other leaders on both sides of the war, were lesser English gentry. They were probably from Bury St. Edmunds, Suffolk, where Moodys had been living since before the days of Henry VIII. The crest that James passed down to his family was granted to Edmond Mody in 1524, for having saved King Henry VIII from drowning.[5] The incident is portrayed on the Moody coat of arms: two vested arms coming together to clasp the red Tudor rose, and below, other heraldic emblems and colours denoting the loyalty and devotion of a faithful public servant to his government and his sovereign. The motto that accompanies it is "Per Varios Casus," or freely translated, "Through Thick and Thin." It is a motto that would suit the American James Moody.

James tells us that his father, John, had been a soldier,[6] and had loved and honoured the profession, but we do not know where he served. Records indicate that he came from England to Little Egg Harbour shortly before James's birth in 1744 with two other families, the Holdens and the Mulliners. After her first husband's death, Mrs. Holden, who already had a daughter Mary, married the now-widowed John Moody and added Rebecca and John to their joint family. There was also a fourth child, Lydia. The Mulliners too remained linked to the Moodys; John Mulliner's sons, Joseph and Moses, grew up to settle in Little Egg Harbour, with Moses marrying Mary Holden and Joseph leading a band of Loyalists during the Revolution.[7]

Little Egg Harbour lies a third of the way up the New Jersey coast, some 20 miles north of present-day Atlantic City. The name referred to the town, now called Tuckerton, and the bay to the north of the mouth of the present Mullica River, the original Little Egg Harbour River. The bay is protected from the fierce Atlantic gales by a series of sand and sedge islands that shift and vanish and reappear under the relentless pounding of the ocean. As a result, the nature of the coast line has drastically changed since the eighteenth century. When James Moody's parents settled there, a small entrance through Little Egg Harbour inlet, through what is now the southern tip of Long Beach and north of present Little Egg Harbour Inlet, permitted vessels to duck into safety from the Atlantic storms and from irate customs officials, and to hide up the river. Though the wide bay provided a secure and spacious harbour, the sailor had to be familiar with shoals and currents around the entrance to get in without mishap.

Today's dense development of holiday resorts and commuter communities makes it hard to imagine the wildness of this land and the abundance that nature provided in the early days of settlement. Along its inner shores, its estuaries and bays and numerous creeks and even up its larger rivers, grew tall, thick salt-marsh grass which gave shelter to vast flocks of water birds — swans, ducks, cranes, gulls, geese, and many others that have since disappeared from the area. The nature reserves there give some of the flavour of the early days, and locals still predict the first snow by the arrival of the Canada geese. Many of the first settlers, coming from England and France, already knew the value of these marsh meadows to fatten their cattle. They reported that the fish were so plentiful that they could almost be caught by hand. Sturgeon and shad migrating up the rivers, and oysters to be dredged at the river mouths, were among the culinary and mercantile delights. Outside the dunes, whales and larger ocean fish swam in huge schools, ready to be plundered.

On the higher sandy ground behind the settlement were endless tangled forests of untouched oak and pine, and great stretches of cedar swamps, red from the iron that the water leeched out from the soil. On harder ground, this iron had formed into collectible nuggets that would form the basis of a bog-iron manufacture, an industry that James would also tinker with in Nova Scotia. With only a little hyperbole, early settlers recalled that the trees, often 160 feet tall, were so intertwined at their tops that a man could travel for three days without seeing the sun. They told of still-standing cedar trunks carted away for house frames, and the pine knots that covered the ground long after the trees themselves had rotted, gathered to use on the fire to give quick light in the long winter evenings. Under the giant oaks there were acorns to feast the farmers' pigs. Here also lived the beasts that must have terrified every early settler — panthers and wolves — and those that would bring him riches — otter, muskrat, and above all beaver. The beaver were so numerous that they not only built dams — the original settler in Tuckerton used a beaver dam to run his grist mill — but also constructed channels through the sedge to make their own travel easier. Land birds to shoot were also plentiful, such as partridge, wild turkeys, and passenger pigeons, the latter so thick in their flight that they darkened the air and so numerous when they settled that they broke the trees they alighted on. Some of the song birds, such as the jewel-like hummingbirds, were totally unfamiliar to Europeans.

Contemporary accounts also dwell on the snakes, beautiful but often treacherous: the wampum snake, black and white like Aboriginal shell money; the graceful black snake that harmed no one; the venomous horned snake, often nine feet long, that when disturbed hissed like a goose; and the rattlesnake that terrified its prey into a hysterical paralysis before striking.

In the forests inland lived the Lenni-Lenape, themselves a part of the wilderness. They belonged to the Delaware family of the Algonquins; their descendants today live in Ohio. Although they had sold their coastal lands to Quaker settlers in the seventeenth century, they were never far away, and when James Moody's family lived there in the 1740s there was still space enough in the interior of the pine forests for these indigenous people.

Not only James's parents from England but many settlers from Pennsylvania and other settled regions of the colonies gravitated toward the area of Little Egg Harbour. The region offered attractions besides a good harbour and inexpensive coastal land. Quakers from New England and Long Island, seeking greater religious freedom, had already established farms, grist mills, schools, and meeting houses. They had built corduroy roads over the old Aboriginal trails that led through the forest to Philadelphia, crossing the swamps with causeways and the fords with bridges, so that the long sea voyage around Cape May was no longer necessary. The new road allowed wagons to carry grain, and the famous local hams, and no doubt oysters to Philadelphia, and even to bring back in these same wagons holiday makers to the beach, as well as more serious Quakers to their monthly meeting. Indeed, shortly after James was born, a local resident, Reuben Tucker (the Tucker of Tuckerton), built a house on Long Beach which became a celebrated "watering place," perhaps the first resort on the Jersey shore. Here young Quakers and others from New Jersey held parties on the beach and danced throughout the summer evenings, to the consternation of their elders.

By the time James's father had established his family in Little Egg Harbour, the early settlers had done the most arduous part of the clearing. People spoke of Little Egg Harbour as "quiet," and its people as decent folk, in contrast to the rascals and scoundrels who inhabited New York. Although the Moodys, Mulliners, and Holdens were Anglican, and some of the new settlers became Methodists, occasionally treated to a service by one of their own itinerant preachers, the Quakers predominated and continued to set the tone for the area.

While James was growing up in Little Egg Harbour, the area was booming. Many local industries had been added to farming. The forest and the sea now provided much of the wealth. Timber, and barrel staves, and fish were the chief exports, usually to New York but sometimes to the West Indies. There was shipbuilding — the beginning of the prosperous shipbuilding of the nineteenth century — at first small boats for coastal fishing and whaling, but soon larger vessels for the Caribbean trade. Money was also made in the transshipment of smuggled goods, offloaded in the secluded harbours.

James's father was a merchant, which meant that he imported goods, such as textiles and luxury items, and sold them locally. He would also have negotiated the sale of local exports with his counterparts in Philadelphia and New York, making a handsome profit as middleman. James, who probably attended the local Quaker school, formed lasting friendships with his Quaker neighbours that would help him in later years. Perhaps he also absorbed their tolerance and sense of sharing. Like any American boy living so close to the forest, he learnt how to survive in the wilderness. At school and at home he studied the Bible. At his father's side he must have learnt accounting and the business practices of the day, and from the tone of his writing, a certain scepticism necessary for dealing with the world. By the mid-1760s he was ready to leave home.

In the eighteenth century, for western New Jersey the great highway into the interior was the Delaware River. Although Little Egg Harbour was on the Atlantic Ocean, its road connection with Philadelphia placed it as part of the Delaware system so that when James's time came to strike out on his own it was natural that he should choose that route. Knowlton Township in newly formed Sussex County was at the northwest corner of the province just before the river passes through the Shawungunk Mountains and makes its great bend northeastward at the Water Gap. It is about 70 miles from New York and twice that distance as the crow flies, from Little Egg Harbour.

Although the records are sparse, it is likely that James came here in 1766, close to ten years before the beginning of his *Narrative*. With the end of the French and Indian War — the war that developed into the Seven Years War for Canadians and Europeans — the conditions were right for settlement in that part of the colony. The large proprietary land holdings were at last being broken up, allowing more modest folk to own land, and the Native People had moved further north and west, making it safe for a farmer to be alone in his fields. James was part of the new American-born generation coming from the more settled parts of New Jersey and the northern colonies, to take up land of their own. Besides Anglicans, there were Moravians and Quakers from Pennsylvania as well as New Jersey, Congregationalists from New England, Presbyterians and members of the Dutch Reformed Church from New York. Their ethnic origins were as varied as their religious denominations — German, English, Irish, Scottish, French, Dutch, and Swedish — combining to make them all, in a generation, Americans.

James's first wife, Elizabeth Brittain, was descended from one of these long-established American yeoman families. On the side of her father, William Brittain, they had been English Dissenters, originally Huguenots, but members of the Dutch Reformed Church when they landed on Staten Island in the seventeenth century. William's branch had moved to Long Island, becoming in the process Presbyterian though still "in harmony" with the Dutch church. He himself had married while underage and had taken up land in central New Jersey. Elizabeth's mother's family, the Collins, had followed a similar pattern in New Jersey, each generation seeking out cheap new sites. Elizabeth was the third of ten children.[8] Now the senior Brittains were living in Knowlton Township, with William surrounded by his younger sons. James's farm was part of this family complex.

Of Elizabeth herself, we know very little, except that she was cherished by her husband. As he is ending his *Narrative* he says that he would gladly forgo the highest military honours "to be once more re-instated in his own farm, with his wife and children around him, as he was seven years ago."[9] Three children were born to the couple: John, on 6 March 1768, a second child whose records have vanished, and Maria, on 28 February 1775, all in Sussex County. The relationship between James and his in-laws was a close one. His father-in-law was an outspoken Loyalist who was often fined and jailed throughout the Revolutionary years for his opinions, and three of his wife's brothers living in Knowlton when the Revolution broke out, served in his regiment during the war.[10] Two older ones joined the American militia in Pennsylvania, and a third did so in New Jersey.

Exactly where James's farm was located in Sussex County is still a mystery. We know that it was in the western part of old Knowlton Township, now a part of Delaware Township, Warren County. Coming from the New York border, the old highway winds down between the hills, through narrow valleys, to New Town (present-day Newton), the county seat and location of the county court house and county jail, to the Moravian settlement of Hope. Here it divides, crossing streams and creeks which would have been familiar to James, the northern branch reaching the Delaware River at today's Delaware Station, the southern at Belvidere, to continue on the other side of the river to York in Pennsylvania. James probably lived a little north of Delaware Station and not far from the Delaware River. A map made a hundred years later shows the same families that James knew in this area.[11] After 1777, many people here and along the length of this highway would shelter and protect him.

The five hundred acres that James farmed was a substantial holding of land, owned in his father's name but for his use. It was not the thousand acres of a very rich man, but neither was it the hundred and two-hundred-acre parcels that the general commonality farmed. It was a generous settlement from his father, probably at the time of his marriage.

Only a small portion of this would have been under cultivation; the rest would be valuable forest on the rocky slopes and untilled pasture in the lowlands. We know he was successfully raising sheep and cattle. Probably he had no more than 30 acres actually cleared. The usual crops for that part of New Jersey were buckwheat as a first crop, then rye, then wheat and flax, which produced not only linen for clothing and bedding, spun on the premises, but also linseed oil and tow (flax fibre) for export. James would certainly have grown oats, timothy, and red clover for his horses and livestock. On his five hundred acres, he had, according to a later claim, four horses, two yoke of working oxen, as well as 15 milch cows, 35 young cattle, and 20 head of sheep.[12]

Nicholas Cresswell, a young Englishman, the son of a land-owner and sheep farmer in Derbyshire, who came out to America to set himself up as a farmer in 1774, wrote about the handsome profits to be gained by agriculture in the years leading up to the Revolution: "I am well convinced that I could have lived much better and made more money, as a Farmer in this country, with five hundred pound, than I can in England, with two thousand. Agriculture is in such an infant state and the value of land so low that anyone with the least spark of industry might make what money they please." [13] To prove his point he drew up a schedule just before the outbreak of the Revolution, of what he could do with five hundred acres in Frederick County in Virginia. He calculated on a very conservative estimate, that he could make a profit of £1,947 Virginia currency or £485 sterling, on his initial investment of £2,434, Virginia currency, a profit of nearly 40 percent.

On the basis of Cresswell's figures and taking into account the fact that James held about one-third less in profitable livestock and slaves (Cresswell puts a figure of £20 each for five men servants and two women, listed between the sheep and the hogs, suggesting that they too were bought), it is reasonable to assume that James earned at least £300 sterling, that is £500 New Jersey currency. Moreover, James had not paid for his land. Cresswell would have needed a minimum of four years to recover his initial investment. In 1777, James had lived in Sussex County for at least nine years.

It is clear that James was a man of substance in Knowlton Township, able to support the fledgling Anglican parish that was being formed, a man others would look to for leadership. His income could be expected to ensure his children's financial future. We can believe him when he tells us in his *Narrative*, that "he was clear of debt and at ease in his possessions."[14]

In addition to the farm, the livestock, and the land, James also had a substantial house. There are many buildings of the period still standing along that road that can give us an idea of what it must have been like. Though not imposing from the outside, they are spacious and comfortable. Typically they are made of neatly dressed stone in front, and rougher stone on the sides and back. The roof is steeply pitched. A distinguishing feature is the two centre doors, one above the other, with a narrow gallery running across the front of the house at the level of the upper door and forming a portico for the lower one.

This device is a practical adaptation to the landscape. Nestled into the rising ground immediately behind them, the houses have two and a half stories like a modern split-level construction. The bottom floor, approached at ground level from the front, was occupied by the kitchen and cellar storage rooms. The first floor, approached at the front by steps that ascended to the gallery and at the back by a door that gave on to ground level, was for the family. With one large and three smaller rooms, this level was heated by two stone fireplaces set into the thick walls and embellished with painted pine panelling. The unfinished attic was where the male servants slept, and was heated by the chimneys from the fireplaces below. An inner circular corner staircase communicated from the cellar to the main floor and attic.

To catch the sun, James's house, like those that still exist, would have faced south, looking toward the low ridge of worn mountains, heavily wooded, that hems in the fertile intervale of farmland sloping toward the Delaware in James's part of Knowlton. One can imagine James, "walking in his grounds," to use his own expression, with his three young children toddling behind down to the duck pond which gave such a pretty aspect from the house. Such ponds, which can still be seen today, served to soak the flax and provide ice for summer storage and perhaps a little winter skating. There was usually an apple orchard, and other fruit trees such as cherry and quince, close to the house, and of course flowers and a vegetable garden which the lady of the house would supervise. The outbuildings would include a substantial barn and perhaps a separate summer kitchen. The fencing around the house would be to keep out the sheep and cattle which would roam free most of the year. .

To run such an establishment, servants were required. There must have been two for the house, probably black since James brought at least two slaves with him to Nova Scotia after the war, and probably another three men to help with the outdoor work. Although life in America was less hierarchical than in England, and master and servant worked together, nevertheless the touches of refinement in their speech and dress and possessions would have marked the Moodys as, if not aristocratic, at least cultivated gentry.

At the beginning of the American Revolution, James Moody was unaware of the tumultuous events that were about to unfold around him. He was even more unsuspecting of the part he himself would play in them. Like most people in agrarian New Jersey, he was, he tells us, "a plain, contented farmer, settled on a large, fertile, pleasant, and well-improved farm of his own, in the best climate and happiest country in the world ... a happy farmer, without a wish or an idea of any other enjoyment, than that of making happy, and being happy with, a beloved wife, and three promising children. He loved his neighbours, and hopes they were not wholly without regard for him." [15] On March 28, 1777, James Moody's idyll was shattered. For others it had happened earlier.

NOTES

1. James Moody, *Lieut. James Moody's Narrative of his Exertions and Sufferings in the Cause of Government since the Year 1776* (London: 1783; repr. New York Times and Arno Press, 1968), 6. Hereafter this volume will be referred to as the *Narrative*.

2. The most recent edition of the *Narrative* was a reprint of the second edition of 1783, by Arno Press in 1968. Among its earlier incarnations was its appearance in 1832 in an issue of *The Excitement*, a book series published in Edinburgh "to induce young people to read." Some

American high school students have read it as part of their American Revolution program.

3. Loyalist Claims, Public Record Office (PRO), Audit Office (AO), vol. 12, no. 99, National Archives of Canada (NAC), microfilm B-1177.

4. This portrait, which is mentioned in the will of the second Mrs. James Moody, was in the Moody family until it was donated to St. Peter's Church in Weymouth, Nova Scotia, from where it was stolen in 1981. Fortunately some excellent colour prints remain.

5. William Reed-Lewis, *Some Genealogical Notes Regarding the Moodys of County Suffolk, and America* (Bedford, NS: privately printed, 1899), 2-3. The story is recounted in Hall's Chronicles of England, the official year-book of its day: "The XVI. yere, the jeoperdy the kyng was in. In this yere the kyng folowing of his hauke lept ouer a diche beside Hychyn, with a polle and the polle brake, and so that if one Edmond Mody, a foteman, had not lept into the water, & lift up his hed, whiche was fast in the clay he had been drouned: but God of his goodnes preserved him."

6. *Narrative*, 51.

7. Leah Blackman, *History of Little Egg Harbour Township, Burlington County, N.J. from Its First Settlement to the Present Time* (Tuckerton, NJ: Great John Mathis Foundation, 1880; repr. 1963), 346. The information concerning James's family is incomplete. My reconstruction is based on the following bits and pieces. Leah Blackman states that the children of John Moody and the former Mrs. Holden were John and Rebecca Moody. She does not mention either James or Lydia. We know from documents that John and Lydia were brother and sister to James, and that John Moody senior, merchant, is the only Moody on the 1773-74 list of ratepayers for Little Egg Harbour. James may have been a son by a first marriage. Rebecca Moody married Thomas Willits, grandson of one of the original Quaker settlers. There is no Quaker record of their marriage, which suggests that it was outside the Quaker meeting. Lydia married William Rose in 1788 in St. Andrew's Anglican Church in Mount Holly, Northampton Township, Burlington County, where the family moved to after the Revolution. He may have been the William Rose, 3rd, that Leah Blackman cannot trace. The Roses of Little Egg Harbour were also Anglican. The Loyalist members of a family tend to be lost, or wiped out, in the nineteenth-century American county histories.

8. Information about the family of Elizabeth Brittain comes from the genealogy of a descendant of her Patriot brother, Samuel (1750 ca.-1792), Mrs. Helen O. Bowman of St. Louis, Missouri. At first this lady was scandalized that any member of her family could have been a Loyalist. In fact, three of the six brothers, and their father, refused to take the American oath of abjuration of the British sovereign. The

three older brothers supported the Patriots. Her information is corroborated by Elmer Garfield Van Name, *Britton Genealogy: Early Generations from Somersetshire, England to Staten Island, New York* (Gloucester County Historical Society Publications, Oct. 1970).

9. *Narrative*, 56.

10. The three younger Brittain brothers settled along the Saint John River in the part of Nova Scotia that quickly after the Revolutionary War became New Brunswick.

11. *County Atlas of Warren, New Jersey* (New York: F.W. Beers, 1874), maps of Hope and Knowlton Townships.

12. Loyalist Claims, PRO, AO, 13/110, p. 245.

13. Nicholas Cresswell, *The Journal of Nicholas Cresswell, 1774-1777* (London: Jonathan Cape, 1925), 195.

14. *Narrative*, 2.

15. *Ibid.*, 1, 2.

2

"THE BLACK CLOUD GATHERING"

TO UNDERSTAND THE CATACLYSM — what James called "the black cloud"— of events that erupted into the American Revolution, one must go back to the beginning of those ten years when James Moody was establishing himself. At the end of the Seven Years War, when the first Peace of Paris was signed in 1763, the British had defeated their arch-rivals, the French, and absorbed most of their empire around the world into their own. They were "a colossus," as Samuel Eliot Morison says, that "bestrode the world."[1] Wealth and happiness for all enterprising Americans seemed assured. However, not only are wars expensive to pay for afterwards, but in peace-time, complacent politicians, caught up in their own scramble for office, can readily lose touch with people outside their constituencies. Unfortunately, the period between 1763 and 1774 saw some of England's more stupid and more venal politicians ruling its empire, directed by an obdurate and bigoted king, and supported by the majority of the limited voting public of Great Britain. As often happens with people at distant headquarters, they lacked the curiosity and the humility to assess and understand the people they were dealing with. Barricading themselves behind what we would today call their political ideology, namely that the central government — their Parliament — was all-knowing, all-wise, and all-sovereign, they attempted to bludgeon a solution to their national debt. This struggle to impose the will of the British Parliament in matters that had previously been left to the colonial legislatures, provoked one of the saddest and perhaps most unnecessary civil wars in modern history. Ironically, it was to be fought by both sides for the "rights of Englishmen," supposedly guaranteed by the unwritten British constitution that had begun with Magna Carta and been reconfirmed less than a century earlier, with the accession to the British throne of Queen Mary and her husband, William III, William of Orange.

Barely one year after the Peace of Paris, while James was probably still living in Little Egg Harbour, the British Parliament initiated a policy to raise revenue in America to pay off the war debt. It reasoned that the American colonies had benefited from the victory and could help pay some of the expenses, ignoring, the Americans felt, their contribution in men and money to this imperial war. It first passed an American Revenue Act, later called the Sugar Act, whose purpose was to reinforce the Trade and Navigation Acts by imposing extra duties on non-British goods shipped directly, or through Great Britain, to the colonies. The act also banned the importing of foreign rum and French wines, a highly lucrative trade that directly affected the merchants on the American eastern seaboard. This was expected to return £45,000 annually. Other measures were enacted to tighten up enforcement of the act and to prohibit any issue of legal tender — that is the minting of coins or printing of money — in any of the colonies. The next year the Mutiny Act stipulated that the colonies were to provide for quartering and billeting British troops in inns, alehouses, and unoccupied dwellings. Adding further aggravation, the Stamp Act, to become effective November 1, 1765, and designed to raise another £60,000, required people in the American colonies to affix a stamp on almost every piece of paper that passed through their hands, from official documents to newspapers and magazines. These amounts represented about a third of the upkeep of the military establishment in America.[2]

The Stamp Act was the first direct tax ever levied by Parliament on the American colonies. No one likes to pay taxes, and the Americans saw themselves singled out to pay money — in their view, probably to corrupt British officials — that they had not voted. Apart from anything else, the Stamp Act was a terrible nuisance in a country where coins were in scarce supply. Already most business had to be done by barter or money drafts against what one hoped were reputable merchants in England. Many people had their houses and land foreclosed for lack of specie to pay the mortgage. Without a coin in one's pocket to pay the tax a person could not get his legal business done. Irritation at the Stamp Act served to focus public resentment on other grievances against the English government.

Reactions in New Jersey were similar to those elsewhere in America. Perhaps the best account of the state of affairs in the colony that summer of 1765 is given by the Attorney General and Speaker of the Provincial Assembly, Cortlandt Skinner, who would later be invited to join both sides in the Revolution but who would opt for the royal cause. In a letter to the ex-governor of New Jersey, Thomas Boone, he strongly criticized the new British policy toward America. He wrote that the Trade and Navigation Acts had ruined the merchants, and drained the colonies of their silver, leaving them with little, after paying the duties, to pay for the goods they imported from England. The reaction of people in the colonies to the passage of the Stamp Law and the Mutiny Bill was frightening. Here he was alluding to what had happened to officials in Massachusetts — including the governor, a descendant of one of the oldest families of Boston — who had been physically threatened and their houses ransacked by a rampaging and encouraged mob. Skinner feared for similar disturbances in New Jersey, and wondered in his letter, how long the local magistrates would be able to keep order.

As for the Mutiny Bill, which would allow for garrisoning troops throughout the colony, he believed it was "a pretence for taxing them."[3] Garrisons might be necessary at Quebec and Montreal, but what occasion could there be for garrisons and forts hundreds of miles in the "Indian country," let alone in American cities, he asked. He ends his letter with these perceptive comments:

Independence is suggested and made the pretence, more than a fear of Indian inroads. Those who make these suggestions are enemies to their country, and are most likely to put the thought into the heads of the colonists by the very means they take to *prevent* dependence. Separate governments and an encouragement to agriculture and settlement, will effectually fix it. Taxes and a restraint on the West India trade are most likely to force the colonists into manufactures and put independence into their heads. *They are in the high road to it now, and though 'tis true that they have not strength to effect it, but must submit, yet 'tis laying in the foundation for great trouble and expense to Britain, in keeping that by force which she might easily do without, and alienating a people which she might make her greatest prop and security.*[4]

Cortlandt Skinner was correct in his apprehensions. The intercolonial meeting which became known as the Stamp Act Congress stated the colonial grievances over the Stamp Act and gave impetus for a non-importation agreement against British goods. The boycott was so crippling that the merchants in England who did business in America brought pressure on Parliament to have the act repealed. But the colonies had tasted power and discovered an effective means of bringing Parliament to heel. For the British government, the issue had become one of sovereignty, a sort of divine right of Parliament. The Declaratory Act that accompanied the repeal of the Stamp Act specifically authorized Parliament to make laws binding on the colonies "in all cases whatsoever."[5]

During the next few years, the British Parliament would foolishly seek, through repressive measures, to exert its will upon the politically very sophisticated colonies. The Townshend Acts imposing import duties and giving notice that Parliament, rather than the colonial legislatures, would henceforth pay the salaries of colonial officials out of these duties,[6] the attempt to bail out the failing East India Company through the Tea Act's monopoly, the ensuing Boston Tea Party, punished by the closing of the port of Boston, the vindictive annulment of the charter of Massachusetts, the sending of more troops — all these served to fan the flames so that what might have been a grass fire became a conflagration. Meanwhile, in Boston and elsewhere "activists," as we would say today, took advantage of the situation for their own nationalistic and economic interests, and orchestrated violence to intimidate the opposition. Each side seemed to behave even more badly than the other, and moderate Jerseyites, who would later be on opposite sides of the quarrel, were genuinely alarmed at the possible destruction of private property should similar mobs get out of hand in their province. They were also appalled that the idea of independence was becoming thinkable. At the same time, in the face of British intransigence, the colonists, through committees of correspondence and, later, the continental congresses, were developing a network of organizations throughout the colonies to oppose the measures they disliked. Soon these bodies were strong enough to enforce a solidarity of action that would in the end defeat the mother country.

The Boston Port Bill became law on March 31, 1774, prohibiting, in almost all civilian cases, the loading or unloading of ships in any part of Boston Harbour until compensation had been made for the loss of the tea dumped into the harbour a few months before. People of good will were outraged throughout the colonies. During May and the ensuing summer months the colonies organized the First Continental

Congress to meet in Philadelphia to take common measures in a boycott of British goods.

The "whole continent," James tells us, was thrown into a ferment,
and almost every part of the country was "maddened" with "*Associations,
Committees, and Liberty-poles,* and all the preliminary apparature necessary to a *Revolt*."[7] In his own county of Sussex, the leading men of
the community got together on July 16, 1774, to choose delegates to
the first New Jersey Provincial Congress, which in turn would choose
a provincial delegation to the First Continental Congress in Philadelphia. These men drew up a set of resolves to be forwarded to that
body. They were fairly typical for all such groups across New Jersey.
They stated:

— That it is our duty to render true and faithful allegiance to George the
Third, King of Great Britain, and to support and maintain the just
dependence of his Colonies upon the Crown of Great Britain, under the
enjoyment of our Constitutional rights and privileges.

— That it is undoubtedly our right to be taxed only by our own consent,
given by ourselves or our Representatives; and that the late Acts of
Parliament for imposing taxes for the purpose of raising a revenue in
America, and the Act of Parliament for shutting up the port of Boston, are
oppressive, unconstitutional, and injurious in their principles to American
freedom, and that the Bostonians are considered by us as suffering in the
general cause of America.

— That it is the opinion of this meeting that firmness and unanimity in
the Colonies, and an agreement not to use any articles imported from
Great Britain or the East Indies (under such restrictions as may be agreed
upon by the General Congress hereafter to be appointed by the Colonies),
may be the most effectual means of averting the dangers that are justly
apprehended, and securing the invaded rights and privileges of America.

— That we will join, with greatest cheerfulness, the other counties of this
Province in sending a Committee to meet with those from other counties, at
such time and place as they shall appoint, in order to choose proper persons
to represent this Province in a General Congress of Deputies sent from each
of the Colonies.

— That we will faithfully and strictly adhere to such regulations and restrictions as shall be agreed upon by the members of said Congress, and that
shall by them be judged expedient and beneficial to the good of the Colonies.

— That the Committee hereafter named do correspond and consult with
the Committees of the other counties in this Province, and meet with them
in order to appoint Deputies to represent this Province in General Congress.[8]

The final resolution named their own committee, ten men, who were for the moment united in opposition to British policy, but who would soon be active in opposition to each other. The prime organizer was William Maxwell, a British army officer originally from Ireland who had fought with Wolfe at the capture of Quebec. A few months later, in May 1775, he would resign his British commission and join the revolution to become in the early part of the war one of Washington's most respected generals. In 1780, he would resign from the Patriot army when Congress passed him over for a promotion.

Another member of the committee was John Cleves Symmes, who drew up these resolutions. He, like Maxwell, was a Presbyterian; his family had emigrated to New England in 1634. He was two years older than James, and had settled in Sussex County a few years before James on several hundred acres of good land in the Flatbrook valley, in Waldeck township, not far from Knowlton. He was one of the judges of the County Courts before the Revolution and as such must have worked in Sussex County with Cortlandt Skinner in happier days. The Revolution would be kind to him. From serving on the county Committee of Safety he would assume command of the Third Sussex Militia Battalion, serve on the Legislative Council, be appointed associate justice of the Supreme Court of New Jersey, and marry as his third wife the younger daughter of New Jersey Governor William Livingston. He would be unrelenting in his pursuit of Tories.

But on that same committee were also men who had no intention of breaking with Great Britain. Among these was Nathaniel Pettit, strong supporter of the Anglican parish, local magistrate, and member of the provincial House of Assembly for Sussex County. Though too old to fight, he would actively support the Loyalists in the area throughout the war, at first openly, suffering imprisonment for his opposition to the rebels, and then secretly in the guise of a cowed neutral. He would leave New Jersey in 1784 to settle in what has now become Ontario. He and Maxwell were both chosen delegates to New Jersey's first Provincial Congress.

The First Continental Congress, which opened on September 5, 1774, brought the crisis between the American colonies and Great Britain to a head. It lasted for nearly two months and held its sessions in secret. Ostensibly convened to work out measures to force Great Britain to rescind its Coercive Acts against Massachussets, it gave the radical opposition a national forum and made the more extreme elements in Whig thinking respectable. Quick political manoeuvring killed moderate imaginative proposals for colonial reform, such as the plan of Joseph Galloway, James's later friend, for a federated union with Great Britain; this was even expunged from the minutes. However, in Great Britain feelings against the colonies had reached such a pitch that it is unlikely Parliament would have considered the proposal any more then than it did later when the plan was forwarded by New Jersey's royal governor, William Franklin. Meanwhile, people like Samuel Adams of Boston were able to push through the purely confrontational measure of a total boycott against Great Britain.

William Livingston, who would soon, as Patriot governor of New Jersey, be James's implacable foe in the ensuing struggle, but who was then only a New Jersey delegate to the Congress, was one of these anti-British Whigs. He later described the mood at the First Continental Congress:

Of these men, her Independence of Great Britain *at all Events*, was the most favourite Project. By these, the pulse of the rest was felt on every possible Occasion, and often upon no apparent occasion at all: and by these men, Measures were concerted to produce what we all professed to deprecate. Nay at the very time that we universally invoked the Majesty of heaven to witness the purity of our Intentions, I had reason to believe the hearts of many of us gave our Invocation the Lie.[9]

Publicly all were swearing loyalty but deep down, secretly or subconsciously, the activist delegates were already plotting independence.

Even more dangerous for the future was that the Congress was devising a system of committees to enforce that boycott, and, in the end, to suppress dissent from that action. The Congress took men who before had hardly known each other and knit them into an intellectual force that would bring about independence. It pushed out those who were for conciliation and it set up an extra-legal structure of government that would replace royal government.

In turn, the year 1775 was to see the attitude of the British Parliament harden, and actual fighting break out between the colonials and British troops at Lexington and Concord in April, and Bunker Hill in June. It would also see the Second Continental Congress assume the role of legal government, annulling all laws and commissions deriving their authority from the king or Parliament, and authorizing an army, including an invasion of Quebec, a navy, and a foreign policy. In New Jersey, Cortlandt Skinner described the year just a week before he was forced to take refuge with the British in New York:

I have always fondly, I may say foolishly, hoped that the unnatural dispute now subsisting would have an amicable conclusion. I find myself sadly disappointed.... They who began had their interest in view, and feared the ruin of their smuggling.... The others, with deeper views, keep it up, and building on the foundation, are attempting a superstructure (a republick) that will deluge this country in blood.... The Congress are our King, Lords, and Commons. They have taken Canada, with the consent of its grateful inhabitants; they block up the Royal army in Boston; they say they have secured the Indians; have appointed an Admiral; are fitting out a fleet, and are universally obeyed. Is this, or is it not independency?... I fear bad consequences will attend the mistaken people who are *so obstinately loyal* as to favour the Royal cause.[10] [Emphasis added]

A week or so later this letter was intercepted. Skinner fled to the British lines just before his Assembly colleague, William Alexander, Lord Stirling, sent a contingent of Continental troops to arrest him in the early hours of the morning at his house in Perth-Amboy.

With the flight of the attorney general on January 7, 1776, and the not very polite apprehension of Governor Franklin, also by order of William Alexander, also in the early hours of the morning, royal government in New Jersey had ceased to exist. The order to arrest and imprison the governor by the New Jersey Provincial Congress on June 16 and the public Declaration of Independence by the Second Continental Congress on July 4 merely made the rebellion official in that colony. The Province of New Jersey became the State of New Jersey and the Provincial Congress changed its name to the Convention of the State of New Jersey. It established what was now a typical oath of loyalty to itself — Quakers needed only affirm — that renounced all loyalty to the King of England, promised to obey the measures adopted by the Provincial or Continental Congresses, and pledged "true allegiance to the government established in this Province under the authority of the people."[11] Anyone holding any office must swear to this new oath, a measure which effectively barred all dissent from power. A law was passed defining high treason as bearing arms against the new government and giving aid and comfort to the British. This was to be punishable by death. Lesser forms of treason such as indulging in seditious speeches or practices, including refusing to take the new oath, would incur fines and imprisonment. In early August, a resolution for sequestering the estates of all persons who had left home to join the enemy was passed. The rebels had moved quickly to quash any opposition.

The attorney general who had feared for the "mistaken" people who would be "so obstinately loyal" to the royal cause, was soon to be their chief military leader, and James Moody one of his stars. The Revolution against arbitrary British rule had become as well a civil war among Americans. In the end, approximately five thousand men from New Jersey would take an active part, either as soldiers or fighters or leaders against the Revolutionary government. They would be supported by more than one-third of the population who would refuse to abjure their British allegiance. In addition, there would be many more Loyalist sympathizers who would never openly declare themselves.[12] Most would lose their land, their possessions, and many their lives. They would be the "mistaken" people who, for seven bitter years and even beyond, would remain "so obstinately loyal."

NOTES

1. Samuel Eliot Morison and Henry Steele Commager, *The Growth of the American Republic* (New York: Oxford University Press, 1942), vol. 1, 127.
2. Richard B. Morris, ed., "1765," *Encyclopedia of American History* (New York: Harper and Brothers, 1953), 73.
3. Cortlandt Skinner to Thomas Boone, 5 Oct. 1765, quoted in William A. Whitehead, *Contributions to the Early History of Perth Amboy and Adjoining Country* (New York: 1856), 103.
4. *Ibid.*
5. Theodore Draper, *A Struggle for Power: The American Revolution* (New York: Times Books/Random House, 1996), 283. Draper's book presents a persuasive thesis that before the Revolution, the struggle between the British government and the colonial assemblies was not about taxes as such, but about sovereignty.
6. *Ibid.*, 377-81.
7. *Narrative*, 5.
8. James P. Snell, *History of Sussex and Warren Counties, New Jersey, with Illustrations and Biographical Sketches of its Prominent Men and Pioneers* (Philadelphia: Everts & Peck, 1881; repr. Washington, NJ: Centennial Edn., Genealogical Researchers, 1981), 49.
9. William Livingston to John Fell, 14 Dec. 1780, Livingston Papers, Box 2, MHS, quoted in "The American Whig: William Livingston of New York," PhD thesis, Columbia University, 1958, 699.
10. Larry R. Gerlach, ed., *New Jersey in the American Revolution, 1763-1783: A Documentary History* (Trenton, NJ: New Jersey Historical Commission, 1975), 165-66.

11. *Minutes of the Provincial Congress and the Council of Safety of the State of New Jersey* (Trenton, NJ: Near, Day and Near, 1879), 560-61.

12. Larry R. Gerlach, *Prologue to Independence: New Jersey in the Coming of the American Revolution* (New Brunswick, NJ: Rutgers University Press, 1976), 354.

3

WHAT IS A TORY?

"*WHAT IS A TORY?*" went a favourite riddle of the day.
"A Tory is a thing whose head is in England, and its body in America,
and its neck ought to be stretched." [1] Presumably with the aid of a noose.

Those who remained loyal to the legal British government, who
were "friends of government" and later "refugees," were labelled by the
revolutionaries as "Tories," after earlier diehard supporters of the
authority of church and monarchy in Great Britain. It was a term of
opprobrium meant to suggest a toady to the Crown, someone willing
to forgo all his own rights in abject support of the king's right to rule
arbitrarily. Though good propaganda, in reality it did not fit most
Loyalists, especially American-born ones. These had also objected to
British colonial policy in America during the decade before 1776, and
while supporting the British government, continued to denounce its
members. On the other side, the revolutionaries, who called themselves Patriots, were labelled by the Loyalists, "rebels," a term denoting
the wickedness of betrayal. To each side, supporters of the other were
said to be "disaffected."

Politically the Patriots were radicals, Whigs, and often Presbyterians, and as the war progressed the British used the term "American."
The Loyalist Americans tended to be more conservative, often Anglican,
sceptical of radical movements, and fearful of the social upheaval such
movements would entail. They represented the American opposition
to the American movement of independence from Great Britain, and

in total (active and non-active) may have comprised only a little less than 30 percent of the population. The rebels probably constituted somewhat more than 30 percent. The uncommitted followed the winning side at any given moment. The American Loyalists were lumped in with the British and their regiments were called provincials by the British. They were, though, like James and his wife, as American as the rebels. Of course, all three sides spoke English, an English more similar on both sides of the Atlantic than now.

However, the distinction, before the Declaration of Independence, was never so clear-cut. Washington, without whose steadfastness, courage, and decency the Revolution would probably never have succeeded, was Anglican, conservative, and fearful of the chaos of mob rule. In 1775, on his way to assume command of the Continental army, he assured the tutor of his stepson, the Reverend Jonathan Boucher, that if Boucher ever heard of him joining in measures toward independency, Boucher had leave to set him down for everything wicked.[2] William Smith, the archetypal New York Presbyterian Whig, finished his life as chief justice of Quebec, a close associate of Sir Guy Carleton, Lord Dorchester, in his second round as governor of that British province. Benedict Arnold, who tried both sides, was in 1764 one of the original Sons of Liberty in Connecticut, and in 1775 — before independence — seized on his own initiative the forts on Lake Champlain for the Patriots. William Alexander, one of Washington's fiercest generals, styled himself Lord Stirling, and probably resented the British for denying the legitimacy of that title as much as for any political reason. Even Benjamin Franklin, as agent of the Massachussets Assembly in London, tried hard to find an accommodation between British parliamentarians and the radical colonials that would avoid the dreaded separation between America and Great Britain. His dismissal from the post of deputy postmaster general for North America by the British government and his deliberate and deep public humiliation at the hands of the British Privy Council in January 1774 turned him irrevocably, in the end, in favour of outright independence.[3] This treatment on the part of British officials partly explains the bitterness of his break with his son, William, and his old friend, Joseph Galloway, both of whom remained loyal to the end of their lives.

For many, what made a man declare himself a Loyalist or a Patriot at the onset of the war was often a matter of chance, a remark in public, a small act of defiance against a local injustice. The political position a man took in his community at the beginning of the American

Revolution began perhaps from temperament and the particular situation in which he found himself. It might depend on whether the people he admired and respected had opted for the rebel or the loyalist cause; whether his experience had encouraged him to fight authority, or whether he saw in legitimate authority the protection of his rights; whether he hated the British, as did so many Irish and Scotsmen, and had inherited from his ancestors, as James said, "the most rooted dislike and antipathy to the constitution of the parent-state,"[4] or whether he admired their administration of order as did many American-born settlers; whether he had old scores to settle, whether he had been bullied by the Tories or by the Whigs, whether he was strongly Presbyterian or strongly Anglican, and more ignobly, whether he saw an opportunity to gain by seizing power, or by maintaining it. All these were subconscious elements that could help to tip the balance. Sussex County, by almost two-thirds, chose to remain loyal.

Two events during the decade before the Revolution must certainly have influenced James, and others in Sussex County, toward the royal cause. The first, in December 1766, was the celebrated trial, in the County Courthouse at Newton, 22 miles from Knowlton, of Robert Seymore, a white man, for the murder and robbery of an Oneida, whose tribe had been part of the Iroquois alliance with the English during the French and Indian War.

Since the peace, several murders of Aboriginals along the frontier had gone unprosecuted. The white settlers were afraid that if this latest criminal were not brought to justice the Native People might launch a new war. The murder was a clear case of racism. The defendant was reported to have declared he would destroy "any Indian that came in his way."[5] The trial was considered sufficiently important to have Attorney General Cortlandt Skinner, also at the time Speaker of the Assembly, and a landowner in the county, prepare the bills of indictment and present the evidence. Governor William Franklin, the popular son of Benjamin Franklin, had offered the substantial sum of $100 for the apprehending of Seymore. Seymore was convicted and hanged. After the trial, Franklin was congratulated by the New Jersey House of Assembly on his vigorous handling of the proceedings and, more importantly, the Iroquois were so pleased with the conduct of the trial that they bestowed upon him the title of Arbiter of Justice. The trial brought these two senior men in the province, the attorney general and the governor, before the people of the county, where they could be judged on a serious local issue.

The other important event for James was the 1769 visit to the county by Thomas Bradbury Chandler, one of the most devoted and well-loved Anglican divines in New Jersey. At the time, he was based in Elizabeth Town and already defending the royal cause during this turbulent decade. Appalled at the state of religion, or rather irreligion, and the resultant "barbarism" in the area, Chandler met the principal Anglicans in the county in November 1769 and advised them on how to set up an Anglican parish.

But Chandler did more than just outline a procedure. He showed that the Anglican Church genuinely cared for people in the outlying districts. He immediately sent them a young man, of an eminent New Jersey family, Uzal Ogden, that he was training as an Anglican missionary, and shortly had him appointed as a catechist and lay reader for Sussex County. He also arranged to have books sent to these deprived people. Ogden reported that there were in the county at least a dozen different denominations among them, including, shockingly, a few Deists, but that people were very keen to have a minister and, poor though they were, even willing to pay for his services. He found himself not only sharing himself between Newton, Knowlton, and Hacket's Town in Sussex and Roxbury in Morris County, parts of northwest New Jersey that during the Revolution remained most loyal, but also reading prayers and sermons during the week in the houses of Dissenters. A third of his adherents lived in James's township, Knowlton. Here he preached once every four weeks and he quickly attracted so many people that in moderate weather the service was held outdoors in a field. Ogden was, in the terminology of the time, "enthusiastic"— strongly evangelical — in his preaching, which no doubt accounted for his wide success. However, the close affiliation between established royal government and the Anglican Church, for which he spoke so eloquently before the war, would also determine the allegiance of many men in Sussex when the struggle for independence began.

For James, putting down his roots in Knowlton just as this parish was being organized, the experience would stand him in good stead in helping to set up a similar parish two decades later in Nova Scotia. Just after the war, in England, fate would bring him into close contact with Chandler. James would also spend much of the Revolutionary war in association with Skinner and William Franklin.

In hindsight, the fundamental difference between the two opposing American sides in the Revolution was deeper than anyone could have guessed before the outbreak of actual fighting. The committed

Loyalist believed that American grievances could and should be redressed within the existing constitution, within existing governmental institutions, by negotiation between men of good will. The Patriot believed that the time had passed for negotiating, that the British were not men of good will, that only armed action would persuade the British to change their colonial policies. This soon turned to independence — secession in later American terms and separatism in still later Canadian terms — and the belief that the colonies would be better off without Great Britain.

But for James and others who would become Loyalists, the colonies had a great deal to lose by separation, especially in terms of the personal freedom and the protection guaranteed by British law. Already, as James said, the Patriot leaders had used the "friendly cooperation" of the "multitude"[6] to make their point and frighten established authority. These gangs, connived at by militant or ambitious Patriots, when they sensed opposition to their ideas of "independency," had burst into decent citizens' houses, looted and wrecked the furniture, pulled out the man of the house, beaten him up or tarred and feathered him and ridden him around the town on a rail. None of these vandals had been prosecuted. Rather, they and their backers had been encouraged to continue their outrages.

"The general cry was, *Join or die!*" James tells us. As he relished neither, he remained on his farm, "a silent, but not unconcerned, spectator of the black cloud that had been gathering, and was now ready to burst on his devoted head."[7] The rebels were seizing the initiative while most Loyalists watched, like James, in stunned paralysis.

These men could not believe that separation would actually take place, and continued to work for reconciliation by constitutional means. It is often ignored that when the results of the deliberations of the First Continental Congress were published in November 1774, support for its actions was by no means universal. Many people objected to the offensive tone of the resolves adopted, and saw danger in a radical mishandling of a serious quarrel that needed resolution.

An anonymous contributor wrote in Rivington's *New York Gazetteer* in November 1774 that the resolutions of the First Continental Congress

have formed no system by which the present differences might be solved, and future contentions avoided, but deliberately have made bad worse, left us no retreat, nor the mother country any opening to advance to a reconciliation....

Had an Act of Parliament formed such an Inquisition by giving power to any man or set of men; to observe the conduct of their fellow-subjects, and as a majority should determine, their neighbour should be exposed to insult and contempt at their pleasure, how should we have heard of the liberty of the subject, his right to trial by his peers, &c. &c. Yet these men at the same time they arraign the highest authority on earth, insolently trample on the liberties of their fellow-subjects; and without the shadow of a trial, take from them their property, grant it to others, and not content with all this, hold them up to contempt, and expose them to the vilest injuries.[8]

More outright resistance was advocated by "A Jersey Farmer" in his declaration in the *New York Gazetteer* of January 26, 1775:

As we never voted or assented to the resolves or proceedings of any town or country meetings, *except such as by law established,* we do not hold ourselves bound by, or pay any regard or obedience to any resolutions or regulations of any congress or committee whatever; that are inconsistent with our acknowledged allegiance to our most gracious Sovereign, the laws of Great-Britain, or those of the province in which we live.[9]

A considerable body of people in Sussex County, where James lived, in Burlington County where he had grown up, and indeed, throughout the province continued to believe that the American grievances could be peacefully reconciled. As late as November 1775, the citizens of Burlington County sent a petition stating:

That in the Opinion of Your Petitioners An Effectual Opposition may be made Against the Measures Now pursueing by the Ministry and Parliament of Great Britain Without changeing The Constitutional Form of Government In the British Empire Established; And that Your Petitioners have not the Least Desire that the Union of the Colonies in that Opposition Should be broken Which they think the Establishment Of An Independency Would Effect.[10]

They urged that a better worded and more properly directed petition through the House of Commons should be tried.

Only tentatively did people opposed to the new Congress begin to form counter-associations, in the spirit of "A Jersey Farmer." Individuals were not roused to organize their misgivings into action until they were themselves personally attacked.

As yet this had not happened in New Jersey. The grievances enumerated in the New Jersey Legislature's petition to George III in

February 1775 — stationing of troops in Boston, elevation of military over civil authority, corruption in the customs service and admiralty courts, abuses of royal office holders, arbitrary dissolution of legislatures, excessive mercantile restrictions, violations of the right of trial by local jury, the Coercive Acts, and Parliamentary taxation — were merely echoing the petition passed by the First Continental Congress only a few months before. They were not describing the local situation. Though the petition had been drawn up largely by the new radical element in the province's politics, including the arch Whig, William Livingston, even it included the admission that "all the Grievances above enumerated do not immediately affect the People of this Colony."[5]

Most people in New Jersey before the Revolution were like James, plain contented farmers, selling their produce through New York or Philadelphia and having very little direct dealings with England. Like James, they were not involved in politics nor even particularly interested in politics. As he said of this period in his *Narrative*: "They felt no real grievances, and therefore could have no inducement to risk substantial advantages in the pursuit of such as were only imaginary. In making this declaration, he is confident he speaks the sentiments of a great majority of the peasantry of America."[11] Living happily on his farm, he viewed the whole debate rather sceptically, seeing it as being worked up by "pretended patriots and forward demagogues" playing on the emotions of the "multitudes who, with little property, and perhaps still less principle, are always disposed, and always eager for a change."[12] He saw an even greater danger to liberty from the displacement of legitimate government than from the constitutional grievances feared by the Patriots. The precedent of allowing a mob of 20 people to ransack a house, and beat up a citizen just because he held a different point of view, seemed to open the door for far more damage politically, and in terms of property, than a few anti-smuggling laws and irritating taxes.

This was to be the Loyalists' mistake. In Sussex County, as elsewhere in the colonies, the rebels had already taken the lead. The "pretended patriots" had been quick to organize an alternative authority. The Sussex County freeholders who had sent their committee representatives to Trenton the previous July, took another decisive step in May 1775 by paying off the royal judges. They thus effectively dismissed, at the local level, any judges who might be inimical to the Patriot cause. In July, two separate groups of Sussex County Patriots met in private houses to form two regiments of militia and to elect the officers for these. Again in August, under Maxwell's chairmanship, the county Committee of Safety was organized with the intention of enforcing the Articles of Association of the First Continental Congress, and particularly, that all men between ages 16 and 50 must sign the muster roll for service in the militia.

At first stunned and then angry, those in Sussex opposed to the work of the Congress began to come together. During the summer we hear of strong royalist rumblings throughout the county. There was a counter-movement among the Loyalists, "a combination and agreement not to comply with any congressional measures." [13] The most recalcitrant region was James's Knowlton Township and the committee was specifically instructed to "get the Association in Knowlton signed as speedily as possible, and to suppress any riot there in its infancy, as threats of a riot from that town had been reported." [14]

The eloquent Justice Symmes described the opposition as, "men who have basely turned their backs upon the sacred cause of liberty and vilely aspersed her true sons, and wickedly endeavored, and do endeavor, to sow sedition, create confusion, and fill the minds of the good people of the county with groundless fear and jealousy, to the great detriment of the public cause." He endorsed the Patriot resolution: "that if any person or persons in any of the towns of this county shall hereafter asperse any of the friends of liberty in this county on account of their political sentiments, or shall speak contemptuously or disrespectfully of the Continental or Provincial Congresses, or of any of the committees of and in this county, or of any measures adopted or appointed to be pursued by the Congresses or committees for the public good and safety," [15] such persons would be arrested and tried, and if found guilty, fined or imprisoned. Dissent was to be rigorously suppressed.

The outspoken James tried to curb his tongue, and "took every precaution, consistent with a good conscience, not to give offence." But in vain. "Some infatuated associations were very near consigning him to death," only because "neither his judgment, nor his conscience, would suffer him" [16] to adopt their resolutions. As a result, he was "perpetually harassed by these Committees; and a party employed by them once actually assaulted his person, having first flourished their tomahawks *over his head in a most insulting manner.*" [17]

In order to enforce these resolutions, it was found necessary to import into Sussex four hundred militiamen from more patriotic counties to round up 40 recalcitrant "Tories." Militia men were always happy to sign up for the "Tory-hunt service," a duty for which they could claim expenses.[18] The word "Tory" was new enough in this American context of non-party alignments to cause Governor Franklin to remark upon it in a letter reporting the event to the British government.

Most of the 40 arrested agreed to take the oaths, but not all. Nathaniel Pettit, the sitting member of the House of Assembly, and his Anglican neighbour, Robert Ellison, required more persuasive treatment. Early in January 1776, these two magistrates were brought before the larger provincial Committee of Safety sitting in Princeton. Here they admitted to considerable previous Loyalist activity, such as signing a Tory association "resolving not to pay the tax ordered to be levied by the Congress of this Province, and not to purchase any goods which might be distrained from persons for their taxes, or for non-attendance at musters."[19] The men were dismissed from their magistratures, fined £50 each, and, seemingly cowed, were allowed, on good behaviour, to return home.

James describes his own feelings at the time: "Of the points in debate between the parent-state and his native country," he states, "he pretended not to be a competent judge: they were studiously so puzzled and perplexed, that he could come to no other conclusion, than that, however real or great the grievances of the Americans might be, rebellion was not the way to redress them." Reflecting a moral tone expressed by many New Jerseyites, he explains: "It required but little skill to know, that rebellion is the foulest of all crimes; and that what was begun in wickedness must end in ruin."[20]

Most eloquently he makes his declaration:

With this conviction strong upon his mind, he resolved, that there was no difficulty, danger, or distress, which, as an honest man, he ought not to undergo, rather than see his country thus disgraced and undone. In spite therefore of incapacity, in spite of disinclination — nay, in spite even of concern for his family — with the most ardent love for his country, and the warmest attachment to his countrymen, he resolved to do any thing, and to be any thing, not inconsistent with integrity — to fight, to bleed, to die — rather than live to see the venerable Constitution of his country totally lost, and his countrymen enslaved.[21]

James had made his decision. He would be among the "obstinately loyal."

NOTES

1. Frank Moore, *Diary of the American Revolution* (New York: 1860), vol. 1, 19.

2. Jonathan Boucher, *Reminiscences of an American Loyalist* (Boston: Houghton Mifflin, 1925), 109. See also Theodore Draper, *A Struggle for Power: The American Revolution* (New York: Times Books/Random House, 1996), 427.

3. See Willard S. Randall, *A Little Revenge: Benjamin Franklin and his Son* (Boston: Little Brown, 1984), ch. 12; Draper, *A Struggle for Power*, 436-38; and Carl Van Doren, *Benjamin Franklin* (New York: The Viking Press, 1938), chs. 17 and 18, esp. 520.

4. *Narrative*, 5.

5. William Nelson, ed., *Documents Relating to the Colonial History of the State of New Jersey: Extracts from American Newspapers, Relating to New Jersey* (Paterson, NJ: The Call Printing and Publishing Co., 1903), vol. 6 (1766-67), 265.

6. *Ibid.*

7. *Ibid.*, 5-6. "Join or die" was the Patriot slogan from the masthead of Paul Revere's *Massachusetts Spy*, taken originally from an earlier cartoon by Benjamin Franklin, which depicted a snake whose divided segments represented the American colonies, in this case facing a British griffin.

8. Larry R. Gerlac, ed., *New Jersey in the American Revolution, 1763-1783: A Documentary History* (Trenton: New Jersey Historical Commission, 1975), 92-93.

9. *Ibid.*, 115.

10. *Ibid.*, 160.

11. *Narrative*, 5.

12. *Ibid.*

13. *New-York Journal*, 28 December 1775, from Newtown, Sussex County, in Gerlac, *New Jersey in the American Revolution*, 171.

14. Benjamin B. Edsall, "Centennial Address," *The First Sussex Centenary*, Benjamin B. Edsall and Joseph F. Tuttle, eds. (Newark, NJ: 1853), 58.

15. *Ibid.*, 59.

16. *Narrative*, 6.

17. *Narrative*, 5-6.

18. Leonard Lundin, *Cockpit of the Revolution: The War for Independence in New Jersey* (Princeton, NJ: Princeton University Press, 1940), 120.

19. *Minutes of the Provincial Congress and Council of Safety of the State of New Jersey, 1775-1776* (Trenton, NJ: Near, Day and Near, 1879), 333.

20. *Ibid.*, 3.

21. *Ibid.*

4

"DISARMING THE DISAFFECTED":

THE POWER OF EXAMPLE

WITH THE DECLARATION OF INDEPENDENCE the die was cast. Each side was committed to war. But there would now be three sides, not just two. There would be the rebels fighting against the British in a more traditional war of one power against another, and there would be an American civil war where two sets of Americans would be fighting each other on ideological grounds. In the war against the British, the recognized rules of war would prevail, with paroles for captured officers and exchange of prisoners. Not so for the American civil war. The American rebels declared that all those Americans who fought with or helped the British were traitors and as such liable to a civilian trial and possible death by hanging. In contrast, the captured British were treated as conventional prisoners of war, and they therefore had no particular interest in the fate of the Loyalist prisoners and were indeed loath to lose a good British exchange to rescue a mere colonial. Nor were the Loyalists themselves, being part of the British forces, in a position to force any kind of retaliation on the American rebel prisoners. This lack of official protection for captured American Loyalists hung over the Revolution, becoming more bitter as the war progressed, until it reached a climax as the war was ending in the very nasty Joshua Huddy affair, which is discussed in Chapter 10. It was a cause of resentment against the British and vicious anger against the American rebels. This three-sided situation was the unhappiest aspect of the American Revolution.

At first the civil struggle between Americans was waged on political, rather than military lines, as between reasonable men, who when the error of their ways was made clear, would naturally join the cause. The Patriot cause — and to the Tory, the Loyalist cause — rested on clear moral principles, the rights of Englishmen and the "glorious Constitution"— English that is — that guaranteed those rights, and the "villainy" and "wickedness" of those who would oppose those rights. For those of the population too ignorant or debased to understand these principles, the good example of men they respected would show them the clear course of duty.

In New Jersey, the two main protagonists were William Livingston and Cortlandt Skinner. Livingston and Skinner would be fighting each other not for personal control but for the restoration of the kind of government each believed to be the best guarantor of American liberty and prosperity. Each would represent on the New Jersey stage the essence of what each side stood for. It is worthwhile to pause a moment to look at these two men.

William Livingston was not originally a New Jersey man. A lawyer by profession, and a biting caricaturist, he was a member of the powerful New York Livingston family and had spent much of his early career in opposition to the office-holding DeLancey faction. Although brought up in the Dutch Reformed Church, and a graduate of Yale, he had as a young man joined the Presbyterian Church. Rather than a Calvinist, he would more properly be called a Christian deist, a rationalist in the tradition of John Locke. He loved good food, particularly oysters, and lobsters "notwithstanding their British uniform when boiled."[1] A voracious reader, he had an extensive library, and had started the New York Society Library. Tall and skinny as a young man, "spindle-shanks" as he called himself, with large brown eyes and large features,[2] by the time of the Revolution, he had changed to a man of "dignified corpulence," a "long-nosed, long chinned, ugly looking fellow ... a man of rueful length of face," he wrote to a relative.[3]

Being against all orthodoxies as exclusively doctrinaire — "sincere men of all sects who imagine their own profession ... more eligible and scriptural than any other"[4] — Livingston hated the Roman Catholics, the Jews, but above all the Anglicans. He saw the Church of England as an extension of royal authority, attempting to eliminate dissent, political as well as religious. Consequently, before the Revolution he

Silhouette of William Livingston, Patriot Governor of New Jersey, as Moody would have known him. His nose and chin are particularly memorable. Courtesy New York Historical Society (33592)

had vigorously opposed the establishment of an American bishopric as well as Anglican control of King's College, present-day Columbia. He had made his fame not in the law, but as a political writer of acerbic wit. By 1772, he had virtually retired from his New York legal practice and New York politics. He had moved to Elizabeth Town, New Jersey to enjoy his books, his family, and his flowers at Liberty Hall, the new manor house he was building for himself. He was the quintessential Whig. He was among those who voiced mistrust of Cortlandt's brother, Stephen Skinner, when this last as provincial treasurer was robbed of the colony's treasury. He was chosen as a delegate to the First and Second Continental Congresses. Royal Governor Franklin saw him in the quarrel with Great Britain as one of the faction opposed to "every Thing which may have even the remotest Tendency to Conciliate Matters in an amicable Way and to omit nothing which may have any Chance of widening the Breach."[5] In June 1776, he was appointed brigadier general to head the Patriot New Jersey Militia and at the end of August he was elected Patriot governor of New Jersey.

By contrast, Cortlandt Skinner, also a lawyer, was a New Jersey man, and had made a distinguished career in the law in New Jersey. The face in his portrait suggests a less gutsy character. His connections were equally distinguished. His father, William Skinner, a MacGregor, active in the Stuart cause, had fled Scotland and changed his name to Skinner before emigrating to America. Here he studied theology and eventually settled as the much-loved first Anglican minister of St. Peter's Church in Perth-Amboy, the capital of East Jersey, where he had the reputation of being "exceedingly kind-hearted, generous and hospitable; and ... very regardless of money."[6] Cortlandt was the eldest son by his second wife, Elisabeth Van Cortlandt of New York. As an Anglican he had supported the establishment of an American bishopric as a means of Americanizing the Anglican Church, allowing American students to be ordained on their own side of the Atlantic, and he resented Livingston's successful campaign to thwart it.

Intelligent and a good speaker, Cortlandt Skinner, in 1754, was appointed attorney general of New Jersey. He was also a member of the provincial Assembly from 1763 till January 1776. During the decade before the Revolution, as we have seen, he had been critical of the British government. The Assembly had twice elected him as speaker, from 1765 till 1770 and then again from 1772 till 1776. In his capacity as attorney general he was well respected throughout the province and had worked with Governor Franklin to establish an equitable standard of justice. Franklin, after his arrest, appointed him as commander of the New Jersey Royal Militia. But Skinner needed more authority to rally the Loyalists in New Jersey than a piece of paper issued by a prisoner. He accepted first the rank of colonel, then on September 4 that of brigadier general, from the British commander in chief, General Sir William Howe, with the commission to raise the regiment known as the New Jersey Volunteers.

Brigadier General Cortlandt Skinner, commander of the New Jersey
Volunteers, often called "Skinner's Brigade." Miniature. Courtesy New York
Historical Society (21018a)

Both these leaders were sincere in their cause, men of integrity,
intelligence, and generosity, who represented for New Jersey the ideals of
each side. Livingston would be backed by Washington, while Skinner's
extension of authority beyond the British lines would be without military support. Tenuous and fragile where it existed, it would be largely
the result of dedication in the face of imprisonment and confiscation.
It was not surprising that Skinner continually tried to capture
Livingston and rebel leaders throughout the state, and that Livingston
tried to destroy Skinner's forces on Staten Island. The kidnapping of

Patriots was a counter to the insistence that New Jersey provincials were traitors punishable by death. Men of the calibre of James Moody were not an inconsiderable part of Skinner's arsenal, and Livingston came to view James almost as a personal enemy.

After the initial successes of the rebels, by September 1776 the British had regrouped their forces and had taken over Long Island. On September 15 they marched into New York, which they would occupy till the end of the war. It was typical that the entry began with a huge fire that devastated large parts of the city, supposedly begun out of vindictiveness by the rebels. This was countered by rumours of a plot by the Tories to kidnap and assassinate Washington. Neither story has ever been proven but they made good propaganda at the time. For the next three months, the British would have the upper hand, pushing Washington's beleaguered and dwindling forces back to the Delaware.

But this was the formal war. The struggle in the civil war would be for men's allegiance, body and soul, and it is here that example — role-model, we would say today — was particularly important. It is here on the local scene that James would play his part. In Sussex County, the Patriots had not by any means won the battle for adherents. Right under their noses, the ex-royal attorney general was sending recruiting instructions for his newly commissioned Loyalist regiment. The very magistrates released on good behaviour from their grilling before the Committee of Public Safety some months earlier, received a letter from him detailing how to go about raising a battalion of 500 men "to serve during the Present Rebellion." It was to be:

Under proper Officers: Four Companys of 50 men Each to be Commanded by a Cpt., Lt. & Ensign. If they Do not Voluntarily inlist, You are then to Detach that Number from the Militia, being Carefull that all Voluntiers or Detached Men are young & healthy & strong. The field & other Officers upon proper recommendation will be Immediately Commissioned, & put on British Pay, as well as the troops they Command. It is hoped that Joseph Barton Esq.'s Appointment to the Command of the Battalion will be Agreeable to the County. Whenever the Battalion is Completed or Companys are formed, they are to March and join the Royal Army, where they will be provided with Arms, Ammunition, Provisions, &c. This action will readily wipe off that Charge of Rebellion that has been entertained of the Province from the Conduct of a few bad men.... It is hoped for the Honour of the County of Sussex in Particular, that the Inhabitants will embrace this Opportunity of showing Loyalty.[7]

Jubilant over the British successes, the Loyalists, like Washington, naïvely expected the British to follow up their advantage with an invasion of New Jersey. During November and December hundreds of recruits poured in to join the loyal regiment. In Pennsylvania across the Delaware and in Sussex County associations were formed to orchestrate a Loyalist uprising when the British troops should arrive. Pettit would later write that they had a plan to "Repair to the Court house with such arms as could be collected and to set up the King's Standard which from the state of the then broken hearted Rebels was Expected it might be Defended." [8]

Now the Loyalists felt they had the upper hand. It was their turn to get a little of their own back, to intimidate and coerce their earlier tormentors, the traitorous rebels, back to loyalty, though nowhere is there mention of turning people out of their houses or tarring and feathering them as the rebels had done before the Declaration of Independence. "The sad affair at Trenton," [9] as Pettit called Washington's surprise victory on Boxing Day, 1776, prevented the taking of the Sussex County Court House though it hardly dimmed Loyalist zeal in Sussex County. It may have raised Patriot spirits, but British recruiting continued here with people from all over the county signing up to serve in the New Jersey Volunteers. The Patriots' over-zealous pursuit of Tories no doubt helped. A worried Washington had already written to Livingston in January about greedy New Jersey militia officers, who "instead of setting a good Example to their Men, are leading them into every Kind of Mischief.... Plundering the Inhabitants, under pretence of their being Tories." Washington felt "A Law should be passed, to put a Stop to this kind of lawless Rapine." Otherwise, "the People will throw themselves, of Choice, into the Hands of the British Troops." [10] Too much zeal by either side tended to throw the victim into the opposite camp.

On that fateful Sunday of March 28, 1777, when the Patriot militia came to his house to arrest James, it was already clear to him that his time at home was limited. The brandishing of the tomahawks in "a most offensive manner" had been a warning. No doubt that Sunday, the topic of conversation as he walked "in his grounds with his neighbour Mr. Hutcheson" [11] was who in the county would support the British and who would risk recruitment and, with it, the possibility of a traitor's hanging at the hands of the Patriots. "From this time, therefore," he continues

He sought the earliest opportunity to take shelter behind the British lines; and set out for this purpose in April 1777. Seventy-three of his neighbours, all honest men, of the fairest and most respectable characters, accompanied him in this retreat. The march was long and dangerous. They were repeatedly annoyed and assaulted: and once they were under the necessity of coming to an engagement with a rebel party considerably superior in number. Men, circumstanced as he and his friends were, could want no arguments to animate their exertions. The attack was sharp, but the Loyalists were successful; the enemy gave way, leaving them at liberty to pursue their route unmolested. The whole company, four only excepted, arrived safe at Bergen, where they joined Lieutenant-colonel Barton's battalion, in General Skinner's brigade. A few whose professions were calculated to render them useful in that department, joined the engineers.[12]

There are many legends about James's activities from this time but most of them are a confusion of later events. We know that in April 1777 he joined Skinner's regiment, as a gentleman volunteer, that is he served without pay, a not uncommon practice in the eighteenth century for a "gentleman" who had not received an officer's commission. His father may have come to America in the same capacity in the War of Jenkin's Ear, the war against Spain in Florida that dovetailed into the War of the Austrian Succession just before James was born. During this first summer of the Revolutionary War in New Jersey, James was recruiting for the brigade not only in Sussex County but across the river in Northampton County, Pennsylvania, and then guiding the men across New Jersey to the British garrison in New York. He was defying rebel coercion, attempting to set an example of loyalty to principles, showing that one need not submit to revolutionaries.

He was not alone. In Sussex County there were at least seven other recruiters scouring the county trying to persuade men to honour their king. But it was a race to the swift. The Patriots, of course, were equally busy, equally determined in the righteousness of their cause, and backed by a militia force from outside the county. Those who would not willingly sign up and abjure the king, were persuaded by less gentle means, such as imprisonment and fines. In July, the Patriot militia all across New Jersey were busy rounding up disaffected persons from lists generously given them by their neighbours.

But not so easily in Sussex, thanks to James and his friends. General Philemon Dickinson complained to Washington that his Sussex Militia were "extremely unfriendly to the cause in general."[13] An irate inhabitant of neighbouring Oxford Township, Charles Green, told the militia lieutenant attempting to sign him up for militia duty, "You and all the rest of the officers may go to the devil and be damned, for I will go for none of you. If the Captain wants me, he may come himself, and if he does I will shoot him. If he offers to take me or anything belonging to me, I have as good a gun as the Captain and as much ammunition and will make as good use of it for I will never take the Oath."[14] He was indicted on a misdemeanour, but managed the next year to escape and join the British.

James's father-in-law, William Brittain, not only refused to take the oath of abjuration, but shouted encouragingly to fellow Loyalists already locked up in the Sussex County jail at Newton: "Fear not Boys. Stand to it, for at the last Battle General Maxwell was beaten back to Washington and beat all to Pieces, and General Washington thereupon retreated; and Lord Stirling was also beaten all to Pieces. It will not be long before the Court-House will be burned and you will be released."[15] Not surprisingly, he was charged "with maliciously & advisedly saying & doing things encouraging disaffection, and manifestly tending to raise tumults & disorders in the state & with spreading false rumours etc."[16] Considered too dangerous to be let back into the community, he was immediately slapped into jail and kept there until his trial came up in November. He then was made to pay the huge sum of £300, and allowed to return to his farm in Knowlton, presumably with the understanding that he would hold his tongue in future.

Sussex County was seen by Washington and Livingston as a hotbed of Loyalism. Much of their correspondence concerns methods of suppressing this dangerous attitude of mind. James, though he plays down the danger in his *Narrative*, was running great risk as a recruiter. In the very month that he enlisted, Washington's aide de camp, Alexander Hamilton, wrote the Patriot governor about Loyalist prisoners from Sussex County:

Several of them have been taken in Arms and others were, beyond a doubt, employed in inlisting men for service of the Enemy. You will readily concur with His Excellency, in the obvious necessity of inflicting exemplary punishment, on such daring offenders, to repress that insolent Spirit of open and avowed Enmity to the American cause, which unhappily is too prevalent in this and other States.[17]

A little further he explains that, "The examination that has been made in this instance is somewhat irregular and out of the common order of things, but in the present unsettled State of government, the distinction between the Civil and Military power, cannot be upheld with that exactness which every friend to Society must wish."

A week later Hamilton was again writing to Livingston:

A spirit of disaffection shews itself with so much boldness and violence, in different parts of this State, that it is the ardent wish of his Excellency, no delay might be used in making examples of some of the most atrocious offenders. If something be not speedily done, to strike a terror into the disaffected, the consequences must be very fatal, among other ill effects. All security to the friends of the American cause, will be destroyed; and the natural effect of this will be an extinction of their zeal, in seconding and promoting it. Their attachment, if it remain, will be a dead, inactive useless principle. And the tories, emboldened by impunity, will be encouraged to proceed to the most daring and pernicious length.[18]

On July 12, Washington was again instructing Livingston about two men from Barton's regiment reported to be up in Sussex County enlisting men for that service, "to have proper measure taken in case of a Discovery, as an Example of this Nature would have a very happy effect."[19] Several such people had been seized and the county was being scoured for others, including James Moody.

James was not caught but a fellow recruiter, Lt. John Troop,[20] was, and his case is relevant because it set the principle that would govern James's treatment when he was himself captured by the Patriots. Livingston and Washington attempted to establish that Troop was a civilian and could thus be tried as a traitor. When captured, although he was a commissioned officer in an enemy regiment, he was not entitled to be treated as a prisoner of war. If he could be convicted and hanged as a spy, it would "set a good example" to other would-be military supporters of the British. It would show them what they could expect if they persisted in their loyalty.

According to Livingston's report to Washington, Troop and two others

were surprised at Dinner at the house of a Farmer who is father to one, & father in Law to the other of the other two.... There they had been for several Days, Troup generally concealing himself in the Woods. He treated the Party who took him very chevalierly, & insisted upon their taking his Parole. When he was brought to me, he appeared insensible of his Danger, and expected to be treated as an officer, & exchanged for one of equal Rank. But what I told him of the Circumstances in which he was apprehended, and my Idea of the Law of Arms in such Cases, with his own reflections the succeeding Day so wrought on him, that the next Evening (his Brother Aid De Camp to General Gates, arriving that day in Town, & increasing his apprehensions) he desired to be examined by the General & me, promising, as the only thing that he conceived could intitle him to your Excellency's Clemency, to make the fullest & most ingenuous Discovery of the Situation of the Enemy. In his Examination he appeared very frank, and, I believe, represented Matters respecting the British Troops to the best of his knowledge. But of the Design of Errand into New Jersey, I cannot persuade myself that he gives us a true Account. That it was only to see his wife ... appears to me incredible.... The two taken with him, being guilty of a capital Felony by our Laws for having gone over to the enemy since October last, & returning without Leave therein mentioned, are to be tried accordingly, unless they agree to enlist on Board any of the Vessels of War belonging to the continental Navy, upon which the Governor & Council of Safety may pardon them. On this they have by the Act six days allowed to consider; Troup being also an Inhabitant of New Jersey at the time of his entering into the British Service might likewise have been proceeded against upon the same Law, but being an officer, it might not have been prudent to point him on board of our Fleet, & your Trials by Courts martial being much more summary & expeditious, are greatly to be preferred.[21]

And a little later in the same letter, Livingston makes the chilling recommendation: "Tho' it pains me not a little to say any thing on so melancholy a subject as that of Lieut. Troup's which may appear to have a Tendency to stop the Interposition of Mercy, I must in Justice to the public, observe, that the People in these parts in general are so greatly exasperated against him that his being treated with lenity will have a very unhappy Effect upon their future military Exertions."[22] The people who were exasperated were of course the rebels. James would later encounter a similar reaction.

But Washington, who saw so much farther than most of his contemporaries, had another concern: he must suppress opposition to the American cause, but he must not corrupt that cause by fostering tyranny. Washington sardonically wrote back to Livingston on September 1 about Troop:

After being so clearly detected, should he escape punishment, it cannot fail to have the disagreeable influence you mention, on the minds of the people, and to be an encouragement to other adventurers. As a similar instance however, has not before come under my direction, I have ordered a Special Court Martial, composed of Men of judgment and moderation to sit upon the occasion, and I have every reason to expect their decision will be dispassionate and well founded. It is doubted whether the Military jurisdiction comprehends a case of this kind; this will be well considered, and if the Court can with propriety go into the Trial and their Sentence should be such, as it is naturally to be expected it will be; I do not think, from my present view of the matter, that it will be in my power to mitigate or remit his punishment, tho' I shall sensibly feel for his friends, who cannot but be deeply affected by his fate.[23]

Here we see the steeliness that helped Washington to prevail in this Revolution.

Although Livingston was very anxious to have Troop condemned, Washington insisted that the acceptable evidence produced was not sufficient to convict him. But neither was Troop released. "He lay in our Provost guard and was marched backwards and forward, till he was naked and almost eaten up with filth and Vermin,"[24] Washington later wrote Livingston. Troop resolved the dilemma himself by escaping back to New York. He lived to fight at the Battle of Eutaw Springs, South Carolina, in 1781 but died from his wounds shortly afterward.

The remarkable thing about this episode — and James's later imprisonment — is that the court attempted to conduct an honest trial. Equally remarkable, though, was the unswerving commitment of the Loyalist prisoners to their own cause.

Throughout the summer of 1777 James tells us that he and his neighbour, William Hutcheson, enlisted upward of five hundred men in expectation of the British army's marching in. Howe had put out a rumour "that while the main army was advancing by land toward Philadelphia, a force of Loyalists under Cortlandt Skinner was to march from Bergen into Sussex County to aid a rising of Tories there."[25] As this seemed supremely logical, Washington stationed troops of militia at points that would intercept any such advance. James was also anticipating this much-wished-for move. He tells us that:

Mr. Moody and his friends had their agents properly placed, to give them the earliest information of the army's moving; when their plan was, to disarm the disaffected, and generally arm the Loyal. Let the Reader then judge of their mortification, when, whilst their adherents were high in spirits, and confident of their ability, at one blow, as it were, to have crushed the Rebellion in New Jersey, they were informed, that General Howe had evacuated the province, and was gone southward.[26]

"This," James wrote into the second edition of his printed *Narrative*, "was the fatal Chesapeak expedition to betray the Loyalists and to ruin Burgoign."[27] As would happen so often during this war, the British commander ignored common sense and any cooperative effort with the Loyalists or his fellow generals. For James and for other Loyalists, the lacklustre conduct of the war was a major reason for British defeat.

James was so disappointed that he could not bear to return immediately to New York. Instead he and his party lingered on in the country "in the hope that some opportunity would still present itself to annoy the rebellious, and to assist the loyal."[28] The best they could do was to gather up as many of the men they had enlisted for the uprising and conduct them safely across the province to British headquarters in New York. Naturally with the pull-out of the British forces, most people were less keen to declare themselves openly for the royal cause, and thereby expose themselves to Patriot anger. Nevertheless, James did, in the short space of 48 hours, in secret and at night, manage to collect one hundred men still willing to risk their lives for the Loyalist cause, and run the gauntlet of a 70-mile march through well-inhabited New Jersey to enlist with the British on Staten Island.

However, such a large body of men was difficult to conceal. Word of their movements soon reached the rebels. The Patriot militia was called out. At first the Loyalists managed to fight them off during several skirmishes but finally the Patriots gathered a strong enough force to stop them near Perth-Amboy. Here, luckily, James and eight others got through to Staten Island, but 60-odd less fortunate were captured. These were confined in the Morristown jail, and "tried for what was called *high treason*." More than half were sentenced to die.

The friends and relations of most of those sentenced petitioned the governor for clemency, arguing that the offenders were young and had been misled. Livingston accepted their pleas and in the end only two men were hanged. He explained his course of action:

View of Staten Island, 1838, from W.H. Bartlett, *American Scenery* (London: N.P. Willis, 1840), vol. 1, 52-53. The fort on the far cliff was where the New Jersey Volunteers were quartered. Courtesy National Archives of Canada (C-139970)

As sound Policy will require the Execution of the Ring-leaders; so Humanity and Mercy will interpose in behalf of the more ignorant and deluded. The latter being the Character of the Majority, I presume they will be pardoned on Condition of their enlisting in our Army, if your Excellency has no Objection against admitting them. As I am convinced they embarked in the Cause of the Enemy from venal Prejudice against ours, but from the delusive and splendid Promises of artful recruiting officers, which they are now persuaded were altogether villainous, I presume they will not upon that account, be the more pious to desert; but probably in order to efface the Ignominy of their former Conduct, & to demonstrate their Gratitude for the Clemency shewn them, be the more studious of manifesting greater Fidelity to the Cause of America.[29]

How wrong Livingston was. James explains: "The love of life prevailed. They enlisted; but so strong was their love of loyalty at the same time, that, three or four excepted, who died under the hands of their captors, they all, very soon after, made their escape to the British army."[30] Among these last were a number of James's neighbours, including his 16-year-old brother-in-law, Joseph Brittain. Much to Livingston's fury, this was to be the pattern in Sussex County.

Moreover, not all the men had been captured. Some managed to escape back to Sussex. The Patriot militia brigadier from nearby Hunterdon County, Philemon Dickinson, lamented to Livingston that "The Officers who have joined the Enemy from the Eastern Parts of this State, will have a very great Opportunity now presented to them, of recruiting their respective regiments, to the irreparable Injury of this State."[31] And indeed James was quick to seize that very opportunity.

On adding up the numbers of those he had set out with, those who had escaped with him, and those who when released into the Patriot services had come back to him, he realized that quite a number must have gone back to their respective homes. He quickly returned "into the country" and came back with 19 more men. But the numbers still did not add up. "Convinced that there were still many more, on whom good advice and a good example might have proper influence," he went back to Sussex County a third time and brought in another 42 men, "as fine soldiers as are in the world; some of whom had but just escaped from jails, where they had been confined for their loyalty."[32] James succeeded in getting all these men safely through to the British lines.

James was clearly brilliant at partisan warfare. To hide and take care of 19, let alone 42, men for several days through enemy territory was masterful, even if much of the land was wooded, and many of the people were friendly. We are told by a British officer recruiting with him, that James left nothing to chance, did his own reconnoitring, and took great personal risks to ensure the safety of his charges at every step of the way. Indeed without his "Vigilance and good conduct," the parties would never have got through.[33] People trusted in his leadership. They were attracted to follow his example to join the British to resist the rebels.

James's successes soon caught the attention of Cortlandt Skinner, commanding the New Jersey Volunteers, and James was granted a commission in the Fifth Battalion of that corps. Capitalizing on these abilities, Skinner would use him for the next three years almost exclusively for special assignments "into the country."

NOTES

1. Quoted in Milton M. Klein, "The American Whig: William Livingston of New York," PhD thesis, Columbia University, 1954, 148.
2. *Ibid.*, 88.
3. *Ibid.*, 162-63.
4. *Ibid.*, 281, quoted from the *Independent Reflector*, preface 31, vol. 28, 29 March 1753.
5. William Franklin to Joseph Galloway, 12 March 1775, New Jersey Archives, 1 ser., X, 575-79, quoted in Klein, "The American Whig," 702.
6. William H. Whitehead, *Contributions to the Early History of Perth Amboy and Adjoining Country with Sketches of Men and Events in New Jersey during the Provincial Era* (New York: D. Appleton, 1856), 100.
7. Orders & Instructing to Nathaniel Pettit, Robert Allison [sic] & Joseph Barton, Esquires, 29 Nov. 1776, NAC, MG 23, H 2, 18.
8. Nathaniel Pettit, letter requesting land grant in Ontario, 12 Aug. 1794, NAC, MG 23, H 2, 18.
9. *Ibid.*
10. Leonard Lundin, *Cockpit of the Revolution: The War for Independence in New Jersey* (Princeton: Princeton University Press, 1940), 239.
11. *Narrative*, 6.
12. *Ibid.*, 6-7.
13. Philemon Dickinson to George Washington, 13 Feb. 1777, Washington Papers, vol. 41, quoted in Lundin, *Cockpit*, 242.
14. *The State vs. Chas Green*, Indictment for Misdemeanor, Sussex Sessions, Aug. 1777, New Jersey Supreme Court, no. 35497, New Jersey State Archives (NJSA), Trenton, NJ.

15. *The State vs. William Britton*, Indictment for Misdemeanor, Sussex Sessions, Aug. 1777, RG Judicial Records, Court of Oyer and Terminer, Sussex County, Subgroup, Clerk's Office, Indictments 1754-1936, Box 1 (1754-1818), NJSA.

16. *Minutes of the Committee of Safety of the State of New Jersey* (Jersey City: John H. Lyon, 1872), 79.

17. Alexander Hamilton to William Livingston, Morris Town, 21 April 1777, Washington Papers, no. 77, p. 69, Library of Congress (LC).

18. Hamilton to Livingston, Morris Town, 29 July 1777, Washington Papers, Reel 23, Series 3C, p. 79, LC.

19. Washington to Livingston, Pompton Plains, 12 July 1777, Washington Papers, Reel 23, Series 3C, p. 120, LC.

20. The usual spelling of this name is Troop, but in some documents including the one cited on this page, the name is written Troup.

21. Livingston to Washington, Morris Town, 15 Aug. 1777, *The Papers of William Livingston* (hereafter *Livingston Papers*), ed. Carl E. Prince et al. (Trenton, NJ: New Jersey Historical Commission, 1980), vol. 2, 32-33.

22. *Ibid.*, 35.

23. Washington to Livingston, Wilmington, 1 Sept. 1777, Washington Papers, Reel 23, Series 3C, pp. 145-46, LC.

24. Washington to Livingston, Valley Forge, 20 Jan. 1778, Washington Papers, Reel 23, Series 3C, pp. 238-39, LC.

25. Lundin, *Cockpit*, 310-11.

26. *Narrative*, 8.

27. *Ibid.*

28. *Ibid.*

29. Livingston to Washington, Princeton, 5 Nov. 1777, *Livingston Papers*, vol. 2, 102-03.

30. *Narrative*, 9.

31. Philemon Dickinson to Livingston, Trenton, 14 Sept 1777, *Livingston Papers*, vol. 2, 70.

32. *Ibid.*

33. Testimony of ensign Ozias Ansley, adj. 1st Battalion, New Jersey Volunteers (NJV), Staten Island, 14 March 1782, Moody Papers.

5

"TO TERRIFY THE ENEMY":

THE SEASONS OF 1778 AND 1779

THE GOOD PATRIOT example having failed to win over the enemy, now a more ruthless policy of coercion would be adopted. The Revolutionary foes must be hunted down, cowed into submission, or forced to leave. They must not be allowed to infect others with "Loyalism." No mercy would be shown. James would be employed in countering these pressures. He, too, would use scare tactics to terrify the local Patriots into good behaviour. In the end, though, he would go further.

Governor Livingston was understandably furious when he discovered that the reprieved men had been spared only to re-enlist in the Loyalist New Jersey Volunteers. On May 29, in an eloquent plea not to adopt a resolution by Congress which would have pardoned Loyalists who returned to the American state by June 10, 1778, Livingston addressed the New Jersey General Assembly:

The thirty-one Criminals lately convicted of the most flagrant Treason, and who, by the gracious Interposition of Government, were, upon very hopeful Signs of *Penitence*, generously pardoned, and then with hypocritical Chearfulness enlisted in our Service, have all to a Man deserted to the Enemy, and are again in Arms against their Native Country.... Whence it is probable that a real Tory is by any human Means absolutely inconvertible, having so entirely extinguished all the primitive Virtue and Patriotism natural to Man, as not to leave a single Spark to rekindle the original Flame. It is indeed against all Probability that Men arrived at the highest possible Pitch of Degeneracy, the preferring of Tyranny to a free Government, should, except by a Miracle of Omnipotence, be ever capable of one single virtuous Impression.[1]

And so on for three pages. Livingston's rhetoric soared in bitter invective. The wily old Whig used propaganda methods that have a very modern ring. Before this speech, he had written to Washington that he had sent to the printer of the *Gazette*, "a number of letters, as if by different hands, not even excluding the tribe of petticoats, all calculated to caution America against the insidious arts of enemies. This mode of rendering a measure unpopular, I have frequently experienced in my political days to be of surprising efficacy, as the common people collect from it that everybody is against it, and for that reason those who are really for it grow discouraged, from magnifying in their own imagination the strength of their adversaries beyond its true amount."[2] It is no wonder that Cortlandt Skinner wanted the New Jersey governor out of office, though James would not yet be called upon for this task.

It is a measure of the high regard in which Cortlandt Skinner was held in all parts of New Jersey that he was able to organize in a short time an efficient and loyal spy network throughout the state, a network that rivalled the equally well-run intelligence network that Washington personally controlled. Skinner had all sorts of people in all walks of life who managed to relay information of the most secret kind as quickly as a horse could carry it which he then passed on to British headquarters. Each week Skinner himself would write his own secret report to the British commander in chief, picking out the highlights of information and making suggestions as to how this information could be used to good advantage for the royalist cause.

Early in May 1778, Sir Henry Clinton replaced Sir William Howe as commander in chief of the British forces. On June 18 he evacuated Philadelphia, abandoning most of the Loyalists there to the mercies of the rebels who would soon make it their capital. Clinton marched across New Jersey with Washington's army nipping at his rear until the two armies met at Monmouth, where both suffered horrendous casualties. After a Pyrrhic victory, Sir Henry stole back to New York and prepared for a new round of fighting in the south.

At this stage of the war, the New Jersey Volunteers were kept out of the main action. Encamped on Staten Island, members of the regiment were used to do the army's less glamorous jobs. It was they who guarded the lighthouse at Sandy Hook and the blockhouse at Bull's Ferry across the North River from present-day 34th Street. They were also assigned to forage for food and fuel in the countryside outside British lines.

But James was now singled out by Skinner for special assignments independent of his regiment. James had spent his first year as an active Loyalist helping to recruit men for Barton's regiment in Skinner's brigade. He had demonstrated his courage, quick-wittedness, and ability to lead men in difficult situations. These qualities would be put to use by his regimental commander in chief.

In the beginning of May 1778 he was sent, he tells us, into the area held by the rebels bordering the Delaware "to render such service to Government, and its friends, as he should have an opportunity for."[3] In a petition in 1780, James is more specific about what this entailed. He came into Sussex County with seven men and was there from May until the end of August. He later testified that he had spent £350 New Jersey currency — £210 sterling — of his own money to keep his men supplied. He also took the opportunity to slip home for a secret one-day visit to his family.[4]

He tells us that to bind his men "to mutual secrecy and fidelity," he always administered to his followers in all his expeditions, an oath:

I, the undersigned A. B. do solemnly swear, on the Holy Evangelists of Almighty God, that I will stand by and be true to the persons joined with me in this expedition, and do everything in my power to accomplish the purposes of it: and I do farther swear, that, in case of our taking any prisoners, I will do my endeavour to treat them as well as our situation will admit of: and I do farther swear, that, in case of any accident should happen to me, and that I should be taken, I will not, even to save life, discover or betray any person joined with me, or any Loyalist who may befriend us with any information, advice, or other assistance; and I do farther swear, that I will not injure nor destroy any property even of a rebel, unless it be arms or ammunition, but faithfully pay the full price of any thing we take from them, if they refuse to sell it: and I do farther swear, that I will not wound nor take away the life of any person whatever, unless they should attempt an escape when in our custody, or it shall otherwise be absolutely necessary for our own defence. *So help me God.*[5]

Perhaps this code of conduct was the main reason why no one ever betrayed him. He was for the county a protector, not a scourge.

In his petition, James explains that to frighten Patriots into more loyal behaviour, he had made incursions into the counties of Sussex and Morris in New Jersey, and Northampton in Pennsylvania. The muster rolls show him as recruiting, but he had undertaken another mission as well. In his petition he says to "Tarefy the most Violent of the Rebels he Surprised them at their own Houses and Threatened them with Death in Case they did not Desist from Persecuting their Neighbours which has had the Desired Effect."[6] These terrifying visits to "disaffected" neighbours would consist of a knock on the door in the middle of the night, and the administration, with a gun held to the rebel's head, of an oath of neutrality for the duration of the war. There was no suggestion, even at the time, that James ever harmed these people. Rather he was applying tactics similar to those used by the rebels, in order to intimidate these last into leaving the Loyalist families in peace.

Like all partisans, James could not have operated without local support. Northampton County, just across the Delaware in Pennsylvania, and Morris County to the east, were adjacent to Sussex, with many of the same families living in all three. In Northampton County, in Mount Bethel Township were the two older brothers of Elizabeth Moody, Nathaniel and Zeboeth Brittain, both Patriots, though how fervent is unknown. There was no permanent rupture in the family: William Brittain senior and his wife joined them in Mount Bethel after the war.

There were also families like the Snyders and the Marrs who had put themselves under James's protection. Out of 34 Loyalist recruits captured the previous August and reprieved from the death sentence on condition that they join the Continental forces, eleven were from Mount Bethel, including four Snyder brothers. Like so many others, the Snyders had promptly deserted the Patriots and joined the New Jersey Volunteers, though their family had sold most of their possessions to provide for them in jail and to pay their fines. James had himself enlisted Elias Snyder.[7] Laurence Marr, a private and later a corporal in James's battalion, was to be on many expeditions with James. He may have been related to James by marriage, for Zeboeth Brittain was married to Elizabeth Marr, daughter of another Lawrence Marr.[8]

Spilling into Sussex County from Morris County was the large extended Swayze family. They were almost a Loyalist unit in themselves. They were prosperous farmers, originally Quakers who had been expelled from Massachusetts in the seventeenth century to Long Island from where they had come to Morris and Sussex a generation earlier. Some, like the ubiquitous Isaac, lived in Roxbury, Morris County, just across the border from James's part of Sussex, and some, like the more sedate Joshua, were immediate neighbours of James.

The Swayzes did not join a provincial corps but acted as Loyalist agents outside the British lines. We hear of them bringing in intelligence to British headquarters, guiding refugees across upper New York, passing continental counterfeit money, and collecting — rustling? — horses for the British troops, being captured, breaking jail, some being killed, but most escaping. After the Revolution most of them settled in Upper Canada in the Niagara district. The Swayzy apple of Ontario was developed by the younger Israel. Throughout the war years, members of the family were continually helping James.[9]

Indeed, in Sussex County itself, all along the highway that still runs through the main valley of the county there were "nests of Tories," to use a rebel phrase. At what is now Ramsaysburg at the Delaware lived Robert Ellison, and Nathaniel Pettit, active Tories from the start. Moving up the road there were James, his in-laws the Brittains, the Swayzes,[10] the Drakes, the Buchners,[11] the Beams, the McMurtries, all of whom would help in the years to come. Above Newton, Joseph Barton, a member of the House of Assembly just before the Declaration of Independence, and now the colonel of the Sussex County battalion of the New Jersey Volunteers, had his house and mill. Then near the New York border lived Joseph Crowell, a man who would remain close to James long after the war was over and they were both resettled, one in Nova Scotia, and the other in New Brunswick. There were others, of course, whose names are now forgotten, but who believed strongly in the royal cause.[12]

Old Greenwich, Knowlton, and Oxford townships were almost solidly loyal, and the rest of the county was very much divided. Washington in his writings made clear that he despaired of any help from there, to the lasting humiliation of nineteenth century historians of the county. After the war, many Sussex residents were so "disaffected" with the new regime that they too emigrated en masse to the Niagara region. It was among these people, and just across the river in Pennsylvania, that James did his recruiting. He must have come to know every family along that road. For the rest of the war, this stretch of country would be James's base. Here, at great risk to themselves, people hid him, sheltered and protected him, whenever he came into the county.

That summer of 1778, James came back to Sussex County like a white knight on a charger, breathing new courage into the hearts of his Tory friends. People were bolder, meetings were organized, midnight visits were paid to obnoxious Patriots. One is conscious of his presence in Sussex, particularly in Knowlton, by the multitudinous charges of misdemeanors and seditious words that were brought before the courts that summer and autumn, and into the next year. In late May, Henry Hoffman, of Knowlton, yeoman, "a disaffected man," got into a political "discourse" with a neighbour at Newton, and blurted out, "You are strong Whigs here. If the Greens[13] and Regulars should come this way, you had better send your boy over to them and perhaps they will not hurt you." In June, members of the Goodwin family of Knowlton "did meet, conspire, etc., and agree to go over and join and to aid and abet the Army of the K. of GT. B." Again in June, a group from Oxford and Knowlton, undoubtedly Swayzes in conjunction with James's other neighbours, worked out a plan to capture several Patriot leaders and carry them off to the Loyalist Colonel John Butler at Niagara. In August, Robert McMurtrie, another "disaffected" yeoman in another argument, boasted that 60 men hiding in the hills — probably escaped British prisoners of war from the Saratoga defeat — were being supported by Knowlton Loyalists. Although large bonds were posted, most of these cases dragged on and were finally dropped for lack of evidence, suggesting perhaps a not unfriendly jury.[14]

Possibly the biggest outrage against true Patriots was Ephraim Drake's overheard remark in July to his son Silas. The remark cost him £500 in bail money. He was encouraging the young man to join the British. Elizabeth Moody, James's wife, was also present. The senior Drake declared, "I have taken the Oaths but I don't regard them more than a fart."[15]

However, the most daring feat planned that summer involved more than words. James tells us in his *Narrative* that "he took prisoner a Mr. Martin, chief Commissioner in that district for the selling of confiscated estates, a man remarkable for his spite and cruelty to the Friends of Government."[16] James's account is laconic in the extreme. The plan concerned not only the hated Isaac Martin but also his fellow commissioner, Samuel Meeker, two of the county's most active and commanding Patriots. Martin, of neighbouring Hardyston Township, in Sussex, was a justice of the peace and acting colonel of the Sussex County Militia, while Meeker was a militia major. Both men were assiduous in testifying against their neighbours. They were also the two commissioners of forfeited estates for the county, empowered to take inventory and to sell the personal property of all persons who had left their homes and joined the enemies of the State of New Jersey. No doubt this second responsibility gave an extra zest to their Patriot zeal.

The Tory scheme was for James to kidnap Martin and Meeker and carry them off to Staten Island, where they would be valuable prizes in the game of prisoner exchange. Silas Hopkins and "divers others" had met on August 28 at Newton to work out the arrangements. Hopkins was to contrive some way to lure the two men out of Martin's house where they could both be captured. Unfortunately, Hopkins had unwisely sought the help of one John De Vore to pilot Moody and his party to Martin's house, and De Vore revealed the plot.[17]

Nevertheless, according to a Patriot witness testifying after the Revolution, James did seize Martin and started off with him to New York. But of course the alarm was up, and "squads of Militia & volunteer citizens" were sent out in hot pursuit. They finally caught up with the abductors "at a place called Sprowles Meadow."[18]

"It was very mortifying to Mr. Moody," James relates in his *Narrative*, "to have this man rescued from him by a large body of the Militia, after having had him in his custody about forty-eight hours. But he relates with pleasure, that the incident had a good effect on this furious oppressor, in as much as his behaviour to his loyal neighbours was ever after much more mild and humane."[19] Obviously the threat of a Moody return had a cautioning effect on the Patriots.

In Sussex County, James could still afford to be humane in his treatment of his enemy, and play the game of who could win the most converts. But conditions on the northwest frontier were far rougher. Here the participants would shoot to kill. Revenge for past wrongs would add to the cruelty from both sides.

James tells us in his *Narrative* that this summer his orders were, more especially,

to obtain precise intelligence from Colonel *Butler*, then supposed to be at Niagara. He employed a trusty Loyalist to go out to Colonel Butler, who fell in with him between Niagara and Wyoming, and was with him at the reduction of this last-mentioned fortress; and afterwards, along with another of Mr. Moody's men (who, having been driven from him, in the disaster just related [that is the capture of the sixty-odd men near Perth-Amboy the summer before] had gone back, and staid with Colonel Butler all the winter, as the only place of safety he could find), he returned with the necessary informations; with which they all went back, and reported them at head-quarters.[20]

The reduction of Wyoming, on the Susquehanna River near modern Scranton, Pennsylvania, has come down in history as one of the most barbarous incidents in the Revolutionary War. In actual fact it was far outshone by the gruesome slaughter of civilians by Mohawk Chief Joseph Brant and his Loyalist Mohawk followers a few months later at Cherry Valley, west of Albany, and the absolute devastation of the whole area by the American forces under General Sullivan the next year. Wyoming was a classic case of revenge, a revenge that only began with its destruction. The incident shows the complexity of people's motives in this as in other civil wars.

The pencil-like but very fertile alluvial valley of Wyoming, 25 miles long by three miles wide, already had a history of violence. Originally Mohawk land in what is now northeast Pennsylvania, it was first set-tled by Pennsylvanians. Both they and the Mohawks still claimed title to the land. About 20 years before the outbreak of the Revolution, the valley had been seized by settlers from Connecticut with the military support of rival land settlement companies. These had burned many of the original houses and were now burning each other's. It was this kind of uncontrolled land grab on the part of white settlers that Cortlandt Skinner had protested against in 1765. By 1778 the population had increased to six thousand inhabitants, most of whom were ardent revo-lutionaries. They had quickly jailed or forced out any Loyalists foolish enough not to have fled. Their rich grain harvest and warlike young men were a great boon to Washington's forces. Many of the displaced settlers were now soldiers in Butler's Rangers.

There were other reasons for ferocity in this northern war which mercifully were not present in New Jersey. Colonel John Butler, who had been the late Sir William Johnson's able assistant when he was superintendent of the Northern Indians, was himself a great friend of the Mohawks. Having commanded in the Niagara district during the French and Indian War, he was used to working with their leader, Joseph Brant. Although he was aware of the difficulty in controlling the Aboriginals and their cruelty to their enemies, he had much sympathy for these Native People ever increasingly ousted from their traditional lands.

Descent into the Valley of Wyoming, 1838, from W.H. Bartlett, *American Scenery* (London: N.P. Willis, 1840), vol. 1, 34–35. The long narrow valley invited military slaughter. Courtesy National Archives of Canada (C-139972)

On a personal level, the northern war among Americans was particularly harsh. Many of Butler's Rangers were fighting for the release of their families. The Patriots in Albany were holding some four hundred Loyalist family members, including Butler's wife and children, as hostages for the safety of the frontier.[21] The Committee of Safety there had remarked significantly, "that as long as their wives and children were in their hands neither Johnson nor Butler would hardly dare to act against them, and if they did their families 'would not be saved from the violence of the people.'" Already the wife and daughter of a Boston Loyalist had been tarred and feathered and paraded through the streets by a mob of women. This might happen to one of them, it was darkly hinted. Even members of Congress were appalled, and one protested, "The brutality offered to the wives and children of some of them ... in taking from them even their wearing apparel, is shocking."[22] The stage was set for something nastier than individual courts martial.

In military terms, the object of Butler's campaign was to reduce the rebel forts on the frontier, to gather supplies for loyalist use, and to keep them out of rebel hands. Specifically, the Loyalists planned to destroy the coming harvest before it could be distributed to the continental army. In the long-term strategy, they were attempting to join forces with the British along the Hudson, to sever Patriot communications between New England and Philadelphia. The Mohawks were delighted to help. In the campaign of 1778, most of the forts in the area capitulated. Wyoming held out and was captured in battle. Only five prisoners were taken, and only six rebel soldiers escaped. The Patriots had lost 302 officers and men, while the Loyalists had one killed and ten wounded.

Colonel Butler wrote:

In this incursion we have taken & destroyed eight pallasaded Forts, and burned about 1000 Dwelling Houses, all their Mills, etc.; We have also killed and drove off about 1000 head of horned Cattle, and Sheep and Swine in great numbers: But what gives me the sincerest satisfaction is, that I can with great truth assure you, that, in the destruction of this Settlement, not a single Person has been hurt of the Inhabitants, but such as were in Arms; to those indeed the Indians gave no Quarter.[23]

Not very pretty. But at least the non-fighting civilians were not massacred. Soon these would not be spared. At Cherry Valley, Brant's followers went on a wild killing spree brutally felling 40 non-combattant men, women, and children as well as surrendering soldiers. Benedict Arnold's scorched-earth policy as he retreated from Quebec in 1777 was perhaps good military tactics; it forced the British to expend half their food supplies for the civilian population and slowed their own invasion of the south. But it set a chilling example for the treatment of civilians in the northern campaigns. It would be 1781 before Mrs. Butler and her family would be released and reach Canada. These cruelties helped no one. Such horrors merely provoked counter horrors. Due to a more generous spirit on both sides,[24] and in no small part to James's example of fair dealing, Sussex County seldom experienced such vengeful acts.

Who the trusty Loyalist was that James despatched to Colonel Butler, or which of his men had escaped to spend the winter at Niagara and take part in the campaign on the northwest frontier, is impossible to say. James was careful in his book not to disclose the names of people who helped him. But piecing together various bits of information that one can uncover from the official papers it is reasonable that the "trusty loyalist" might have been Isaac Swayze. Swayze had acted as a guide for the British troops in upper New York and maintained steady links with Colonel Butler at Fort Niagara.[25]

It was September before James got back to his regiment on Staten Island. A month later an important event in New York gave new hope and impetus to the Loyalists gathered there. This was the return of the royal governor of New Jersey, William Franklin. At last released from the misery of his solitary confinement in his filthy vermin-ridden room, in Connecticut, he was exchanged toward the end of October for John McKinley, former governor of Delaware. His loyalty unshaken, perhaps deepened through embitterment, he made the decision to stay in America rather than take refuge in England, being as he said, "averse to quit the scene of action in a time of danger and difficulty."[26] Here was a Loyalist leader of stature, who understood the situation and had access to power. In the end, he was as helpless as the rank and file, but in the autumn of 1778 he brought long needed vigour to the Loyalist cause.

Franklin's story is among the most poignant in the Revolution. He was the American-born, illegitimate but acknowledged, son of Benjamin Franklin. He was a taller, more polished version of his father with the same high convex brow, strong nose and chin. Intelligent and cultivated, he charmed those around him with his wit and kindness. A

William Franklin, royal governor of New Jersey and illegitimate son of Benjamin Franklin, painted by Mather Brown. Courtesy Mrs. Jackson C. Boswell, Arlington, VA, on loan to the Frick Collection, New York

contemporary Englishman had described him while he was studying law in England, as "one of the prettiest young gentlemen he had known."[27] While in England, to his father's chagrin, he had fallen in love and married the "golden skinned"[28] daughter of a rich plantation owner from the West Indies, a gracious, fragile lady, devoutly Anglican who gave generously to the new parishes in New Jersey. As a young man he had been close to his father, a partner in his scientific as well as his political activities. Appointed governor on his own merit in 1763, he had proved himself honest and conscientious, representing the interest of his people to the British government, and encouraging the prosperity of New Jersey. A loyal public servant, he parted company with his father in his support of the British government. It was a decision Benjamin never forgave.

In his imprisonment by the Revolutionaries, William Franklin was denied all contact with those outside and was not even allowed a brief visit to his dying wife in New York, an unusually harsh punishment for a man of his rank. The British were too insensitive to have him quickly exchanged and the Patriots — Benjamin Franklin and George Washington among them — were only too happy to keep so respected a Loyalist leader out of action.

In New York, Franklin at once offered his services to Clinton in any capacity. On his own, he set about organizing the twenty thousand-odd Loyalist civilians who by this time had sought refuge in New York. Scattered across the city, separated from their families, they were often living in squalid conditions. The lucky ones survived on British rations or odd jobs. Most were unsuitable for regular military service, poor and without employment, frustrated and humiliated in their state of dependency on British handouts. At the same time, their advice and their talents were ignored with contempt by the British military authority.

Franklin immediately cheered Loyalist morale by bringing about an exchange of eight captured Connecticut Loyalists who had been on the point of facing trial for treason and, of course, death. He did this by chivvying the commander in chief — reluctant because of possible retaliation against British Burgoyne prisoners — into threatening that whatever was done to the Connecticut Loyalists would be done to the Connecticut rebels held by the British.[29] The Loyalists felt that at last someone with influence cared about them.

One of the first organizational things Franklin did was to establish the Refugee Club where Loyalists from different colonies could meet.

From the commander in chief, Sir Henry Clinton, with some nudging from the British Peace Commission which was just completing its unsuccessful mission, he obtained the use of a house in King Street. The business of helping distressed Loyalists was seen to be so urgent that the club held meetings almost every day. Franklin also made a point of inspecting the camps where the Loyalists lived, both in the city and on Long Island.[30]

The membership of the club was military and civilian, "composed of the first Characters from the different Provinces."[31] Franklin, with other members, was anxious to form an official cadre of Associated Loyalists that could organize employment for the refugees in harassing the enemy. It was either here, perhaps brought along by his regimental commander, Cortlandt Skinner, or at headquarters on general business, that James first met Franklin. The Loyalist governor testified six years later that he did not know anything of Moody till 1778 when he found him at New York. "He was a Sober, steady, brave Man and distinguished himself in going on Expeditions from New York,"[32] Franklin recalled. The expeditions in which James was engaged during 1779 were the sort of thing that Franklin was advocating at headquarters, perhaps coordinating his ideas with those of Cortlandt Skinner.

Much to Washington's discomfiture, Franklin had been urging a raid on Monmouth County all during the winter, and the one that James was sent on was the second of three that spring and summer. It took place in June 1779. The purpose of the raid was to secure supplies of cattle and livestock that had been collected for the rebel army in Monmouth County, and to kidnap some of the leading rebel militia officers who were making life difficult for the Loyalists there, as in Sussex County. The Loyalist force was made up of 56 men and officers from various battalions of the New Jersey Volunteers, and a Lieutenant John Buskirk of Colonel Ritzema's regiment. According to a contemporary newspaper account, the main body of the force was conveyed on June 9 by boat from Staten Island, where they were normally stationed, to the outpost that guarded the lighthouse at Sandy Hook. Here, some of the other New Jersey Volunteers who did guard duty at the Hook joined them. The idea was to sail to the Gut, some four miles away, and transfer to smaller boats that would take the men across to the mainland. Because of high winds, the landing had to be postponed until the next day, when they were deposited on shore in the evening. Marching under cover of darkness, the men were led undetected by a local Loyalist of the party, Lieutenant Thomas Okerson, to the town of Tinton Falls, a few miles south of Shrewsbury.

Not being quite sure where the main rebel guard was stationed, the group was split into three in order to surround three houses. James, despite his inferior rank, was put in charge of the one that was to seize Colonel Hendrickson. James volunteered for the expedition but made sure he had a nucleus of men he could count on. Again, his laconic account is misleading, and really describes only his part in the raid:

On the 10th of June 1779, an opportunity of rendering some service to his country now offering, having first requestd Mr. Hutcheson and six men, and some guides, to be of the party, he marched, with sixteen of his men, from Sandy Hook to Shrewsbury. They eluded the vigilance of a Rebel Guard, and gained a place called **The Falls**. Here they surprised and took prisoners, one Colonel, one Lieutenant Colonel, one Major, and two Captains, with several other prisoners of inferior note, and, without injuring any private property, destroyed a considerable magazine of powder and arms. With these prisoners and such public stores as they were able to bring off, Mr. Hutcheson was charged, whilst Mr. Moody brought up the rear, with his sixteen men, to defend them. They were, as they had expected, soon pursued by double their number, and overtaken [that is, Moody's detachment to the rear].

Mr. Moody kept up a smart fire on his assailants, checking and retarding them, till Mr. Hutcheson, with their booty, had got a head to a considerable distance. He [Moody] then also advanced, making for the next advantageous station; and thus proceeded, from one good spot to another, still covering the prisoners, till they had gained a situation on the shore at Black Point, where the enemy could not flank them. But, just at this time, the pursuers were reinforced with ten men: so that they were now forty strong. Mr. Hutcheson, with one man crossed the inlet, behind which he had taken shelter, and came to Mr. Moody's assistance: and now a warm engagement ensued, that lasted for three quarters of an hour. By this time all their ammunition, amounting to upwards of eighty rounds of cartridges, was expended; and ten men only, three of whom were wounded, were in any capacity to follow their leader to the charge. The Bayonet was their only resource; but this the enemy could not withstand: they fled, leaving eleven of their number killed or wounded.

The rebel account reported two men killed and ten wounded. James continues his story:

Unfortunately, Mr. Moody's small, but gallant, party could not follow up their blow; being, in a manner, utterly exhausted by a long harassed march, in weather intensely hot. They found the Rebel Captain dead, and their Lieutenant also expiring on the field. There was something peculiarly shocking and awful in the death of the former. He was shot by Mr. Moody, whilst, with the most bitter oaths and threats of vengeance, after having missed once, he was again levelling his piece at him. Soon after the engagement, one of the party came forwards, with an handkerchief flying from a stick, and demanded a parley. His signal was returned, signifying the willingness of the Loyalists to treat with him; and a truce was speedily agreed on; the conditions of which were, That they should have leave to take care of their dead and wounded; whilst Mr. Moody's party was permitted, unmolested, to return to the British lines. Happily none of the wounds, which any of his men received in this expedition, proved mortal. The publick stores which they brought away with them, besides those which they had destroyed, sold for upwards of five hundred pound sterling; and every shilling of this money was given by Mr. Moody to the men, as a small reward for their very meritorious conduct.[33]

The expedition was a lucrative one.

James's next assignment was again something Franklin had been urging, namely, sending a "suitable person in New Jersey ... to Washington's Camp where he has several Acquaintance among the Officers."[34] "About the middle of October following," James tells us, he "was again sent into the interior parts of the Rebel Country, to obtain intelligence respecting Washington's army. He succeeded; and his intelligence was communicated to General Pattison."[35]

It was at this point that James made a very close friend, John Le Chevalier Roome, a distinguished New York lawyer and secretary to Major General Pattison, then commandant of New York. Roome wrote later that he met Moody when this last came in with intelligence reports for the general, and that "from this time an intimacy commenced between us." Roome offered to lend him money for one of his expeditions, stood as witness to his second marriage, and handled affairs for him in New York when James was later in London. Roome's father emigrated to Nova Scotia after the war, as Roome had himself intended to do. Roome said of his friend, "I know that Mr. Moody has, at his own expence and credit, supported those, whose health from a participation of toil and fatigue with him, on these excursions, have been impaired."[36]

"Again, about the middle of November, he was desired to find out the situation and circumstances of an army under the Rebel General Sullivan, which had lately been on an expedition to the westward against the Indians," James continues. General John Sullivan had been ordered by Washington to "carry the war into the heart of the country of the Six Nations, to cut off their settlements, destroy their next year's crops, and do them every other mischief which time and circumstance will permit."[37] It was the absolute in revenge for the Loyalist campaigns the year before against the settlements of Wyoming and Cherry Valley. Throughout the summer, with the help, among others, of a brigade from New Jersey under General Maxwell, General Sullivan accomplished his mission with horrifying effect, laying waste the populous villages of the Iroquois, burning and destroying as ruthlessly as his enemies had the year before, and forcing Brant and Butler into what is now Ontario.

It was on this expedition that one of the Patriot officers wrote in his diary: "At the request of Maj. Piatt, sent out a small party to look for some of the dead Indians. Toward morning they found them and skinned two of them from their hips down for boot legs; one pair for the Major the other for myself."[38]

James writes:

He went eighty miles into Pennsylvania, close by Sullivan's camp; and obtained an exact account of the number of men and horses with which he went out from Easton [across the Delaware from Knowlton Township], on this Indian expedition; and the number also that he returned with.

From thence, he went to Morris County, where Washington then lay with his army. And here he had the good fortune to obtain, from their own books, an account of the rations which were drawn for them. He next went to Pumpton, where General Gates then was [returning from the triumph of victory at Saratoga against General John Burgoyne], on his march to the southward [to join General Greene against Sir Henry Clinton's invasion of the Carolinas]; and here also he gained the exactest information, not only of the amount of the force then with him, but of the numbers that were expected to join him. And now, having pretty well gone through the business entrusted to him, he returned to New York, and continued there till next year.[39]

This cryptic account leaves the reader to wonder how and with whose help he strolled so uninhibitedly through enemy lines reading documents and counting resources. James was always scrupulous about not divulging names, though again the evidence suggests that at least one of his spies was probably Isaac Swayze.[40] We know that in James's first assignment concerning Washington's army he spent £150 Pennsylvania currency, which he translates into £90 sterling. Again in November he paid out £320 local currency or £192 sterling.[41] It is likely that he paid others to bring him information, though to receive it he needed to infiltrate the enemy's lines. James had now established his reputation. He was, Franklin said later, "the most distinguished Partizan we then had."[42]

NOTES

1. Address by William Livingston to the New Jersey Assembly, Princeton, 29 May 1778, *Livingston Papers*, vol. 2, 349.
2. Livingston to Washington, Chatham, 27 April 1778, *ibid.*, 313. See the simpering letter of May 6, 1778, signed "Belinda," 322.
3. *Narrative*, 9-10.
4. John Bakeless, *Turncoats, Traitors and Heroes* (New York: J.B. Lippincott, 1959), 158.
5. *Narrative*, 44-45.
6. Memorial of James Moody, New York, 28 Sept. 1780, Moody Papers.
7. Petition of Patrick Campbell and Others to William Livingston and the Legislative Council on behalf of the Snyder brothers, Nov. (1-30), 1777, NJSA, Reel 6, no. 030. Claims of Elias and Peter Snyder, Fraser, *Second Report Bureau of Archives*, Ontario, 1904, part 1, 271. James kept in his possession Elias Snyder's New Jersey pardon on condition that he enlist in the Continental army; it is now in the PANS. The family was from Mount Bethel Township, Northampton County, Pennsylvania. The Snyders, Swayzes, Slaghts (Slacks), Drakes, Titmans, to name but a few of James's Sussex County neighbours, are to be found in T.F. Chambers, *Early Germans of New Jersey: Their History, Churches and Genealogies* (Baltimore: Genealogical Publishing Co., 1969).
8. The Brittain genealogy comes from Mrs. Helen Bowman of St. Louis, MO, a descendant of Samuel Brittain, a brother of James's first wife. The letter is in the possession of John Wentworth Moody, Ottawa. Mrs. Bowman's information was corroborated from Elmer G. Van Name, *Britton Genealogy: Early Generations from Somersetshire, England to Staten Island, New York* (Gloucester County Historical Society

Publications, Oct. 1970), NJSA Library. The Mount Bethel Township, Northampton County, PA, 1775 tax returns show the two eldest Brittain brothers, Nathaniel and Zeboeth, as living there. The Pennsylvania Census for 1790 for Northampton County shows the widow of Zeboeth Brittain as Elizabeth Marr. Zeboeth's will was filed July 8, 1790.

9. Benjamin Franklin Swasey, *Genealogy of the Swasey Family, which includes The Descendants of the Swezey Families of Southold, Long Island, New York, and The Descendants of the Swayze Families, of Roxbury, now Chester, New Jersey* (Cleveland, OH: privately printed for Ambrose Swasey, 1910). This book gives the connection with other Loyalist-leaning families in James's neighbourhood, like Silas and Peter Hopkins, who married two Swayze sisters of James's generation. *Documents Relative to the Revolutionary History of the State of New Jersey, November 1, 1779-September 30, 1780*, vol. 4, "Newspaper Extracts," 648, prints an offer of $5000 dollars reward for the capture of two escaped Swayze cousins. Court records for Sussex County in the NJSA were another source.

10. Besides Swayze, the name is sometimes also spelt Swase, Swasey, Swazey, Swaze, Swazy and Swezey — an indexer's nightmare.

11. In another indexer's nightmare, members of this family also turn up as Bruchner, Buggineer, Boughner, Brugler, and Bugler, in addition to Buchner.

12. These names are taken from Sussex County court cases and Loyalist claims.

13. The Greens are Skinner's Greens, the Loyalist provincial regiment, the New Jersey Volunteers, commanded by Cortlandt Skinner. In the early years of the Revolution they wore green uniforms, like many other provincial regiments, for better camouflage in the woods. They later changed to red coats, like the British. James's picture shows him wearing a red coat. The Regulars are the British troops, the redcoats. Information about the New Jersey Volunteers' uniforms comes from Albert W. Haarmann, "Some Notes on American Provincial Uniforms, 1776-1783." *Journal of the Society for Army Historical Research* 49, no. 199 (Autumn 1971): 148.

14. These are all New Jersey Supreme Court cases, first tried in the Oyer and Terminer of Sussex County, Hoffman, no. 36007, Goodwin, no. 35473, McMurtrie, no. 37079, NJSA.

15. *The State vs. Ephraim Drake*, Indictment for Misdemeanor, Sussex Sessions, May term 1779, RG Sussex County, Clerk's Office series, Indictments 1754-1936, Box 1 (1754-1818), NJSA.

16. *Narrative*, 10.

17. Sussex County Oyer and Terminer, September 1778, no. 35979, NJSA. Silas Hopkins is an interesting example of the clandestine support that

much of Sussex County gave to James. Hopkins was married to Mary Swayze, sister of Joshua, and aunt of Isaac. He was one of the first captains to command a company from Sussex County in the New Jersey Volunteers. He had, though, soon taken advantage of the Patriot amnesty of 1777 and returned to his property in Newton. However, he and his brother, Peter, married to another Swayze sister, Mehitabel, continued to help James and other Loyalists in the area. Peter Hopkins and Joshua Swayze represented Sussex County in the General Assembly in 1781.

18. Declaration of Benjamin Sutton, February 24, no year, to apply for a pension allowed by Act of Congress, 7 June 1832, courtesy of the David Library of the Revolution, Washington Crossing, PA.

19. *Narrative*, 10. The commissioners also excited the anger of Patriot citizens of Sussex County, as evidenced by their petition to the State Assembly accusing Martin and Meeker of renting confiscated property at cheaper rates to their friends. See New Jersey Assembly Petitions, Bureau of Archives and History, Manuscript Collection, Box 14, Item no. 40, NJSA. The exasperated William Brittain exclaimed a year later, "I will give any Man two hundred & fifty Hard Dollars to take Isaac Martin to Staten Island & I will pledge my Estate for the performance of my promise." *The State vs. William Britton*, Indictment for Misdemeanor, Sussex Sessions, May term 1779, RG Judicial Records, Court of Oyer and Terminer, Sussex County, Subgroup. Clerk's Office series, Indictments 1754-1936, Box 1 (1754-1818), NJSA.

20. *Ibid.*, 10.

21. Ernest Cruikshank, *Butler's Rangers* (Welland, Ont.: 1893), 42. Cruikshank does not give his sources though his information is reliable. For a fascinating and impeccably researched account of these northern campaigns, see Howard Swiggett's moving *War Out of Niagara: Walter Butler and the Tory Rangers* (Port Washington, NY: Empire State Historical Publication 20, Ira Friedman, 1963).

22. *Ibid.*, 31. The Congressman was General Roberdeau.

23. Major John Butler to Lt. Col. Mason Bolton, Tioga, 18 July 1778, passed on to Sir Henry Clinton and Whitehall. Sir Henry Clinton Papers, Box 41, Folio 20, William L. Clements Library, University of Michigan, Ann Arbor.

24. For instance, Major Robert Hoops, of Belvidere, though a committed Patriot, strived for conciliation rather than harsh measures in dealing with local Tories. He consistently pled for more lenient treatment and even their release when circumstances seemed to warrant it.

25. Benjamin Franklin Swayze, *Genealogy of the Swasey Family*, 235. Isaac is depicted in a newspaper account of one of his escapes from jail as being "about 30 years of age (he was 24 at the time), five feet 8 or 9 inches high, sandy complexion, and had a scar of a bullet or swan shot

in one of his temples." William Nelson, ed., *Documents relating to the Revolutionary History of the State of New Jersey*, vol. 4, Extracts from American Newpapers Relating to New Jersey, Nov. 1, 1779-Sept. 30, 1780 (Trenton, NJ: State Gazette Publishing, 1914), 648.

26. Governor William Franklin to Lord Germain, 10 Nov. 1778, *Documents of the American Revolution, 1779-1783*, vol. 15, Transcripts, 1778, ed. K.G. Davies (Dublin: Irish University Press, 1976), 247.

27. Willard S. Randall, *A Little Revenge: Benjamin Franklin and His Son* (Boston: Little, Brown, 1984), 129. See also William H. Mariboe, "The Life of William Franklin, 1730(1)-1813, 'Pro Rege et Patria,'" PhD thesis, University of Pennsylvania, 1962, for another excellent account of this man's life.

28. *Ibid.*, 173.

29. Mariboe, "The Life," 489.

30. *Ibid.*, 465.

31. Isaac Ogden to Joseph Galloway, New York, 15 Dec. 1778. Balch Loyalist Letters, New York Public Library.

32. William Franklin testifying on behalf of James Moody, 8 June 1784, before the Commission for Enquiring into the Claims of the American Loyalists (hereafter Loyalist Claims), PRO, AO 12/13, p. 76. Microfilm B-1157, NAC.

33. *Narrative*, 10-12.

34. William Franklin to Sir Henry Clinton, New York, 11 June 1779, quoted in Mariboe, "The Life," 493.

35. *Narrative*, 13.

36. *Ibid.*, appendix 6.

37. George Washington to Gen. Horatio Gates, 6 March 1779, forwarded to Gen. John Sullivan, Washington Papers.

38. Journal of Lt. William Barton of Maxwell's Brigade, *Proceedings of the New Jersey Historical Society* 2 (1846-47): 31.

39. *Narrative*, 13.

40. This is the same Isaac Swayze mentioned in note 25. In his memorial of June 5, 1783, he states that he spied for Generals Howe, Clinton, and Knyphausen for secret intelligence, NAC, British Headquarters Papers, vol. 4, no. 7897, NAC.

41. Loyalist Claims, PRO, AO 13/110, pp. 257-58. Microfilm B-2213, NAC.

42. Loyalist Claims, PRO, AO 12/13, p. 76. Microfilm B-1157, NAC.

6

"LURKING IN THE COUNTY," 1780

JAMES HAD SO FAR SUCCESSFULLY completed every mission he had been assigned. His next task would test all the partisan skills he had acquired since his first involvement in the war. He was now selected to capture the biggest New Jersey prize of all, William Livingston. As one of the New Jersey governor's supporters wrote, the Patriots had no prisoner of corresponding importance they could trade back for him. If kidnapped he might languish for years in unspeakable misery, like his royal counterpart, William Franklin. Events would not unfold as James had planned them, but his reputation as a partisan would gain new lustre.

Threats against Livingston had been a constant feature of his life from the time he was first elected governor. As early as October 28, 1777, Congress had made provision for him to have a "Guard for the Security of his Person." It was to consist of six light horsemen and six militiamen, as he thought necessary. Throughout the war, Livingston lived mostly in the saddle, shifting his place of residence, hardly daring to spend more than a few nights in any one location. As his letters attest, this was a constant worry to him, both because he was leaving his own family and possessions unprotected, and also because he fully realized the propaganda coup his capture would afford the enemy. With Franklin's plans for the Associated Loyalists "to bring off a number of Committee men and other rebels to keep as hostages for their own security and in case any of their body should happen to be taken prisoners,"[1] Livingston had justifiably felt personally threatened.

Already, in late February 1779, a British force under Lieutenant Colonel Thomas Sterling had descended on Elizabeth Town and surrounded Liberty Hall. But "the Rebel Governor Livingston had notice sent him & left his House before we got there," Sterling reported.[2] In late March, Livingston had written to Clinton that he was "possessed of the most authentic proofs of a General officer under your command having offered a large sum of money to an inhabitant of this State to assassinate me, in case he should not take me alive." Livingston concluded his letter with the veiled threat, "I give you this opportunity for disavowing such dark proceedings if undertaken without your approbation, assuring you at the same time that if countenanced by you, Your person is more in my power than I have reason to think you imagine." In the autograph draft, Livingston had originally written "life" for "person."[3]

Clinton had written back:

Had I a soul capable of harbouring so infamous an Idea as assassination, you, Sir, at least would have nothing to fear; for be assured I should not blacken myself with so foul a crime to obtain so trifling an end.

Sensible of the power you boast of being able to dispose of my life, by means of intimates of yours ready to murder at your command, I can only Congratulate you on your amiable connections.[4]

Needless to say, Livingston replied and a Loyalist propagandist, probably Jonathan Odell from the tone,[5] continued the correspondence under the name of Pluto, each side thoroughly enjoying its own rhetoric, as they had done in the more peaceful days before the war. But in May another plot to kidnap the governor had been confessed to, with the added assertion that the mayor of New York, David Matthews, was said to have told a group of Loyalists, "that it was a Pity they could not lay some Plot and bring that Rascal Governor Livingston; and that they replied they had planned matters so, in *that Quarter*, that they would have him in less than two months. That they had proper Connections in *that Quarter* for that purpose."[6]

In sending James out in 1780, the British High Command had presumably decided the job required a professional. James took care in his preparations. He consulted his friend John Roome on the practicality of the excursion. "Mentioning his want of cash to carry into execution so essential a service," Roome testified, "I offered to supply him with twenty-five guineas for this purpose, and to be his security, or to borrow at interest a larger sum it being out of my power to advance more."[7] In the end James secured 30 guineas from Major General Robertson and scrounged a little more. He chose, to accompany him, men from his own neighbourhood in Sussex County, including his brother-in-law, Sergeant William Brittain, Corporal Joseph Lowery, Jr., Henry Buchner,[8] and Laurence Marr, these last two from his own battalion. He then set off to surprise Governor Livingston, "a man," James insisted, "whose conduct had been, in the most abandoned degree, cruel and oppressive to the loyal inhabitants of New Jersey."[9]

James set out in mid-April and "with all necessary secrecy" got into Livingston's neighbourhood and "penetrated very near to one of Mr. Livingston's lurking places." There he found that the governor was in Trenton with the Assembly, but had to be back for an appointment. James "led his party into Sussex County and there left them; himself only retiring to a proper situation, till his plan should be ripe for execution."[10] Unfortunately, or fortunately, one of the corporals, Joseph Lowery, Jr., was discovered by the rebel, Major Robert Hoops, assistant deputy quartermaster general in the Continental army, near his house at Belvidere, in present-day Warren County, then Sussex County. Hoops had been advised "that there were disaffected persons in the neighbourhood,"[11] probably by John O'Neil, a soldier of the Patriot 2nd Regiment of New Jersey, who had infiltrated the local Loyalists by passing himself off as bringing intelligence from New York to the Aboriginals.

James says that Hoops "extorted" a confession from the corporal that Moody was in the country, and, as he imagined, in quest of some person of note, who lived near Morris Town. The newspaper account gives the details:

On Sunday morning the 4th instant, about one o'clock, Major Hoops discovered a fellow in company with a woman near his house; he immediately questioned them; the woman prevaricated, and the man hesitated in his answers, gave him suspicions; upon which he desired them to walk into the house, that he might be fully assured of what they told him. Major Hoops on his way to the house looking round, found the man running away; he pursued and took him, not without wounding the fellow through the arm with a small sword, upon seeing a cocked pistol in his hand. He was discovered to be a Levy soldier in his regimentals, belonging to the corps of Jersey Volunteers; on bringing him to the light, the Major presented one of the pistols he had taken from him to his head, and resolutely declared he would put him to death if he did not inform him of his designs in coming to this part of the country. He said that about three weeks ago he came out with Lieutenant Moody, and another, from New York, who had received instructions from General Knyphausen, but he kept them secret, only hinting that he was to take some person off within two miles of Morris-Town, but finding that he was not at home nor would be before the 15th of this month, they came up here in order to pass their time away till the person returned: that he had liberty to go to his uncle's, one Matthew Lowrey, where he was then going had not Major Hoops disappointed him: and that he was to meet Moody and his companion on the top of Jenny Jump mountain on Thursday night, when they were to proceed on their intended expedition.[12]

Lowery was put under guard and a rebel group gathered to give chase to James. As James remarks, "This blasted the whole project; the intelligence was instantly sent to Livingston, who too justly, concluded himself to be the person aimed at; and, of course, took every precaution to prevent a surprise."[13] "So strict a search was made that he was obliged to retire," he said in his 1780 petition, adding that "One of the Governor's Council was Privy to and had Promised his Assistance in accomplishing the above Design."[14]

James warms to his story:

Still, however, Mr. Moody flattered himself he should yet be more fortunate and do something, notwithstanding the alarm that was now spread through the country. The first plausible thing that offered was, a plan to blow up the magazine at Suckasunna, about sixteen miles back of Morris Town; but this also proved abortive: for, notwithstanding his having prevailed on some British prisoners, taken with General Burgoyne, to join him in the enterprise, the alarm was to become so general, and the terror so great, that they had increased their guard around this magazine to the number of an hundred and upwards; so that he was under the necessity of abandoning his project.

Returning again into Sussex County, he now heard that several prisoners were confined, on various suspicions and charges of loyalty, in the jail of that county; and that one of them was was actually under sentence of death. This poor fellow was one of Burgoyne's soldiers charged with crimes of a civil nature, of which, however, he was generally believed to be innocent. But when a clergyman of the Church of England interposed with his unrelenting prosecutor, and warmly urged this plea of innocence, he was

Sussex County Courthouse, Newtown (Newton), NJ, 1765, drawn in 1842. The lower part of the building was the jail from which Moody released imprisoned Loyalists. *Historical Collections of New Jersey: Past and Present* (New Haven, CN: published by subscription, John W. Barber, 1868), by John W. Barber and Henry Howe, 472

sharply told, that, though he might not perhaps deserve to die for the crime for which he had been committed, there could be no doubt of his deserving to die, as an enemy to America.

There was something so piteous, as well as shameful, in the case of this ill-fated victim to republican resentment, that it was determined, if possible, to release both him and his fellow-prisoners. For this purpose, Mr. Moody took with him six men; and, late at night, entered the county town, about seventy miles from New York. The inhabitants of the town were but too generally disaffected. This suggested the necessity of stratagem. Coming to the jail, the keeper called out from the window of an upper room, and demanded what their business was? The Ensign instantly replied, "he had a prisoner to deliver into his custody." "What! One of *Moody*'s fellows," said the Jailor? "Yes," said the Ensign. On his enquiring, what the name of this supposed prisoner was, one of the party, who was well known, by the inhabitants of that place, to be with Mr. Moody, personated the character of a prisoner, and spoke for himself. The jailor gave him a little ill language; but, notwithstanding, seemed highly pleased with the idea of his having so notorious a Tory in his custody. On the Ensign's urging him to come down, and take charge of the man, he peremptorily refused; alleging, that, in consequence of Moody's being out, he had received strict orders to open his doors to no man after sun-set; and that therefore he must wait till morning.

Finding that this tale would not take, the Ensign now changed his note; and, in a stern tone, told him, "Sirrah, the man who speaks to you is Moody; I have a strong party with me; and, if you do not this moment deliver up your keys, I will instantly pull down your house about your ears." The jailor vanished in a moment. On this, Mr. Moody's men, who were well skilled in the Indian war-whoop, made the air resound with such a variety of hideous yells, as soon left them nothing to fear from the inhabitants of New Town, which, though the county town, consists only of twenty or thirty houses. "The Indians, the Indians are come!"— said the panic-struck people: and happy were they who could soonest escape into the woods. While these things were thus going on, the Ensign had made his way through a casement, and was met by a prisoner, whom he immediately employed to procure him a light. The vanished jailor was now again produced; and most obsequiously conducted Mr. Moody to the dungeon of the poor wretch under sentence of death.

It may seem incredible, but it is an undoubted fact, that, notwithstanding all the horrors and awfulness of his situation, this poor, forlorn, condemned British soldier was found fast asleep; and had slept so sound, as to have heard nothing of the uproar or alarm. There is no possibility of describing the agony of this man, when, on being thus suddenly aroused, he saw before him a man in arms, attended by persons, whom, though they were familiarly known to him, so agitated were his spirits, he was utterly at a loss then to recognize. The first, and the only idea that occurred to him was, that, as many of the friends of Government had been privately executed in prison, the person he saw was his executioner. On Mr. Moody's repeatedly informing him of his mistake, and that he was come to release him in the name of *King George*, the transition, from such an abyss of wretchedness to so extravagant a pitch of joy, had well nigh overcome him. Never before had the Writer been present at so affecting a

scene. The image of the poor soldier, alternately agitated with the extremes
of despair and rapture, is, at this moment, present to his imagination, as
strong almost as if the object were still before him; and he has often
thought, there are few subjects on which a painter of taste and sensibility
could more happily employ his pencil. The man looked wild; and
undoubtedly was wild, and hardly in his senses: and yet he laboured, and
was big with some of the noblest sentiments, and most powerful passions,
by which the human mind is ever actuated. In such circumstances, it was
with some difficulty that the Ensign got him away. At length, however, his
clothes were got on; and he, with all the rest who chose to avail themselves
of the opportunity, were conducted into safety, notwithstanding a warm
pursuit of several days.[15]

"The mournful sequence of this poor soldier's tale," James relates, was
to be caught again, and accused of a robbery which was later confessed
to by "a less conscientious loyalist ... acting on the principles of retaliation and revenge."[16] On refusing a reprieve if he would but name
Moody's confederates, he was hanged.

James later reported that in addition to the condemned man,
Robert Maxwell, he released the other prisoners, including a neighbour, James Slack (Slaght, etc.). He then locked up the jail and pock-
eted the key. Slack was in prison for harbouring and helping a number
of Burgoyne's escaped British soldiers. These were troops captured in
October 1777 at the Battle of Saratoga. They were supposed to be sent
back to England but the Americans refused to let them go, reasoning
that they would soon be back as new troops. Many had escaped and
were roaming the countryside, sheltered by Loyalists.

The local Loyalists showed themselves equally courageous in taking
in James and his party. James and his sergeant, Henry Buchner,
together with the other men James had brought with him, camped
near Slack's house, in present-day Byram County off Route 206, and
were furnished with provisions by the Slack family during their stay
there. The Slacks were not the only ones to help James. When Hoops's
militia was chasing James, the group fled to Mathias Buchner's house
"where they were concealed and hospitably entertained and further
Supplied with Ammunition, fire Arms & provisions";[17] Buchner's
father also sheltered the party. Jacob Beam (after whom Beamsville in
present-day Ontario is named), another kind Loyalist, took in Buchner
and hid him in his house for almost a month, and also supplied the
Moody party. And of course the Swayze family, whom we have met

before, was represented by Isaac whose father, Caleb senior, lived at Roxbury. There must have been others who chose to remain anonymous. Most of these people were subsequently arrested, jailed, and fined. After the war, many of them fled to Canada.

Having liberated the occupants of the Sussex County jail in Newton, James then turned his attention to the obnoxious people living outside the jail. His little group now numbered seven, and he hoped to immobilize opposition in the county and thus help what he probably expected as the long-awaited British invasion of New Jersey, by "securing as many as he could of the Rebel militia." [18] On the night of June 23, the group managed to seize 13 men, including a major, a captain, two lieutenants, and two sergeants, who opted for signing 15-day paroles, after which time, they promised to surrender themselves at headquarters in New York. Another swoop captured five militia men, to be held as prisoners of war, as opposed to prisoners of state, until an appropriate exchange could be arranged. On another occasion he visited Justice Bright and committee man, James McClennon, "Violent Rebels and far advanced in Years to whom he administered an oath of Neutrality." [19] By July 17, he was exhausted with camping in hiding, and the 30 guineas he had brought was nearly all spent. Gathering more stray Burgoyne soldiers so that his contingent now numbered 13, he set off with his men to work their way back to New York.

The rebels in Sussex County also felt they had had enough of James and sent a complaint to the Governor's Council, then sitting at Preakness, that Ensign Moody was "lurking in the said County enlisting men in the British Service." The minutes continue, "And as he has Opportunity impelling people to Sign Paroles, the Board advised His Excellency to direct Colonel West to call out of his Regiment Forty men to Serve as Scouts to apprehend the said Ensign Moody and his party or prevent their further Operations." [20] Closer to home, the militia colonel, Aaron Hankinson, was to scout out the neighbourhood with ten of his men. It will come as no surprise that Governor Livingston refused to honour the paroles, let alone allow the men to pass into New York.

As for James, he tells us that like David in the Bible, "the Ensign was again pursued and sought, according to the strong expression of Scripture, 'as a partridge in the mountains.' [21] But 'wandering in deserts, and in mountains, and in dens and caves of the earth,' by the blessing of God, he still eluded all their researches.... But his former good fortune now forsook him; and he himself was soon doomed to feel all those bitter calamities, from which it had been the object of his exertions to extricate others."[22] James's capture was, to use the rebel general, Anthony Wayne's expression for his defeat that July 21, "by the most malicious fortune."[23] James had the bad luck to arrive with his men at the Loyalist post of Bull's Ferry at the very time when the whole neighbourhood around the blockhouse, up and down the Hudson River, in the mountains close by, and along the road was "infested"— he might have said — with enemy troops.

Situated on the Bergen side of the Hudson River, halfway between Fort Lee and Paulus Hook, today's Jersey City, the post had been built as protection for the New Jersey Volunteers whose duty it was to gather forage and wood in the neighbourhood for the British garrison in New York. It consisted, as the rebels discovered to their sorrow, of a wooden fort constructed of very thick sturdy walls, "surrounded by an Abbatis & Stock to the perpendicular rocks next North River — with a kind of Ditch or parapet serving as a Covered way."[24] To further ensure safety, the only entrance to the blockhouse was a subterranean passage through which only one man at a time could pass.

To get rid of this enemy nuisance, General Anthony Wayne, with the First and Second Pennsylvania Brigades, four pieces of artillery belonging to Colonel Thomas Procter's Regiment, and Colonel Stephen Moylan's Continental Dragoons, had been ordered to seize and destroy the refugee stronghold. Two Patriot regiments were also hidden along the shore with orders to rush the enemy with bayonets should they attempt to land reinforcements from across the river, and Brigadier General William Irvine was posted where he could watch the British movements on the other side of the river. All these troops had been carefully placed before the first light of day. The rebels pulled up their cannon to within 60 yards of the fort and bombarded it mercilessly, while the Loyalists kept up an unremitting return fire from inside.

Into this assault walked James with his 12 men. With his usual presence of mind, he probably hoped that in the confusion of cannon smoke he could slip into the blockhouse. But the rebel attack was so fierce and so well mounted that the inmates dared not open the entrance. As James succinctly put it, "Resistance was vain, and retreat impracticable. Mr. Moody, and the greater part of his men, were now obliged to submit to captivity."[25] Indeed James and his companions were the only prisoners taken by the Patriots that day, and their only triumph as they abandoned the attack after an hour and a half of fruitless bombardment.[26]

The young New York militia officer, Jonathan Lawrence, who captured James and his men, reported the next day to the New Jersey governor:

Inclosed you have the Original Paroles of Several Gentlemen of the State of New Jersey Captured by an Ensign or Capn Moody with the Copy of his orders from Genl Kneephausen. He has been in the State of Jersey from the 10th of May till he fell into my hands yesterday Morning near the Enemy's Block House. He is the person that released the Prisoners from Sussex Gaol the Key of which will be handed your Excellency with this letter. Should there be any provision allowed for the taking him I hope your Excellency will think of the men under my Comd. I have sent the Prisoner to Major Genl Howe in the Highlands.[27]

A rebel newspaper announced exultantly a week later:

We have the pleasure to assure our readers, that Ensign Moody, a refugee from Sussex to the British army, and who was lately sent from New-York with a party of ruffians for the purpose of burning Sussex gaol, of taking or assassinating Governor Livingston and the persons who were active in apprehending the three spies lately executed and of inlisting our inhabitants in the service of the British tyrant, was lately captured himself by the vigorous exertions of Capt. Lawrence of the New-York state levies, near the English neighbourhood — The instructions found upon Moody, in order to give the better colour to his private directions for inlisting and assassinating, and to prevent his being treated as a spy from the military stile, what he was to produce, in case of his being taken prisoner, was in the following terms:

Head-Quarters, May tenth, New York, 1780.

Sir

You are hereby directed and authorized to proceed without loss of time, with a small detachment into the Jerseys, by the most convenient route, in order to carry off the person of Governor Livingston, or any other acting in publick station whom you may fall in with in the course of your march, or any person whom you may meet with, and whom it may be necessary to secure for your own security, and that of the party under your command.

Should you succeed in taking Governor Livingston, you are to treat him according to his station, as far as lies in your power; nor are you, upon any account, to offer any violence to his person. You will use your endeavour to get possession of his papers, which you will take care of, and, upon your return, deliver at head-quarters.

> By order of his Excellency Lieutenant-General Knyphausen.
> George Beckwith, Aid de Camp.

To Ensign Moody, 1st battalion
New Jersey volunteers.

It is said that all Moody's party, except one, who attempted to swim the North river in his flight and is supposed to be drowned, have been either captured or killed by the activity of our inhabitants; and as to the famous or infamous *Ensign* himself, the great taker of Governors and general gaol deliverer of Sussex, he is at present safely lodged at West-Point and if he has justice done him, it is generally supposed, as our correspondent observes, that he will be hanged for a spy, for inlisting our citizens in the British army, and coming with a party so small as nine, and with weapons concealed, either of which are, according to the present construction of all the nations of Europe, characteristic of a spy.[28]

The prose is worthy of Livingston himself.

Here was the dilemma regarding James's military status: could he be treated as a spy, and therefore hanged, and the country rid of him, or must he be considered a prisoner of war and eventually exchanged? It was the same situation that had faced John Troop three years before. For James, the next two months were to be months of agony, physical and mental, as the argument was played out between members of the rebel civil and military authorities in copious correspondence between Washington and his officers, and Washington and Livingston. James, like Troop, and other prisoners, would be alternately harried and cajoled in an effort to frighten a damning admission from him.

The newspaper announcement of James's capture was certainly music to rebel ears, but it must also have afforded some comfort to the Loyalists, for it announced that James was not yet dead, as the swimmer across the Hudson had reported when he got back to British headquarters. Lawrence had James and two of his men confined with their hands tied behind their back at the headquarters of the New York militia, at Tappan Sloat, and then, as he says, sent them on to the rebel general, Robert Howe, a kindly, elderly southerner who was just about to give up his command of West Point. The general, James relates, treated him with great civility and permitted his servant to attend him.[29] On seeing his orders and commission, the general issued him with a parole and sent him on to the rebel commissary of prisoners at Fishkill, where he was given permission to circulate within a three-mile limit of Kingston.[30] For the next ten days all seemed normal. He was being treated as a prisoner of war.

But once Livingston was informed of James's capture, the rebel governor brought pressure to bear on his military colleagues to ensure that James did not escape. During this week, he must have written to Washington about James for on August 2, shortly after the newspaper account appeared, the prisoner was suddenly seized and thrown into "the Dungeon" at Poughkeepsie and then returned to the Commissioner of Prisoners at Fishkill. Here he spent a week in the Provost — the military jail — "a strong room," he tells us,[28] "guarded by four soldiers, two within the door, and two without."

Here the first harsh measures were introduced. James writes:

The Serjeant, in the hearing of the Ensign, gave orders to the sentinels who were in the room with him, to insist on his lying down on a bed, and instantly to shoot him if he attempted to rise from it. On this, he requested and insisted to see the Commissary. The Commissary came; and was asked, if these orders were from him: his answer was, "The Serjeant had done his duty; and he hoped the men would obey their orders." Mr. Moody remonstrated, and urged, that it was no uncommon thing with him to rise from his bed in his sleep: he requested therefore only, that, if he should happen now to be overtaken with such an infirmity, the men might be ordered to call him by his name, and at least to awake him before they fired. All the answer he could obtain, from this tyrant-minion of tyrant-masters, was a cool and most cutting repetition of his former words.[31]

But James's sufferings were only beginning. Nor did he realize how dangerous his situation was. Both Washington and Livingston were determined to be rid of him. In the correspondence of the next few days there is panic that he might slip through their grasp. Washington's instructions to the Deputy Commissioner of Prisoners were received on August 7. He was to send to West Point "Ensign Moody a Prisoner of War There to be Kept Closely Confined, His Conduct in Jersey having been Such as Perhaps may Cost him his Life." Colonel William Malcolm, the officer commanding at West Point, was enjoined to have him "Strictly Attended to, as he is a Person of a Very Enterprising disposition."[32] At the same time, a letter was despatched from William Duer, a New York delegate to Congress, also directed to the commanding officer at West Point, expressing Livingston's great concern over Moody's being on parole and that he would "probably soon make his escape from (to) the enemy; and thereby escape the fate, he so richly deserves, of being hung as a spy." Colonel Malcolm was not only "to give orders for securing this person, 'til he can be tried by proper authority," but he was also to inform Livingston that he had Moody in his custody, as Livingston "apprehends at present that he has made his escape."[33]

By August 8, James was being confined at Fort Putnam, one of the dilapidated bastions that protected West Point. He gives us a description of the powder magazine that served as his military jail for the rest of that month: "The above-mentioned dungeon was dug out of a rock, and covered with a platform of planks badly jointed, without any roof to it; and all the rain which fell upon it immediately passed through, and lodged in the bottom of this dismal mansion. It had no floor but the natural rock; and the water, with the mud and filth collected, was commonly ankle-deep in every part of it. Mr. Moody's bed was an old door, supported by four stones, so as just to raise it above the surface of the water." Not surprisingly, Colonel John Lamb, the officer in charge of defences, immediately ordered repairs to make the prison doubly secure. Moreover the only food James received was

stinking beef, and rotten flour, made up into balls or dumplins, which were thrown into a kettle and boiled with the meat,[34] and then brought to him in a wooden bowl which was never washed, and which contracted a thick crust of dough, grease, and dirt.... The clothes on his back were seldom dry, and at one time were continually wet for more than a week together.[35]...
Orders were given that he was to have no liquor, even at his own expense, and an Officer was sent to take away his money which he refused to give up.[36]

But these discomforts were minor. James now found himself with his hands manacled and his legs shackled in irons. Irons were usual treatment for suspected traitors, not only to hobble the prisoner but also to humiliate him, a technique still used in many countries for political prisoners. In addition in James's case, whether by design or not, the handcuffs were ragged on the inside causing his wrists "to be much cut and scarified" as a fellow prisoner later testified.[37]

However, the irons on his legs were the real issue, and these posed a moral dilemma for the Patriot officers. Washington had not stated the charge against him but had ordered that he be "closely confined."[38]

By international convention, irons were legal only if James was considered a spy, but not if he was a prisoner of war. On the other hand, given the ruinous state of the bastion and the ingenuity of the prisoner, gentler treatment might lose him. Seeking clarification, Lamb sent a note to Benedict Arnold, who had taken over the command of West Point from General Howe, urging him to get instructions from Washington himself.

In the meantime, James managed to procure pen and paper and get a letter to Arnold, probably with the money he had refused to give up. In it he gave the details of his capture and subsequent treatment. He pleaded for a speedy trial that he might "not lie under that Scandal which I am innocent of any long time in this insufferable condition." He added that when he had been "in the country" he had "marched all the time" in his uniform, and arms, and "likewise did all" his men,[39] showing that he was a prisoner of war and not a spy. James's protests and bravado were the prisoner's way of showing that he was not, nor would be, cowed. Of course James had been a recruiter and a spy, but his blustering and bluffing had time and again saved his life. He had sown doubt in his captors' conscience. It was his only hope in his present situation.

Arnold, who at this point was in the middle of negotiations over his defection to the British, sent James's letter to Lamb with a note saying, "I don't think it justifiable to put prisoners of war in irons as a punishment, and on no other principle but retaliation or when it is absolutely necessary to secure them.... I believe Moody a bad man, but considered as a prisoner of war, no discrimination can be made, if he has observed his parole.... I could therefore wish they [the irons] might be taken off by you, without his knowing that I have interfered in the matter."[40] James was never to know of this intervention and characterizes Arnold as a cruel man in his *Narrative*. Lamb argued very forcefully that the irons be retained:

I have to observe, that as Moody was formerly parolled by General Washington, the General must certainly have been informed of some criminality on the part of the prisoner, which had not come to his knowledge before.... For my part, I view him in the light of a spy, from every circumstance respecting him. And as he was brought into the garrison in open day light, and has had an opportunity, (from the simplicity of the guard, and the facility of conversing with them) of knowing the state of the garrison; at least what kind of troops it is composed of; I think it will be highly improper to take off his irons, and let him escape; which he undoubtedly will do, in forty-eight hours if he is unshackled.... I think this garrison a very improper place to send prisoners of his enterprising spirit to, and I wish you would write to General Washington on the subject as soon as possible.

Every method ought to be taken to prevent the enemy from knowing the real state of this post. For altho' they may not at present have it in contemplation to attack it; yet when they are informed what kind of troops are destined for its defence, it may become an object. And should they embark their troops, and finess, as if they were going elsewhere, and embrace the opportunity of pushing up the river with a strong southerly wind, (after landing a sufficient body of troops in Jersey to draw General Washington's attention that way), I know not what could prevent it falling into their hands.[41]

Lamb's biographer erroneously remarks that this was precisely the plan that Clinton afterward adopted. Indeed, the weak state of the West Point garrison was being deliberately arranged by Arnold for just such a British takeover, but Clinton never got around to it.

Arnold concurred in the shackling until Washington's orders could be received. Meanwhile, the other prisoners were moved by water to King's Ferry and from there to Washington's headquarters near Orange-Town, leaving James and William Buirtis, a New York Loyalist prisoner, in Fort Putnam. Lamb in his frustration sent a message by Colonel William Alexander Livingston, who must also have informed Washington of James's circumstances, to the governor asking what was to be done with this prisoner. On August 17, Washington announced to Livingston the he had set September 1 as the date for Moody's court martial. He added, "If your Excellency knows of any material evidences against him, be pleased to direct them to attend."[42] A few days later he wrote to Arnold to keep Moody "without Irons except he should make any attempt toward an escape," until the end of the month, and then to send him down to him under the care of an Officer and party. Washington added, "If what is alledged against him be true, he has departed from the proper line of conduct of an Officer and must expect to be treated accordingly."[43] James was not informed that he was to be tried as a spy, nor were his irons removed.

Still protesting, James managed to get a second letter to Arnold, which resulted in a visit from one of Arnold's aides. His fellow prisoner described the occasion: on seeing Lieutenant Moody, the officer asked if that was the *Moody* whose name was a terror to every good man? on his replying that his name was Moody, he (the Aid de Camp[sic]) replied in a scoffing manner, "*You have got your self into a pretty situation*"; on his (Lieutenant Moody's) saying the situation was disagreeable, but he hoped it would not be of long continuance; he answered, he believed not, as he would soon meet with justice (pointing at the same time to a gallows that was erected in the sight and view of the dungeon); and also added, *there* is the gallows ready erected, which he (meaning Moody) had long merited. Lieutenant Moody answered, he made no doubt he (the Aid de Camp) wished to see every Loyal Subject hanged, but he thanked God, the power was not in *him*; but if he (Lieutenant Moody) was hanged, it could be for no other reason than being a Loyal subject to one of the best of Kings, and under one of the best of Governments; and added, if he had *ten* lives to lose, he would sooner forfeit the ten as a Loyal Subject, than *one* as a Rebel; and also said, he hoped to live to see him (the Aid de Camp), and a thousand such other villains, hanged for being Rebels. The officer then said he was sent to examine his irons, as he (Lieutenant Moody) had been frequently troubling General Arnold with his petitions. On examining the irons, he said *they were too bad*; and asked, who put them on? — saying, *Irons were intended for security, not for torment; but if any one merited such irons, he* (Lieutenant Moody) *did in his opinion.*[44]

James remained shackled throughout his four weeks at West Point, and very nearly for longer, in spite of Washington's and Arnold's orders. Presumably the guard was afraid of losing his prisoner and dared not risk any slackening of his security.

James, on September 1, still unaware of his impending court martial, now postponed for lack of credible evidence, was sent to Washington's camp near the Liberty Pole. Here the commander in chief's adjutant general, Colonel Alexander Scammel, came to supervise his reshackling in the new cell. By this time James's legs were inflamed and bleeding, sorer even than his wrists. He complained to the colonel about this treatment, adding again "that death would be infinitely preferable to a repetition of the torments he had just undergone."[45] An idealistic young officer, much mourned by his men and his fellow officers when he died shortly after the Battle of Yorktown a year later, Scammel was himself shocked. He immediately ordered that the irons be left off until the prisoner's legs could heal. When the army moved over the New Bridge, James was brought along, taking the opportunity to observe the enemy forces in detail, just as Lamb had feared he would. James says:

Everything seemed smooth and fair; and he felt himself much at ease, in the prospect of being soon exchanged; when, very unexpectedly, he was visited by an old acquaintance, one of their Colonels, who informed him, that he was in two days time to be brought to trial; that *Livingston* was to be his prosecutor, and that the Court Martial was *carefully picked* for the purpose. He subjoined, that he would do well to prepare for eternity, since, from the evidence which he knew would be produced, there was but one issue of the business to be expected.[46]

The colonel told him that he would be accused of assassinating the two officers that had been killed the year before in the skirmish near Tinton Falls. And anyway, the colonel insisted, "you are so obnoxious; you have been, and are likely to be, so *mischievous* to us, that, be assured, we are resolved to get rid of you at any rate. Besides, you cannot deny, and it can be proved by incontestable evidence, that you have enlisted men, in this *State*, for the King's service, and this, by our laws, is *death*."[47]

The *Narrative* continues: "Ensign Moody affected an air of unconcern at this information; but it was too serious and important to him to be really disregarded; he resolved, therefore, from that moment, to effect his escape, or to perish in the attempt." The dramatic account which follows could make a film script:

Every precaution had been taken to secure the place in which he was confined. It was nearly in the centre of the rebel camp. A sentinel was placed within the door of his prison, and another without, besides four others close round, and within a few yards of the place. The time now came on when he must either make his attempt, or lose the opportunity for ever.

On the night, therefore, of the 17th of September, busy in ruminating on his project, he had, on the pretence of being cold, got a watch-coat thrown across his shoulders, that he might better conceal, from his unpleasant companion, the operations which he meditated against his hand-cuffs. While he was racking his invention, to find some possible means of extricating himself from his fetters, he providentially cast his eye on a post fastened in the ground, through which an hole had been bored with an auger; and it occurred to him that it might be possible, with the aid of this hole, to break the bolt of his hand-cuffs. Watching the opportunity, therefore, from time to time, of the sentinel's looking another way, he thrust the point of the bolt into the above-mentioned hole, and by cautiously exerting his strength, and gradually bending the iron backwards and forwards, he at length broke it. Let the reader imagine what his sensations were, when he found the manacles drop from his hands! He sprung instantly past the interior sentinel, and rushing on the next, with one hand he seized his musquet, and with the other struck him to the ground. The sentinel within, and the four others who were placed by the fence surrounding the place of his confinement, immediately gave the alarm; and, in a moment, the cry was general —"*Moody* is escaped from the Provost."

It is impossible to describe the uproar which now took place throughout the whole camp. In a few minutes every man was in a bustle; every man was looking for Moody, and multitudes passed him on all sides — little suspecting, that a man whom they saw deliberately marching along, with a musket on his shoulder, could be the fugitive they were in quest of. The darkness of the night, which was also blustering and drizzly, prevented any discrimination of his person, and was indeed the great circumstance that rendered his escape possible.

But no small difficulty still remained to be surmounted. To prevent desertion, which at that time, was very frequent, Washington had sur-rounded his camp with a chain of sentinels, posted at about forty or fifty yards distance from each other; he was unacquainted with their stations; to pass them undiscovered would certainly be fatal. In this dilemma Providence again befriended him. He had gained their station without knowing it, when luckily he heard the watch-word passed from one to another —"Look sharp to the chain — Moody is escaped from the Provost." From the sound of the voices he ascertained the respective situations of these sentinels; and, throwing himself on his hands and knees, he was happy enough to crawl through the vacant space between two of them, unseen by either. Judging that their line of pursuit would naturally be toward the British army, he made a detour into the woods on the opposite side. Through these woods he made as much speed as the darkness of the night would permit, steering his course, after the Indian manner, by occasionally groping and feeling the *white-oak*. On the south side the bark of this tree is rough and unpleasant to the touch, but on the north side it is smooth; hence it serves the sagacious traverser of the desert, by night as well as by day, for his compass. Through the most dismal woods and swamps he continued to wander till the night of the 21st, a space of more than fifty-six hours during which time, he had no other sustenance than a few *beech* leaves (which, of all that the woods afforded, were the least unpleasant to the taste, and least pernicious to health), which he chewed and swallowed, to abate the intolerable cravings of his hunger.

In every inhabited district he knew there were friends of Government; and he had now learned also where and how to find them out, without endangering their safety, which was always the first object of his concern. From some of these good men he received minute information how the pursuit after him was directed, and where every guard was posted. Thus assisted, he eluded their keenest vigilance; and, at length, by God's blessing, to his unspeakable joy, he arrived safe at *Paulus-Hook*.[48]

NOTES

1. William Franklin to Lord George Germain, 5 Feb. 1779, quoted in *Livingston Papers*, vol. 3, 49.
2. Thomas Sterling to Sir Henry Clinton, 26 Feb. 1779, PRO, Colonial Office (CO) 5/97, quoted in *Livingston Papers*, vol. 3, 50, n. 5. Sterling (also spelt Stirling), Clinton, and Howe are but three of the confusing examples of the same name being held by unrelated prominent people on opposing sides in the American Revolution.
3. William Livingston to Sir Henry Clinton, Elizabethtown, 29 March 1779, *ibid.*, 49.
4. Sir Henry Clinton to William Livingston, New York, 10 April 1779, *ibid.*, 54.
5. See William Smith, *Historical Memoirs from 26 August 1778, to 12 November 1783 of William Smith* (New York: Eyewitness Accounts of the American Revolution, Series III, New York Times and Arno Press, 1971), 95 for a discussion of who the Loyalist writer might be. Other candidates were the Reverend Samuel Seabury, Clinton's old schoolmate and later to be the first Episcopalian bishop of the United States, and Loyalist governor, William Franklin.
6. William Livingston to William Livingston, Jr., Raritan, 24 June 1779. *Livingston Papers*, vol. 3, 124-25.
7. *Narrative*, appendix 6.
8. See note 10 in Chapter 5 for the wide variety of spellings of this name.
9. *Narrative*, 14.
10. *Ibid.*
11. *Documents Relating to the Revolutionary History of the State of New Jersey*, ed. William S. Stryker (Trenton, NJ: 1901). Extracts from American Newspapers (hereafter Newspaper Extracts), vol. 4, 435.
12. *Ibid.*
13. *Narrative*, 14.
14. Moody Memorial, 28 Sept. 1780. The identity of this British spy was never discovered.
15. *Narrative*, 14-18.

16. *Ibid.*, 21.
17. Petition of Mathias Bugginer, *Research Papers*, Ontario Historical Society, vol. 24, 32.
18. *Narrative*, 21.
19. Moody Memorial, 28 Sept. 1780. Moody Papers.
20. 17 July 1780, *Minutes of the Governors' Council, 1779-1789*, ed. David A. Bernstein, *New Jersey Archives*, 3rd ser. (Trenton: 1974), 160-61.
21. "For the king of Israel is come out to seek a flea, as when one doth hunt a partridge in the mountains." I Samuel 26:20.
22. *Narrative*, 22.
23. Anthony Wayne to George Washington, 22 July 1780, Washington papers, Ser. 4, Reel 68, LC.
24. *Ibid.*
25. *Narrative*, 22.
26. The engagement was another example of Loyalist bravery. There were a hundred men in the fort resisting an assault by some seventeen hundred Patriots. The battle lasted one hour and a half and resulted in four killed and ten wounded for the refugees and 30 rebels dead and another 40 wounded. Sir Henry Clinton went over and thanked the men and Major John André wrote the poem, "The Cow Chase," which extolled the bravery of the defenders and satirized the rebel leaders.
27. Jonathan Lawrence, Jr., to William Livingston, 22 July 1780, New York Public Library.
28. Newspaper Extracts, 2 Aug. 1780, vol. 4, 553.
29. In the eighteenth century, to have one's servant taken away was a severe blow and a sure sign of still worse things about to happen. Mme de Sévigné wrote to M. de Pomponne when Nicholas Fouquet, Finance Minister to Louis XIV, was arrested and his two servants taken away from him, "cette cruauté ... c'est une chose inconcevable; on en tire même des conséquences fâcheuses dont Dieu le préserve." Manuscrit du XVIIIᵉ siècle, dépôt de l'Association "Les Amis de Vaux-le-Vicomte."
30. The other name for Kingston at the time was Aesopus, and this is the name James uses in the *Narrative*.
31. *Narrative*, 23.
32. G.H. Van Wagenen to Col. William Malcolm, 7 Aug. 1780, Washington Papers, Ser. 4, Reel 69, LC.
33. Isaac Q. Leake, *Memoir of the Life and Times of General John Lamb* (Albany: Joel Munsell, 1850), 246.
34. A south German specialty, and leaden at the best of times.
35. *Narrative*, 28-29.
36. Memorial, 28 Sept. 1780.
37. The Testimony of William Buirtis, 11 May 1782, quoted in the *Narrative*, 26, but also among the Moody Papers.

38. Col. John Lamb to the Officer Commanding the Guard at Fort Putnam, West Point, 9 Aug. 1780, Lamb Letter Book, Lamb's Papers, New York Historical Society (NYHS).
39. James Moody to Benedict Arnold, West Point, 11 Aug. 1780, Lamb's Papers, Reel 2, no. 94, NYHS.
40. Arnold to Lamb, 11 Aug. 1780, quoted in Leake, *Memoir*, 247.
41. Lamb to Arnold, West Point, 12 Aug. 1780, *ibid.*, 248.
42. Washington to William Livingston, 17 Aug. 1780, *Livingston Papers*, vol. 4, 39.
43. Washington to Arnold, 19 Aug. 1780, *The Writings of George Washington from the Original Manuscript Sources, 1745-1799*, ed. John C. Fitzpatrick (Washington, DC: 1931-44), vol. 19, 395.
44. *Narrative*, 27-28.
45. *Ibid.*, 30.
46. *Ibid.*
47. *Ibid.*, 31.
48. *Ibid.*, 31-34.

7

NEW YORK, 1780-82

JAMES HAD ARRIVED SAFELY BACK to his regiment on Staten Island. Once more his life was to take a new turn. He was about to leave the barracks and move to New York, to be charged with assignments that would be even more dangerous. The move would bring him into contact with senior British officers and make him more painfully aware of their sluggish, wasteful conduct of the war. He would also experience living in an occupied city, in a society of refugees and exiles, his movements watched by enemy spies.

Until now James had operated mostly in his own territory of Sussex and its adjoining counties. Although he was often gathering intelligence, he was acting on local New Jersey issues, attempting to reduce the rebel pressure on his Tory neighbours. The enemy was the Patriot Jersey government of Governor Livingston, rather than the Continental forces of George Washington. This focus was about to change for him. His reputation as a daringly successful leader of small important missions had been steadily growing. Sir Henry needed a man of his calibre to bring him direct information about the enemy. It was probably after he made his escape from Washington's camp in late September 1780, that James was seconded from his regiment on Staten Island to come directly under the commander in chief's command at headquarters.[1] A few months later, we find him being paid a per diem allowance to live in New York.

Though still as eager to do his utmost for the Loyalist cause, he was beginning to chafe at administrative neglect. He had, as he said, been happy to serve for nothing as he had not the least thought of becoming a soldier and expected to be back on his farm before the first year was out. Money had not been a concern. But now, three years later, the war still showed no signs of ending. His property had been confiscated. Like many other Loyalists, he had spent his own fortune, including in his case £1,200 left him by an uncle, in enlisting and paying men for public service. He had had to borrow money for the Livingston expedition. Inflation was rampant and he had family responsibilities to consider. He must now ask to be paid his due.

Before going out to capture Livingston he had taken the precaution of procuring certificates claiming back pay as an ensign from October 25, 1777 until February 1778. This was the period during which he was on the muster rolls but before his warrant was changed to an ensign's commission in July 1778. He had, of course, served without pay as a "gentleman volunteer" during the spring and summer of 1777 when he was recruiting and escorting men through New Jersey to New York. When he came back in late September 1780, he attached to his intelligence report a summary of his activities up to that time, and followed it with a reminder a week later that he still had received no money. He also asked that he might be considered for one of the vacant lieutenancies in the New Jersey Volunteers.

James slipped into New York on September 27, presented his report the next day, and his memorial for back pay and a lieutenant's commission on October 2. But his superiors had other preoccupations. On September 17, the day James broke out of the Liberty Pole prison, Major John André, Clinton's young adjutant general, had been arranging to meet the rebel general, Benedict Arnold, near West Point. What should have been a brilliant coup for the British, with the handing over of the strategic fort of West Point on the Hudson River, its men and arms, possibly ending the war in a bloodless victory for the British, turned into a humiliating sprint to the British lines on the part of Arnold, and personal tragedy for André. While James was making his way back to freedom, André was captured, tried, and condemned as a spy. He was hanged on September 30, two days before James submitted his request for a promotion.

Everyone who knew André had hoped that he could be saved. Colonel John Graves Simcoe, the British officer commanding the provincial corps of Queen's Rangers, and after the war, Lieutenant Governor of Upper Canada, had put forth a daring plan involving James. Reasoning that Washington would send André to Philadelphia to be tried, he and James, with a small band, would swoop down on the prisoner's escort and pluck André from his American captors. He did not know James personally but his reputation was such that Simcoe felt that he was the one person who might actually succeed in such a mission.[2] He could not have realized that James had himself just escaped from captivity. In any case Clinton summarily dismissed the scheme.

Nor did James's request receive immediate attention. In view of the heavy preoccupation of British headquarters at the time, this is not surprising. However his wait seems to have been unnecessarily long. Only in mid-March of the following year did he have "justice done"[3] him at the Inspector General's Office. Although he was not promoted to lieutenant until then, he was, as we have seen, already in 1780 being addressed as captain, even by the rebels. The British military establishment had little confidence in the Loyalist Americans, barely distinguishing them from their Patriot opposites. They considered them self-pitying and undisciplined and endeavoured to keep them in their place. They resented the Loyalist provincial regiments and insisted that their own field officers outrank provincials of the same grade. This was a colonial humiliation that had also disenchanted Washington when, as a young man, he had served as colonel of the Virginia Regiment on the Virginia frontier in 1754.[4]

The New York that James moved to in that year comprised only the tip of Manhattan. One can wander through the winding streets that are now the financial district and, with willpower, imagine one is back with James. The shoreline of his New York followed the lines of Pearl Street, to the Bowling Green and up Greenwich Street, which was the edge of the North River. The main docks were where Water Street is now. Going north, the city extended only a little farther than St. Paul's Chapel on Broadway. James would have recognized the chapel, but not the spire or the portico on the Broadway side, which were added in 1794. Just to the south from the Bowling Green, James would see the ramparts of now-vanished Fort George, and beyond the harbour to the southwest, bucolic Staten Island, where the new Jersey Volunteers were quartered. Directly across the North River section of the Hudson was Paulus Hook, the haven where a boat could carry him swiftly back to the safety of New York after a special mission.

The Bowling Green is still there at the foot of old Broadway, a small island of green surrounded by towering skyscrapers. Before the Revolution there had been, at its centre, a gilded lead equestrian statue of George III — today replaced by an ugly concrete fountain — that was toppled by an enthusiastic mob on the night of July 9, 1776, just after Washington announced the Declaration of Independence to his troops. The original wrought-iron fence, though blunted, still surrounds this little oasis: its palings were divested of their charming crowns in the same patriotic exuberance. Even without its statue, the Bowling Green was enjoyed and played on during the British occupation. This was the fashionable residential area that had escaped the terrible fire of 1776. Sir Henry had his headquarters — as did Washington and Carleton, and other commanders on both sides — in the elegant Kennedy house at Number One Broadway, just across the street. Benedict Arnold lived next door. Their gardens behind, sweeping down to the water's edge, gave an uninterrupted view across the river to the Jersey shore. Both these houses have long since been demolished. However, an eighteenth-century building among today's skyscrapers that James would still recognize is Fraunce's Tavern, known to New Yorkers of the Revolution as Black Sam's after its West Indian owner, Samuel Fraunce. It was then the Queen's Head Tavern, and had originally been the house of the first Stephen DeLancey, built on a water lot facing Staten Island. It has since become famous as the place where Washington, on December 4, 1783, took tearful leave of his still-serving principal officers, a week after the final handing over of New York City to the Americans by Sir Guy Carleton, an event James was no doubt glad to have missed.

New York had been, before the Revolution, a thriving port fast on its way to overtaking Philadelphia in its commercial activity. It had been a charming architectural mixture of seventeenth century, high, Dutch houses and later English Georgian mansions. But by 1780, when James moved in from the barracks on Staten Island, much of the city had become a smelly, disintegrating slum, a city of refugees, soldiers, and camp followers. Ravaged by two fires, and despoiled by two occupying armies, two-thirds of the city was now a "Canvass Town" of flimsy rubble lean-tos huddling against the charred ruins of once elegant buildings. It was "a place of refuge, for drunkenness, prostitution, and violence ... the resort of sailors from the ships-of-war in the Harbour, of Negroes who fled from the neighbouring provinces, and others brought from the south by the troops in their southern expeditions."[5] Lovely old trees, planted a hundred years before by the Dutch, remained only as blackened stumps. Any other trees that had survived

View of the Bowling Green, northwest side at Broadway, 1826. The first house on the left is No. One Broadway, where Sir Henry Clinton had his headquarters as British commander in chief while Moody operated out of New York, 1780-82. Courtesy New York Historical Society (32267c)

the fires had been cut down for heating or cooking fuel during the unspeakable cold of the previous winter.

A contemporary Englishman, Nicholas Cresswell, is eloquent in his disgust at what he saw and smelled:

Ditches and fortified places are full of stagnate water, damaged sour Crout and filth of every kind. Noisome vapours arise from the mud left in the docks and slips at low water, and unwholesome smells are occasioned by such a number of people being crowded together in so small a compass almost like herrings in a barrel, most of them very dirty and not a small number sick of some disease, the Itch, Pox, Fever, or Flux.... If any author had an inclination to write a treatise upon stinks and ill smells, he never could meet with more subject matter than in New York, or anyone who had abilities and inclinations to expose the vicious and unfeeling part of human nature or the various arts, ways and means, that are used to pick up a living in this world, I recommend New York as a proper place to collect his characters.[6]

With no civil government, the army patrolled the streets, helping themselves to what came their way. Fences, window frames, doors were plundered from Loyalist as well as Patriot property, to reappear in a fire or a British officer's converted and requisitioned barn. The elegant hospital, the Dissenting churches, were crammed with sick soldiers or despairing prisoners. The university and the charity schools were closed. On the ruins of the lovely old Gothic-style Anglican Church of the Trinity a summer theatre had been built and tombstones had been torn up to make the entrance way wider. Close by, destitute women, turned prostitute, tried to make a few shillings for their families.

New York was a city almost entirely of men, a city under siege with all the longing and dissoluteness that such situations engender. Fortunes were made in government contracts by skimping on rations, particularly for prisoners, and military supplies for the men. The senior officers made money through graft and perks. They lived in requisitioned houses, assigned to people on the favour of the officer in charge, with the government paying no rent for houses that had belonged to rebels and, despite contrary regulations, often not paying anything to the Loyalist owner either. A host of unsavoury people catered to their wants as men far from home.

The troops thro idleness fall into all manner of the worst of vices, contract illnesses, which take off many. Thus they dwindle away by that means, and by small excursions which answer no real purposes. After campaigns which have accomplished nothing, more troops are required. The general language even of the common soldiers is, that the war might and would have been ended long before now, if it was not for the great men, who only want to fill their purses; and indeed it is too apparent that this has been and is the ruling principle in all departments, only to seek their own private interest, and to make hay while the Sun shineth, and when they have got enough then to retreat or go home — let become of America what will![7]

The commander in chief, Sir Henry Clinton, set a particularly inglorious example. A bad-tempered man who would shut himself away with a small retinue of intimates for several days at a time, he consoled himself in his widowhood with his married housekeeper, by whom he had a second family, which to do him justice he supported afterward in England. Nor did her sergeant husband suffer from the arrangement. Clinton loved drag hunts, which in New York gave him the exercise he craved. William Smith disgustedly described these. "I saw him," Smith wrote in his diary, "at three o'clock pass my window with several horsemen, as I have often this winter, following a Hessian jager who dragged a bone pursued by a dog, all full speed over fences, through fields, etc. Perhaps the packet will be detained tomorrow that he may enjoy this unmanly sport this afternoon!... He never played this low game till the commissioners were gone, though he was daily on horseback."[8] Even Clinton's love of music was tarnished. At his country residence, the Beekman mansion at Turtle Bay on the East River, the group, which included André and the young Oliver DeLancey, would play the violin and sing and impersonate those they did not like until they became too drunk to stand.

Although Clinton had shown military energy and skill when he campaigned on the Hudson under General Sir William Howe, it was as if once in full command himself, he was no longer able to make decisions. He seemed afraid to make a move for fear it would be the wrong one, and afraid to let anyone else take action because they might attain more glory than he. Instead of working with his generals and civilian leaders, he became secretive, paranoic, and jealous of his peers, with his will and his judgement paralyzed, never continuing "in one mind," as one contemporary wrote, "from Breakfast till dinner, or from dinner till bed-time."[9] Franklin described him as "weak, irresolute, unsteady, vain, incapable of forming any plan himself, and too weak or rather too proud and conceited to follow that of another." [10] For the Loyalists, the contrast was all the more painful with Washington, upright in his private life and decisive as a general.

For the Loyalists it was a heartbreaking time. Families were broken up, some not to find each other until after the war. The officers and men who had enlisted in the provincial corps had often fled to the British lines leaving their wives and children behind in the country. These were likely to be forcibly evicted from their houses, like the wife of Joseph Galloway in Philadelphia, and often harassed like the family of James's Connecticut friend Jesse Hoyt, whose wife and five small children were dragged out of their house in winter in their sleeping clothes, and whose small baby died as a consequence. Those who tried to salvage any of their possessions were escorted to the edge of the British lines. Many wives died far from their husbands, of a broken heart, like William Franklin's, or of an accident, like James's, leaving small children to be cared for in a war-torn city. Getting the family into New York required rebel permission, which, ironically, was not always forthcoming. Some men, like James Budd, the father of James's future daughter-in-law, Margaret, brought their families into New York a few at a time. In this case, the little girl was boarded with a family for three months until her mother and the rest of her own family could be fetched. Then her father was killed while recruiting in White Plains and the family had to struggle on alone in New York. Quite apart from the acute shortage of money and accommodation, the anguish of separation was felt by all.

Jonathan Odell expressed this feeling in some deeply felt, even if not altogether accomplished, verses that he wrote to Mrs. Odell, entitled "A Loyalist in Exile from his Family sends a miniature picture to his disconsolate wife." He describes a frightful dream — no doubt recurring — that he has had:

> The ruthless Tyrant, with untimely haste,
> Pointing his lance, and near thy pillow plac'd —
> Thy Bed surrounded by an orphan train,
> Where Tender cries to Heaven ascend in vain!
> While speechless agony and Horror shake
> My trembling frame, till from the trance I wake —

And he prays:

O Providence Divine
O'er Anna's dwelling let thy banner shine,
Protect the Mother and her Infant care,
Be thou her Guard, her Refuge from Despair,
Subdue the bloody rage of civil strife.
Restore me to the Mother and the Wife.[11]

Or another in a lighter vein, entitled "Veridicus":

My stocking comes, lest I shou'd tear it,
For you to mend it ere I wear it.
"A stitch in time" — (you know the adage)
But every laundress, in this *badage*,
At best is but a mere pretender,
An awkward clumsy-fisted mender:
Then kindly lend *your* needle's aid,
Nor let the favor be delay'd:
For, to be free, my stock is small,
And, more or less, wants mending all.[12]

For James the time must have been particularly painful. His own family affairs seemed to be in crisis.

After the defiant Loyalist outbursts that had accompanied his successful recruiting in Sussex County in 1778, the rebels proceeded to redress the political balance. Throughout 1779, members of the Drake family, friends and neighbours of the Moodys, were hauled into court, Ephraim for having urged his son to join the British, and for his own irreverent outburst against the oaths of allegiance and abjuration, and his wife, Mary, for giving food to an enemy soldier. In both indictments, Elizabeth Moody was named as the only witness. In the first instance, her father, William Brittain, gave £100 surety for her appearance at the next quarter sessions of the court. William himself was indicted for his "seditious words" concerning Isaac Martin, and Joshua Swayze put up a bond for him for £200. But Elizabeth Moody was not mentioned in the records of the actual court hearings. Did she in fact appear? Or was she discarded as an unhelpful witness for the prosecution? James would have worried about her, and he must have felt very alone.

One catches glimpses of James in New York during his leisure time. He attended the Anglican Church services, and met a number of senior military and civilian officials. Here he made a lifelong friend in Charles Inglis, the rector of Trinity Church. Ten years older than James, Inglis was a serious, very devout man, and also a warm, affectionate, and kindly person, devoted to his family and his church. He was descended from a long line of Scottish and Irish Anglican clerics, had lost both his parents at an early age, had come to Philadelphia as a private tutor, and then had gone on to teach school and study on his own to qualify as an ordained minister. His first wife had died in childbirth but he was now happily remarried with four young children with him in New York. Like many committed Loyalists, he had opposed the Stamp Act and the right of Parliament to tax the colonies.

But now, Inglis was the most senior Anglican divine in America. James must have listened to his moving, well thought out, rather evangelical sermons in Saint Paul's Chapel, upholding the cause of loyalty against rebellion but also insisting on Christian behaviour even in war, aspects of the struggle that James passionately believed in. No doubt he contributed to the funds that Inglis raised at Christmastime for needy widows and orphans.

Perhaps it was here that he met and fell in love with the cultivated and kind young widow, Jane Robinson Lynson, a Loyalist from Newark in her early twenties, the only daughter of Captain Robert Robinson. The Lynsons were a New York merchant family. Perhaps she gathered up his motherless children when they came to New York, for in later life they certainly loved her as their own mother. Perhaps the legend is true that she hid him when he escaped from Washington's camp. Jane was herself a devout Anglican.

James was also a Master Mason in Lodge 169, the Boston Lodge of York Masons that had regrouped in New York in 1779. Here were friends like John Le Chevalier Roome and John Thompson, a fellow officer who had been captured with him at Bull's Ferry. William Franklin probably also belonged to this lodge. James continued to be an active Mason for the rest of his life.

Like all cities in wartime, New York offered many amusements both private and public. With James's sense of humour and sense of the dramatic, which emerge so clearly in his *Narrative*, he must have enjoyed the London plays put on by the British officers to raise money for poor families. He liked good company and good food. We can presume that he attended some of the many balls held that winter, such as the one Joanna Robinson breathlessly described to her brother, Beverley, in Virginia, a ball given by Mrs. B., "vastly elegant a crowd of gentlemen and fifteen Ladies Mrs. Arnold was there and looked like an Angel the company broke up at two o'clock we should perhaps have gone away earlyer if it had not been for the entertaining Miss Williams who said so many *good things* that it was impossible to keep from one continual laugh." [13] Perhaps he shared in the amusement at seeing Prince William Henry, the future King William IV, a visiting midshipman under Admiral Robert Digby's tutelage, "essaying very awkwardly to skate, supported by generals, admirals, and their supporters," [14] on the broad expanse of frozen water that extended behind the city to the North River. Perhaps he and Jane Lynson skated there too, though the night that all New York feted the arrival of the royal prince, James was out on a special mission.

James must certainly at this time have got to know better William Franklin and other members of the Board of Associated Loyalists, as well as some of the officers being sent out by it. We know that Franklin took comfort in the company of fellow active Loyalists and found himself impatient with those highly placed New Yorkers who had not suffered from the war. [15] James won the respect of the senior officers and military people who later testified on his behalf. He is described as being of "undeviating probity and honour," [16] but he also comes across as entertaining and fun, a man who can tell a good story, and is not afraid to take a risk.

Most of James's time, however, went into the war. No mention is made of what he did at headquarters, but one wonders if he were not in some way organizing spying expeditions. The city teemed with agents, Loyal and Patriot. Although both sides — Washington and Skinner with William Franklin — had good spy networks, Clinton's intelligence was always poor, and his use of it worse.

With André's replacement by his friend and fellow stage buff, Major Oliver DeLancey, as adjutant general, the British secret service became more closely associated with the Loyalist community. DeLancey, though an officer in a British regiment, was a member of one of New York's most influential families, high Anglican Tories that had opposed the Livingston Whigs. He was the son of Brigadier General Oliver DeLancey, commanding DeLancey's brigade from New York and senior Brigadier General of Provincials, and grandson of the Huguenot immigrant Stephen (in French, Étienne) who had arrived in New York after Louis XIV's Revocation of the Edict of Nantes, with a small bag of precious gems to establish his fortune and his family. A first cousin of young Oliver was Colonel James DeLancey who now headed the

West Chester Light Infantry, a detachment of refugees who won renown and opprobrium as the "Cow boys," because they were particularly skilled at rounding up other people's cattle for British provisions (the term "cowboys" did not acquire its modern, Western sense till 1867).[17] Oliver was also the brother of the Stephen DeLancey who was colonel of James's battalion at this time. James would meet these last two many times again after the war.

In his new capacity, Major Oliver DeLancey was assisted by Colonel Beverley Robinson, another Loyalist, whose father owned the country seat on the Hudson opposite West Point where Arnold had lived when commander there; and by Captain George Beckwith, member of a distinguished British military family, who as aide de camp to General Knyphausen had sent James out to kidnap Governor Livingston.

These three men attempted to set up a structured intelligence network for Clinton. They drew up in early 1781 "Proposals for a Plan of Gaining Intelligence." The document stated what had already been evolving under André, that they would "endeavour to open a correspondence with persons of consequence in different parts of the country.... All persons employed by us and who produce passes from us or either of us should neither be examined nor detained by any officers at the advanced posts, either in going out or returning."[18] James permanently had such a pass. It was Beckwith who prepared the intelligence items for DeLancey, who then passed them on to Sir Henry. Both young men later wrote glowingly of James's contribution to the Loyalist cause.

These men were at last doing what Washington had done from the outset of the war. As they hoped to do, he had kept a tight control over his own networks. Early on, he had outlined in detail the spy's task to his chief operative in New York, Robert Townsend, code-named "Culper junior," beginning crisply: "C——— Junr. to remain in the City, to collect all the useful information he can — to do this he should mix as much as possible among the officers and Refugees, visit the Coffee Houses, and all public places. He is to pay particular attention to the movements by land and water in and about the city especially."[19]

Another of Washington's agents, John Vanderhovan, who had probably also been planted in New York shortly after the departure of the Americans, followed this excellent advice. Like modern security-minded intelligence services, most of these spies operated independently of each other in little networks of their own, but Vanderhovan occasionally used Culper's organization to get his information out of New York. Vanderhovan, under the code name "Littel D.," was detailed to follow James just after his escape back to New York. By making friends with James, Vanderhovan was gathering crumbs of information on British intelligence. Here is what he sent off to John Hendricks, another agent, on October 24, 1780, in his deliciously phonetic spelling that was obviously designed to conceal his identity:

I have had the Good forain to Introduce my Self to a Certain George Frustner of Lankister Brother in law to a Certain Capt. Rankin in Browne Coar who formerly Kept a Ferry at that Place and who was often out with Andre as he Informs me, this Mr. Frustner was Sent out the fifth Day of this month by Gennoral Clinton to Meet Some officer of Distinction of your Army.

Mr. Moody Introduced Mr. Frustner to me Moody and I are on Veery Good terms and I often Give Him an Invitation to Come and dine with me and Sup and So fourth.

I am working on Mr. Frustner and Leut. Moody Every Night and I Belive that I shall find out all theyre Secrets in a time as Moody Has Informed me that One of the Goveners own Counsel Sent Him Word Every Day while He was out after Him and I intend to find out His name in a Day or two and His Guide I now know as he has told me his name which you Shall Know as Soon as I can fix a time with you.[20]

Two days later we learn that "Mr. Frustner is out and Mr. Moody's Man the[n] left this yesterday morning." The spy writes: "I wish to See you on Some particular Business and wish you would Send Some trusty person — to posts next Saturday night about Six O'clock as I wish to Get of from this Side Before the Gards are Set out pray do not fail as I wan to Communicate Something that Cannot be Done with out —." From Vanderhovan we get a picture of the excitement at British headquarters when a mail is captured:

Since yesterday I have Been at Head Quarters and find that a Mail is Intercepted and Brought into town By a Refugee as is Said hear I saw the man & his Guide is a Lusty pumkin Man a Very Villain in his Eyes the Mail was Brought to town the twenty third at night Ever Since they are Verry Busey at the Adgedent Gen. office three of them writing as fast as possible and it is Said that a frigate is to Sail to morrow morning with Despatches for England.[21]

And we find that Furstner has further unbent himself, for "Littel D."
sends off another dispatch:

Another Cutthroat General amongst you don't know who he is he and two
collenals met one Fustner a Duthm who Clinton Snt out By the way of
Shroesbury within ten or twelve Days last and fostner told me he Brought a
number of letters from them fostner would not tell me his name But I am
trying to work it out of him they Met at one Clarks near Bordentown this
fostner has Long Been Imployed in the Business and three times out with
André to Arnold he formerly lived in Merraland and is Brother-in-law to
Mr. Bisket.[22]

How vulnerable these men were.

Furstner, whose Christian name was Andrew and not George, was
the Loyalist courier between Philadelphia and New York, and was, as
the Patriot spy was discovering, employed by André to carry letters destined for Arnold. Another huge man, he was a German farmer who
first offered his services to the British under Howe as they approached
Philadelphia, in 1777. In 1778, before James sent his "trusty Loyalist,"
Furstner had taken dispatches to Colonel John Butler at Niagara. He
was also the contact man between British headquarters and a group of
Loyalists in Lancaster County, Pennsylvania, and other Philadelphia
spies such as Christopher Sower, a printer, Joseph Stansbury, a poet
and owner of a china shop, and Samuel Wallis, a shipping agent, who
had been recruited probably by Joseph Galloway while the British
occupied Philadelphia. In addition, Furstner ran messages between Sir
Henry and a group of Loyalists in York County on the northern frontier of Pennsylvania, headed by his brother-in-law, William Rankin.

James must have been drawn to these Pennsylvania men now
forced to seek refuge in New York. Most of them, like James in Sussex
County, had tried to maintain in readiness, in Pennsylvania, a secret
force sympathetic to the British. Rankin is particularly interesting. He
was an influential landowner in York County, a justice of the court of
common pleas and quarter sessions, and a colonel of the local militia.
He had, in 1776, represented York in the Pennsylvania Assembly under
the new constitution, but with the Declaration of Independence, like
a number of other Whigs in America, he had balked at waging a war
of separation. Instead he kept his command of the militia and secretly
offered his services to the British, including the loyalty of five hundred
men, who, like Moody's recruits, would be prepared to rise up and

seize control of the countryside as soon as Sir Henry ordered. In this he was acting in concert with a captain of the Northumberland militia, while a colonel of the Lancaster militia was also promising help. These Loyalists wanted to join forces with Butler on the northern frontier against General Sullivan in 1779, and help in seizing the Rebel magazine at Carlisle, but Sir Henry refused to endorse the plan.

In May 1780, Rankin had six thousand men he felt he could count on, "spread all over the country," not only in Lancaster, York, and Northumberland, and but also in Delaware and Maryland, across the Pennsylvania boundary. Franklin had agreed to lead a "New Jersey Provincial brigade and such other Provincial corps as will turn out voluntarily" plus as many refugees as he would be allowed to raise along the way, with the help of a British diversion "to keep off Mr. Washington's army ... to penetrate into the loyal county of Sussex in New Jersey, reinforce himself, and form a junction with those people on the frontiers of Pennsylvania."[23] One senses a Moody presence here.

The letters that Furstner told Vanderhovan about may well have been Rankin's address of October 14, 1780, to King George III, sent via Simcoe, then commanding the provincial corps of Queen's Rangers. The address stated that Rankin and his associates of Pennsylvania, Delaware, and Maryland, now numbering seven thousand, needed only confidence and support to make them highly useful to the royal cause. They hoped that Simcoe, as one of the few British officers they trusted to carry through an enterprise, would lead an expedition to the Chesapeake that would join forces with the Loyalists in the region. But Clinton refused all such suggestions and used Rankin and the others only for intelligence. Eventually in 1781 Rankin also fled to New York.

In spite of excellent intelligence supplied by Loyalist agents, the British commander in chief does not seem to have paid careful attention to it. Warnings against rebel spies and leaked confidential information were largely ignored. William Smith complained that Clinton never bothered to interview rebel informers. "How can a General ever acquire what is of so much Importance in all Wars, and especially a Civil one, when no enquiries are made?" Smith railed. He considered Clinton "totally negligent as to the Use of the Means for procuring Intelligence."[24] Perhaps the effort of reading through the memoranda and of pulling all the information together into a coherent intelligence estimate was beyond his capacity in his paralyzed state of mind. Perhaps he found the necessary concentration on picayune detail too taxing. In any case, by the spring of 1781 Sir Henry was turning more and more to intercepted dispatches to give him information about the rebels. They told the full story at a glance. The only problem was to find a quick dependable man to do the capturing. For this the daring Ensign Moody was the obvious person. James was about to embark on the most hazardous adventures of his career so far.

NOTES

1. Loyalist Claims, PRO, AO 12/99 and certificate of Cortlandt Skinner, *Narrative*, appendix 2.
2. Draft letter of John Graves Simcoe, Wolford Lodge, to an unknown friend, 15 June 1783, Simcoe Family Papers, Archives of Ontario, microfilm F47-6-0-1.
3. Covering letter from James Moody to Major Oliver DeLancey, with his memorial to Sir Henry Clinton, New York, 11 March 1781, Moody Papers. James is asking that his previous petition be reconsidered and that he have "justice done."
4. Willard Sterne Randall, *George Washington: A Life* (New York: Henry Holt, 1997), 90 and following.
5. William Dunlap, *History of the American Theatre* (New York: 1833; repr. 1963), 79.
6. Nicholas Cresswell, *The Journal of Nicholas Cresswell, 1774-1777* (London: Jonathan Cape, 1925), 244-45.
7. Occupation of New York City by the British from the diary of the Moravian Rt. Rev. A.A. Reinke, entry for Dec. 16, 1780, *The Pennsylvania Magazine of History and Biography*, 10 (1886): 434.
8. William Smith, *Diary*, 1 March 1779, quoted in William B. Wilcox, *Portrait of a General: Sir Henry Clinton in the War of Independence* (New York: Alfred A. Knopf, 1964), 266, note 5.
9. William H. Mariboe, "The Life of William Franklin, 1730(1)-1813, 'Pro Rege et Patria,'" PhD thesis, University of Pennsylvania, 1962, 496.
10. *Ibid.*, 532.
11. Jonathan Odell, Poetry, notebook no. 2, 1766-1814, New York, 23 March 1780, microfilm, University of New Brunswick, Loyalist Studies, Roll 7.
12. *Ibid.*
13. Joanna Robinson, 1 May 1781, to Lt. Col. Beverley Robinson, New Brunswick Museum, Reel 180, Packet 18, Shelf 128, Box 3.
14. Dunlap, *American Theatre*, 83.
15. *Historical Memoirs from 26 August 1778 to 12 November 1783 of William Smith*, ed. William H.W. Sabine (New York: Eyewitness Accounts of the American Revolution, Series III, The New York Times

and Arno Press, 1971), 250. Smith recounts that Royalist Governor William Tryon "speaks acrimoniously of Governor Franklin as fond of low Company when he may figure as the Head." He must be alluding to Franklin's work with the refugees and the Refugee Club.

16. *Narrative*, Appendix 7.
17. Bill Bryson, *Made in America: An Informal History of the English Language in the United States* (New York: William Morrow, 1994), 127.
18. Carl Van Doren, *Secret History of the American Revolution* (New York: Viking Press, 1941), 406.
19. Corey Ford, *A Peculiar Service* (Boston: Little, Brown, 1965), 192.
20. *Ibid.*
21. *Ibid.*
22. *Ibid.*
23. Van Doren, *Secret History*, 224-25.
24. Smith, *Memoirs*, 65.

8

CAPTURING THE MAILS:

SPRING AND SUMMER, 1781

DURING THE NEXT YEAR James was to be sucked into a game of wit between Washington and Clinton. He was about to be launched on a new career. "On the 6th of March 1781," James tells us, "Colonel Delancey, the Adjutant General, requested Mr. Moody to make an expedition into the rebel country, for the purpose of intercepting Mr. Washington's dispatches." [1] These were being sent by post rider from Washington's headquarters in New Windsor, north of West Point, to Congress in Philadelphia. For the next few months, James or people under his direction would harass Washington's communications with remarkable results.

In a memo he wrote to Sir Henry before setting out, James requested an explicit order from him to "Execute the business" as a precaution against accusations of spying. As well, he desired "two men lightly armed, as artilleries men, a good fusee for himself, and some cash in order to defray Expences." [2] He also asked to be landed in Jersey.

The expedition began easily enough. Travelling after dark, they covered 25 miles the first night and hid in a swamp the next day. But the second night their guide refused to take them any further. He was probably one of the men associated with Claudius Smith and his sons of the Clove neighbourhood of Orange County, New York, through which the party would travel. In his rage, or what he calls "the first transports of indignation," James was on the point of shooting the man, when he suddenly remembered "that the poor devil had a wife and family who depended on him for bread,"[3] and instead took him back to New York as a prisoner.

But James was not to be stopped. Pausing only long enough to see that the man was detained in total isolation, James set off again immediately with a new guide from the same region, convinced that the enemy would least expect this course of action. We have the second guide's account of the affair, which despite appalling discomforts and risks did succeed in its objective:

Benjamin Kelly — Says — That on the 8th March last [1781] he was applied to by Ensign Moody of the 1st Battn. New Jersey Volunteers to go with him to the upper part of Smith's Cove as a Guide, that they left the City in Company with Jonathan Gage a Corporal in the same Regimt. and Stephen Roblin putting themselves under the Command of Mr. Moody. They Travelled that night as far as Paramus and lay by next day. On the night of the 9th they Travelled about five Miles further, but were prevented by the darkness of the Night from proceding any further. That on the night of the 10th they reached Haverstraw Mountains, and on their way heard that the Post had pass'd by that day — that night there fell a heavy snow — that they press'd forward on the 11th hoping to cut him off — that in the Course of this days Travelling they overheated and fatigued themselves very much, their Cloaks hung wet thro' with Sweat — that they were disappointed in their Expectations of cutting off the Post as he had got the Start of them — That on the 12th, 13th, and 14th they lay in the Mountains, way laying the Road the whole day from Morning till night — Sleeping in a Swamp every night at some distance from the Road — That on the afternoon of the 15th they took the Post Rider Benjamin Montanye with the Mail — That the Horse having been shot in the Leg to prevent an Escape they were obliged to drage him some distance in the Woods where they left him, and prepared for their Return to New York — That they Travelled this Night with the Post and Mail to the lowere part of Haverstraw Mountains and lay by the 16th. That on the Night of the 16th they Travelled very hard and arrived at Hoebuck in the Morning of the 17th, at which place they cros'd to New York bringing the Mail and Post Rider with them — That from the time they left New York till their Return they lay constantly in the Woods and Swamps — had very bad Weather, a great part of the time, & four falls of Snow, a good deal of Rain and very cold weather — they were most part of the time in want of Provisions — That the deponant from lying out in Snow, Rain and Cold Weather, as well as from the fatigue of the Journey hath that [sic] Contracted disorders which he fears he will never get the better off.[4]

James is more laconic: "The inexpressible hardships which the party underwent in this adventure, both from hunger and cold, were fatal to the health of most of them."[5] Indeed he was more specific in a later memorial: two of his associates had since died, the third continued in a bad state of health, and he himself found his own constitution sensibly impaired.[6] Kelly continued his partisan activities but did not survive the war; he was shot by the rebels in July 1782, in the New York Highlands as he attempted to escape after a raid. The other members of James's party, Gage and Roblin, were also from the Cove area.

A British officer, Frederick MacKenzie, wrote at the time in his diary that Moody's party took the mail near New Windsor, New York, and that "Moody received 100 Guineas for executing this enterprize." He also noted that the mail contained "a great number of letters, amongst which are several from Mr. Washington, from whence no doubt the Commander in Chief has received very material information." There were also letters from "Rhode-Island and Providence, but in all their letters and papers not the least mention is made of an Action between the fleets; nor is there any account of the French fleet having returned to Newport."[7]

In December 1777, France had agreed to recognize American Independence. Entering into a formal alliance with the Americans early the next year, the French were now supplying them with money and naval support. Knowledge of the whereabouts of the French navy was essential to the British high command.

It was not surprising that the mail contained very little about the movements of the French fleet, but mostly informative letters from Washington. It seems that the shrewd rebel general was again using cunning over arms to harass the British commander in chief. Washington was concerned about the British campaign in the south and unable to bring much help to his beleaguered forces. But what he could do was keep Sir Henry's soldiers pinned down in New York. By putting it about that he might be contemplating an attack on that city, he was able to keep Sir Henry too anxious for its safety to send reinforcements to Cornwallis. The ploy of false information and judicious leaks is as old as time. By now Washington had taken the mental measure of his opponent. Five years after the Peace he wrote:

It was determined by me, nearly twelve months before hand, at all hazards, to give out, and cause it to be believed by the highest military as well as civil officers, that New York was the destined place of attack, for the important purpose of inducing the eastern and middle States to make greater exertions in furnishing specific supplies, than they otherwise would have done, as well as for the interesting purpose of rendering the enemy less prepared elsewhere. It never was in contemplation to attack New York, unless the Garrison should first have been so far degarnished to carry on the southern operations as to render our success in the siege of that place, as infallible as any future military can ever be made. That much trouble was taken and finesse used to misguide and bewilder Sir Henry Clinton, in regard to the real object, by fictitious communications, as well as by making a deceptive provision of ovens, forage, and boats, in the neighborhood, is certain; Nor were less pains taken to deceive our own army; for I had always conceived, where the imposition does not completely take place at home, it would never sufficiently succeed abroad.... Many circumstances will unavoidably be misconceived, and misrepresented. Notwithstanding most of the papers, which may properly be deemed official, are preserved; yet the knowledge of innumerable things, of a more delicate and secret nature is confined to the perishable remembrance of some few of the present generation.[8]

And finally there is the version of this affair by Montaigne, the intercepted messenger, who told a friend who told the person who wrote it down. The story goes, that "when Washington gave him the package [of letters] he carefully pointed out the route designed for him to take, and then resumed his writing, for the great man was busily employed at a small table. Montaigne saw at once the way would lead him directly under a battery of the enemy, who at that time held what is called the Clove or Ramapo Pass. He remained at the door, hesitating to obey, and fearful to explain the difficulty. Washington lifted up his head — 'What, not gone, sir!' he cried. Montaigne then said: 'Why General, I shall be taken, if I go through the Clove!' Washington bent his eyes sternly upon him, and brought his foot down heavily upon the floor — 'Your duty, sir, is not to talk, but to obey.'" The story is no doubt apocryphal and told in hindsight, but the bare bones may indeed be true.[9] Although the British did not have a battery at the Clove, the area was very much in the control of Loyalist freebooters.

On May 15, James, with four men, was again sent out to capture dispatches. But this time the rebels were waiting in several ambushes for him. Spies, perhaps John Vanderhovan himself, had informed the rebels of James's intended expedition. If Washington was indeed anxious to deceive the enemy, in this incident he must have figured to gain no matter how the incident turned out. His letters would get through, or he would capture Moody.

The first ambush happened the second night and found James and his men cornered between enemy soldiers and a rock. They chose the rock and by rare good fortune were able to jump from it onto soft ground and escape to a swamp. But once they crossed this they found another body of men waiting for them. Fortunately, they saw the enemy first and hid, lying on their stomachs, in the bushes on a little hill. "What he and his men felt, when they beheld so superior a force marching directly toward them, till at last they were within fifty yards; or when, in this awful moment, they had the happiness to see them, without being discovered, take another course; no person of sensibility will need to be told," James recounts.[10]

At this point the Loyalist party backtracked to the North River, within four miles of New York, and breathed a sigh of relief at now being out of danger. But this was not quite so. Suddenly, to their consternation 70 men poured out of a house and made straight for them. Despite James's scepticism, their guide was absolutely sure they were Loyalists, and, with another of the party, went forward to meet them. Their welcome was a volley of shot. Meanwhile a large detachment ran after James and got to within 50 yards of him, and in their turn began shooting. "The bullets flew like a storm of hail all around him; his clothes were shot through in several places; one ball went through his hat, and another grazed his arm. Without at all slackening his pace he turned round, and discharged his musket, and by this shot killed one of his pursuers; still they kept up their fire, each man discharging his piece as fast as he could load."[11] However, James managed to "give them the slip." He got back safely to New York, where, no doubt to his amusement, he found the news again circulating that he had been killed.

Nothing daunted, James set out again the very next night, on the theory that the rebels would least expect him to go out so soon again. Travelling with four men, he spent the first night at Secaucus and crossed the Hackensack River in a canoe he kept hidden there; he was then nearly taken by a party of rebels, but frightened them off by fooling them into thinking he had a large reserve coming up in his rear. By this time he was at Saddle River, which the group waded across in the dark, upstream from the road bridge which was guarded by rebels.

They learned that the whole countryside was out looking for them. To draw the enemy off, James "dispatched a trusty Loyalist to a distant part of the province" — perhaps to Little Egg Harbour to William Giberson or Joe Mulliner? — "directing one of them, whose person, figure, and voice most resembled his own, to pass for him but a single hour; which he readily did." 12

In this friend's neighbourhood, lived a pompous and important Justice of a Peace, who was a cowardly fellow, and of course had been cruel. At this man's house, early in the evening, the person employed raised an alarm. The Justice came out, and espying, as it was intended he should, **a tall man**, his fears convinced him it was Moody; and he instantly betook himself to the woods. The next day the rumour was general, that Moody was in that part of the country: and the militia was brought down from the part where he really was, to pursue him where he was not.13

James's party lay hidden in wait for five days near Newton, only a few miles from his own home, again helped with food by a Swayze, a sister of Isaac's.14 They seized the mail on June 1, and then brought it into New York on the evening of the 4th. By coincidence, Joshua Hett Smith, the brother of Justice William Smith, and the person who accompanied Major André on his last fateful ride, had just made his escape from a rebel prison in Kingston where he had been kept because of his possible collusion in Arnold's defection. He too was coming into New York that night and he gives an account of what James must have passed through to get back to New York, and of meeting James at the ferry.

Smith is describing the last stage of the journey of his escape:

On the evening of the 4th of June, 1782 [sic], my two pilots crossed this river [Passaic or Second River] in a small cedar canoe, or boat, to the opposite shore, which was a salt meadow, sometimes overflowed by the tide, which leaves a muddy slime, over which a light boat may easily be drawn. We passed a large tract of meadow, some miles in length before we came to another river, called Hackinsack River, on the opposite shore of which, near the foot of Snake Hill, we discovered a party of men who hailed us, not answering they fired several shot, but they fell far short of us. We now judged it prudent to hide the boat, in the hedges, and retire, as they could not pass to us; this being done, we hid ourselves, — and soon afterwards heard several vollies, appearing to us as if two parties had been attacking each other, this ceasing, we again ventured to the margin of the river, and observing no person on or near the opposite shore, we boldly launched our bark, knowing that no parties but British would venture to stay there long in broad day-light; we crossed in safety and soon reached the town of Bergen, where halting a few minutes for refreshments, we proceeded to Pryor's Mill, near Paul's-hook, and were informed by the man of the house that owing to fresh orders that had been given by Sir Henry Clinton, no person would be permitted to enter New York by that post.... While detained here Captain Moody came in with a captured mail of general Washington's despatches; and soon after, a serjant and file arrived to carry us across the ferry.

Smith convinced one of the officers who had known André, who he was, and was then permitted to cross with James and went with him to Clinton's headquarters.[15] The British officer, Frederick MacKenzie, wrote in his diary:

The information obtained by the Commander in Chief from the despatches and letters found in this Mail, is of the utmost consequence, as they contain the particulars of the conference held the 17th of May at Weathersfield in Connecticut, between Washington and Rochambeau, and the whole plan of their operations for the ensuing Campaign. The Capture of this Mail is extremely consequential, and gives the Commander in Chief the most perfect knowledge of the designs of the Enemy. Ensign Moody [whom he called Ensign John Moody] received a reward of 200 Guineas for this Service. General Knyphausen, and Lieut Genl Robertson, met the Commander in Chief this afternoon, to examine the papers taken.[16]

The next day MacKenzie added:

It appears certain by the intercepted letters, that The Rebels and French intend making an attack on this place. About 300 men belonging to the Corps in Virginia, under orders of embarkation, are countermanded. The Cavalry in Virginia are to be brought from thence immediately.... It is hoped, from The knowledge The Commanders by Sea and Land now have of the designs of the Enemy, we may be able in the course of this month to give them a severe blow.
... The French have not yet moved from Rhode-Island, but they have embarked all their heavy Cannon there, and certainly intend leaving it soon.[17]

James wrote in as a footnote to copies of the second edition of his *Narrative*:

A few days after this Genl. Clinton told him, that the Letters were of great consequence, that the taking of them was a most important service. But that he had now done enough; that he would not suffer him to venture himself in any more of such hazardous Enterprises; and that he would take care to provide for him. Mr. Moody does not doubt but that he then intended it; but these and his other Intentions seldom lasted longer than the day.[18]

At the conference at Wethersfield, Connecticut, between Washington and the French General Rochambeau and Commodore de Barras, the decision to invade New York had not been nearly so clear. The French had favoured sending troops and ships to reinforce Lafayette and Green, fighting in Virginia against Lord Cornwallis, while Washington had suggested that the moment was opportune to attack New York since so much of its garrison had been sent off to help Cornwallis. In a more personal letter to Lafayette, Washington left the impression that his opinion had prevailed. Little did they know. Washington was hitting the enemy on several fronts, sowing discord as well as false information. One has the same feeling that Cassandra must have had when the Trojans opened their gates to the wooden horse. Of course, it is just possible that Washington is still fooling us.

In any case, Sir Henry was jubilant and told everyone about his coup. Loyalist Captain Joseph Lee wrote to two of his fellow officers in the Third Battalion of the New Jersey Volunteers holding the Fort of Ninety-Six in South Carolina. "Moody has made another excursion into Jersey & taken a Rebel mail which contains some very Capital Intelligence (so says the Com'der in Chief). I wish he may benefit by it, for we do nothing here at present, Arbuthnot is at the Hood again and lets the French get as much Flour from Philadelphia as they want."[19] The event, like James's first mail capture, was written up in the London *Political Magazine,* and some of the captured letters were even printed. If nothing else, the feat cheered Loyalist morale. It was the fourth mail to be taken thus far, Hugh Gaine printed in his *Mercury,* though only two of these at this stage had been brought in by James.

Having frightened Sir Henry out of sending relief to Cornwallis in Virginia, Washington took action to protect his future despatches, which he presumably no longer intended for enemy eyes. On June 6, he wrote to Samuel Huntington, president of the Continental Congress, sending him a duplicate of his last dispatches and urging him to send all letters in future by express. "The communications by the post from hence to Philadea. has become so dangerous that I cannot in future trust any dispatches of importance by him and I beg you will observe the same rule. — The parties which are sent out know the exact time at which he may be expected, and cannot fail of securing him. They have not the Same opportunity of intercepting Expresses as their times of riding are uncertain." [20] The next day he wrote to the delegates from Maryland, "The danger to which letters are exposed upon the communication between this and Philada. render undesirable to enter into details upon paper." [21]

James organized the capture of two more mails, the first by a man named Meyers, earlier in the year, and the second in August. "In the second of these little expeditions his brother commanded, a young man, whose fearless courage, in the very teeth of danger, he had repeatedly witnessed. The younger Moody succeeded in his attempt, so far as to intercept the mail; but, after seizing it, he was attacked by a superior party, and two of his men were taken; yet he himself had the good fortune to escape, with that part of the papers which was in his own custody. Pennsylvania was the scene of this enterprise," [22] writes the elder Moody. This attempt took place in August. According to John Turner, one of the three men John Moody had with him, the mail consisted of dispatches from Congress to Washington. [23] It was seized at Brandywine Creek, Pennsylvania, where the rider had to ford the stream, and then taken to Little Egg Harbour, where the men embarked for New York. Along the way, though, two enemy whale boats captured the party and their craft. Turner was three times hanged by the neck to extort a confession, but in the end, he and the others escaped.

We read of another attempt in a letter from the rebel General William Heath on September 27. "Moody waylaid the last mail from the Southward — but finding it under escort did not attempt to seize it. He afterwards seized and carried off Several persons and horses between Paramus and Judge Coe's." [24] This letter may be a garbled account of John Moody's August expedition.

Horses were a valuable strategic commodity and in short supply on both sides of the Revolution. Cresswell had hoped to make money breeding them, and during wartime they were essential for private and military transport as well as for cavalry and all forms of swift communication. In moments of acute need, the rebels "requisitioned" horses, preferably from Loyalists or luke-warm neutrals, while Loyalists "stole" them from rebels and then sold them to the British. By the summer of 1781, the rebels of New Jersey attempted to call a halt to the Loyalist trade. Already people like Caleb Swazey had been jailed for the offence, but in July, Silas Condict wrote to Governor Livingston urging more concerted action:

We have direct information from N. York & Staten Island, The trade of Horse stealing flourishes amazingly, and I think it adviseable and for the good of the State to offer a pretty hansome reward for apprehending Caleb Sweasy Isaac Sweasy Nathan Horten junior James Ohara John Moody: and there is one Gibertson from Monmouth whose Christian name I am not certain of ... also a certain Burney, who passed a large quantity of Counterfeit Money near Pluckamin ... and a number more carrying on the business with too great success, and I think we ought to give encouragment to Such as may take pains to apprehend them, for without it they are not like to be taken.[25]

The result of this appeal was a proclamation by Governor Livingston, dated August 8, 1781, which appeared in the *New Jersey Gazette* and other Whig newspapers:

WHEREAS it has been represented to me that the persons herein after mentioned have been guilty of atrocious offences, and have committed divers robberies, thefts and other felonies in this state: — I have therefore thought fit, by and with the advice of the Honourable Privy Council of this state, to issue this proclamation, hereby promising the rewards herein mentioned to any person or persons who shall apprehend and secure in any gaol of this state, any or either of the following persons or offenders, to wit, Caleb Sweesy, James O'Harra, John Moody and Gysbert Gyberson, the sum of TWO HUNDRED DOLLARS of the bills of credit issued on the faith of this state.

Given under my hand and seal at arms, at Trenton, the third day of August, in the year of our Lord one thousand seven hundred and eighty-one, and in the fifth year of the independence of America.
Wil. Livingston

By His Excellency's Command.

Gysbert should have been William, nephew of Gysbert,[26] and accordingly a retraction and new proclamation was issued in the *New Jersey*

Gazette of October 17. At least three of these men, and probably the fourth, William Giberson, were known to James. James O'Hara was one of the three men sent off with John Moody, this same month, to intercept the rebel mails from Philadelphia, and Caleb Swayze was a brother of Joshua and cousin of Isaac. Already in the previous December, our indefatigable rebel spy Vanderhovan, alias Littel D., was warning that Giberson had recently left New York with a party of 12 men from Monmouth County to kidnap Governor Livingston and another prominent Whig. It seems inconceivable that such a man in New York on such a mission would not have talked it over with James before setting out.

James answered Livingston's proclamation with a satirical one of his own:

From James Moody

HUE and CRY

TWO HUNDRED

GUINEAS

REWARD

August 25, 1781

Whereas a certain WILLIAM LIVINGSTON, Late an Attorney at Law, and now **A Lawless Usurper, and incorrigible Rebel**, stands convicted in the minds of all honest men, as well as in his own conscience, of many atrocious crimes and offences against God and the King, and among many other treasonable practices, has lately, with malicious and murderous intention published a seditious advertisement in a rebel news-paper, offering a reward of what he calls Two Hundred State Dollars to an Assassin who shall take and deliver me, and three other Loyalists into the power of him the said William Livingston.

I do therefore hereby promise to pay the sum of Two Hundred Guineas, **true money**, to the person or persons who shall bring the said William Livingston alive into this city, and deliver him into the custody of Capt. Cunningham, so that he may be duly lodged in the Provost, till the approaching exstinction of the rebellion, then to be brought to trial for his numerous crimes and offences aforesaid. In the mean time, if his WHOLE person cannot be brought in, half the sum above specified will be paid for his

EARS and NOSE

which are too well known, and too remarkable to be mistaken. Observe, however, that **his life** must not be attempted, because that would be to follow **his** example of exciting the villainous practice of **Assassination**, and because his **death**, at present, would defraud **Jack Ketch** of a future perquisite.

> Given under my Hand and Seal at Arms, in New-York, this Twenty Third Day of August, 1781.
>
> **(A stile which I have surely as much right to assume as William Livingston, or any other rebel usurper)**

J. Moody

The several Printers on the continent are requested to insert the above in their newspapers.

James, in writing of "assassination," is referring to the letters of April 1779 between Livingston and Clinton, discussed in Chapter 5. Cunningham was the British Provost Marshal of prisoners in New York City, and Jack Ketch was slang for a hangman or executioner. Needless to say, none of the rebel newspapers of the time printed James's proclamation.

In the meantime, history was being played out. Sir Henry had called for reinforcements from Cornwallis, who had entrenched himself overconfidently in Yorktown waiting for British naval help. The rebel troops marched down to Virginia, the French came by sea, and Cornwallis was cornered. On October 19, he capitulated. Washington refused his request to have the Loyalists under his command considered as prisoners of war and not be punished for having joined the British army; their fate was a matter for the civil authorities. Sir Henry turned back at sea. The rebels had in effect won the war.

But James's part in the revolutionary struggle was not yet over. After Yorktown, in spite of Sir Henry's earlier assurance that he had done enough, he was once more called upon to risk his life in what certainly today seems a stupid enterprise. "It was nothing less than to bring off the most important books and papers of Congress"[27] by going to Philadelphia and stealing them from the secretary of that body. The expedition was to end in disaster, and personal sadness for James.

NOTES

1. *Narrative*, 35.
2. Clinton Papers, William L. Clements Library, Box 149, Folio 44, erroneously dated March 16, 1781. The date should be March 6, 1781. "Artillery" also had a now obsolete meaning of "munitions" or

"military equipment" in the general sense, and "fuze," in addition to its modern meaning, could also be a variant of "fusee," meaning "light musket."

3. *Narrative*, 35.
4. Benjamin Calley, sworn Oct. 2, 1781 before John Le Chevalier Roome, Moody Papers.
5. *Narrative*, 36-37.
6. Memorial of James Moody to the Lords Commissioners of the Treasury, Oct. 14, 1782, Moody Papers.
7. *Diary of Frederick MacKenzie, Giving a Daily Narrative of his Military Service as an Officer of the Regiment of Royal Welch Fusiliers During the Years 1775-1781 in Massachusetts Rhode Island and New York* (Cambridge, MA: 1930), vol. 2, 498. The diarist erroneously dates this a week later, and attributes the leadership of the expedition to Lt. John Moody of the 4th Battalion, New Jersey Volunteers. John Moody was James's younger brother, a private first in the 4th Battalion, but by this time in James's 1st Battalion. There was often confusion between the two.
8. Morton Pennypacker, *General Washington's Spies on Long Island and in New York* (Brooklyn: Long Island Historical Society, 1939), 212-13.
9. *Ibid.*, 213-14.
10. *Narrative*, 38.
11. *Ibid.*, 39.
12. *Ibid.*, 41.
13. *Ibid.*, 41-42.
14. Memorial of Isaac Swayze, 10 July 1783, British Headquarters Papers, no. 8392, NAC.
15. Joshua Hett Smith, *An Authentic Narrative of the Causes which led to the death of Major André, Adjutant-General of his Majesty's Forces in North America* (New York: 1809), 163-65.
16. MacKenzie, *Diary*, vol. 2, 536.
17. *Ibid.*, 537.
18. *Narrative*, 42.
19. Capt. Joseph Lee to Lt. Col. Isaac Allen, New York, 18 June 1781, *The Papers of the Continental Congress*, compiled by John Butler, 1978, vol. 3, National Archives, Washington, DC.
20. Washington Papers, Ser. 4, Reel 78, LC.
21. *Ibid.*
22. *Narrative*, 42.
23. *American Loyalist Claims*, ed. Peter Wilson Coldham (Washington, DC: National Genealogical Society, 1980), claim of John Turner, vol. 1, 496. The other two were James O'Hara (wanted by the State of New Jersey for horse stealing), and Richardson Davenport (Devenport).
24. Maj. Gen. William Heathe to Thomas W. McKean, Continental Village, 27 Sept. 1781, *Papers of the Continental Congress*.

25. Silas Condict to William Livingston, Morris Town, 20 July 1781, *Livingston Papers*, vol. 4, 242-43.

26. Both were Tories, originally from Monmouth County, NJ. See David Fowler, "Egregious Villains, and London Traders: The Pine Robber Phenomenon in New Jersey during the Revolutionary War," PhD thesis, Rutgers University, 1987, for a full account of the Gibersons, and William, Jr., in particular.

27. *Narrative*, 43.

9

THE PHILADELPHIA EXPEDITION:

AUTUMN, 1781

THE IDEA OF STEALING the secret papers of Congress was not a new one. In the summer of 1779 when André was negotiating with Arnold, he had dreamed of placing an agent in the office of the Secretary of Congress who would send him regular reports, probably through Furstner; and he had arranged the release of a Philadelphia rebel named Edward Fox to work with a man in the Secretary's office for this purpose. The happy prisoner merely regained his freedom, and the scheme was never put into effect.

Nevertheless, the idea remained with the office of the adjutant general. In January 1781, Samuel Wallis wrote on the subject from Philadelphia to Captain Beckwith in New York, that he had "an Affair now on hand, which if I can but succeed in I shall be able to do something handsome for you."[1] Throughout the summer, the plan was discussed through Rankin and Brigadier Skinner, though, by September, Wallis seemed more doubtful about its success, especially if Cornwallis were defeated in the south. Nevertheless the project was to go forward.

Again an ex-clerk from the Secretary's office was to be released and returned to his former job in Philadelphia. This one, named Thomas Addison, annoyed at not receiving an increase in salary, had quit his job and gone on board a rebel boat when he had been taken prisoner and brought to New York. After a few months, he had offered his services to Beckwith to steal "all the most interesting private papers of

Congress, their letters and instructions to their Ministers at Foreign Courts, etc., etc." 2 He had been recruited by Benedict Arnold, who perhaps had some knowledge of him from his own Philadelphia days. The fact that he was an Englishman may have made Beckwith more trusting, though large sections, not to mention several generals, of the Continental army were made up of men born in Great Britain. Presumably Beckwith had been assured from Philadelphia of the young man's credentials. The spy was to be paid a reward adequate to the importance of the service and the risk he would be running. Perhaps he was Wallis's agent, or perhaps he was, from the beginning, a rebel plant.

James, we are told, "was abundantly careful, and even scrupulous, in his inquiries concerning the man's character; on which head Major Beckwith expressed the most entire confidence; and observed, that Addison was equally cautious respecting the characters of those who were to attend him." 3 James took the precaution of not telling Addison that he was to be on the expedition, lest the man find the temptation to betray him too great. He requested that his brother and private Laurence Marr, who had often accompanied him, make up his party. "Their first instructions," he tells us, "were to wait on Addison, and to bind him, as they themselves had just been bound, to mutual secrecy and fidelity, by an *oath*, which the Lieutenant had always administered to his followers in all his expeditions, when the importance of the object rendered such an additional tie necessary." 4 This oath, quoted in Chapter 4, bound each person in the party to silence concerning themselves or other Loyalists who might have helped them in their mission.

James tells the story himself:

After taking this oath, a certain number of nights was agreed on, in which Addison was to expect them; and a certain place also appointed, where he was to meet them. In such an adventure, it was impossible to be exact to any time; but it was agreed, that if they failed of being at the place in any of the specified nights, he should no longer expect them; and they farther promised, by proper means, to apprise him, if possible, if any accident should befall them, so as either to delay, or wholly put an end to their project.

Things thus settled, Addison left New York in due form and manner, as was generally supposed, in order to return to his former friends and employment; and, at the proper time, Lieutenant Moody and his friends followed him. The manner and the circumstances of their march, it is not material nor proper here to relate: Suffice it to say, that, on the night of the 7th of November, the first in the order of those that had been appointed, they arrived in the neighbourhood of Philadelphia, but on the opposite side of the river. They found Addison already on the spot, waiting for them, according to appointment.

The prudent James

kept a little back, at such a distance as not to have his person distinguished, yet so as to be within hearing of the conversation that passed. His brother, and *Marr* his associate, on going up to Addison, found him apparently full of confidence, and in high spirits; and every thing seemed to promise success. He told them, that their plot was perfectly ripe for execution; that he had secured the means of admission into the most private recesses of the State-house, so that he should be able the next evening to deliver to them the papers they were in quest of. They, on their parts, assured him, that every necessary precaution had been taken to secure and expedite their retreat; and that they had with them *a sure friend*, who would wait for them on that side of the river, who, as well as themselves, would die by his side, rather than desert him should any disaster befal them. He replied, that they should find *him* as true and faithful to them and their cause, as they themselves could possibly be. Soon after they crossed the river together to Philadelphia; and it is probable that, on the passage, Addison was for the first time informed, that this friend was Lieutenant Moody.

Whether it was this discovery that put it first into his head, or whether he had all along intended it, and had already taken the necessary previous steps, the Lieutenant cannot certainly say; but he assures himself, that every generous-minded man will be shocked when he reads, that this perfidious wretch had either sold, or was about to sell them to the Congress.

As the precise time in which they should be able to execute their plan could not be ascertained, it was agreed that Lieutenant Moody should remain at the Ferry-house, opposite to Philadelphia, till they returned. On going into the house, he told the mistress of it, by a convenient equivocation, that he was an officer of the *Jersey Brigade*, as he really was, though of that Jersey Brigade which was in the King's service. The woman understood him as speaking of a rebel corps, which was also called the Jersey Brigade. To avoid notice, he pretended to be indisposed; and, going up stairs, he threw himself upon a bed, and here continued to keep his room, but always awake, and always on the watch.

He was wise to do so, for the next morning

about 11 o'clock, he saw a man walk hastily up to the house, and overheard him telling some person he met at the door, that "there was the devil to pay in Philadelphia; that there had been a plot to break into the State-house, but that one of the party had betrayed the others; that two were already taken; and that a party of soldiers had just crossed the river with him, to seize their leader, who was said to be thereabouts." The Lieutenant felt himself to be too nearly interested in this intelligence, any longer to keep up the appearance of a sick man; and, seizing his pistols, he instantly ran down stairs, and made his escape.

He had not got a hundred yards from the house when he saw the soldiers enter it. A small piece of wood lay before him, in which he hoped at least to be out of sight; and he had sprung the fence in order to enter it. But it was already lined by a party of horse, with a view of cutting off his retreat. Thus surrounded, all hopes of flight were in vain; and to seek for a hiding place, in a clear, open field, seemed equally useless. Drowning persons are said to catch at straws; with hardly a hope of escaping so much as a moment longer undiscovered, he threw himself flat on his face in a ditch, which yet seemed of all places the least calculated for concealment, for it was without weeds or shrubs, and so shallow, that a quail might be seen in it. Once more he had reason to moralize on the vanity of all human contrivance and confidence; yet, as Providence ordered it, the improbability of the place proved the means of his security. He had lain there but a few minutes, when six of his pursuers passed within ten feet of him, and very diligently examined a thickety part of the ditch that was but a few paces from him. With his pistols cocked, he kept his eye constantly on them, determining, that, as soon as he saw himself to be discovered by any one of them, he would instantly spring up, and sell his life as dearly as might be; and, refusing to be taken alive, provoke, and, if possible, force them to kill him. Once or twice he thought he saw one of the soldiers look at him, and he was on the point of shooting the man; but reflecting that possibly though the soldier did *see*, yet he might have the humanity not to *discover* him, as he would fain hope was really the case, his heart smote him for his rash resolution; and he thanks God that he was restrained from putting it into execution.

From the ditch they went all around the adjacent field; and, as Lieutenant Moody sometimes a little raised up his head, he saw them frequently running their bayonets into some small stacks of Indian corn-fodder. This suggested to him an idea, that if he could escape till night, a place they had already explored would be the securest shelter for him. When night came, he got into one of those stacks. The wind was high, which prevented the rustling of the leaves of the fodder, as he entered, from being heard by the people who were at that time passing close by him into the country, in quest of him. His position in this retreat was very uncomfortable, for he could neither sit nor lie down. In this erect posture, however, he remained two nights and two days, without a morsel of food, for there was no corn on the stalks, and, which was infinitely more intolerable, without drink.

He goes on to say:

He must not relate, for reasons which may be easily imagined, what became of him immediately after his coming out of this uneasy prison; but he will venture to inform the reader, that, on the fifth night after his elopement from the Ferry-house, he searched the banks of the Delaware till he had the good fortune to meet with a small boat. Into this he jumped; and having waited a little for the tide of flood, which was near, he pushed off, and rowed a considerable way up the river. During this voyage he was several times accosted by people on the water; but, having often found the benefit of putting on a fearless air, he endeavoured to answer them in their own way; and recollecting some of the less polished phrases of the gentlemen of the oar, he used them pretty liberally; and thus was suffered to pass on unsuspected. In due time he left his boat; and, relying on the aid of Loyalists, some of whom he knew were every where to be found, he went into a part of the country least known to him, and the least likely for him to have thought of; and at length, after many circuitous marches, all in the night, and through pathless courses, in about five days, he once more arrived safe in New York.[5]

The expedition had been a disaster. The two young men, for whom, as James said, there was not a ray of hope of escape or pardon, were immediately tried as spies under a court martial appointed by the Board of War. It was presided over by the Marquis de LaFayette, who happened to be passing through Philadelphia on his way from Virginia home to France. The prisoners were interrogated for two days, convicted as spies, and on Sunday, November 11, both condemned to die. John Moody was to be hanged on the 13th while Laurence Marr was given a reprieve until the 23rd in the hope that he would disclose more information.

The trial caused quite a stir. The French minister, the Chevalier de la Luzerne, wrote to his foreign minister, the Comte de Vergennes, that the prisoners had revealed "a number of accomplices and ill-affected persons, inhabitants of the Jerseys, whose houses have served for a resort to bands of villains who frequently come from New York to commit all sorts of acts of disorder in the neighbouring states."[6] The plot was attributed to the machinations of Benedict Arnold, who, according to the French diplomat, had offered Addison a large reward for his part in the business.

Luzerne must also have written to a number of newspapers, including the *Boston Gazette* and the *Boston Independent Chronicle,* and the news was picked up by the *Newport Mercury* and abroad by the prestigious *Gentleman's Magazine* and *Gazette de Leyde.* The Philadelphia *Freeman's Journal* of Wednesday, November 14 reported, as seems to have been standard for the times, that "from Saturday evening until yesterday, the criminals were both attended by a gentleman of the clerical order, who gives us ground to hope they were real penitents, as from the beginning of their confinement they manifested the greatest contrition for all their sins, political and moral." It added that "the enemy, who at this period seem equal to no exploits superior to robbing mails and stealing papers, may thank the monster Benedict Arnold, their beloved friend, for the untimely death of this young man, who was only in his 23rd year."[7]

When James Moody got back to New York, the *Royal Gazette* informed New Yorkers: "The report of the death of Lieut. James Moody, proves a mistake, he being now in this city, but his brother John Moody, after being seized at Philadelphia, was put to death by the rebels, and his body carried for interment to his distressed father, and relations at Egg-Harbour."[8] Marr was reported hanged on November 23 by the *Boston Gazette* of December 3.

John Moody, as a good Christian about to meet his Maker, was contrite, but not for any political sins. The night before his execution he wrote a last letter to James:

Dear Brother,
Let me Entreet you not to Grive at my fate and the Fate of my Brother
Soldier for we are Both Condemned to Die to morrow. Being taken for
Spies being Betrayed by the man who we Depended to Execute the plan
proposed by Captn Beckwith but pray forgive him as I do & likewise
Laurance Marr Also & all I pray for is forgiveness from my Maker & this

one Request I have to make to you and that is that you will take warning by my fate and never attempt any more to Come out of the British lines. I am now in Irons but thanks be to the Almighty I have the liberty of my tounge. O Lord Direct me to make a Good Use of it to thy praise pray Guive my love to all my Accuaintances in the British lines & Laurance Marrs likewise. Now I must prepare for Eternity having but a few Hours to Repent of Upwards of twenty three years Sin O Lord have mercy upon me a miserable sinner and prepare my Soul to Come before the Judgment Seat of that Great God in Whom All must put his trust if he Expect Salvation thanks be to Almighty God I now feel Some Ease in my mind since the sentence of Death is pasd. which has not been pasd. two Hours but I have prayed to My God since & Seem to be Quite Cheerfull. May the Lord make me Exceptable in his most Hevenly sight I Every moment a minister here so I must Conclude with Saing the Lord have mercy on your Soul my Dear friend & Brother may he be your Guide Hereafter Amen

John Moody

P.S. As to what property I have in N. York my Desire is to have it Sent to my father in Egg Harbour to be for his Use and my mother & Sister Lydia N.B. the Cash I Mean for the Cloths are but trifling & you may Do what you Se best with them.
P.S. Laurance Marr & my love likewise to Captn. Cougle and Company and all the Bttn. Both Officers & Soldiers.[9]

Although the rebels claimed hundreds of names had been revealed, in reality there were only six. Richard Peters, secretary to the War Office, wrote Governor Livingston while the trial was in progress:

We have received Information that James Moody is now with a Party of thirty or forty Refugees arrived at Little Egg Harbour. About one half Mile from the Meeting House "up the Mill Swamp on the West Side at a little Branch running from the Westward into the main Swamp there is a Small Cabbin formed by the Refugees." These are the Words of our Informant & we thought it necessary to inform your Excellency thereof as we have no Troops to send on the Service. We dispatched a few of the City Light Horse after one Hulings who was concerned in the Plan of which you have no Doubt heard for siezing the public Papers; but he being in Philadelphia heard of the Apprehension of the Spies now in Custody & has made his Escape to New York.[10]

In spite of what James thought, this letter suggests that the two prisoners never did reveal that he was with them, but rather gave the
impression that Samuel Hewlings, who had guided all three to the
meeting place at Cooper's Ferry, was the third man. They must have
told Addison that James Moody was at Little Egg Harbour, safe inside
Loyalist territory, for we know that James was still in his haystack until
the night of the tenth, whereas Peters' letter quoted above was written
on the ninth.

Moreover, Laurence Marr was not hanged. On November 13,
Peters asked Governor Livingston if Marr could be further reprieved
beyond November 23 to "be useful in detecting or bringing to Justice the
disaffected Persons mentioned in the Confessions."[11] There is no record
of further revelations in connection with the Philadephia expedition.
But Laurence Marr does reappear in the Sussex County Court of Oyer
and Terminer in February 1782 giving testimony in a number of cases
of misdemeanors committed by the people who had hidden James and
his party in 1780. The other witnesses are Joseph Lowery, the man
Major Hoops took into custody, and Hoops himself. The miscreants
pleaded guilty and were released with insignificant fines. Perhaps the
kindly major used the occasion to obtain for both young men a permanent reprieve from hanging. At the evacuation of New York, Marr
went to New Brunswick with the other members of his battalion, and
finally settled in Upper Canada.

Information from sources at British headquarters, accounts in contemporary newspapers and the later court cases that were tried as a
result of the prisoners' revelations tells us that the three Loyalists left
New York on November 2, and slipped down to Little Egg Harbour in
two well-armed whaleboats which then immediately returned to New
York. The men may well have been landed at Gaunt's Point on the Bay
shore, below the village, on the night of Monday, November 5, for the
court records affirm that Joseph Gaunt of Little Egg Harbour, whose
brother owned the point, received and hid them, and then guided
them northwest through the woods to Evesham Township, where with
the help of others, Hewlings took them on to Cooper's Ferry opposite
Philadelphia.

The son of a prominent Quaker, Joseph Gaunt was only a few years
older than James and the two must have known each other before
James moved to Sussex County. One of his sons later married a niece
of the two Moody brothers, Rebecca Mulliner, daughter of Mary
Holden Mulliner.[12] Three members of the Peacock family of Evesham,

as well as Samuel Hewlings, were also later indicted for helping James's group on this expedition.[13]

As for James's return journey, as soon as he ventured out of the haystack he took refuge with Jersey friends, whom he would endanger by identifying, around Little Egg Harbour. When he heard about his brother's hanging, he decided he was too well known in the area and must move to a safer place. His rowing up the river was to get to Philadelphia where no one would ever think of looking for him. There he stayed hidden with a sure friend, and when the rebel search for him had cooled down he made his way back, as he describes, "through pathless courses," to New York.[14]

Thomas Addison too had his troubles. In spite of the jubilation in the newspapers, a number of his neighbours seem to have given him a hard time. On November 30, he wrote to Congressman James Lovell:

Sir,

A Sincere desire to avoid the censure of my countrymen induces me to address you at a period which to me is truly alarming. Willing to give the fullest assurance of my attachment to the liberties of America & the rights of mankind, I exposed to view with the greatest candour a Scheme pregnant with the most Serious & dangerous consequences to these States. Those of my countrymen who were influenced by principles of reason undoubtedly approved of my conduct; others venomously influenced by their passions I believe condemned, or at least censured me; both impatiently waited for the determination of Congress, a determination which in my critical circumstances (for the public are highly censurious) should have been of the greatest moment. To my extreme mortification I was informed this day that Congress (for what reason I am ignorant) had not brought matters, in respect to me, to a conclusion, and my mortification is the more Severe, by frequent interrogations which I am Sorry, I cannot possibly answer.

In fact, Sir, in every Sense, I am pushed to the extreme, & can only hope for your intercession in Congress to provide a Speedy resolution in favor of

Sir,

Your Most Obedt. Servt.

T. Edison[15]

Five days later Addison (Edison), was awarded "two hundred and sixty-six dollars and two-thirds of a dollar" for "an essential service to the United States and a singular proof of his fidelity to their interests." [16] What had Clinton offered him? Not enough. The *Boston Independent Chronicle* ended its description of the affair with a final flourish of rhetoric: "This account, and an hundred others of the same kind, afford a demonstration of the weakness and debasement into which Britain has fallen; seeing her forces vanquished on all sides by the defenders of our honourable cause, she has nothing left but to employ those disgraceful means, at which any nation would blush that had not enrolled an Arnold among it's Generals." [17] It was a sad and humiliating time. For James and the Loyalists the next six months would prove even worse.

NOTES

1. Samuel Wallis to Capt. George Beckwith, 13 Jan. 1781, Clinton Papers, Box 140, Folio 34, William L. Clements Library, University of Michigan, Ann Arbor.
2. Frederick MacKenzie, *Diary of Frederick MacKenzie: Giving a Daily Narrative of his Military Service as an Officer of the Regiment of Royal Welch Fusiliers During the Years 1775-1781 in Massachusetts Rhode Island and New York* (Cambridge, MA: Harvard University Press, 1930), vol. 2, 698-99.
3. *Narrative*, 43.
4. *Ibid.*, 44.
5. *Ibid.*, 45-50.
6. Chevalier de la Luzerne au Comte de Vergennes, Philadelphia, 10 Nov. 1781, *Correspondance politique*, Etats-Unis, fol. 235-42, Archives Nationales, Paris.
7. Louis Gottschalk, *Lafayette and the Close of the American Revolution* (Chicago: University of Chicago Press, 1942), 337; *Philadelphia Freeman's Journal*, 14 Nov. 1781, repeated in the *Boston Gazette*, 3 Dec. 1781.
8. *Royal Gazette*, 21 Nov. 1781.
9. John Moody to James Moody, 12 Nov. 1781, Moody Papers. Part of this letter is included in the *Narrative*, 52.
10. Richard Peters to William Livingston, War Office, 9 Nov. 1781, *Livingston Papers*, vol. 4, 327.
11. *Ibid.*, 13 Nov. 1781, 329.
12. Leah Blackman, *History of Little Egg Harbour* (Tuckerton, NJ: Great John Mathis Foundation, 1880; repr. 1963), 326, 346.
13. A sixth man was Samuel Evans, who was called as a witness with Samuel Hewlings against Joseph Gaunt. The indictments are from the files of the New Jersey Supreme Court in the New Jersey State Archives in Trenton.

14. MacKenzie, *Diary*, vol. 2, 699.
15. Thomas Edison (Addison) to James Lovell, Philadelphia, 30 Nov. 1781, *Papers of the Continental Congress*, No. 78, Vol. 8, Fol. 375, M247, National Archives, Washington, DC.
16. 5 Dec. 1781, *Journals of the Continental Congress: Edited from the original records in the Library of Congress* (Washington, DC: U.S. Government Printing Office, 1912), vol. 21 (July 23-Dec. 31, 1781), ed. Gaillard Hunt, p. 1160.
17. *Boston Independent Chronicle*, 6 Dec. 1781.

10

NOT WITH A BANG BUT A WHIMPER:

SPRING, 1782

JAMES HAD ONCE MORE ESCAPED the rebel net. But he came back to New York this second time a devastated man. When he added up the reckoning, his losses were terrible. His brother had "perished by an ignominious death." Now his father, heartbroken at the hanging of this son of his old age, was losing his reason. He and many Loyalists must have sickened at the price they had paid: the loss of loved ones, the dispossession of property that would have ensured a future for their children, and the humiliation of being tied to such lacklustre leadership as the British were giving.

After 1780 the nature of the war in New Jersey had changed. The fighting between the two main armies had moved to the south; the debacle at Yorktown, with the British surrender of Loyalist troops as prisoners of state, could only deepen Loyalist bitterness. As the struggle continued, the skirmishes and raids between Loyal and Patriot Americans became more bitter and more personal. In places like Monmouth County, they had become a blood feud between Tories and Whigs.

Outside the lines, in the country, there were many Loyalists who had not chosen to seek shelter in New York. These dispossessed men, often from a common family, were hidden and supported by less conspicuous friends and relatives, some in good standing with the rebels. By 1781, these groups had formed into quite solid bands, which under a forceful leader often controlled whole sections of the countryside. In New Jersey and adjoining New York, James was in touch with three such clans: the Swayzes in Sussex and bordering Morris counties, who not only helped James but gathered intelligence in upper New York State; the Smiths at the Clove in the Haverstraw Mountains, who guided James as he waylaid Patriot dispatches; and the Gibersons in the vicinity of Little Egg Harbour, who probably passed him on through Monmouth County after his escape from Philadelphia.

These men were the counter to the rebel militias, except that unlike these last, they seldom slept in their own beds. They acted as guides to regular military groups, like James's, or passed counterfeit Continental currency to undermine the Patriot economy and help cash-strapped Loyalists pay their taxes, or alleviated the British horse shortage at the expense of their less friendly neighbours. As the war progressed, particularly obnoxious or successful individuals were singled out by each side for capture, and often death. It also became highly profitable to sweep down on someone's house and rob him in the name of "Liberty"— old style or new — and if one had a captive, one could also collect a ransom from his relatives. In some areas like Long Island Sound or Little Egg Harbour, the two sides almost seemed to work in collusion. These private Loyalist operators were variously and understandably styled by the Patriot authorities as "egregious villains," horse thieves and wood robbers, and given no quarter when caught by a detachment of Patriot militia. It is interesting to note that in the two areas where James was directly connected with the inhabitants, Sussex and Burlington counties, the struggle was never so vengeful. Nor was James ever betrayed in these parts of the country where he was personally known.

Since the Loyalists could not pressure the British forces into any military action under William Franklin's leadership, they lit upon the idea of organizing a private force of their own, under their own Board of Associated Loyalists. This could at least harass the enemy with hit-and-run raids along the coast, sallies that today would be called "commando" or "terrorist" raids, depending on which side one favours. These would also give its members a livelihood as the expeditions were to be financed out of rebel plunder. Moreover, the Associators would keep their own prisoners to exchange or use as hostages for good treatment of their captured comrades. Franklin was their obvious president, with a Board made up of other influential Loyalists. The New Jersey, Connecticut, and Rhode Island coasts were to be the prime targets.

Each action must be approved by the Board and by the British commander in chief. Sir Henry, no doubt jealous of Franklin's initiative and reluctant to endorse rival military activities, may also have shown one of his few flickers of good judgement in stonewalling for two years the official sanctioning of this doubtful private retribution.

In any case, the Board of Associated Loyalists did at last become legal in December 1780. Its incorporation also gave a legal status to the irregular Loyalists. Many of these, like Joe Mulliner and William Giberson who operated around Little Egg Harbour, were given commissions by the Board. Mulliner, who commanded a whaling boat along the coast, gave out paroles, like James, which similarly were not honoured as soon as his back was turned. He also managed to bring in a few prisoners to New York for exchange or ransom. When these Loyalist raiders were caught by the rebels they were usually tried by a civilian court and hanged as traitors. Interestingly, the indictment was usually for robbery and causing mischief, but seldom for murder. Thus, the stage was set for the Huddy disaster in Monmouth County.

Briefly stated, the Huddy affair was one of naked revenge. It was characterized by some of the same cruelty that had marked the struggle between Loyalists and Patriots in upper New York State, though without the Native People and without the soldiers of the two major armies. Fortunately, it was confined to a few related families. It began when Stephen Edwards of Eatontown, who had enlisted with the British in June 1778, was surprised by the rebels on a clandestine visit to his wife. He was convicted of spying and hanged from a tree two days later. It ended in 1782 with the murder — after several others committed by both sides — of militia captain Joshua Huddy, Edward's hangman, on the beach near where he lived. The following note was pinned to his chest: "We, the refugees, having with grief long beheld the cruel murders of our brethren and finding nothing but such measures daily carrying into execution, we therefore determine not to suffer without taking vengeance for numerous cruelties and thus begin and have made use of Capn. Huddy as the first object to present to your views, and further *determine* to hang man for man as long as a refugee is left existing. Up goes Huddy for Philip White."[1] As is well known, Washington threatened to retaliate by hanging a British officer prisoner chosen by lot, Captain Charles Asgill of the Grenadier Guards. Fortunately for everyone, Asgill had connections with the French royal family and the hanging was abandoned.

The court martial of Captain Richard Lippincott, the Associated Loyalist considered responsible for the murder of Huddy, and brother-in-law to Edwards and White, was held shortly after Clinton's departure. Here it was alleged that the ex-commander in chief had approved the retaliation. This seems highly unlikely as Sir Henry, for all his faults, had consistently opposed such revenge tactics by the refugees. It was also intimated that William Franklin had given a direct order to carry out the business. This also seems unlikely. The action was probably approved without Franklin's knowledge. There was strong evidence of this at the court martial and such outright cruelty was not in his nature. But there is no doubt that once the decision was taken he must have agreed not to oppose it. Perhaps he was even persuaded that the hanging would have a salutary shock effect on the Patriots, as the threat of retaliation had done in 1778. But holding hostages, and threatening equal treatment for prisoners, gives warning, whereas murder to avenge another murder is still murder, all the more repugnant when it has an official sanction. In a struggle which was about the rights of man under the British Constitution, a man of Franklin's training as a lawyer and experience as a governor should have foreseen the ethical and political consequences of such an act, an act that tarnished his own good name and cast a distasteful shadow over the Loyalist movement. It must be pointed out that had Washington carried through on his plan to hang Asgill in retaliation for Huddy, he too would have earned the opprobrium of history.

There is no suggestion that James was in any way involved in the activities of the Associated Loyalists. But he knew the members of the Board, and he expressed his support for their dilemma when he added by hand to the second edition of his *Narrative*:

Was not the taking Arms against the King, at least as high Treason, as the fighting against their new formd self created States? Yet our Generals suffered these Executions of the Loyalists to go on; without ever attempting to put a stop to them by threatening to Retaliate. Nay they would not permit the associated Loyalists to save their Friends, by threatening to Execute any of those Rebels, whom these Loyalists had taken prisoners, and whom they then held in their own Custody.[2]

The sad truth is that the British were not concerned about Loyalist prisoners, and the Loyalists felt driven to reprisals to protect their own.

It was not James's way to murder but, after the hanging of his brother, the Patriots feared that he might attempt some coup. They had word that he was planning Livingston's capture again. The latter informed Washington on January 1, 1782:

I have intelligence of James Moody's being again out with a party of six or seven men. He lately declared that he intended to take one of the Members of Congress in Philadelphia to revenge the death of John Moody not long since executed as a Spy, which to a Fellow of his Enterprize & so cherished by the Tories as he is not impracticable. Other Intelligence from New York represents his object to be a person of less consequence in the Town.[3] At any rate from the mischief he has already done, & his intimate knowledge of every part of this Country together with his extensive connections with the disaffected amongst us, it would I think be worth some pains to prevent his further progress.[4]

Washington wrote back sympathetically:

It is a pity but that Villain Moody could be apprehended lurking in the Country, in a manner that would bring him under the description of a Spy. When he was taken before, he was in Arms — in his proper uniform — with a party — and had his Commission in his pocket. It was, therefore, a matter of great doubt whether he could be considered otherwise than a prisoner of War. It was said he had been inlisting men in the Country but no proof of the kind ever appeared.[5]

Is this consolation after the event? Or did the colonel who visited James in his cell merely do so to frighten him into some sort of confession? Or was he warning him that he must try to escape? We shall probably never know.

In any case, James makes no mention of any intentions or attempts to avenge his brother. He may very well have said in Rivington's coffee house, over a glass of rum, that he would like to carry off a member of Congress or kidnap Livingston, but there is no evidence that any such attempts were made by anyone. Like many other Loyalists, not only had he lost everything he owned, but even his health had been worn out by the hard exposure to snow and swamp and hunger that his campaigning had forced upon him. Indeed, James had other preoccupations during the early part of 1782. He had his three motherless children to care for. Family tradition states that Elizabeth Moody died during the war when she was thrown from her horse. This could not have been earlier than late February when she appears as a witness in two cases in the Sussex County Court of Oyer and Terminer. James hastily turned to his charming friend, the widowed Jane Lynson. The two were married on March 21 by the elderly Isaac Brown, former rector of the bride's church in Newark, a dear gossipy man, much loved by them both. The witnesses were James's good friend, John Le Chevalier Roome, Mary Bell, and John Grigg, a New York spirits retailer turned tallow chandler, and Hannah, his wife. Jane had no children of her own. James's children must have come to New York at this time.

A few days later, Sir Henry received word that his resignation as commander in chief had been accepted, and that Sir Guy Carleton was to be his replacement. On May 1, hostilities were ordered to cease at all ports held by the British and the refugees were told not to go out any more without orders. Unknown to most people, Sir Guy had been appointed to make the final peace arrangements. He landed in New York on May 5 with great fanfare. The *Mercury* reported that as he stepped ashore his arrival was announced with a discharge of cannon from Fort George; "he was received ... by a Party of Horse and Foot, the gentlemen of the Army, most of the respectable Inhabitants of the City, and a numerous concourse of People, who all testified their joy in his happy Arrival." [6]

In a moment of expansion, Sir Henry asked James to return to England with him, and according to several colleagues assured James that he would do something for him. James was exhausted in mind and body and gladly accepted the invitation. William Franklin, writing his friend Joseph Galloway that week, wondered at Sir Henry's sudden generosity. One presumes it was Sir Henry's substitute for the captaincy he had earlier promised James. The next few days James spent scurrying around to his friends, collecting letters of introduction to people in England, and certificates attesting to his character and the risks he had run in his fighting for the Loyalist cause. He also took the precaution to obtain a certificate of introduction from his Lodge of Masons. His wife was to remain in New York with his father and the three children.[7] As things turned out she would join him in London in the autumn of 1783. On the evening of the 11th, Sir Henry was bid farewell by the principal officers of the army at "a splendid Entertainment" at Roubalet's Tavern attended by Sir Guy, Rear Admiral Digby, and many other officers and persons of distinction.[8] James must surely have been there too.

On the 13th, Sir Henry's party was escorted to his ship with much the same pomp and ceremony that had greeted Sir Guy's landing a week earlier. The retiring commander in chief and Lieutenant General Knyphausen, accompanied by a large number of officers, and James, one presumes, walked from headquarters to the water through an honour guard of British and Hessian troops which lined each side of the street. Cannon shots were fired and at about noon the two generals and their party stepped aboard *The Pearl*, sloop of war, to begin their journey to England.

Most Loyalists were glad to see Sir Henry leave but it must have been a tearful, apprehensive little family that watched James step off the dock onto the waiting vessel. So much had been lost in the last five years: friends, family, livelihood, the land they loved and had helped to shape. So many sacrifices had been made, and in the end, for nothing. In little more than a year, all the active Loyalists would have left New York. James, like them and so many refugees since, was about to begin a new life.

NOTES

1. See Willard S. Randall, *A Little Revenge: Benjamin Franklin and His Son* (Boston: Little, Brown, 1984), 468-74, and William H. Mariboe, "The Life of William Franklin, 1780-1813: 'Pro Rege et Patria,'" PhD thesis, University of Pennsylvania, 1962, 536-48, for a dispassionate account.
2. *Narrative*, "Author's Notes," 8.
3. Livingston means himself.
4. William Livingston to George Washington, 1 Jan. 1782, *Livingston Papers*, vol. 4, 357.
5. Washington to Livingston, Philadelphia, 12 Jan. 1782, David Library of the American Revolution, no. 2206.
6. *The Journals of Hugh Gaine Printer*, ed. Paul Leicester Ford (New York: Dodd Mead, 1902), vol. 2, 150. Guy Carleton had been the able governor of newly-conquered New France, 1766-78, and responsible for the Quebec Act of 1774, which guaranteed to French-speaking Catholic Quebecers their language, religion, and civil law. Created Lord Dorchester, he would return to Quebec as governor in chief of all mainland British North America, 1786-96.
7. James Moody to Mr. Foster, 19 May 1784, London, PRO, AO 13/110, p. 253.
8. Gaine, *Journals*, vol. 2, 149-50.

II

ENGLAND (1782-86)

(8)

province, and was gone to the fouthward †. Notwithftanding this difcouragement, Mr. Moody and his party ftill continued in the country agreeably to their inftructions, in the hope that fome opportunity would ftill prefent itfelf to annoy the rebellious, and to affift the loyal. But no fuch opportunity offering immediately, they foon received orders to join the army with the men they had enlifted, or could enlift.

In confequence of thefe inftructions, they fet forwards with about 100 Loyalifts (not more than that number, from the change of profpects, were then to be prevailed upon to leave their own country; or, if it had been otherwife, the time was too fcanty, being not more than 48 hours, to collect them together, which, it muft be obvious, was to be done only with great caution and fecrecy), on a march of upwards of 70 miles, through a well inhabited part of the province. The rebels purfued them; and, after feveral fkirmifhes, at length came upon them in fuch force, near Perth-Amboy, that they were obliged to give way and difperfe. More than fixty of the party were taken prifoners; eight only, befides Mr. Moody, got within the Britifh lines. Thefe prifoners, after being confined in Morris town jail, were tried for what was called *high treafon*; and above one half of them were fentenced to die. Two, whofe names were *Iliff* and *Mee*, were

† This was to the Chefapeak expedition. *fatal*

to betray the Loyalifts & to ruin Burgoign. actually *Was not the taking Arms againft the King, at leaft as high Treason, as fighting againft their New form'd self created States? yet our Generals suffer'd thefe Executions of the law, [illegible] to go on, without one attempt to*

Page 8 from the second edition (1783) of *Lieut. James Moody's Narrative of his Exertions and Sufferings in the Cause of Government since 1776*. The annotations are in Moody's handwriting. Courtesy Columbia University Rare Books and Manuscript Library

11

LONDON: SETTLING THE PAST

IN LONDON THERE WOULD BE two important tasks that James would set himself. The first would be to work for a better understanding of the Loyalists in the minds of the British public. The second would be to procure the means of establishing himself in another part of British North America. The first would take the form of a booklet and the second would entail endless petitions to the British Treasury. The two would go hand in hand, and happen almost by chance.

James arrived in Portsmouth on Wednesday, June 12, 1782.[1] The voyage had taken just over four weeks, very fast for the period. Sir Henry and his suite, of which James was a member, hurried up to London, as most of us still do. Sir Henry rejoined his sister-in-law and his legitimate children in Harley Street, and James went straight to his friend, Charles Cooke, at 97 Wardour Street in Soho, a new part of London where rents were cheaper. This house remained his address for the next year.

Cooke was an affable Irishman who had come out to America in 1766 and established with his brother Robert a flourishing import-export business in Crosswicks, Burlington County, near the Delaware River. He had collected provisions for the British army, before being captured by Washington's forces just after the Battle of Trenton, and had then spent three years as a prisoner of war first in Philadelphia and later in Lancaster. While on parole in Philadelphia he had shrewdly bought up close to £2,000 worth of flour, "in hopes of reserving them for the use of the British Army, Who was then expected, Shortly, to take possession of this City."[2] In 1779, he was exchanged and allowed to rejoin his brother in New York. It is here that he and James must have met. He had come to England in January and had made himself the banking agent for a number of New York and New Jersey Loyalists. James relied on him from the outset.

With his usual foresight James arrived in London armed not only with certificates and affidavits as to his services as a Loyalist during the war, but also with letters of recommendation to a wide variety of Loyalists living in England. These included a letter from William Franklin to his friend, Joseph Galloway, the distinguished Philadelphia lawyer and politician who had in earlier, happier days worked with Benjamin Franklin in the Pennsylvania Assembly, and two letters to the Reverend Thomas Chandler who had been responsible for setting up the Church of England parish in Sussex County. These last two from James's clerical friends in New York, Isaac Brown and Charles Inglis, were ecstatic in their praise. Brown wrote: "You will receive Mr. Moody as my particular friend, and as one most firmly attached to his Majesty, and the constitution both in church and state. He has both done and suffered great things from a principle of loyalty. You may give full credit to all he says, and if he tells you some things seemingly incredible, still you are to believe him. He is honest, sober, and firm — never intimidated by danger, and of undeviating probity and honour."[3] How could anyone have resisted such an introduction?

Chandler lost no time in presenting James to another Loyalist Anglican divine, Jonathan Boucher, who had been the tutor of George Washington's stepson and rector of churches in Virginia and Maryland. A passionate, self-educated Englishman nine years older than James, from the Scottish border country of England, he was considered one of the best preachers of his time. It was in Queen Anne Church in St. George's County, Maryland in 1775 that he held a band of Patriots at bay with a pair of loaded pistols on the cushion of the pulpit, as he delivered his last sermon in America. He had married Nelly Addison, member of a prominent Maryland family, who was already dying when James first met the family.

Boucher welcomed James into his circle of High Church Anglicans, and these in turn were charmed by James. This group included the people close to Boucher at his school in Paddington and his new rectory at Epsom, people like the Parkhursts and the Calverleys, and above all William Stevens, the rich and thoughtful hosier who was treasurer to

The Reverend Thomas Bradbury Chandler. From the Collections of the New Jersey Historical Society

Queen Anne's Bounty, a fund from which the livings of poor British clergy were supplemented. Stevens had been instrumental in having Boucher nominated as undersecretary to the Society for the Propagation of the Gospel, introduced him to important clerics, given him business advice, and helped him throughout his life. Boucher, expressing his admiration for this layman's theological knowledge,

The Reverend Jonathan Boucher, painted by David Gardner, n.d. From the
Mabel Garvan Collection, courtesy Yale University Art Gallery (1946.401)

described Stevens as "not only pious and charitable to an uncommon
degree, but also a man of very considerable learning, and one of the
ablest divines I am acquainted with."[4]

When James arrived in London short of cash Boucher immediately
lent him £25, probably borrowed from Stevens, since Boucher too at
this period was hard pressed for money. It was undoubtedly Boucher,
Stevens, and Chandler who encouraged James to publish the narrative
of his own experiences during the American Revolution. Someone else
lent him another £10. James was to need all the help he could get.
London was even then a very expensive city to live in and James's half-
pay as lieutenant at two shillings and fourpence per day would not take

him far. In spite of Sir Henry's professed high opinion of James's "Zealous, active and Spirited conduct,"[5] it was early evident that the ex-commander in chief would make no move to aid him, despite his promise in New York. James must look elsewhere. Cooke and others no doubt advised him to petition for financial assistance from the British government, as other Loyalist refugees stranded in England had been doing since the outbreak of the war. James's services surely entitled him to something extra.

With the change of ministries in the spring of 1782, came the end of hostilities and the opening of negotiations for a peace settlement with the American colonies. In the desire to end the war, and the expense of the war, the treaty only "recommended" to the new states that the Loyalists should be able to obtain restitution for their confiscated property and rights, a recommendation, which, needless to say, was never even intended to be honoured by the winning side. This was the famous Clause V of the treaty which, with Clause VI, supposedly guaranteeing no future harm to any Loyalist, seemed to be a sellout by the British of the Loyalists who had sacrificed so much for the British cause.

At first, the relief in Britain that the war was over at last was so great that the Loyalists were all but forgotten. For Lord Shelburne, the new prime minister, the government's concern was to put some limit on the allowances that had been granted to Loyalists who had earlier sought refuge in England. Shortly after James arrived in London, a small Parliamentary enquiry consisting of two members of Parliament, John Eardley-Wilmot and Daniel Parker Coke, was set up to review these temporary pensions and to deal with any new ones on a more rational basis. Independent of either political party, but on the whole, sympathetic to the American cause rather than to the Loyalists, they saw the assignment as taking two, or possibly three months to complete.

It was to these men, through the Lords of the Treasury, that James appealed in mid-October for financial help. He asked that as he now had nothing to subsist on, some immediate relief might be granted him, and that such further compensation might be made to him, as his services and sufferings might be found to deserve. In preparing his petition James had considerable previous experience. By now he had the form well in hand. In succinct prose he detailed his experiences and his achievements, and appended certificates testifying to the truth of his petition. Some, as we have seen, he had collected a few days before leaving New York, but others, such as that of Major General James

Pattison, were written after his arrival in London to support his request for help, and Chandler as early as August had passed on to him the flattering extracts from Brown's and Inglis's letters. The petition with the certificates was forwarded with "Mr. Townshend's particular recommendation of Mr. Moody to their Lordships compassionate consideration," on October 30.[6]

In drawing up his appeal, James must have consulted Chandler and Boucher, and probably Stevens. One sees the three men at Paddington in the Boucher house asking James about the details of how he opened the Sussex County jail in Newton, how he escaped from Washington's camp, how he evaded capture after the fiasco of the Philadelphia expedition. As Boucher was to write him later, his life during that period had been "a series of Wonders," and he must look back upon it "with such sentiments as a ship-wrecked Mariner would feel on looking on a tempestuous Ocean from which he had just escaped."[7] Surely someone in the group said to James, "You must write it up. You must tell others what it was like, so that people in England will understand." Perhaps it was Chandler, himself a great propagandist, who could see the value of having this exciting and moving story told.

In any case, at some point during the autumn James did sit down and write the *Narrative of His Exertions and Sufferings in the Cause of Government since the Year 1776.* The mood is not one of relief at having escaped, it is more a vindication of Loyalism, taking his own experiences as typical of those of a Loyalist. He begins in the leisurely manner of the eighteenth century, like a Jane Austen novel: "Choice and plan, it would seem, have seldom much influence in determining either men's characters, or their conditions. These are usually the result of circumstances utterly without our controul. Of the truth of this position, the Writer's own recent history affords abundant proofs." He continues:

Seven years ago, few human events seemed more improbable, than that he, a plain, contented farmer, settled on a large, fertile, pleasant, and well-improved farm of his own, in the best climate and happiest country in the world, should ever beat his plough-share into a sword, and commence a *soldier*. Nor was it less improbable that he should ever become a *writer*, and called upon to print a *narrative* of his own adventures. Yet necessity and a sense of duty, contrary to his natural inclination, soon forced him to appear in the former of these characters; and the importunity of friends has now prevailed with him to assume the latter.[8]

With the same dry humour and sparse prose, he goes on to tell his story, how he was situated at the beginning of the war, how he felt about the situation, how others felt about him, and the details of his adventures until he sailed for England. Much of this has already been quoted. James ends his book with a plea that the many thousands of Loyalists in the colonies who were Loyalists by conviction, will not be deserted by Government:

It is with the utmost concern Mr. Moody has heard of the doubts and debates that have been agitated in England concerning the number and the zeal of the Loyalists in America. It might be uncharitable, and possibly unjust, to say, that every man who has entertained such doubts, has some sinister purposes to serve by them; but it would be blindness in the extreme not to see, that they were first raised by men who had other objects at heart than the interests of their country. Men who have performed their own duty feebly or falsely, naturally seek to excuse themselves by throwing the blame upon others. It would ill become an obscure individual to obtrude his opinion upon others; but any honest man *may*, and, when he thinks it would serve his country, should, relate what he has seen. The writer of this narrative has already disclaimed all pretensions to any extraordinary share of political sagacity; but he has common sense — he can see, and he can hear. He has had more opportunities than most men of seeing and hearing the true state of loyalty in the *middle* colonies; and he most solemnly declares it to be his opinion, that a very great majority of the people there are at this time loyal, and would still do and suffer almost any thing, rather than remain under the tyranny of their present rulers. Let but the war be undertaken and conducted on some *plan*, and with some spirit; let but commanders be employed who will encourage their services, and leave them under no apprehensions of being deserted and betrayed; and *then*, if they do not exert themselves, and very effectually, let every advocate they have had, or may have, be reprobated as a fool or a knave, or both together — and let the Americans continue to feel the worst punishment their worst enemies can wish them — nominal independency, but real slavery.
  Perhaps the honest indignation of the Writer may have carried him too far; but, on such a subject, who, in *his* circumstances, could speak coolly, and with any temper.... He has given the strongest proofs of his sincerity: he has sacrificed his all; and, little as it may be thought by others, it was enough for him, and he was contented with it. He made this sacrifice, because he sincerely believed what he declares and professes. If the same were to do over again, he would again as cheerfully make the same sacrifice....

He trusts he shall soon be able, and he would rejoice to be called *by the Service*, to return to America. He would go with recruited spirits, and unabated ardour; for, rather than outlive the freedom of his country, it is his resolution, with King William of glorious memory, even *to die in the last ditch.*[9]

The work was dated November 1782, and was published at that time. The war was of course over, but James's slim volume had an instant success. The *Political Magazine*, an opinion-maker like today's *Economist*, immediately featured the second half of the book, beginning with the summer of 1780, in its issue of January 1783. In the same volume, the extract from James's *Narrative* was followed by "Extracts from Sir Henry Clinton's Narrative" together with a highly critical review of the latter's work. This issue also contained articles on the provisional treaties with France, Spain, and America, and debates in Parliament on the treaty, as well as accounts of the recent campaign in the Carolinas and Virginia. James's moving personal account of his war experience appeared not only as the peace treaty was being negotiated, but also as every vessel from America was bringing more and more destitute Loyalists to the shores of England. It highlighted the vivid contrast between the Loyalists who had stayed in America to fight for legitimate British government, and those who had spent the war in safe and relatively comfortable exile in England. People like the Boston Loyalist, Samuel Curwen, who kept a detailed diary of his war years in London, rushed to get his copy of the magazine.[10]

After an abortive hearing in early December, James's petition was given consideration in February, 1783. He was called to testify on oath on the 12th. He brought to the interview not only his just-published *Narrative* and his old certificates, but also a new one from William Franklin who had now himself arrived in London and was living just a short distance from James. Without hesitation, the two commissioners accepted his petition. "This is a Case of great Merit & great Exertions in his Majesty's Service," they commented. "His Real & personal Estate was worth about £1500 Sterling. He makes a Demand for a Sum of Money amounting to about £1500 part of which there might be Doubts about; but his Services were so great & so well attested that we think him intitled to a Payment after the Rate of £100 a Year from the 5th July last."[11] The commissioners had established that they would not compensate for debts incurred during the war. James had asked to be reimbursed for the money he was out-of-pocket, but the commissioners justified their recommendation on an assessment of his assets. The assistance was based on his merit rather than on his losses during the war.

James lost no time in distributing copies of his *Narrative* to anyone interested. He sent one copy to Sir Henry, who protested that he had never promised to do anything for him, as Charles Inglis was claiming, but had only said that James deserved public recognition. He also sent a copy to John Graves Simcoe, who had commanded the provincial corps of Queen's Rangers, with the accompanying note: "The attention shown by you to that unhappy class of Men, in America who have attempted to support the Authority of Government & have been consequent Sufferers, induces me to offer to you the Accompanying Narrative.... I am convinced that myself & All other Loyal Subjects have to lament, that every officer serving in America was not Activated by a Zeal & attention, similar to yours, otherwise, that Country must now have been part of the British Empire."[12] As we have seen, Simcoe was equally admiring of James. He wrote to a friend that he believed everything in the *Narrative* was true.[13] Elizabeth Galloway, in England with her father Joseph Galloway, listed on the flyleaf of her copy titles of other Loyalist works she owned, as if the five were particularly precious to her.

The bookseller soon ran out of copies and a second edition was printed in 1783. Like most of us, James had a few after-thoughts, and these he wrote in by hand in a number of the copies of this edition that he distributed, as footnotes at the bottom of the appropriate pages. They included three sharp criticisms of the British High Command, and may be seen in the copy now in the Library of Congress Rare Books Collection, and his own copy now in the rare books library of Columbia University.

The work clearly had an immediate influence on the public and the members of the government. No sooner were the provisions of the peace treaty passed by Parliament in January, than the new ministry and the Opposition vied with each other in proclaiming their concern for the plight of the Loyalists. Even the king mentioned the subject in his speech from the throne at the opening of the current Parliamentary session, trusting that the members would agree with him "that a due and generous attention ought to be shewn to those who have relinquished their properties or professions from motives of Loyalty to me, or attachment to the Mother Country."[14]

In June, at the initiative of the new chancellor of the exchequer, Lord John Cavendish, the two-man Parliamentary Enquiry was turned into a five-man Commission. Its mandate was "to enquire into the Losses and Services of all such Persons who have suffered in their Rights, Properties, and Professions, during the late unhappy Dissentions in America, in consequence of their Loyalty to his Majesty and Attachment to the British Government."[15]

Loyalty, Wilmot later wrote, was to be the cornerstone, the groundwork of the whole. The Act establishing the Commission was passed without opposition in July 1783. All claims were to be submitted by March 25 of the following year. Now meeting refugees who had willingly risked their lives, and lost not only their health but their property, possessions, and many of their relatives for their loyalty, the members of Parliament and the British public came full circle in their attitude toward the Loyalists. They had turned from a contempt for these colonials to an admiration for what they had suffered for the British cause. They now felt a sense of responsibility for what the Loyalists had sacrificed. Although the country was greatly in debt, it was felt these brave people could not be abandoned, rather in the way that hard-bitten Canadian Parliamentary committees after World War II were moved by the returning veterans to approve much more generous rehabilitation and education help than anyone had dared to dream possible.

For the moment, though, James had a greater worry even than finances. He had left his new wife in New York with his children, and under the articles of the peace treaty, the Loyalist forces must leave New York. Without government help, his family would have no means of support or place to live. At the end of May, he again appealed to the Treasury for reimbursement of the money he had advanced in the service of government in order to be able to return to New York to take charge of his family. He also asked for the confirmation of his annual allowance of £100, which he was finding far from adequate, even should he be out of England. There is no evidence that James's request elicited a reply but no doubt the idea of compensation for loyalty was already taking shape and it may have been felt that such appeals would be taken care of in the enquiry that was soon to be organized.

In any case, Jane Moody came to England on her own. She must have left New York in the second half of July. On the 16th, through John Le Chevalier Roome, £59 14s, New York currency, is made over to James's father, with the acknowledgement of another £20 6s having been received earlier. This presumably the senior Moody had lent Jane while her husband was in England. The children stayed with their grandfather in New Jersey, in the hope that they would help to console him for the loss of his younger son whom he was still mourning. Jane left her effects, including a loom, with Mercy Millidge to be shipped with this lady's things to Nova Scotia.

Mercy's husband, Thomas Millidge, was the major of James's battalion. Before the Revolution, he had been a deputy surveyor general in New Jersey, working in Bergen, Essex, Morris, and Sussex counties. He had also been appointed a justice of the peace for Morris County just before the outbreak of the Revolution. He probably drew, from memory, the map of northern New Jersey that John Hills later published in his collection of Revolutionary maps of New Jersey.[16] The Millidges went directly from New York to Nova Scotia, in the summer of 1783. They and the Moodys would work closely together later in Nova Scotia.

The Moodys' thoughts were now on settling in Nova Scotia. James had already indicated to the Parliamentary Enquiry, that if any lands should be granted in Canada or Nova Scotia, he would be glad to have a portion; it would give him an opportunity to provide for some of the men, about 15, whom he had raised in America and who were now under circumstances that made it impossible for them to live there.[17] James had written to Millidge in the summer to tell him about the new Act setting up the Loyalist Claims Commission and recommending Charles Cooke as a trustworthy agent to submit petitions and collect any money that might be forthcoming. He also asked about conditions in Nova Scotia.

Millidge wrote back a vivid account of his new land:

I am with my family at a place called Digby, named after the Admiral who has been pleased to Suffer it named after him — the lands are pretty good here but rough full of what is Calld. Cradle hills — these apear to have been made by the blowing up of Timbers a long time ago — hard Maple, Beach, Birch, Firs, Hemlock & Spruce grow here; this place is distant 18 miles from Annapolis Royal — an exceeding good harbour for Shipping. Fishery may be carried on to advantage & some Lumber if moneyed & spirited men were here. — there is a great many of the refugees here and I am in hopes that the place will come to something. Mr. Rome & his Family are here — his Family had a very bad passage were out nine weeks and were drove to the necessity to Cut Down their Masts & were drove into a Small River where they continued untill they hired a small schooner to bring them to this place — the lands are hard to be cleared and very Expensive before the lands may be used to advantage — the Regiment is gone up the St. John River, the best accounts of that part of the country I am able to procure is that there is very good lands high up the river — that one month its Impossible for the Ice in the River, that its Froze up about 3 months, and 1 month breaking up and after this it over flows the lands near the River for a Considerable time.

The best parts of this Province that I am yet able to find out is Cornwallis Cumberland & Horton — all Kinds of Provisions is extravagantly dear here potatoes Excepted which are here in great Plenty and very Good — if you wish to send anything here to make a Proffit let it be Check linnen, Cheap Coarse Cloths, Soap & Candles, good uper & Sole leather much wanted here, if you wish to have a lott in the place You had best Employ some person to draw it & take care of it for you — half acres have sold here for twenty Guineas but believe me its not so Easy to live here as in London.

We are Just informed that the Evacuation at New York Took place the 25th of Novr. that on the Entrance of the Rebels many Loyalists yet Remained who were Treated very ill.[18]

But the immediate task for the Moodys and the other refugees in London was to submit their claim to the new commission. Only with some capital, as Millidge pointed out, could anyone hope to make much of the situation in Nova Scotia. The deadline was set for March 25, 1784. There was a hectic scramble among all Loyalists to prepare their petitions. As loyalty, and not losses, was to be the criterion, though losses of course were what they were seeking compensation for, the old petitions that had appealed for temporary assistance must be honed with loyalty in mind. It was especially important to get people of rank and credibility to vouch for one's sentiments as well as one's conduct from the very beginning of the war. It was one thing to impress the commissioners with one's derring-do, but in the new enquiry, with so many more people applying, one must present an even better case. There was also the penalty that fraudulent evidence automatically disallowed any claim.

We see this shift in the petition James presented to the commissioners, dated March 15, 1784. He begins, "your Memorialist who was ever a lover of peace and good order, and loyal on principle, was, on that account driven from his property," etc., and again "your Memorialist, during the long course of his exertions, being most zealously engaged in promoting the great cause of government, attended but little to his own private interest," and so on. In his *Narrative* he had set out clearly what little money he had received throughout the war:

During the first year he served for nothing, not having the least thought of becoming a soldier, or the least doubt of General Howe's suppressing the rebellion long before the end of it. In the second, third and fourth, he received pay as Ensign; and in the fifth, as Lieutenant. Beside his pay, upon his taking the first mail, he received one hundred guineas, which he divided equally with his three associates. Upon his taking the second mail, he received two hundred guineas, one hundred of which was for himself. And this was the whole of what he ever received — except thirty guineas advanced to him by General Robertson, in order to fit him out for the expedition for the taking of Governor Livingston. He does not mention twenty-two guineas he has received here in England, because that was merely to pay a bill of charges incurred in one of his expeditions.[19]

In all, this amounted to £170, which he deducted from his total losses in his claim. This statement was to lay to rest Sir Henry's suggestion that James was asking for money twice over.

We see James scurrying around London for the next year gathering more support. Having met with a very lukewarm response from Sir Henry Clinton, and the suggestion that he was not being quite truthful, he had in July 1783 obtained a certificate of support from Brigadier General Alexander Leslie, a senior British officer who had served in America throughout the whole war. In January 1784, Daniel Cox, who had sat on the Board of Associated Loyalists and owned a large tract of land in Knowlton Township in Sussex, certified to the existence of his farm. In March, Sir Henry's adjutant general at the time that James was capturing enemy despatches, Major, now Colonel, Oliver DeLancey, repeated that Sir Henry had indeed intended to promote him and that he deserved better than a lieutenant's half-pay. James continued, almost compulsively, to collect certificates over the next two years.

In the meantime he was being called in by the commissioners to corroborate land values in Sussex County. On February 17, he gave evidence on behalf of Joseph Galloway, on March 27 for Cortlandt Skinner, and on May 3 for Col. DeLancey's father, Brigadier Oliver DeLancey, who had raised three battalions in New York. The claimants had the right to produce their own witnesses, but Wilmot explained that "whenever we could find out any Persons of character possessing knowledge of the subject matter, we have of our own authority sent for and examined them."[20] The witnesses were all examined under oath and separately from the claimant. James qualified on both counts.

In spite of his allowances, now amounting in all close to £150 a year, the Moodys, like most of the American refugees, could barely make ends meet in London. That first year together must have been particularly difficult. James owed £35 in England, and paid £80 New York currency to his father in America, leaving barely £50 for other expenses. It is not surprising that he was anxious to leave England and get back to some kind of normal life.

In May, James put in a special plea for an early hearing of his case so that he might set sail for Nova Scotia. His three children left with his father in New York were "in a most forlorn and distressed situation." His father, "in the late unfortunate War," had lost most of his property and through grief for his younger son's death was "nearly deprived of reason, and unable to afford the children necessary support or necessary Education." James was concerned that no land could be allotted to him until he got there, and that when he did get there he would find himself "far distant from those Friends & Fellow Soldiers with whom" he "had been accustomed to share the enjoyment of peaceful society, & the toils and perils of Warfare." Moreover the sooner he was established in Nova Scotia, with a little assistance from Government, the sooner he would be able "to raise an asylum against the inclemency of the weather & by industry & the knowledge of Agriculture which Experience had taught him, be able to make a comfortable provision for his family."[21]

His request was speedily granted. On June 8, he was called before the commissioners. His petition was brief and referred to his printed *Narrative* for the details of his services. He also presented a schedule of his property losses, and the next day brought an account of the expenses he had incurred in his intelligence-gathering and other expeditions behind the enemy lines. Major General James Robertson, who had been commandant of the city of New York, appeared before the Commission to corroborate the truth of James's publication, adding that James was always enterprising and would engage in services which others thought impossible, but in which he would nevertheless be successful. William Franklin went further. He not only praised his character but added that the *Narrative* described only some of what James had done, and, that, very modestly. Lieutenant Colonel Watson, former aide de camp to Sir Henry, offering to appear, wrote: "I conceive Mr. Moody's Services are so notorious & the Testimony of his Certificates so very ample that I presume it is scarce in the Power of an Individual to add anything that can give additional weight to his Merit.... The Services he has rendered & the risques he has run to serve this Country are such as make such an Individual *invaluable* to a General whilst commanding in a Country where he is acquainted & entitle him to as handsome a recompence both in justice & policy as a Country in the distressd state of our own can afford."[22]

The Board agreed immediately to allow the £1330 that he claimed for monies expended in raising men and other services, "being satisfied that he expended the whole of his property in rendering material Services to the British Govt. & on this Acct. they are induced to break their resolution on this Head," that is, of not compensating for out-of-pocket expenses incurred during the actual Revolution. Moreover, they added a note that "the Board desired him to inform them when he goes to Nova Scotia in order that they may recommend him to the Gov'r."[23] Sir Henry's aspersions on the veracity of his accounts were wiped away.

The commissioners, however, were only establishing the extent and the worthiness of the claim; the actual payment would have to be decided by Parliament. There were so many claims — 1,724 by April 5, 1788 — that the work of the Commission was extended. The Act finally died only in 1789. Two commissioners were even sent to Canada and Nova Scotia in 1785 and 1786 so that those Loyalists who could not travel to England could also personally present their claims. From time to time James put in an official plea for the speedy settlement of the money owed to him, or at least to receive enough reimbursement to allow him to cross the Atlantic. The commissioners were working as fast as they could, investigating claims during the day, and in the evenings, examining requests for temporary relief for those whose situation had left them destitute. But in the end there was nothing for any of them to do but wait.

Joanna Robinson wrote wryly to her brother in Nova Scotia,

What a charming country this would be if we had but the means of living well in it, as it is it requires a great deal more philosophy than I am Mistress of to be content. I am afraid papa is not so sanguine in his hopes of getting a support from government as he was some time ago. but really the great people quaril so much among themselves, that they have not time to think of such little people as *Loyal subjects* — we see a number of our American acquaintance daily and all very civil and attentive, but I am astonished to find, that those whom I expected most from, are the least friendly of all ...

— we live very comfortably, here, in very decent lodgings tho rather in the cottage style — the house belongs to a baker who inhabits part of it, and supplys the whole world with bread.[24]

The Loyalists rented rooms or part of a house over a business as Joanna Robinson describes. None of them could afford half the space they had been used to at home and they moved frequently within the same neighbourhood. The Moodys moved three times in three years, never more than a few blocks away. James and his friends lived in the area just north of Oxford Street, just west of the upper end of Great Portland Street, a section of London that was just being developed. The Moodys' last address in London was 4 Quick Set Row, on the north side of what is now Euston Road at the corner opposite today's Great Portland Street tube station. Behind the house stretched open fields and hedgerows.

Not all the waiting was unpleasant. James had been among the first of the genuine veterans to arrive in England. As the fighting ceased, he was followed by many more. William Franklin arrived in September, Inglis in December, Roome also in December of 1783, Cortlandt Skinner and his brother Stephen, Colonel James DeLancey of "cowboy" fame, and hundreds more soon after, so that many old acquaintanceships from New York were happily renewed.

The visiting and the calls were a part of everyone's life. While some people were disappointing in their neglect, still, as in all times of distress, others, equally unexpectedly, came forward to help. The Moodys' clerical friends were always close. The friendship with the Bouchers ripened and when Nelly, Jonathan's wife, died, Boucher's sister, Jinny, continued to be devoted to the Moodys. We find Jane cheering Dr. Chandler by sending him a currant pie, baked by herself in true American fashion, no doubt. Chandler was being considered for bishop in Nova Scotia, but he was also suffering from a painful cancer of the nose, which in the end prevented him from accepting the appointment.

Inglis was another friend who needed cheering. Though he would eventually be given the bishopric, he was at this time working hard to rebuild the American Episcopal Church, negotiating between England and America for an ordaining bishop in the new country. His second wife had died just before leaving New York and he had had to leave behind, with his mother-in-law, one of his daughters, who was too ill from measles to travel. He felt bereft, and uncertain of his own future.

Like James, he wanted to go to Nova Scotia as soon as possible, but must wait for the settlement of his claim. James brought diversion. Inglis records in his Journal in October 1785, that "he spent the evening at Capt. Moody's with Governor Franklin, Col. Stephen DeLancey, Mr. Boucher and Mr. Cooke who had dined there." In December, when his two children in London were very ill, and he was himself coming down with the same sickness, Inglis again wrote that "Capt. Moody called & insisted on his dining with him." It must have been another great dinner, for Franklin, James DeLancey,[25] Boucher, and Cooke were all there. James could sympathize with the widowed Inglis in his anxiety, and his loneliness. Indeed, during this time of stress in December 1785, James brought him money and called almost daily, one evening over-staying until 10 o'clock in his concern.

And there were James's seafaring friends from New York, men who would continue to be important to James after he left England. These were: Thomas Yorke, privateer owner from Philadelphia, now transporting Loyalists from England to Nova Scotia and New Brunswick; his captain, Thomas Miller, a company commander in Colonel Banestre Tarleton's Legion who had fought in the last, disastrous Southern campaign; and Jesse Hoyt, chief pilot for the Connecticut coast — one of the people the Patriot agent "Littel D." had reported on — just come in the autumn of 1785 from the new settlement of Sissiboo, present-day Weymouth, in Nova Scotia, to present his claim before the Loyalist commissioners.

Yorke, born in Lancaster, Pennsylvania was, like James, an American. By 1775 he was a partner in a sail loft, a sail-making business, and was becoming established as a shipbuilder in Philadelphia. By the time he was proscribed in 1779, and had fled to New York, he had an interest in at least five vessels. Admiral Digby had praised him for being "very assiduous and active in suppressing the American Trade."[26] When he settled his family in England in 1784 he still owned *The Fair American*, the privateer that New York Loyalist ladies had helped to outfit in 1779.[27] He had his wife and at least one son who later skippered one of his ships; they were neighbours of the Moodys and of William Franklin, who testified on his behalf.

Hoyt, from Norwalk, Connecticut, was "in the Merchants Service at the commencement of the troubles" and "came away with his vessels to New York in 1776." Throughout the war he acted as chief pilot to the British fleet along the Connecticut coast, and commanded the armed brig, *Sir Henry Clinton*, under the jurisdiction of the Associated

Loyalists. After the war, the Hoyt family had been evacuated to Nova Scotia and had settled "in that Remote and Unfrequented place," Sissiboo.[28] Hoyt had had the misfortune to cut himself in the leg with an axe. The wound had festered, necessitating the amputation of the limb, so that he now walked with a wooden leg.

In London, these three, with Cooke, must have held many meetings in the coffee houses that were so popular in the late eighteenth century. The Loyalists, living in cramped conditions, took advantage of these comfortable establishments that made up for not having a proper livingroom of one's own, much as the Viennese still do today. They served the new fashionable drink of coffee, but also dispensed simple main courses and sweet confections. A man could spend the entire day, if he so chose, reading the newspapers provided by the management, and meeting friends, who would know at what table and what coffee house to find him. The Loyalists soon chose their favourites, the New Englanders frequenting one, the Middle Colonials another, and so on. Here they wrote out testimonies for each other, discussed anxiously the Commission investigating their claims, speculated over new ministries in the British Parliament, traded the latest news from America, and made business plans for the future. They were like exiles the world over, sharing their frustration in the present and their hope of turning their lives to something purposeful in the future.

There was comfort in numbers, and a childish pleasure in revenge, toothless though it might be. When the revolutionary leader, Reverend John Witherspoon, the Presbyterian president of Princeton, appeared in town to raise money for his college, he was publicly heckled from coffee house to coffee house. "A man saw him at the New York Coffee House, and spoke of him with a loud Voice, and the opprobrious Epithets, of Villain, Rascal etc., that had the Impudence to beg Money in this Country for the Jersey College. The Doctor made no Reply, but soon went out to the Philadelphia Coffee House where this Man followed him & treating him in the same Manner, the Doctor left that House very soon."[29] This scene, reported by the Philadelphia Loyalist Quaker, Samuel Shoemaker, obviously caused great merriment among Loyalists all over London.

There were other less vindictive sights to take one's mind off the anxious waiting. On March 12 two manned balloons rose up over London, watched by an immense crowd as they slowly ascended into the sky. A 47-year-old Polish dwarf who could speak English and French was another sensation. The theatre was a particular delight, with Mrs. Siddons moving her audiences to tears in such tragic parts as Lady Macbeth, and Lady Randolph in John Home's now-forgotten Scottish drama, *Douglas*. Excursions to the country, visits to the Houses of Parliament and the Tower of London, attendance at the myriad different churches were also edifying.

And for the colonials, art came to play a new part in their lives. Their education in this field could be enhanced by attending the frequent public auctions of European paintings — William Smith's brother bought Rubens' *Judgment of Paris* for six guineas. They could visit the studios of such renowned artists as the Philadelphian, Benjamin West, who not only could be seen in his white woollen gown and yellow satin slippers, painting his own large historical canvasses, but who also had a very fine collection of Old Masters hanging on the walls of his unusual gallery. This had been added to his house at 14 Newman Street, and was built around a grass plot and over an arcade decorated with busts of Roman Emperors. West was at this time in great favour with George III for whom, among other subjects, he painted portraits of the royal family. A very generous man, he befriended and helped the other half dozen American painters who were working in London just after the Revolution, and was in close contact with most of the Loyalists there. West is now best remembered in North America for his painting of the *Death of Wolfe*.

Perhaps it was here that James was persuaded to have his portrait painted, not by West of course, but by one of the many talented portrait painters of the day, perhaps someone like Robert Arnold who painted the portraits of Judge Thomas Jones and his wife, the daughter of John Peter DeLancey and first cousin of Colonel James DeLancey, or even Gilbert Stuart, future portraitist of Washington, who had just begun to make a name for himself under West's tutelage. James's portrait was stolen in July 1981 from the very Nova Scotia church he had worked to found. Fortunately, colour photographs of it remain. The work of a skilled artist, it was an oil painting on canvas measuring approximately 30 by 20 inches. James is portrayed in the scarlet dress coat of an officer of the New Jersey Volunteers; the strong expressive face, set off by the powdered hair, frizzled in the latest London fashion, is highlighted by the white lace jabot and the officer's gold epaulette. It is wonderfully alive, and was obviously much cherished as Jane mentions it in her will.

James's *Narrative* continued to have a vogue, and in 1786 a large engraving was printed depicting his releasing the condemned Maxwell from the jail in the Sussex County Court House, the very scene on

A romantic reconstruction of Moody's 1780 freeing of Robert Maxwell from the Sussex County Court House jail, by Robert Pollard, 1785. Courtesy National Archives of Canada (C-81756)

which he enjoins a "painter of taste and sensibility" to employ his pencil. Never mind that the jail had Gothic vaulting, the print sold in vast numbers and was republished in both its large version and in a smaller one for some years afterward.

But no matter what the distractions, the urgent need to be gone was always present. News from America concerning James's children and his father was ever more distressing; the sense of opportunities slipping by was ever more pressing. At last release came. In June 1785, Parliament took pity on the hundreds of Loyalists like James, whose claims had been approved and who were stymied in their efforts to become self-supporting as they waited for compensation. At the urging of the commissioners, who saw such payments as "a most seasonable relief to the Individuals" and as "aiding the progress and improvement of their infant Settlements," [30] it resolved to distribute in part payment £150,000 to those American Loyalists whose claims had already been decided upon by the Board. The balance would be given out when all the claims had been heard. James was allowed £1608 on his original petition for £1719 10s. This claim included the amount he was out of pocket in his incursions behind the enemy lines, and some £300 for stock and household effects. He was paid £634 4s as a first instalment; £16 10s was deducted from the total on account of his temporary pension. When the claim was finally settled he received an ongoing pension of £47 9s per year, in addition to his half-pay pension as a lieutenant. This gave him, in all, £88 19s sterling.

In March 1786, he was ready to sail. After four intense years in England, he and Jane had made many good friends. Jinny Boucher wrote a heart-rending letter to the Moodys that they kept all their life. It is stamped Epsom, March 21:

And is it come to this at last that you are going so speedily, & so unexpectedly by me: for I was athinking now the weather was opened Again, we should be favoured with Another Visit from you, Agreeable to promise & pleasing myself that I should have it more in my power to be a little Entertaining than I could possibly show the last for then it so happened I had the will only to show my Gratitude, & Attachment to you. My Brother urges me to come to you tomorrow to say only that Cruel word *farewell* — indeed I cannot. I will save both yourselves and me the Pain — If any body in this World are entitled to my good wishes, tis you — and you have them. May every Blessing Attend you, and fill the Greatly Swelling Sail to bring you to your desired Haven & there may you be happy, happy as is or can be the Lot of Mortals here — What am I talking, we are not parted forever No! we shall meet in *Eternity* there I hope (if it is permitted) be useful & Servisable to each other & where pleasures have no End. I do nothing but cry now Mrs. Moody — then judge what a Meeting, if I had come — What a parting — think not of me till you get to Nova Scotia & then never forget me More.

Had I been near you, what plesure should I have had collecting little things for you that you might want particularly, physic I think you will want some for Change of Climate, and some good Warm clothing I fear you will Stand in Need of in Yonder Dreary Climes.

All sorts of Tools for Maam & Sir for they now must be industrious. I wish I had my little Hammer for I have now got two, and I hope I would forever part with half my Morsel for you, however I feel now if I had £1000 you should never go there. Oh if Fate should determine that we are ever to Come, how will I run to your house before my own! Did my Bro'r say anything About your Bed at Paddington, but he will be in presently & I will ask him. We have been twice to Church this day, & he is not Catechizing the Children. If you shou'd ever neglect writing to us, depend upon by time all Love will naturally die away, if it is not your own faults I am sure I shall write to you While I live. Give my best compliments to the good Dr. Seabury & to any other enquiring friend you may meet — If ever you see a Rev'd Mr. Barker an Irishman in that Country — remember he is a friend of Mine.[31]

She then goes on to press them to "go to Paddington and take the best Bed we left there with Bedstead furniture & Chairs or any thing else of ours in the house that you want." She insists that she and her brother always intended one of those Beds for them. She concludes with greetings from the Calverleys, the Parkhursts, poor Golding, and Mr. Stevens — "you are followed by every body's best wishes and every body joins in God Bless you with J.B."

Two weeks later they were aboard the *Lord Middleton* bound for Halifax. In saying goodbye to England, they were also laying to rest the hurt of the Revolution. London had allowed them to reexamine the past, to understand more clearly what they had fought for, what values were most important to them. A new awareness made them realize that they were neither the new America nor the old England. They had rejected the activism of the emerging American nation, and had been expelled by the rebels; yet they were too American to accept the rigidity of the English social structure. They must build something that blended the two.

NOTES

1. *Gentleman's Magazine* 52 (June 1782): 307.
2. Petition of Robert Cooke on behalf of himself, and his Brother and Co-partner, Charles Cooke, late of Crosswicks, in the Province of New Jersey in North America, Merchants, New York, 30 Oct. 1779, British Headquarters Papers, 9962 (16), enclosure 20, NAC, microfilm M-367.
3. *Narrative*, Appendix 7.
4. Jonathan Boucher, *Reminiscences of an American Loyalist* (1797; repr. Boston: Houghton Mifflin, 1925), 146.
5. Sir Henry Clinton to Lt. Moody, 24 May 1783, Moody Papers.
6. Evan Nepean to George Rese, Esq., Whitehall, 30 Oct. 1782, Moody Papers. Thomas Townshend was at this time Home Secretary responsible for the colonies.
7. Jonathan Boucher to James Moody, 30 July 1788, Moody Papers.
8. *Narrative*, 1.
9. *Ibid.*, 54-57.

10. Samuel Curwen, *The Journal of Samuel Curwen, Loyalist,* ed. Andrew Oliver (Cambridge, MA: Harvard University Press, 1972) vol. 2, 886. Entry 1 Jan. 1783.

11. Loyalist Claims, PRO, AO 12/99, f. 4, NAC, microfilm B-1177.

12. James Moody to Col. John Graves Simcoe, 31 May 1783, Moody Papers.

13. Draft letter of John Graves Simcoe, Wolford Lodge, to an unknown friend, 15 June 1783, Simcoe Family Papers, Archives of Ontario, microfilm F47-6-0-1.

14. John Eardley-Wilmot, *Historical View of the Commission for Enquiring into the Losses, Services, and Claims of the American Loyalists, At the Close of the War Between Great Britain and her Colonies, in 1783* (Boston: Gregg Press, 1972), 31.

15. *Ibid.,* 42-43.

16. John Hills, *Collection of Plans of New Jersey* (London: Meriden Gravure, 1777-82), Geography and Map Division, LC.

17. Loyalist Claims, PRO, AO 12/99, p. 54, NAC, microfilm B-1177.

18. Thomas Millidge to James Moody, Digby, 8 Nov. 1784, Moody Papers.

19. *Narrative,* 56.

20. Eardley-Wilmot, *Historical View,* 66.

21. James Moody to Mr. Foster, undated but probably a rough draft of the shorter letter sent 19 May 1784, Moody Papers.

22. Loyalist Claims, PRO, AO 13/110, pp. 255-56, NAC, microfilm B-2213.

23. *Ibid.*

24. Joanna Robinson to her brother, Lt. Col. Robinson, Nova Scotia, Mortlake, 6 Feb. 1784, New Brunswick Museum, Packet 18, Shelf 128, Box 3, Reel 180.

25. This is not the Col. James DeLancey then in Annapolis, but a younger relative.

26. March 15, 1784, Certificate accompanying claim submitted 29 Jan. 1785, PRO, AO 13/72, NAC microfilm B-2438.

27. *Lloyd's Registry,* 1784.

28. Claim of Jesse Hoyt, PRO, AO 12/101, p. 257, NAC microfilm B-1178, and AO 13/96, p. 542, NAC, microfilm B-2200.

29. William Smith, *The Diary and Selected Papers of Chief Justice William Smith, 1784-1793* (Toronto: Champlain Society, 1965), vol. 1, 23.

30. Eardley-Wilmot, *Historical View,* 127.

31. Jinny Boucher to Mr. and Mrs. Moody, n.d., Moody Papers.

III

NOVA SCOTIA (1786-1809)

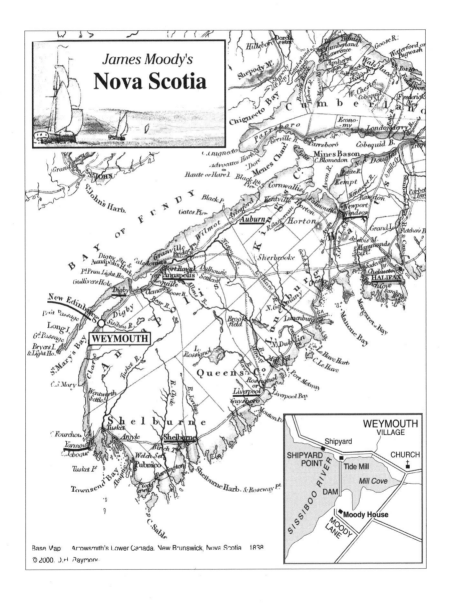

James Moody's **Nova Scotia**

Base Map   Arrowsmith's Lower Canada, New Brunswick, Nova Scotia   1838

© 2000 J.H. Raymond

WEYMOUTH VILLAGE

Shipyard

SHIPYARD POINT

Tide Mill

CHURCH

Mill Cove

DAM

Moody House

MOODY LANE

SISSIBOO RIVER

12

ARRIVING IN NOVA SCOTIA, 1786

JAMES SAILED INTO HALIFAX heralded as a wartime hero. On May 16, the day after he landed, a short paragraph announced in the *Royal Nova Scotia Gazette*: "Yesterday afternoon arrived the ship *Lord Middleton* in forty-one days from London, in which came passenger (among several others) Mr. Moody who several times during the late war, at the risk of his life intercepted the mails from the enemy's headquarters to Philadelphia etc."[1] James was one of the most celebrated Loyalist partisan of the Revolution. His name would have been familiar to all the Loyalists of Halifax and Nova Scotia.

But his military exploits were no longer relevant. He must now refurbish his civilian skills. In coming to Nova Scotia, he was returning to the familiarity of British American colonial life, with much that he had been used to in New Jersey, but also with new challenges that would require all his energies. After six years of fighting and four years of exile, at 41 he was taking up in a new location, the pastoral story that had been cut short in New Jersey, the story of "the contented farmer," happy with "a beloved wife" and "promising children." He was to settle in Sissiboo, a remote village in Annapolis County, in western Nova Scotia. It is worth examining the nature of the society the Moodys were coming to and what they would have seen on their journey across this new land that first summer.

First, and this was a devastating shock to the arriving Loyalists, was the poverty of the province. Except for the Annapolis valley, the shores of the Annapolis Basin, and the area between Windsor and Horton around the southern bay of the Minas Basin, most of Nova Scotia is not farmable. By and large, the interior of the province still consists of dense forest, growing out of bog and thin acid topsoil sitting on rock. The great wealth of Nova Scotia, until very recently, lay in its fisheries close to the offshore fishing banks, and lumber with its added potential for ship building. Moreover, in the eighteenth century there were very few roads so that the communities, which were small and struggling, were cut off from one another, socially and economically.

There was another feature of the country that might not have been so apparent at first glance but which very much affected the people who were there. In the 33 years before the arrival of the Loyalists, Nova Scotia and what is now New Brunswick had gone through a complete remaking of the ethnic composition of its population. Although the British were awarded peninsular Nova Scotia by the Treaty of Utrecht in 1713, they took a more aggressive control of the province after 1748, when the great French fortress of Louisbourg on Cape Breton Island, dominating the sea route to New England, was returned to France. To counter the menace of further incursions from the Catholic French, the British began almost immediately a policy of making the province Protestant and secure. Between 1751 and 1753, some three thousand Lutherans from the German Palatinate and Upper Rhine, with a few Swiss Calvinists, were brought to the colony.[2] Between 1755 and 1762, as military raids in America dovetailed into Europe's Seven Years War, most of the thirteen thousand Acadians — the original French settlers — were forcibly deported, in an eighteenth-century version of ethnic cleansing. These French-speaking farmers had colonized this buffer zone between New France and New England since the first half of the seventeenth century. They had been dispersed in little groups throughout the English-speaking American colonies lest they form a single threatening block.

However, after the war, some two thousand Acadians were allowed to return, not to their former homes but to resettle certain less desirable areas of the province, such as the inhospitable south shore of Saint Mary's Bay, near where James intended to settle. By the time he arrived in neighbouring Sissiboo, their community here numbered close to eight hundred and stretched almost as far as Yarmouth, making up the township of Clare, the westernmost section of Annapolis County. Called Frenchtown at the time, it is now known as the French Shore. These Acadians would be very much a part of James's life in Nova Scotia.

Meanwhile, about seven thousand New Englanders, with a small contingent of Presbyterian Scots-Irish from Londonderry, New Hampshire, and Londonderry, Northern Ireland, were invited to take the place of the Acadians. These new Yankee "Planters" flocked to the now-deserted and buildingless Acadian farms, and other empty areas of the province, some as farmers, some as fishermen. In the early 1770s, another thousand people came from Yorkshire, soon followed by several hundred Highland Scots. By 1783 the non-native population of Nova Scotia, including what is now New Brunswick, had been completely made over. Long-settled, French-speaking, Catholic Acadians had been replaced by predominately newly arrived, mostly English-speaking, Protestant settlers of British origin, over half from New England. In all, the new inhabitants numbered close to thirty thousand people, a little over twice the number deported.

When the American Revolution formally ended, an even greater population change took place in Nova Scotia. Nearly forty thousand Loyalist refugees suddenly flooded the province. Sheltering in New York City, the only safe enclave left, they had nowhere else to go but British territory when the city was handed over to the American forces. Most of them came by ship, in two main groups under escort of the British navy, in a brilliantly organized evacuation that took up much of the year. James had left New York a year earlier. Happily for him, he was arriving in Nova Scotia after the turbulence of the first inundation had subsided.

In 1786, when James sailed into the port of Halifax, the town, with a population of five thousand, was a tiny and very distant outpost of empire, not the busy charming city the visitor sees today, nor the boom-town it would become in the next 20 years in the prosperous times that followed the new Loyalist settlement. It had been founded in 1749 as a naval supply station. As the new capital of Nova Scotia, it replaced the old fort of Annapolis Royal on the other side of the penin-sula. Its fortifications were intended to checkmate the French base of Louisbourg. The site had been chosen to take advantage of one of the finest protected deep-sea harbours in North America, a harbour large enough to have been used in both World War I and World War II as a collection point for transatlantic convoys. A contemporary diarist described the city a year after James's arrival:

The town of Halifax is prettily enough situated on a hill side, at the top of which there is a citadel and block-house. The houses are all built of wood, and in general painted white or yellow, which has a very pleasing effect, particularly in summer. The streets extend from north to south along the side of the hill, and are intersected by cross streets, extending from the shore up the hill toward the block-house. The Governor, Parr, and the Commissioner of the dockyard have both very good houses. There are three barracks, which would contain from 600 to 1000 men. There are also two churches, both very neat buildings of wood, and one or two meeting-houses. There is a square in town called the Grand Parade, where the troops in garrison parade every evening during the summer; and where all the belles and beaux of the place promenade, and the bands remain to play as long as they walk.[3]

The town had not completely recovered from the sudden invasion of thousands of Loyalist refugees. The Common, somewhat reminiscent of war-time New York, still had remnants of a tent town and abandoned spruce wigwams where the poorer American refugees had camped after their evacuation from that city three years before.[4] It also had many of the less appealing characteristics of an eighteenth century port city. Doing a lively trade were the prostitutes and disreputable taverns that lined Barrack Street heading up from the harbour. Dusty in dry weather and muddy in wet, the uncobbled streets and lanes were lit at night by lanterns hung on posts some eight feet high, an easy target for mischief-makers and those whose business preferred the darkness. As in wartime New York, drunken soldiers and sailors, barely touched by civilian law, roamed the streets breaking up fences, beating up the casual stroller, and attempting to rape any young woman unfortunate enough to be unaccompanied at night, or at times even in broad daylight. The stench of the daily sewage being trundled down to the harbour added to the city's attraction. Shortly after James arrived, bush fires broke out on the outskirts, casting a pall of smoke over the town.

With his recommendation from the Loyalist commissioners, it was James's duty to call immediately on the governor, John Parr. A short, dapper military man, Parr was psychologically ill-equipped to deal with the immense problems of the sudden invasion of these American hordes who had descended on him. Mostly destitute but highly vocal, they clamoured for shelter, for immediate and precise land surveys, and for the proper distribution of food and tools to build communities in the inhospitable wilderness. James must have sighed as he took the measure of the man, another of these rather mediocre British commanders, lazy and self-serving, with whom he and the other Loyalists had had to cope in New York. Though overwhelmed by these extra responsibilities, Parr was basically a decent man who had wanted to enjoy the plum of the governorship of a small colony, and amass enough money to retire comfortably to an estate in England. He probably did not think too much of the energetic James either. But the visit must have at least given James a picture of the Loyalists' first three years in Nova Scotia, and told him who else was in town.

Among the prominent people that James would have known in New York and called on at his arrival was the Philadelphia merchant and wool manufacturer, Philip Marchington, whom Cresswell had described before the war as "an extravagant fop."[5] Marchington had succeeded in coming away from New York with £35,000, with which he was able to rebuild his business and buy up much of Halifax's choice commercial real estate. He would have dealings with James on shipbuilding, and would, incidentally, reform himself into an ardent chapel-goer. Another highly placed acquaintance was Attorney General Samuel Salter Blowers, formerly from Boston but solicitor-general of New York during the war and secretary to the Board of Associated Loyalists. He was a jolly, friendly man, with a highly intelligent, inquisitive mind.[6]

There were other refugee acquaintances not so fortunate, like the 60-year-old Isaac Longworth whose now pathetically crippled wife, Catherine, was a sister of the eminent Loyalist, Judge David Ogden. Jane had known them all in Newark before the Revolution as well as in New York during the war. Destitute, Longworth had come up from New York to present his claim before two of the commissioners for enquiry into the Loyalist losses who had been sent out the previous November.[7] On May 22, just six days after his arrival, James wrote a letter to the commissioners attesting to the man's loyalty and good character. The commissioners would make the tour of Nova Scotia in the next few months and again James's name would be used to bolster an old friend's claim.

However, the Moodys did not linger in Halifax, but rather pushed on to Sissiboo on the opposite side of Nova Scotia. Their baggage would have been sent around the coast by boat. The first part of their own journey was overland by carriage to Windsor, permitting them to look in on Isaac Brown who had married them four years before. The next stage was to Horton on horseback, over a tolerable road that passed through good agricultural land, thickly settled by both Planters and Loyalists. The road, leaving the area near the Minas Basin and winding its way beside the upper reaches of the Annapolis River, then brought them into Annapolis County, and down through the fertile valley of the Annapolis River to Annapolis Royal, the county town at its mouth at the upper end of the Annapolis Basin.

Annapolis was one of the largest counties in Nova Scotia. In 1786, with a population of over five thousand, consisting mostly of farmers. Loyalists outnumbered the New England Planters three to one. These "old" settlers tended to be Congregationalist, with some Methodists and Baptists, many recently converted to the New Light movement, while the "new" settlers searching for order after their wartime experience often favoured the Anglican Church.

Annapolis Royal was (and still is) a charming place, with its neat gardens and pretty New England-style clapboard houses. Three years earlier, it had gone through the upheaval of thousands of Loyalist refugees temporarily camped among its inhabitants. The little town's resources had been strained to their breaking point as new arrivals sorted out landholdings and destinations. In 1786, with a little over three hundred inhabitants, it was still two and half times the size it had been four years before.[8]

Originally the French Port Royal, named after Champlain's "Habitation" of 1605 on the opposite shore, Annapolis Royal had been the capital of both Acadia and Nova Scotia, under alternate French and English governments throughout the seventeenth and early eighteenth centuries. At the close of the War of the Spanish Succession in 1713, when the English took definitive possession of the area, the town was renamed Annapolis Royal after Queen Anne. It still had buildings dating from its days of earlier importance, including its Vauban-style earthenwork fort which exists today only slightly altered by later British additions.

The area had been the heartland of old Acadia. These early French-speaking settlers were the descendants of a small number of families, mostly from different parts of France but also mixed with a few Scots and local indigenous peoples. Throughout the last hundred and fifty years, they had spread up the lower Annapolis River, around the shores of the Minas Basin and the upper reaches of Chignectou Bay, raising cattle on the long marsh grass that grows in these protected estuaries. With great skill they had built dykes as high as two metres which had enabled them to transform the tidal marshland into very fertile farm-

View of Annapolis Royal, by J.F.W. Des Barres, 1781. Courtesy National
Archives of Canada (C-2705)

land on which they grew grains and legumes. In Annapolis Township,
they had drained the salt marshes along the lower reaches of the
Annapolis and Lequille rivers where some of the dykes and outlines of
their farms can still be seen. Here access to the sea had always allowed
the inhabitants to ship their products to market. It is no wonder that
this area drew the densest settlement in the county among the succeeding Planters and Loyalists.

When James passed through the town of Annapolis Royal in 1786,
the immediate area was now almost completely English-speaking. It
had attracted a number of more substantial Loyalists, among whom
James found many old acquaintances. Here was Colonel James
DeLancey, of Westchester, New York, the dashing officer who during
the war had commanded one of his uncle Oliver's battalions, then his
own Light Horse, and then the West Chester Light Infantry (nick-
named the Cowboys). He had gained a reputation for courage and
ability in the field. He had built a house at Round Hill, overlooking
the Annapolis River upstream from the town. He, too, had returned to
his prewar occupation of farming. James could bring him news of his
jurist cousin, Stephen, lieutenant-colonel of James's battalion in the
New Jersey Volunteers and recently elected member of the House of
Assembly for Annapolis Township, but still in London attending to his

Town of Digby, E. Woolford, *Sketches in Nova Scotia*, 1817. The church is Trinity Anglican Church, consecrated July 31, 1788. One of the first churches built by a Loyalist community in Nova Scotia, it follows the American meeetinghouse style and with the added feature of the hexagonal tower at the west end, is in sharp contrast to the classical style of St. Mary's Auburn. Note the blockhouse. Courtesy Nova Scotia Museum (N-8263)

father's estate.[9] Also living close by was the able doctor, James Van Buren, of Bergen County, New Jersey, who when captured and threatened with hanging for his loyalty, was released on the petition of his women patients.[10] His son, also a practicing physician, became the Moodys' family doctor.

From Annapolis Royal, the Moodys boarded a schooner for an easy passage to Digby at the other end of the Annapolis Basin, passing numerous prosperous farms sloping down to the shore, also settled by a mixture of New Englanders and Loyalists.

Digby was a small fishing port now swelled with Loyalists to a population of over a thousand,[11] situated just inside the Basin's entrance to the Bay of Fundy. Here was James's friend and battalion major, Thomas Millidge, who had brought Jane's loom with him at the evacuation of New York, and who had resumed his profession of land surveying for the new settlements in the vicinity. He had just been elected to represent the new township of Digby in the provincial legislature and was getting ready to go to Halifax to be sworn in on June 8. The two men would have exchanged stories about the evacuation from New York, the stormy journey in the little boats under escort of Admiral Robert Digby, after whom this fast-growing community had been renamed, about the moments of despair as they all faced the first winter in "Nova Scarcity," about the confusion over escheated land lots that Millidge was resurveying, about building a house and at last being settled enough to run as a member of the House of Assembly. They would have talked too about the beauties of the great city of London, the vexations of being short of money, the sense of rootlessness and lack of "place" in that highly structured society, the snobbery and lack of understanding of the English, the increasing sympathy of the Loyalist commissioners, and the many old friends that had gathered there after the war. One wonders if James brought the red calico and other goods that Millidge had recommended in his first letter from Digby. Millidge could advise him about procedures for acquiring land, and how much to pay for it.

The final leg from Digby to Sissiboo, made by a roundabout sea route, took another three or four days. Digby Township stretched from Digby to Sissiboo, and included the long peninsula and islands that separate Saint Mary's Bay from the Bay of Fundy. Before the arrival of the Loyalists it had been settled by only a tiny handful of New England fishing families. Although a rough trail across the isthmus between the Annapolis Basin and Saint Mary's Bay connected Digby to Sissiboo, it was hardly suitable for new arrivals laden with even light baggage. The same vessel from Annapolis Royal that regularly made the circuit from Annapolis Royal and Digby, around the south shore to Halifax, probably took the Moodys to their new destination, and certainly would have brought their heavier effects from Halifax. The voyage from Digby consisted of sailing southwest along the rocky, sparsely settled south shore of the Bay of Fundy, around Digby Neck through the swirling tidal currents of the Petit Passage, into the calmer Saint Mary's Bay, and then back up to the mouth of the Sissiboo River, where James hoped to settle.

At Sissiboo James must have felt he had come home, almost to New Jersey again. The challenges facing the newly arrived settlers were the same he had faced in his early manhood in Sussex County, and the site had much in common with Little Egg Harbour, where he had grown up. The settlement was similarly situated on a sheltered bay of the sea, a bay also attractive to smugglers. There was the same abundance of fish, cod and herring in Sissiboo, and "oysters and lobsters in plenty" as Stephen Skinner had reported on his visit in August 1783.[12] There was the same dark forest of pine and spruce and oak, and also birch in Sissiboo; the same sparse top soil, too thin for heavy crops. Even the friendly Mi'Kmaq,[13] like the Delaware, were Algonquin speakers and less warlike than the Iroquois who had sided with the British during the Revolution. The tides were higher and the climate was colder — but the snakes were fewer. A new feature for James were the resettled Acadian French further down the coast, with their frame houses strung out along the high ground, perched to look down over their fields to the sea, the dense forest at their backs.[14] They raised cattle and fished and lumbered.

Here James again found himself among friends and military colleagues. Except for six New England families, and a few Acadians, everyone was Loyalist. The settlement along both shores of the river barely numbered a hundred people. In the whole area, not counting the Acadians there could not have been four hundred.[15] Apart from Hoyt, foremost were the Griggs, John and Hannah, who had been witnesses at James's and Jane's wedding in New York. James Cosman was another fellow Loyalist that James had probably known in New York. From Orange County, New York, home of the Smith gang that had helped James in capturing Washington's dispatches, Cosman had early been indicted for supporting the British, and then, like Miller, had joined Tarleton's Legion to fight in the South.[16] His land included the little creek named after him, that empties into a bay protected by the coastal ridge, before it becomes part of the Sissiboo River at its mouth. He would soon not only be James's neighbour but also a business associate. He and his brother were witnesses to James's first land purchase, as was also Captain Benjamin McConnell, another veteran whose descendants, famous for their Ontario seed and nursery business, still have in their possession James's sword. There was John Taylor, before the war an extensive landowner in Monmouth County, New Jersey, then a captain in James's battalion, and now owning seven hundred acres of land, mostly on the south side of the river, that he exploited with the help of seven slaves. In conjunction with a Loyalist neighbour, James Journeay, he had already erected a sawmill to serve the neighbourhood. There was also another comrade at arms, Reuben Hankinson, a fellow officer in his battalion of the New Jersey Volunteers.

James had arrived in Nova Scotia at the best possible time, when the refugees were becoming established and the province was poised to begin its commercial expansion. He had friends throughout the province, he had standing, and he had capital. His experience in New Jersey, growing up in a coastal hamlet not unlike Sissiboo, and then farming rocky rugged soil on the old province's northwest frontier, would help him to understand the problems that now faced him and allow him to quickly establish another farm and a profitable business in his new country. His qualities as a wartime field officer would further contribute to his position as a leader in the community. During the next few years James's successful ventures would greatly enhance the prosperity of this little settlement.

NOTES

1. *Nova Scotia Gazette and Weekly Chronicle*, Tuesday, 16 May 1786.

2. *Historical Atlas of Canada: The Beginning to 1800* (Toronto: University of Toronto Press), vol. 1, plates 29-32. All the figures, for this chapter are from these plates, unless noted otherwise.

3. *Dyott's Diary, 1781-1845: A Selection from the Journal of William Dyott, Sometime General in the British Army and Aide-de-Camp to His Majesty King George III*, ed. Reginald W. Jeffery (London: Archibald Constable, 1907), vol. 1, 30.

4. Thomas H. Raddall, *Halifax: Warden of the North* (Toronto: McClelland and Stewart, 1948), 104 and following.

5. Nicholas Cresswell, *The Journal of Nicholas Cresswell, 1774-1777* (London: Jonathan Cape, 1925), 153.

6. See Chapter 10, page 138, for James's connection with members of the Board of Associated Loyalists.

7. They had been sent out from London to hear Loyalists who had not been able to get their petitions to London before the original expiry date of 25 March 1784.

8. These figures are taken from letters by the Rev. Jacob Bailey, quoted in W.A. Calnek, *History of Annapolis County* (Toronto: William Briggs, 1897; Canadiana Reprint Series no. 30, Belleville, Ont.: Mika Publishing, 1980), 169.

9. Col. James DeLancey of Round Hill was the son of Peter DeLancey, and cousin of both Oliver DeLancey, Clinton's adjutant that James dealt with when he was sent out to capture enemy mails, and Col. Stephen DeLancey mentioned here, both sons of Brig. Oliver DeLancey. Col. Stephen was married to Cornelia Barclay, Thomas Barclay's sister. Col. James also had a brother Stephen, at this time in Canada, who came to Annapolis a few years later, after cousin Stephen was appointed chief justice to the Bahamas in 1789, and a sister Susannah married to Thomas Barclay. See also Chapter 7, pages 103-04.

For a portrait of the members of this important but confusing family who came to Annapolis Township after the Revolution, see George DeLancey Hanger, "The Life of Loyalist Colonel James DeLancey," *Nova Scotia Historical Review* 3, no. 2 (1983): 39-56.

10. E. Alfred Jones, *The Loyalists of New Jersey: Their Memorials, Petitions, Claims, Etc., from English Records*, Collections of the New Jersey Historical Society, vol. 10 (Newark, NJ: New Jersey Historical Society, 1927), 224.

11. This figure was reached by counting the town lots listed in the "Book of Proceedings kept by the Board of Agents while locating Loyalists in the town of Digby, during the years 1783, 1784, 1785," quoted in Isaiah Wilson, *A Geography and History of the County of Digby, Nova Scotia* (Halifax, NS: Holloway Bros., 1900; Canadiana Reprint Series no. 39, Belleville, Ont.: Mika Publishing, 1985), appendix E, part 1, 393.

12. Diary of Stephen Skinner, 1783-87, p. 22, Public Archives of Nova Scotia (PANS) Reports, 1968-74.

13. The new, phonologically more correct spelling of the word Micmac.

14. Their system of landholding was not the seigniorial system of New France (Quebec), but rather an apportionment of marsh, farmland, and woodlot, with communally made weirs, etc. In Clare, the land grants were soon divided as the families grew.

15. This figure is based on the number of families Bishop Inglis mentions as being there in 1788, allowing seven people per family. Charles Inglis, Journal, 26 Aug. 1788, p. 11, NAC, MG 23, C6, ser. 1, vol. 5, file 2.

16. E.M. Ruttember, and L.H. Clark, *History of Orange County, New York* (Philadelphia: Everts and Peck, 1881), vol. 1, 70.

13

BUILDING SHIPS, 1786-87

JAMES'S FIRST PLAN had been to go back to farming, but by the time he arrived in Nova Scotia he had another enterprise in mind as well. It was to build ships. James had already organized a consortium for this purpose before he left London.

His intention to settle in the Digby area must have been half-formed as early as 1783, when he sent his effects with the Millidges. Although his arrival three years after the evacuation of New York, when the best farming land had already been taken up, might have seemed a handicap, there were other advantages to coming a little late on the scene. The first chaos of the arrival of the mass of Loyalists refugees was over. Those who could not adapt to the difficulties of life in Nova Scotia were already moving on, either back to the United States or to new lands being opened up in what was to become Ontario. Others were now settled in proper houses, on farms that were beginning to produce, however meagrely. They had money to spend beyond the necessities, opening up possibilities for commerce. New industries such as lumber and fishing were begging to be developed by men with skill and capital. While James was too late for a grant of land where he might want it, he had a substantial sum of money from his claim to buy what he needed.

Millidge's mention of good hard and soft wood for timber, and Hoyt's knowledgeable description of his own area of Sissiboo, with friends and suitable shore land, probably determined James to choose Sissiboo as the place he would settle. Here his family could be happy and ships could be built successfully.

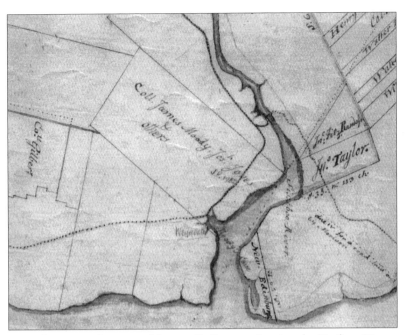

Part of a manuscript map of Annapolis County, showing the Sissiboo River
and the Weymouth area, by John Harris, ca. 1816. Moody's Cove is where
Moody had his shipyard and tidal mills. John Taylor had an earlier sawmill,
which would have supplied the lumber for Moody's first ship, on a little
creek in the middle of his property. The Upper Falls on the Sissiboo (top) is
where Moody had an interest in yet another later sawmill. Courtesy College
of Geographic Sciences Map Library, Lawrencetown, NS

It was a good time to get into the shipbuilding business in Nova
Scotia. American ships were now excluded from trading with the
British West Indies and England. Moreover, there was a shortage of
vessels after the war on both sides of the Atlantic. The American shipbuilding industry had been all but destroyed during the Revolution.
One Loyalist gleefully described what he saw on the waterfront at New
York when he revisited that city as late as 1787: "Not one single ship
on the stocks in the whole Town. Poor Devils! tho' they richly merit
every evil they yet feel and will feel, for they have many more to come,
yet, I can't help commiserating them a little."[1] In England, where timber was scarce and expensive, American ships had developed a high
reputation for craftsmanship and efficiency. At the time of the
Revolution about a third of all ships owned in England had been built
in the American colonies. Their lack was now acutely felt.

It was natural that the Loyalists in Nova Scotia and New Brunswick should attempt to fill the gap. Many of them were the same skilled entrepreneurs who had operated in America before the Revolution, and certainly there was plenty of first-quality timber available in their new land. As a further incentive, in 1785, the Nova Scotia Government instituted a bounty of 10 shillings per ton for vessels constructed in the province over a certain minimum tonnage.[2]

Building a large seagoing vessel in the eighteenth century was an enterprise of great accomplishment. It required special skills and knowledge, not only of boats but also of men. The builder must have "connections" to raise the necessary capital. He must find a suitable construction site. Finally, he or one of his associates must have a sense of the business market, and, of course, a knowledge of the sea. To achieve an ocean-going ship on a remote inlet on the edge of the English-speaking world, would be a challenge. Perhaps James had dreamed of just such a venture from his days at his father's wharf in Little Egg Harbour.

With the payment of Loyalist claims, there was, for the first time in some years, the prospect of private money to invest. Stephen Skinner, a man with whom James was later to do business and a brother of Cortlandt Skinner, James's commander in chief of the New Jersey Volunteers, wrote from Shelburne that if full compensation were to be made to the Loyalists in the spring of 1789, James's London agent, Charles Cooke, would have in his hands £3,000 in a lump sum and so would be well able to accept drafts for fairly large amounts.[3] Drafts were important in Nova Scotia, as in pre-Revolutionary New Jersey, because no money was minted in the colony and specie to make the initial outlay for lumber and workmen must be bought in England with a draft on a reputable banker who was known to have substantial sums at his disposal.

James probably formed his consortium in the autumn of 1785, when Jesse Hoyt had come to London to present his claim and brought a first-hand report of the favourable conditions for shipbuilding in his part of Nova Scotia. The group consisted of James and three others. James would be the organizing energy at the site. His banker, Charles Cooke, who had close contacts with government and money people, was a natural choice to handle the financial arrangements and the cargo. Another obvious partner was James's shipowning friend Thomas Yorke, who like most Loyalists had maintained his American business connections, and who was anxious to get back into the seagoing trade.

He could see to the London insurance, registration, and eventual sale of the vessels.

The fourth investor was the wealthy John Dick, who was probably introduced to the group by Cooke or Franklin who, with his father, had stayed with other members of the Dick family as a young man. His contribution would have been in the form of capital and "connections." A generation older than the others, he came from an eminent Scottish family, had served as British consul general at Leghorn (Livorno), and was a good friend of James Boswell, who had succeeded in more or less legitimizing a baronetcy for him.[4] In 1781, he was appointed head auditor and comptroller of the accounts in the War Office. He had considerable financial experience and at least a sentimental interest in Nova Scotia. As a young man in the 1740s he had started his career as a merchant in Rotterdam and his firm, Dick and Gavin, had been chosen in 1749 as agent for the British government to transplant Protestant settlers from the German Palatinate to Nova Scotia.[5] Childless and extremely rich at this time, he was a man who supported people who were willing to sacrifice themselves for their beliefs.[6] He had undoubtedly read James's *Narrative* and was probably intrigued by James's war exploits and was looking for an interesting investment in a field he understood.

Finally there was Jesse Hoyt, who though he had no money to put into the business, did have long experience with ships, and as the actual working mariner, would have invaluable advice to give. Hoyt could describe Sissiboo as remote but he could also recognize its commercial potential. He undoubtedly invested in shares in the cargo. He would be the captain of their first ship. Hoyt had made his last appearance before the Loyalist claims commissioners barely ten days before James sailed and one suspects that he was one of the "several others" who were on board the *Lord Middleton* when she docked in Halifax that May.

James lost no time in getting his business started in Sissiboo. His plan was to build first a ship — a three-masted square rigger — and to begin in the spring. Hoyt surely walked with him along the shore at the mouth of the river and introduced him to the widow, Bethiah Strickland, a pre-Loyalist New England settler whose land he would buy for his shipbuilding operation. Her lot included a stretch of beach that continued to be used as a shipyard well into the twentieth century, long after the Moody connection had been forgotten. It was on the sheltered southern side of the point outside the tidal pond that is a continuation of Cosman's Creek, just inside the mouth of the Sissiboo River, before the river empties into Saint Mary's Bay.

Although the deed with Mrs. Strickland was not registered until January 30, 1788, it is obvious that James was already in possession of his site in that first summer. With the rigours of the climate, ships were built during the warm months, begun as soon as the weather permitted in May. It was the custom for a prudent businessman to arrange for his timber and plank the season before and have it dry over the winter on the site.[7] James was in luck. He arrived to find a glut of local timber due to the lack of ships that could carry it to foreign markets. This would reduce his costs. It also augured well for his enterprise.[8] To be ready, James must have spent most of that first summer lining up his materials.

Equally important were the workmen, and these too would have had to be spoken for in the previous autumn. Again the timing was right. By 1786, the refugees were settled with functioning houses and gardens and were looking for extra income above subsistence from their land, so that skilled tradesmen, like carpenters and blacksmiths, were happy to sign up for extra wages. These were usually paid in kind, in provisions such as flour and corn, and necessaries for their families, bought from the shipbuilder's stores and calculated at "reasonable rates" on the basis of so much money per day. A skilled ship's carpenter would be working at the rate of 5 shillings per day.[9] The main meals were also provided: breakfast, dinner, and half a pint of rum for locals, and full board and lodging for people who lived farther away.

Many of the craftsmen would be blacks — some slaves rented out by their masters and some free — who had practised these trades before the Revolution, and who being poorer than their white counterparts were willing to accept lower pay. There was a relatively large settlement of black Loyalists between Digby and Sissiboo. Other workmen would be French-speaking Acadians from farther down the coast of Saint Mary's Bay who had been building small wooden fishing vessels since their arrival in the New World nearly two hundred and fifty years earlier. We know, for instance, that the knees for James's vessels were ordered from the French shore.[10]

James was also lucky to find in Digby a highly skilled master shipwright. This was Griffith Jenkins, a Loyalist from Newark, Jane Moody's home before the Revolution. All sorts of details would have to be worked out: the woodwork in the cabin; the carving, if any, of the head; what kind of cargo the hold should be fitted out to carry, what proportion of fish to lumber, to dry goods like sugar and rum; and so on. James and Jenkins must have spent long hours pouring over plans for this first vessel.

During that summer, there was a frenzy of construction so that all would be in place for work to begin early the following spring. In addition to cover, wharves and two landing places with access roads from the water to the shipyard were constructed. The timber was rafted downstream from John Taylor's new sawmill a short distance away. The southern exposure of the Strickland beach was ideal for drying the wood over the winter, and the wide bank gave ample room for the ship stocks and saw pits, and the oxen dragging up the huge planks to the shipyard. The tide there is always at least 15 feet, easily accommodating a vessel with a draught of as much as 13 feet. James must also have had built part of the access road around the creek outlet that still connects with the highway from Digby.

There was great excitement in the whole county over the ship. Already in December 1786, from as far away as Annapolis Royal, Thomas Walker, a Loyalist member of an eminent New England shipping family, was writing to a colleague in New Haven, Connecticut,

I hope to See you in the Spring a jaunt to this Country may I think be not prejudicial to you or your House, in your Commercial Matters I mean — Many Excellent Vessels are already at Sea Built in different parts of this Province and Brunswick and esteem'd to Be as Good as any Built in the United States — and By those who are good judges too, I am convinced that when you come here you will be able Clearly to point out so many Great advantages to your Father, that will arise from Being concern'd in Navigation that he will See the efficacy of it and immediately Build a good Vessel. There is now Building in Sissiboo a Ship of about 300 Tons and many of the Digbyites talk of Setting up Large vessels in the Spring So that you see we begin to flourish.[11]

The keel for James's ship was laid May 30, 1787. On June 29, Captain Pierre Doucet shipped for James from Annapolis Royal on board his schooner *Betsie* one barrel of pork, nine bushels of potatoes and sundry articles, which were probably provisions for the workmen.[12]

By the end of the summer the vessel was almost completed. She had a capacity of 193 tons, not quite what the letter writer boasted but still a good average size for a merchant vessel of the day built for foreign trade. Her hull measured 84 feet overall, 69 feet on the keel and 24 on the beam. She had two decks, a square stern and under her bowsprit a carved knee. Described by the surveyor as "staunch, well built and strong," she was made of Nova Scotia timber throughout, with black birch for keel and planking, and undoubtedly, white pine for her three masts and her cabin, so much admired by contemporaries.[13] We know that the cabins of these Maritime square-riggers were famous for the beauty of their interiors. Completely panelled in wood, usually white pine, they were embellished with gracefully carved designs, often beaded or with scrolls, even on the beams.

In New Brunswick, across the Bay of Fundy, she was heralded in an item in the Saint John paper dated September 20: "The Ship, building at Sissibou, is almost finished and will be launched in about a month: she is said to be a very handsome vessel, and an exceedingly good one. This is the second ship built in this province."[14] Again the writer was a trifle over optimistic. It would not be until the following summer that the new vessel would be launched. But James had established in "that remote place" an industry that would grow into many more sea-going vessels during the next six years.

NOTES

1. Benjamin Marston to Edward Winslow from New York, 8 Sept. 1787, *The Winslow Papers, 1776-1826*, ed. W.O. Raymond (Saint John, NB: The Sun Printing Co., 1901), 347.

2. Stanley T. Spicer, *Masters of Sail: The Era of Square-rigged Vessels in the Maritime Provinces* (Toronto: McGraw-Hill Ryerson, 1968), 23.

3. Stephen Skinner to Samuel Worthington, 23 Jan. 1789, Stephen Skinner Letterbook, 1780-93, NYHS.

4. James Boswell, *The Earlier Years, 1740-1769*, ed. Frederick A. Pottle (Toronto: McGraw-Hill, 1966), 370-71.

5. Winthrop Pickard Bell, *The Foreign Protestants and the Settlement of Nova Scotia* (Toronto: University of Toronto Press, 1961), 127-28.

6. In his will he left £200 per annum to "Col. Pleydell, in approbation of his attachment to the Duke of Gloucester." *Gentleman's Magazine* 74 (1805): 1175-76.

7. Stephen Skinner to Thomas Maddy, 22 May 1790, Stephen Skinner Letterbook.

8. See "The Loyalists in the Economy," in Neil MacKinnon's excellent book, *This Unfriendly Soil: The Loyalist Experience in Nova Scotia, 1783-1791* (Montreal: McGill-Queen's University Press, 1986).

9. *Diary of Simeon Perkins*, 1790-96 ed. Charles Bruce Ferguson (Toronto: Champlain Society, 1961), Sat., 5 Oct. 1792, vol. 3, 183.

10. The Account Book of Jovite Doucette, 1787-1806, shows among other items for the account of James Moody, June 22, 1789, "To 8 knees for the vessel @ £2." Centre Acadien, Collège Sainte Anne, Church Point, NS, MG3, b1-d3.

11. Thomas Walker to Peter Totten, 21 Dec. 1786, PANS, MG1, vol. 93A.

12. Capt. Peter Doucet, "Logg Book for Schooner Betsie for 1784-87," Collection of Anselme Doucet, Centre Acadien, Church Point, NS.

13. Petition of Philip Marchington and others, 4 March 1790, PANS RG5, Series A, vol. 3.

14. Date-lined Shelburne, 20 Sept., in *Royal Gazette and New Brunswick Advocate*, 25 Oct. 1787.

14

PUTTING DOWN ROOTS, 1787-89

THE YEAR 1787 SAW JAMES establish himself in other ways in Sissiboo. There is a charming letter written to Jane Moody in October by Elizabeth Galloway, the daughter of William Franklin's great friend, Joseph Galloway, who had accompanied her father into exile in England after the evacuation of Philadelphia in 1779. As noted earlier, they had become good friends of the Moodys in London, and the letter bears testimony to the warmth of the relationship between the two families. It gives the atmosphere of resettling that the Moodys must undertake and that Elizabeth Galloway as an American could understand so well.

The letter is an answer to one that Jane had written some time earlier, perhaps during that first winter, as it is addressed only to Mrs. Moody, Nova Scotia. "Judge not by my silence my dear Mrs. Moody, that I have ceased to remember or love you," Elizabeth Galloway begins, then explains that a dear friend has died, and continues:

Do not write me a condoling letter. Tell me that *you* are happy, you know that will give me sincere pleasure. The greatest alleviation to the pain I feel in being *separated* from those I love in this world is the hope of meeting them in a *better*.

I was obliged to leave this letter a few minutes and I am now returned determined to finish it without any more of the dismals. Apropos — have you seen the Bishop. [Elizabeth Galloway is referring to James's friend

Charles Inglis who had just been appointed first bishop of British North America, and bishop for life of Nova Scotia and its dependencies.] I hear he is to be quite brilliant.

I hope by this time you are *comfortably* settled and can entertain his *lordship* with due dignity if he should deign to visit your cottage. I am sorry that Capt. Moody hurt his side but I hope he has not sprained his right wrist, I begin to fear some accident has happened to him or his letters as we have not received a syllable from him. However to tell you the truth I had rather hear from you than him, as I know you will be more particular in your accounts. How many rooms have you in your house? how many cows have you got? will your poultry live through the winter? have you any society that you like? have you got the children from Jersey yet: and how do they promise? but above all can *I* do any thing here for you?

Pray tell Moody I desire he will cut my name in the first chair he makes for you that you may both remember on a winters evening one who tho removed from the contemplation of your virtues will ever retain a sincere regard for you. My father desires his best wishes may be tendered to you, tho he did expect to have heard from Capt. M. before this time.

You know I am yours sincerely,

E.G.[1]

Between the two ladies' writing, many changes had taken place in the Moody family. After the evacuation of New York, James's father had moved from Little Egg Harbour to Mount Holly, in neighbouring Northampton Township, Burlington County. In the spring of 1787 he died, leaving a small inheritance to his wife Anne, and £20 to his daughter Lydia. One of James's children, probably the middle one, also died during this period. An inkling of these impending sad events may have reached James and Jane in London and may have been an added reason for their precipitous departure from England.

How the remaining two children made the journey to Nova Scotia we do not know. It seems highly unlikely that James himself went to collect them in New Jersey as, even in 1786, his name would have excited revenge from his enemies. Perhaps the children travelled with one of the black retainers who came with the family at this time. In any case, by early March 1787,[2] even before this letter was written, and well before January 1788 when James registered the deed for the first land bought in Nova Scotia, the remnants of the family had at last been reunited.

There was also to be a new beginning for Lydia who, until then, must have been the mainstay of her aged parents and her brother's children. On November 21, 1788, she was married in St. Michael's Anglican Church in Mount Holly, Burlington County, to Samuel Rose. It is likely that this was Samuel Rose III from Little Egg Harbour, the Samuel Rose lost to the American family genealogists because he had been a Loyalist.

James was very soon in possession not only of the Strickland lot but of two more on the north side of the river, above the creek, so that his land adjoined that of his friend Jesse Hoyt. He built his house, not a "cottage," but a "hospitable mansion,"[3] as a later visitor was to describe it, on the first of the new lots. The building is believed to have burned down by the mid-nineteenth century. Today, a large hole, the remains of the cellar, is still discernable, and until the 1920s, local children used it as a skating rink in the winter.

A house built a few years after James built his, by a man of similar circumstances in the neighbourhood, gives us a clue as to what the Moody house looked like. It was probably two and a half stories, in the latest Georgian style with very simple outside trim, perhaps a fan light and classical pediment framing the front door, offset by symmetrically placed windows on either side and across the upstairs and back of the house. Inside, more spacious and more elegant than the Sussex County house, the main floors would have had two rooms on either side of a central hallway running almost the full length of the house, ending in a small room that could be used as a closet. Light and airy, each main room being on a corner would have had three windows, and a fireplace for winter comfort, with handsome pine panelling and mantelpieces in the two lower front rooms. The attic, reached directly from the kitchen, would have housed the domestic servants, including the several slaves, both men and women, that we know accompanied the Moodys to Nova Scotia. They had also brought a cook from England. The commodious basement with its brick flooring would be suitable for storing cases of madeira and porter, and the Souchong and Hyson tea ordered in bulk from England, and rum, molasses, and sugar imported from the West Indies, as well as the local fruit and root vegetables.[4] With James's shipyard close by, it would be normal for him to have bricks baked and iron hinges, door handles, and locks forged there.

We have a more accurate account of his furniture as this is listed in the probate inventories for both his own and his wife's estates. One room was furnished with a bureau desk and bookcase above with books, an easy chair, probably a wing chair, four occasional chairs, and two tables. There was also another set of 12 chairs, two more expensive tables, two elegant looking glasses, pictures, including of course the portrait of James, carpets, beds and bedsteads with curtains, bedspreads, brass candlesticks, silver and pewter and china, and so on. James owned a riding chair — a light, open, one-horse-drawn carriage. The picture is one of comfort and a certain elegance.

We know that beside the house James planted an orchard of cherry and apple trees, and in the stretch of fertile fields behind he undoubtedly grazed his sheep and raised a little hay. He also grew gooseberries and currants, and the usual peas and beans and root vegetables, and of course excellent potatoes.[5] There must have been flowers — roses which grow so well in Nova Scotia — and shrubs like hawthorns, and laburnum and lilacs that one still sees about the old homestead sites.

And birds! Bishop Inglis in his journal mentioned with delight the beauty of an early June morning in the country, "made more agreeable by the great variety of singing birds that chanted their music from every quarter." He then continued, "I had not heard so many singing birds since I left Pennsylvania. Every tree and spray seemed to be vocal."[6] James too must have sighed nostalgically over the sweetness of his American past before the cruel disruption of the American Revolution intervened, and he must have hoped that at last in Nova Scotia it could be recaptured.

From his front door, James could look out from the mouth of the Sissiboo River across the five miles of blue sea of Saint Mary's Bay to the great red cliffs on the other side. At high tide he could see the swollen river as it opens into a wide waterway between the raised sandy bank on the Sissiboo side where his house stood and the high stony bluff on the New Edinburgh side, and at low tide as the seascape changed, the long red mud flats reaching forth on either shore shrinking the river, and enlarging the sheltered cove just inside its mouth, where Cosman's Creek trickles in. Below him, at the water's edge, were his two private wharves with a road leading up to the house. Directly across the Sissiboo River he owned another wharf. Inside the mouth of the river on his side across the little creek, was his shipyard with two more wharves, far enough away that the clang of the workmen was muted at the house. During these years he also acquired land on the other side of the bay, at Sandy Cove opposite Sissiboo, and on Long Island, a fish lot and a farm lot, as well as four hundred acres of wilderness land on Digby Neck. To his old friend John Grigg, he sold the lot above the Hoyt land. As he had hoped, he was comfortable and surrounded by people he cherished.

A Design to represent the Beginning and Completion of an American Settlement or Farm, by Paul Sandby, n.d. This was printed as publicity to encourage settlers to America before the American Revolution. Much of it a visitor would recognize visiting the Moodys in Sissiboo: the forest, the mill, the canoe, the axeman squaring logs for timber, the black slave cart driver, the sailboat in the river estuary, the dock and warehouses, and the house. Courtesy Library of Congress (312001 USZ62 31185)

And then a wonderful thing happened, the sort of thing that happens in fairy tales but rarely in real life. An Englishman named Henry Niols had read James's *Narrative* and was so moved by his story, that he left him in his will five thousand pounds. Niols had never met James, but he "believed him deserving (as he certainly is) of his generosity."[7] Who Niols was we do not know. Although the Niols will was probated at the end of 1787, James could not have been aware of the legacy before April 1788. Only then did a notice appear in the Saint John newspaper asking that he be located and informed.

The London friend who had put the notice in the paper was Jonathan Boucher. James wrote to him immediately. His shipbuilding was coming along nicely; one vessel was almost finished, another was planned. He had named the point where his shipyard stood after their friend, William Stevens. His financial needs were not for the moment so desperate and he wanted to use this wonderful legacy to help those around him who were not as fortunate as he.

Boucher's answer, dated July 30, 1788, is instructive:

I return You many thanks for your obliging Favour of the 13th of April last, and shall always consider it as an obligation to hear of You, whenever your leisure will permit. The very handsome legacy left to you gave very general Joy to all your Friends here, & to none more than to my Sister & myself. It was an extraordinary Event; & I am happy to hear, that it has made the proper Impression on your Mind; which however I always knew & said it would not fail to do. For the last ten or a dozen years indeed, the whole of your life has been a series of Wonders ... now You are once more settled & in easy Circumstances.... Freely & honourably as this Money was given to You, it does great Credit to You to have shown Yourself equally liberally in assisting your less fortunate Neighbours. But, your Assistance, will be very handsome, & proper, if, when You have accommodated any of your Neighbours with Assistance that may want it, You are duly careful, as I hope You will be, to take proper Security. You may be generous to them, without being unjust to Yourself. I rely, that You will not only take in good Part this well-meant Hint, but also regard & make the proper use of it.

After sending news of his sister, and greetings from her and their other friends, he adds: "Mr. Stevens continues just the same honest, cheerful worthy Character He always was; & goes about the Country now, in his Way, laughing & saying, He now has no Occasion either to buy Potatoes, or to marry & beget Children; for that Captn. Moody has immortalized him by calling his Ship-Yard Point Stevens."[8]

Alas, a highway bridge now obliterates the site.

Ever generous, James lent considerable sums of money to his neighbours in Sissiboo and along the shores of Saint Mary's Bay, and to people whom he considered deserving, from as far away as Bear River. Following Boucher's advice, he would take a mortgage but never seems to have foreclosed nor even worried the borrower to return his money. However, before he knew of his legacy, he was being described as "a public benefactor to the settlement."[9] The new money merely enabled him to be more so.

James was also helping in other ways. One of the first things he did in Sissiboo was to work toward the establishment of an Anglican parish. To the Anglican, the Church of England stood for moderation, the mean between the "tyranny" of church doctrine of the Roman Catholic Church and the "chaos" of the free individual interpretation of the Bible by the Dissenters, especially the Baptists. In political terms, the Anglican Church stood for moderation also, the glorious unwritten English constitution, the king held in control by Parliament, controlling the established church, in a rational hierarchical universe. In contrast, in Anglican eyes, the Catholics were for the divine right of kings, the Presbyterians were for no king, and the Dissenters were revolutionaries. The turmoil of the seventeenth century in England, with its civil war, restoration of the monarchy, and finally the Bill of Rights and the establishment on the throne of Protestant William of Orange and his wife Mary, the Protestant daughter of James II, had settled this English framework. It was this role of the Church of England as an arm of the English political establishment that had caused the American Whigs like William Livingston to adamantly oppose the creation of an Anglican bishopric in America before the Revolution. Among Loyalists after the Revolution, it was this same upholding of the constitution that made them eager to see the Anglican Church firmly established throughout their new settlements. It would educate against revolution.

Through the Venerable Society for the Propagation of the Gospel in Foreign Parts (called familiarly the "Venerable Society" or simply the SPG), the role of the Church of England in the colonies had been to send out well-educated, carefully chosen young men as resident clergymen who, with their families, would set a good example and help "civilize" the "rude" colonists on the frontiers of the empire. These missionaries taught religion in "church" schools and also established lay schools open to everyone, especially the poor. They always included blacks among their parishioners, both slave and free.

Looking back to his New Jersey days, James would have said that one of the reasons that his own Sussex County, and particularly Knowlton Township, had remained loyal was because of the early establishment of the Anglican Church there. James must certainly have agreed with his friend Inglis's description of the pre-Loyalist Nova Scotia inhabitants when he arrived in 1787 as the first bishop in the colony:

The old settlers in this province are generally poor, owing to some unfortunate circumstances. The first British inhabitants were mostly fishermen, or emigrants from New England, and indolence was the general characteristic of both. Agriculture which claimed the first care, was little attended to. Poverty was the natural consequence of this; as a laxness of morals was of the want of a sufficient number of regular clergymen. The people seem now to be sensible of these evils. A spirit of industry has been introduced by the Loyalists, which is caught in many places — indeed in most — by the old settlers; and I found a general inclination to have Divine worship regularly established everywhere, according to the mode of our excellent church.

It will certainly be prudent in Government to cherish this disposition — every motive of good policy calls for it, wherever the principles of our church prevail, they naturally byass the mind toward the constitution, and incline it to loyalty; by diffusing those principles, we consequently increase the number of those who are loyal to the sovereign, and attached to the constitution.[10]

The bishop knew that most of these New England settlers were Dissenters — Congregationalist, Baptists, and Methodists — whose religious "enthusiasm," he believed, might lead them to a more "independent" way of thinking. The Church of England, with its stress on the established order, would be a bolster against any latent republicanism.

The new settlers in Sissiboo were as eager as the bishop to see a church established there. Only six months before James's arrival in Nova Scotia, the first Loyalists at Sissiboo and Saint Mary's Bay had already petitioned for a missionary. The newly arrived Anglicans explained that "for want of an Orthodox Clergyman," they were "in danger of losing their religion by the industry of Fanatic Teachers pouring in upon them from New England."[11]

These were the New Lights, followers of Henry Alline who, like George Whitefield 40 years earlier in the American colonies, preached a new personal and ecstatic relationship with God. Early in 1775, at the age of 27, Alline had undergone a profound spiritual conversion, the New Light New Birth of a complete regeneration. "My whole soul was filled with love, and ravished with a divine ecstasy beyond any doubts or fears," he wrote, "for I enjoyed a heaven on earth, and it seemed as if I were wrapped up in God."[12] Alline, himself a Nova Scotia "Yankee" brought to the Minas Basin area with his parents at the age of 12, preached throughout the Congregational settlements of Nova Scotia during the years of the American Revolution, until he died in 1784 on a trip to Maine. His successors, some from New England but most like himself from Nova Scotia though of New England origin, were carrying on his work.

To withstand this "enthusiastic" message, the Anglicans of Sissiboo requested an exemplary clergyman, plus some Bibles and prayer books to properly meet their needs — a cry repeated in every newly founded Loyalist settlement, as it had been in frontier New Jersey.

However, to attract qualified men and to allow them to live respected by the community, the SPG insisted that the missionary be assured of a decent salary. In new Loyalist settlements in Nova Scotia, a tract of land known as the glebe, usually a thousand acres minus land for a school, was granted to the Church of England to be a continuing source of revenue for the incumbent minister. In addition, before appointing a man to a parish, the members of the congregation must guarantee an annual income of £30 raised by subscription from his future parishioners. The SPG would supplement this with an additional £50 sterling and often the British government with another £75 per annum allowance. It was Sissiboo's lack of financial resources that had hindered the appointment of a full-time Anglican minister.

Governor Parr had twice blocked their appeal. He had first written to the SPG that, though they were "truly to be pitied both in a temporal and spiritual view, many of them having never had divine service since they came into the province," the settlers were too busy forming their settlements and too few to be able to contribute to the support of a minister.[13] Furthermore, he had added later, Sissiboo was a "small place," with "no roads to any other new settlement, the only communication being by water which is always expensive and sometimes impracticable."[14] Ironically, it was perfectly practicable for the new Loyalist minister at Digby, 20 miles away, to add Sissiboo and Sandy Cove across Saint Mary's Bay to his already quite large religious circuit.

But James's establishment in the community, as well as the appointment of his friend as bishop of British North America, gave the Anglican inhabitants new hope. On the Sundays when no Anglican clergyman was there, which was most of the year, James read prayers and a sermon in his own house to a number of his neighbours. In this he was repeating the practice he had experienced in his younger days in Knowlton, where a leading lay member of the congregation would take the service when the minister was required to attend elsewhere, and indeed where people of other denominations would also take part, so anxious were they for some religious guidance. A new application for a clergyman was made to the bishop, and James engaged to furnish a house — probably Mrs. Strickland's former house — until a parsonage could be built.

Bishop Inglis wrote to the SPG in the spring of 1788, that he had informed the inhabitants of Sissiboo "of the Society's good will and actual appointment of a Missionary for them." He continued: "They are numerous, but scattered widely over an extensive tract of country.... They have begun a subscription for the support of a missionary, and they will set about building a Church next summer.... In the meantime I shall apply to the Governor for a Glebe. The new inhabitants are Loyalists, very respectable, and worthy of the Society's attention."[15] The SPG promptly voted "that the Society are ready to erect a Mission at Sissiboo, when a proper person can be found."[16] James had many friends in the SPG, not least of which were Stevens, Boucher, and Franklin. With the bishop's endorsement, the Society quickly supported the request. Unfortunately, it would be some years before such a person was found, and even longer before a glebe was settled. As Parr had written, the small number of widely scattered parishioners could hardly muster the necessary financial support. These difficulties would hinder the formation of a parish for far longer than anyone could have anticipated.

However, in this summer of 1788, every endeavour of James's seemed headed for success. His first ship was launched on July 5. She was named *The Loyalist*. We have no record of the launching ceremony but from other accounts[17] we know it was the custom for the owner on that day to host a large dinner for all the yard workers and friends from the area. If the weather was fine — on this occasion it was early July — tables would be set out under trees by his house and spread with platters of roasts and pies and cakes, to be washed down with lashings of rum and madeira, and beer. Much of this food would be contributed by the women of the parish and sold to raise money for a local project. Toasts would be drunk to the royal family, the governor, and the people involved in the building. Perhaps, like others, James gave master builder Griffith Jenkins a silver bowl, and received in return the building model of the vessel. An air of festivity lingered on throughout the summer and, when Bishop Inglis visited Sissiboo seven and a half weeks later, it was still felt.

The bishop did deign to visit James's "humble cottage" and stayed three days in the community. Indeed, he would visit the Moodys many times during the next 20 years and enjoy their company in his own house at Aylesford. On this first rather official occasion he came in company with three leading men from Digby, the Reverend Roger Viets, Thomas Millidge, and Isaac Bonnell. A graduate of Yale, Viets was a Loyalist clergyman from Connecticut, who had two years before taken on the parish at Digby. Like James, he had only recently reunited his family in Digby. He was an extraordinarily energetic and well-organized minister. He had an active congregation made up of many wartime members of Inglis's Trinity Church in New York. Together they were able to complete the church in Digby by 1789. Viets worked his farm, and engaged in a little trade, and in the summer, almost once a month, managed to visit Sissiboo and the villages along the 40-mile stretch of the other side of Saint Mary's Bay. He also ministered to communities to the east of Digby on the Annapolis Basin, sometimes in these early years going as far as Granville near the mouth of the Annapolis River. His sermons were excellent and like his counterpart, Jacob Bailey, in Annapolis Royal, he wrote poetry, some of which was published in Nova Scotia as early as 1788. He was married twice and had numerous gifted children.

Bonnell was a Loyalist from New Jersey. Before the war, he had been sheriff of Middlesex County, and a close friend of William Franklin. He also owned a half-share in a sloop impressed during the Revolution to carry fuel for the army and eventually captured by the Americans. He early joined the British and held the job of barrack master on Staten Island during the war. James may have known him there. In Digby he was prospering as a merchant and starting his own shipbuilding business. The two families would soon have a bond through their children's in-laws.

The journey from Digby to Sissiboo was unpleasantly arduous. Inglis complained about the six miles of road from Digby to the head of Saint Mary's Bay and the still worse one along the shore and in the

Bishop Charles Inglis, by Robert Field, 1810. The Bishop's lawn is very
evident. Courtesy John Ross Robertson Collection, Metropolitan Toronto
Reference Library (T 31584)

woods, "the worst road he had ever travelled," he expostulated to the
SPG secretary. It fitted the Reverend Jacob Bailey's description of the
road out of Annapolis, "encumbered by rocks, holes, roots of trees
windfalls and deep sloughs," leading through "dismal woods," under
"overhanging precipices," and along "stoney beeches."[18] The bishop
recorded in his diary that they got caught in a heavy rain and the

"jaunt" became "disagreeable and dangerous."[19] Drenched, the riders slid their way to a tavern kept by a Mr. Reid, who warmed and fed them, and then when the rain let up, carried them in his boat to Sissiboo. One imagines that they were very happy to dock at James's wharf, slip into the comfort of his new house, and dry their boots in front of his generous fire.

The next day was better. One senses that the sun was shining. The bishop was taken across the river to have a tour of New Edinburgh, the settlement on the west side of the Sissiboo River, which had been chosen in the original survey as the location for a town. It was here that the grant of church and school lands was situated. It was also at the eastern edge of the Acadian settlements. There was a moving service conducted by Viets for the baptism of eight babies and two adults, including the infant son and the wife of the Loyalist blacksmith Samuel Doty, who lived on the New Edinburgh side. The congregation took the opportunity to speak to Inglis about the kind of missionary they wanted. "They most earnestly entreated me to send them a good man, or send them none," he wrote to the Archbishop of Canterbury.[20]

The day before, the bishop had already decided on the Sissiboo side as the proper site for a church, judging it also accessible for the settlers living on the north side of Saint Mary's Bay. He noted that the village of New Edinburgh consisted of four or five farm houses with a total of 17 families on that side of the river. On the east side lived Capt. Moody and five or six other Loyalists; the number of Loyalist families settled on the Sissiboo side and within five miles of the river was 38. He also remarked that there were living in New Edinburgh several French families with their own priest.

Inglis had never been intolerant of Roman Catholics, but he vehemently resisted what he saw as "Papist designs" toward the legal recognition of a Catholic hierarchy in Nova Scotia.[21] Though a firm defender of the Anglican order, steadfastly believing in the superiority of his Church, he was also cooperative with Dissenters, like the Presbyterians and other Calvinists. However, he had little tolerance for what he called "enthusiasts," the Protestant sects that preached salvation only through revelation, such as the later separating Methodists and the New Lights. He objected strongly to shutting out non-Anglicans from attending the new King's College at Windsor.

In a special ceremony the bishop christened a new Hoyt baby, "James Moody Hoyt" in honour of the child's father's friend. This boy was the first of several James Moodys born throughout the next ten years. Inglis visited Point Stevens and not only went on board the *Loyalist* and pronounced her cabin "very beautiful," but also visited the 190-ton brig, the *Three Friends*, set to be launched the next summer. He commented in his journal, "The country here is beautiful, the soil good and the inhabitants very industrious. It abounds in excellent ship timber." [22] The next day saw the baptism of John Cosman, son of the Moodys' neighbour, James Cosman. Then the bishop departed, taking the precaution of going by boat to the head of Saint Mary's Bay and only from there returning on land to Digby. The visit had seemed a smashing success.

It was not until November 18 that the *Loyalist* was completely rigged and sent to sea. Perhaps Yorke delayed in sending out the sail-cloth and ropes from England, as was necessary in Nova Scotia at that time. There must have been great excitement in the settlement on that day. Hoyt sailed her, with James on board, around the South Shore to register her in Shelburne on November 27.[23] Here they arranged for a cargo of fish and lumber.[24] Then Hoyt took her on a voyage to the West Indies, and from there to England.

The year 1788 ended with a great sense of accomplishment. One ship had been completed and begun its mercantile career, another vessel was on the stocks almost finished. The first concrete measures toward establishing a church in the community had been set in motion. The Moody family had put down roots in the new settlement and shown a determination to help build it into a happy, prosperous and decent society. Viets rhapsodized that year about Annapolis Royal, but he could have been writing about Sissiboo:

> On each fair Bank, the verdant Lands are seen,
>   In gayest Clothing of perpetual Green:
> On ev'ry Side, the Prospect brings to Sight
>   The Fields, the Flo'rs, and ev'ry fresh Delight:
> Herbs, Fruits and Grass, with intermingled Trees
>   The Prospect lengthen, and the Joys increase:
> To higher Grounds, the raptur'd View extends,
>   Whilst in the Cloud-top'd Cliffs the Landscape ends.
> Where Trees and Plants and Fruits themselves disclose;
>   Where never-fading Groves of fragrant Fir,
> And beauteous Pine perfume the Ambient Air;
>   The Air, at once, both Health and Fragrance yields,
> Like sweet Arabian or Elysian Fields.

The decent Mansions, deck'd with mod'rate Cost,
  Of honest Thrift, and gen'rous Owners boast;
There Skill and Industry their Sons employ,
  In Works of Peace, Integrity and Joy;
Their Lives in social, harmless Bliss, they spend,
  Where Truth and Charity abound,
Where God is sought, and heav'nly Blessings found.[25]

NOTES

1. Elizabeth Galloway to Jane Moody, 28 Oct. 1787, Moody Papers.
2. The Moody family appear on "A Return of the Men, Women and Children and also those qualified to bear arms in the Township of Digby, County of Annapolis, taken the 11th March 1787 by order of His Excellency Lieutenant Governor Parr," *Letter Book of Edward Brudenell, 1784-1786-1787-1788*, Digby Museum, Digby, NS, pp. 250, 271. They are listed with other Weymouth inhabitants, such as Jesse Hoyt and John Grigg.
3. Eliza Inglis to Jane Moody, 31 Aug. 1803, Moody Papers.
4. See Inglis Family Papers, Charles Inglis letters to Brooke Watson and Co. (known in Halifax as Foreman, Grassie, Goodall, and Turner), 24 May 1792, 1 Jan. 1799, and many others for items ordered, NAC. Also Stephen Fountain Account Book for an account with James Moody, 1789, 1790, NAC, MG23 C27, Reel M-2313.
5. Margaret Budd Moody to Elisha William Budd Moody, Yarmouth, 27 July 1820, Moody Papers. The land beside the house was called the Orchard for many years after the Moodys left Sissiboo.
6. Thursday, June 3, 1790, Journal of Charles Inglis, Inglis Family Papers, NAC, MG23 C6, Ser. 1, vol. 5.
7. *Philadelphia Independent Gazette*, 11 April 1788, cited in Thomas B. Wilson, *Notices from New Jersey Newspapers, 1781-1790*, Records of New Jersey, vol. 1 (Lambertville, NJ: Hunterdon House, 1988), 434. The same notice appeared in the *Nova Scotia Gazette and Weekly Chronicle*, Tuesday, 8 April 1788, 3, but without the laudatory comment.
8. Moody Papers.
9. Charles Inglis to Dr. Morice, 7 April 1788, Inglis Family Papers, NAC, MG23 C6, Ser. 1, vol. 1, p. 56.
10. Charles Inglis to Mr. Cumberland, Halifax, 26 Sept. 1788, NAC, MG23 C6, Ser. 1, vol. 1, p. 98.
11. Inhabitants of Sissiboo and Saint Mary's Bay to SPG, 10 Jan. 1786, *SPG Journal*, NAC, MG17 B1, vol. 24, p. 285, Reel A-156.

12. George A. Rawlyk, *Champions of Truth: Fundamentalism, Modernism, and the Maritime Baptist.* Winthrop Pickard Bell Lectures in Maritime Studies, 1987-88. Published for the Centre for Canadian Studies, Mount Allison University (Montreal: McGill-Queen's University Press, 1990), 7.

13. Gov. Parr to SPG, 27 April 1787, *SPG Journal,* NAC, MG17 B1, vol. 24, p. 413, Reel A-156.

14. *Ibid.,* 13 Sept. 1787, vol. 25, p. 20, Reel A-157.

15. Inglis to Dr. Morice, 7 April 1788, Inglis Family Papers, NAC, MG23 C6, Ser. 1, vol. 1, pp. 55-56.

16. General Meeting, SPG, 23 May 1788, *SPG Journal,* NAC, MG17 B1, vol. 25, p. 80, Reel A-157.

17. Brooke Hindle, ed., *Material Culture of the Wooden Age* (Tarrytown, NY: Sleepy Hollow Press, 1981), 111.

18. Jacob Bailey to Samuel Peters, Annapolis, 14 May 1787, Jacob Bailey Letters, no. 22, Carleton University, microfilm F16.m32, Carleton University Library.

19. Inglis, Journal, 26 Aug. 1788, Inglis Family Papers, NAC, MG23 C6, Ser. 1, vol. 5, p. 11.

20. *Ibid.,* Charles Inglis to Archbishop of Canterbury, 18 Dec. 1788, vol. 1, p. 126.

21. In 1803, Inglis had a terrible altercation with the Irish Roman Catholic resident priest in Halifax, Edmund Burke. See Brian Cuthbertson, *The First Bishop: A Biography of Charles Inglis* (Halifax, NS: Waegwoltic Press, 1987), 214-17.

22. Inglis, Journal, 27 Aug. 1788, vol. 5, p. 11.

23. PRO, CO, 193, Shelburne, NS, Shipping Registries, 1788.

24. Stephen Skinner to James Moody, Stephen Skinner Letter Book, 27 Jan., 26 June, and 22 July 1789, New York Historical Society; Stephen Skinner Ledger, 19 June 1789: "To lumber for 100 oars," PANS.

25. Roger Viets, *Annapolis Royal: A poem, 1788* (Halifax: A. Henry, 1788; repr. Kingston: Loyal Colonies Press, 1979), 1-5.

15

THE PROSPEROUS YEARS, 1789-92

AS WITH MOST LOYALISTS throughout Nova Scotia, the next three years were good ones for James and his family. There would be many changes, not least the emergence of the new name Weymouth, for Sissiboo. James threw himself into the development of the little settlement with the same enterprise that he had shown in his partisan warfare during the Revolution. Here again he became a leading force in community life. His shipbuilding flourished; he pushed for the construction of an Anglican church; he had a guiding hand in local agriculture and commerce. His family were together and happy.

The summer of 1789 was a season of weddings in James's family circle. On May 11, his oldest child and only son, John, married Margaret Budd. John was now 21, and Margaret exactly six months older. James bought the lot upstream and adjoining his own land for them. John was making his first tentative venture into a business of his own. In August, Margaret's older brother, Elisha Budd, was married to Mary Ann Bonnell, daughter of William Franklin's friend, Isaac Bonnell. Elisha Budd had been an ensign in his father's regiment. He had fought in Georgia and South Carolina, and taken part in the successful defence of Savannah. He too had settled in Digby. In 1789 he was a successful merchant, on the point of going into business with his father-in-law. Both these weddings must have been grand affairs, judging from the large sum of 23 shillings and four pence that Viets was paid to perform the ceremony.[1]

The Budds were typical of political divisions within American families during the Revolution. James Budd, the father, came from a well-to-do family of Anglican Loyalists from White Plains, New York. His wife, Elizabeth Brown Budd, on the other hand, came from a large land-owning family at Rye, Presbyterian and "rather rebelliously inclined."[2] Despite pleadings from his brother-in-law not to join the villainous British, James Budd stood up for the Loyalist side. Immediately a price of $900 was put on his head, "dead or alive." He sent his wife to Rye for safety among her Whig relations, where the local rebels took the opportunity to accost her with "pointed" bayonets, demanding that she reveal the whereabouts of her husband. Though frightened out of her wits to the extent that she refused to go outside her room for the next six weeks, she nevertheless gave them no information. An old friend of her father's, who was a senior officer in the rebel forces, was so shocked by the soldiers' behaviour that he ordered a sentinel to be posted outside the front door to protect her from further attacks.

Meanwhile James Budd escaped to Boston, then made his way to New York and there joined the King's American Regiment as a captain. Here, after some months, he managed to reunite his family. Unfortunately, he then went back to White Plains on a recruiting expedition, and there he was surrounded and shot by his rebel neighbours in front of his own house. Elizabeth Budd was allowed to come down from New York to nurse him during his dying days. She spent the rest of the war in New York. Here she met and married a Loyalist from Virginia, Charles Coulbourne, a lieutenant in the Loyal American Regiment and quartermaster of the corps. Coulbourne brought his new family to Digby in 1783, and during the next ten years captained ships to the West Indies.

James's master shipwright, Griffith Jenkins, was also married on May 11, and soon settled in Sissiboo, where he could be nearer to James's shipbuilding. Sadly, that day also saw the burial of one of James's black men, who died following the amputation of his leg.

Beyond James's immediate circle there were other significant developments. Although his own children were too old to benefit, James was pleased to see the opening in 1788 of the King's College School at Windsor, which still exists as the now coeducational King's-Edgehill. In 1790, King's College also opened, again at Windsor where, on the model of Oxford and Cambridge, the students could study away from the distractions of the city. Both these institutions were founded with the vigorous encouragement of his friend Bishop Inglis, to enable boys to receive a superior education in the province without having to go to England. The curriculum was designed to train them for the church and the professions, much as pre-Revolutionary King's College had done in New York. Sissiboo would soon have a small school that would serve in the early years for James's grandchildren, who in turn would encourage the academy in Yarmouth.

Of more immediate cultural interest to the Moody family in 1789 was the founding of *The Nova-Scotia Magazine and Comprehensive Review of Literature, Politics, and News*, a literary magazine of original stories and articles, reprints and excerpts of English and American and classical works. While it only lasted for three years — its founder and editor, the Anglican scholar, William Cochran, from New York, was lured away to head the new King's College — the magazine set a literary standard for the province that continued to be felt into the next century. During its brief existence, it published the debates of the House of Assembly and acted as the vehicle for the newly formed Agricultural Society, promoting agriculture in the province, and publishing letters and articles from that association. Much richer and more diversified than its contemporary English counterparts, *The Gentleman's Magazine* or *The London Magazine* or present-day equivalents like *The Atlantic Monthly*, the publication contained everything to keep a cultivated gentleman living in Halifax or Annapolis or even in a tiny village like Sissiboo informed and stimulated. It presented serious but also diverting material, like plays and short stories, and passages from history, that could be read out loud in front of the fire on a blustery winter's night. It circulated among the élite of the province. James was its westernmost subscriber.[3]

The formation of the Society for Promoting Agriculture in the Province of Nova Scotia, already alluded to, was another landmark in that year. Under the impetus of American Loyalists like John Wentworth, the former governor of New Hampshire and still surveyor of the King's Woods, and particularly Bishop Inglis, who was shocked by the unscientific methods of farming practised by his pre-Loyalist neighbours, the society was formed to exchange the best available information among farmers throughout the province. Inglis himself was continually experimenting in methods of husbandry, and was responsible with his fellow Loyalist from Wilmot Township, General Timothy Ruggles, for developing the yellow "Bishop Pippin" apple.[4]

Articles were copied from agricultural societies in Great Britain and members were invited to share their knowledge in the form of papers which were published in the *Nova Scotia Magazine*, and later in several volumes entitled *Letters and Papers on Agriculture*. These ranged in topic from preparing seed wheat to prevent smut, to raising calves, avoiding foot rot in sheep, making cider, and improving worn-out land, to name but a few. It was also intended to help people procure from Europe and America the best in seeds, plants, and trees. In this way there would be "not only an increase of useful knowledge, of industry, and of provisions of every kind," but also "a great advance in the value of lands, which is the certain consequence of the former."[5] The original fee, a guinea a year, was soon reduced to half that, and anyone could join. At first, nearly half the executive was from Halifax, but by the next year there were 48 directors, only six of whom were from the capital. It comes as no surprise to find James as a director for Digby Township. Even when the society ceased to hold regular meetings he and the bishop and the governor continued to exchange information on agricultural subjects.[6] The demise of the *Nova Scotia Magazine* in 1792 was a blow to the society.

During these years, James, like many other Nova Scotia Loyalists, maintained his close personal links with Britain. In September 1789, his ship, the *Loyalist*, completed its trade cycle with the West Indies and arrived in England, bringing his old friends letters and presents. The vessel was insured and registered with Lloyds in the name of Thomas Yorke. Charles Cooke took care of the cargo and made the English deliveries. Rebecca Thompson, the widow of a Massachusetts Loyalist shipper whom the Moodys had befriended while they were in London, wrote ecstatically to Jane Moody:

I have been on board The Ship Loyalist & feasted my eyes with the sight
of The production of Nova Scotia which was worked up under the Super-
intendency of your dear better part. I did not think any of the produce of
that country Half so Beautifull — I was not well the day we was on board
but could not help dancing when we entered the Ship —... I kisst the peaces
where I thought you or your better part had laid your hands — there we
spent the Day with pleasure & Festivity — I believe I can answer For all the
party — which consisted of the two Mr. Cooks, York, Stevens, Larrence,
Bell, Capt. Hoyt & Son.... Capt. all complacency — you may Suppose the
Conversation Turned chiefly on your dear selves & the country you Live in.

She then went on to comment on the French Revolution which had just broken out, and which soon would affect all their lives. She wrote:

"I do not pretend to meddel in politics — only must observe the French Swallowed a wonderful draught of american rebellion which would not digest — it has staid in their stomakes. Till now they have brought it up in double portions among themselves — I wish them joy with it etc."[7] She ended by sending greetings from a host of English friends that she names. Her letter was to return on the *Loyalist*.

Of course there was something for Jonathan Boucher, now rewidowed but about to marry for the third and last time, and his sister, Jinny, who was so fond of the Moodys. Boucher was away in northern England courting his intended bride, and Jinny wrote: "I saw Mr. Cook Yesterday, who tells me I can ship this off tomorrow, and I am happy in the Opportunity, for I long to have a little Chat with you: in the first place thank you for the Plank and the sweetmeats, which I got safe & sound and excellent, yesterday. Surprised I was, & my Heart overflowed with Gratitude at your kind remembrance of me." After giving news of mutual friends, including William Stevens, she added, "I think I shall distribute your bounty amongst some of them." She ended with a P.S.: "I should be happy to have an invitation to the christening when I mean to challenge you for snuffing, but I do suppose, Moody will challenge us both, tho I assure you I am an excellent hand. I am told the planks are most beautiful wood & I flatter myself my Bro'er will have them made to the Greatest advantage. I think after the invitation, I have given myself to your christening I cannot omit, saying how happy I would be to see you upon such an occasion at Epsom."[8]

Throughout these years, up every estuary that had a beach and timber nearby, sailing vessels, large and small, were being built as fast as the men could steam the planks and hammer the nails in. This energy was seen around the Annapolis Basin in Digby, in Annapolis, up the river in Bridgetown, and as far as Paradise, the head of tide. Around the shores of Saint Mary's Bay and on the Fundy side, in places where the banks were not too high, the same industry was evident. Until just a few years ago, one could still see the construction of wooden fishing boats, some quite large, on these shores. The only difference in method was that the present-day tools were all electric.

In the same year that the *Loyalist* reached London, the Moody shipyard launched the brig the bishop had seen on the stocks, the *Three Friends*, 190 tons. This went to Thomas Yorke who immediately sold it. In 1790, three more vessels were completed, the ship *Yorke*, 310 tons, for Thomas Yorke, the brig *Jane*, 101 tons, for James's son John, and the schooner *Experiment*, 91 tons, probably for Stephen Skinner. The larger ships would take a cargo to the West Indies and then to England to be sold within a year or two of having been built. Unusually, Thomas Yorke kept his *Yorke* for six years. For a short time in 1791, the ship's captain was Thomas Yorke, junior, presumably a son learning the trade. In all, a few months before the outbreak of the war with France in 1793, the Moody shipyard would produce in tonnage a little over half of the shipping capacity built in Digby Township up to this time.[9]

Some records remain of the cargoes of these vessels. The *Jane* made a round trip from Sissiboo to the Caribbean that lasted from November 1792 to May 1793. It was typical in its cargo and its itinerary for many Nova Scotia trading vessels. The brig left Shelburne with 216 quintals of dried fish, 45 barrels of mackerel and herring, 44,000 board feet of lumber, 10,000 feet of shingles and clapboards, 23 spars, and vessel stores. It spent two and a half months in Nassau, selling off the cargo and buying, among other things, 405 bushels of salt, needed for preserving and shipping fish. After stopping in Bermuda, the vessel proceeded to Sunbury, some 70 miles up the Saint John River in New Brunswick, picked up another 45,000 board feet, sold this in Nassau, and sailed home to Sissiboo in ballast. Other ships carried short-haul cargoes, such as shad in season to Boston, or apples and onions later in the year. James's son, John, imported coffee and cotton in bulk.[10] A favourite to England was sugar.

As one would expect, 1790 also saw a rash of baptisms, though not all of infants. In January, there was the second of the many James Moodys, this one the son of Abraham Lynson, of New Jersey, a relation of Jane's first husband. In July, James's daughter Maria was baptized into the Anglican Church. Born in 1775, when Sussex County was in turmoil at the outbreak of the American Revolution, she had missed out on receiving this first sacrament. It was her christening that Jinny Boucher was referring to. It took place in the Moody house and was an occasion to give thanks for all the blessings the family had received after so many years of suffering and separation. On October 20, James's first grandson was baptized and named James Budd Moody.

The summer of 1790 saw other launchings. James had kept up his membership in the Order of Ancient Free and Accepted Masons ever since he had left New York. Then as now, members of the secret brotherhood helped each other and swore to look after surviving widows and children should a fellow Mason die. By the eighteenth century the society had ceased to have any architectural or engineering role but included in its membership the leading men of English and American society. Masons were bound to believe in God, to behave in accordance with the Ten Commandments, and never to reveal what went on in their meetings. In the English-speaking world, politics and sectarianism were forbidden topics at the meetings. These began with a general prayer. On special occasions, like St. John the Baptist Day — the summer solstice and for this reason by some believed to have come down from very ancient times as the society's special feast day — sermons were preached.

In colonial America, the membership included people with widely divergent views. Such men as George Washington, Benjamin Franklin, Thomas Jefferson, William Franklin, Cortlandt Skinner, Jonathan Boucher, Roger Viets, and James Moody, were all Masons, as was later Governor John Parr in Nova Scotia. By 1781, the Loyalist refugees in New York had regrouped their lodges under a new Provincial Grand Lodge. After the Revolution, Lodge 169, the leading one from New York and the one that James had belonged to, had carried its membership to Nova Scotia and New Brunswick. Although Halifax had had St. Andrew's Lodge since 1768, with the arrival of the Loyalists a Grand Lodge was instituted for all of Nova Scotia in September 1784. Five days later this body issued a warrant for the formation of Digby Lodge, Number 6 of the Grand Lodge, and this lodge in turn held its first meeting the following January 22, attracting Masons from the surrounding area, including Sissiboo. The Loyalist brethren all over the province were re-associating themselves "in private gatherings where recreation and improvement could be enjoyed."[11]

When James arrived in 1786, he at first attended the meetings in Digby. But in the summer of 1790 he pushed for the formation of a new lodge in Sissiboo. In October, at the request of the Halifax Grand Lodge, the Digby Masons solemnly gathered at James's house in Sissiboo to inaugurate Union Lodge, Number 20 in the province. They even voted a present to the new branch, which was to meet there on the second Wednesday of each calendar month. The secretary was James's old friend Reuben Hankinson, an ensign in his battalion, who now lived at the first bend of the Sissiboo River. Another member was John Grigg.

Yet another enterprise for James that summer of 1790 was the launching of the building fund for the new Anglican Church in Sissiboo. The SPG had allotted two hundred pounds Nova Scotia currency — £150 sterling — to the community from a fund for the construction of Anglican churches. This money, controlled by the bishop, who decided where and when the churches should be built, and often advised on the architecture and size of the building, was doled out at three stages in the construction. This ensured that the full sum was not received until the structure was complete. For Inglis, community support from the parish was essential before a clergyman would be sent, and this included building the church and providing a guaranteed income for the minister. In addition, the community must provide a house, but this last could be lent or rented for him, until a proper one was built. The church and the income could not wait.

On June 15, a deed was drawn up giving 1 and 3/8 acres of land "for the sole purpose of erecting a Church thereon." James, with Jane's consent since the gift involved her dower rights, donated this land "in consideration of my good will toward the Inhabitants of Sissiboo River, and to promote as far as in me lies the Establishment of the Church of England, in said place."[12] At a public meeting, a committee consisting of James, Stephen Jones, a Massachusetts Loyalist, and John Taylor, were appointed to supervise the building of the church. Fifteen members of the congregation stepped forward to help in "so laudable and Christian like [an] undertaking."[13] James led off with £15, to be followed by John Taylor giving £7, and Stephen Jones £5. Others contributed what they could, some cash, others labour, twelve days in the case of Reuben Hankinson, though the six that Benjamin McConnell pledged was more usual. Cerano Upham Jones, a cousin of Stephen,[14] offered as well five days of ox-work, rather like five days of tractor use today.

Construction moved at such a pace that in the next year at the end of August, James and Thomas Millidge rode up from Granville where Millidge now lived, to the bishop's house at Aylesford farther up the Annapolis Valley, to tell Inglis that the church at Sissiboo was "raised and partly covered in."[15] This meant that the frame and sides and roof but not the steeple were finished: the church would soon be eligible for the second instalment of money.

It was just as well that James had inspired these men to come together to work on the church. In September, there arrived the first serious rival to the Anglican establishment in Sissiboo, and that within a mile of James's own house. It came in the person of the 21-year old Joseph Dimock, an itinerant New Light Baptist preacher passing on his way from Granville to Yarmouth. Dimock, converted by the inspirational message of Henry Alline, was in turn to convert many of the old New England Dissenter settlers in Annapolis County, and also some of the Anglican Loyalists in Granville and Digby townships.

In Sissiboo, he was welcomed by the Sabean family, Congregationalist fisherfolk, who, after the expulsion of the Acadians, had first gone to Yarmouth with the Strickland family from Connecticut, and then had finally settled with them at the mouth of the Sissiboo, on the same side of the river as James. Dimock describes in his journal, his experience in Sissiboo and his near brush with some-one who could only be James:

I spent the Lord's day and preached at the house of a Mr. Sabine. Both Mr. S. and his wife appeared to be pious; two of their children, a son and daughter, were, I hope, savingly converted, and many others appeared deeply affected. In my prayer during the forenoon service, the Lord I believe put it into my heart to pray for the leading man of the settlement, (whom I then supposed to be at home a mile from our meeting,) that he might be blessed in his person and his family, and that his influence might be used for the promotion of piety and good order in society. I afterwards learned that he was present at the time, and that in going out of the house he was heard to say He makes a pretty good prayer, but I don't want to encourage any such renegades to come here. He then addressed several young fellows, who had assembled at the door to play some trick upon me of which he knew, on my going out, saying —"He is a simple, good kind of fellow enough, perhaps it is not worth while to take any notice of him"— when they dispersed with others who have [sic] come to see the sport, without offering me any injury.

The anticipated roughing up that Dimock refers to was quite common in urbanized communities — Anglican and Presbyterian — that were out of sympathy with itinerant evangelical preachers. James's more moderate attitude, after his characteristic original outburst, was part of his New Jersey ecumenical experience — and perhaps a little flattery. In colonial New Jersey, as in Nova Scotia, people of different denomi-nations would turn out to hear a notable itinerant preacher, some of course from curiosity, but many from spiritual need. A godless, churchless community was seen by nearly all elements of the popula-tion in the English colonies as leading to barbarism and anarchy. Because of SPG and government support in Nova Scotia during these early years, the Church of England could secure for the community an educated minister quickly, especially as there were already a number of ordained clergymen, refugees like themselves, ready to serve. After people were established, they could be more choosy. And indeed in a few years the families of some of these contributing Anglicans did also join the new Baptists.

James's son, John, and his family were now launched on their own in Sissiboo. John had built a house next door on the land his father had bought for him. This property, which James never did make over to John, was farmed in common with that of his father. We find him vestry clerk in the parish, keeping track of the pledges toward the construction of the new church, helping with the accounts at the shipyard, and supervising some of the construction. He was also doing business on his own in Digby.

Throughout 1792 the boom for the Moodys continued. Again it was a year of babies important to the family. In February, Elisha Budd's son was baptized James, Elizabeth Coulbourne stood as godmother to baby Mary Viets, Griffith Jenkins had a daughter Anne. But the most exciting event was in the Moody household at the end of July. On the 28th, John and Margaret Moody's second child was baptized Elizabeth Jane, elegantly named after her three grandmothers. The next day, Maria Moody, James's daughter, was married to James Taylor, a professionally qualified sea captain who had been navigating vessels across the Atlantic since the close of the Revolution.

Two more ships from the Moody shipyards were registered that year in Shelburne. The *Mary*, 210 tons, was a particularly beautiful vessel, square-sterned with galleries on her quarter bridges. Probably a first for a ship in Nova Scotia, she had a female figure carved at the head. One wonders whether the lady was a classical figure or did she wear an old-fashioned bonnet like the one Simeon Perkins complained of ten months later ordered for his brig *Minerva*?[16] Unlike all James's other ships, the *Mary* did not pass through Thomas Yorke's hands, but went directly to Glasgow to the firm of George Oswald, nephew of the Scottish merchant who had helped negotiate the peace in Paris with Benjamin Franklin. For some years afterwards, Taylor captained the *Mary* between Greenock and Maryland, importing American tobacco for the Oswald firm and, of course, stopping off to spend time with his family at Sissiboo.

The second ship that year was the *Governor Wentworth*, 325 tons, registered in July in Shelburne, and destined to Thomas Yorke. The name was a compliment to the new governor, John Wentworth, a Loyalist from one of the earliest families in New Hampshire. The unpopular John Parr had died unexpectedly the previous autumn.

The new governor was particularly well suited to the post. Before the Revolution, Wentworth had spent two years in London broadening his education. There, under the patronage of a distant cousin, Charles Watson Wentworth, Marquis of Rockingham, a leading Whig politician and twice prime minister, he was able to move in the highest of English social circles. At this time, he gained his first experience in dealing with the English power structure when he acted as New Hampshire's agent for the Stamp Act Congress in presenting a petition to have "that cursed" act repealed. At the age of 29 he succeeded his uncle as surveyor of the King's Woods and as governor of New Hampshire. Rather like Sir William Johnson of New York, he built himself a large mansion in the forests of his native province. Forced to flee to New York by the rebels, he attempted to raise a regiment, and when this failed he joined his elegant, rather worldly wife in England. After the war, he settled in Halifax and continued as surveyor general of the King's Woods for seven years, tramping through the forests of eastern British North America marking pines for the navy.[18]

When Parr suddenly died in 1792, Wentworth was in England. He was appointed lieutenant-governor, gossips said, through the influence of Prince William Henry who had sought solace in his lady's arms on the prince's several naval stopovers in Halifax. Actually, Wentworth had been promised the governorship in 1782 but a change of ministry had given it to Parr. In 1792, it was his friend John King, just appointed permanent undersecretary at the Home Department, then responsible for colonial affairs, who suggested him to his cabinet minister, Henry Dundas, the home secretary. Dundas was impressed with Wentworth's record as Loyalist governor of New Hampshire. William Franklin had also been mentioned for the post before Parr's death, though he was never seriously considered for the appointment. Nova Scotian Loyalists like Moody were overjoyed at the naming of a civilian, who was both an American and a Loyalist, a man who knew the province and who was experienced at governing a colony and dealing with the English bureaucracy. The new settlers had feared yet another English military governor; Wentworth understood the problems of a young colony and was anxious to make a success of this one.

In Halifax, the governor's wife had been appreciated for other qualities. A very pretty, well-educated woman, who came from an old Bostonian family, Frances Wentworth — her maiden name was also

Sir John Wentworth, Lieutenant Governor of Nova Scotia, by Robert Field, 1808. Courtesy Government House, Halifax

Wentworth — was his cousin, whom he had married precipitously — within a week of the death of her first husband, another first cousin.[17] Like her husband, she had spent several years in England with the English Wentworths with whom she continued to maintain close contact, and was used to moving among "people of the first fashion." During these early years in Halifax, her only son at school in England

Lady Wentworth as a young woman, after a portrait by John Copley, n.d.
Courtesy National Archives of Canada (C-27695)

and her husband often away for long periods surveying the king's trees, she must have been bored to tears. One of her admirers described her as "a most charming woman, but unhappily for her husband, rather more partial to our sex than her own. But he, poor man, cannot see her foibles, and they live very happy." Then, commenting on the salacious gossip of the town when Prince William Henry visited Halifax in 1787, he remarked to his diary, "I believe there was a mutual passion which subsisted between his Royal Highness and her," and while "the ladies of Halifax are a little scrupulous of their virtue and think it in danger if they were to visit Mrs. Wentworth, for my part I think her the best-bred woman in the province."[19] As time went on, Frances Wentworth settled down to respectability. As governor's wife she did show herself as "the best-bred woman in the province."

Despite Fanny Wentworth's doubtful reputation — in any case a former intimate relationship with a member of the royal family has always lent a certain titivating glamour — both the Wentworths, when they returned from England in May 1792, were joyously welcomed in their new position.

Immediately, they brought style to the little capital. Just before Christmas of their first year they gave a ball, gushingly written up in the Halifax *Gazette* as "altogether the most brilliant and sumptuous entertainment ever given in this country." The whole house was thrown open with each room splendidly lit and decorated. Upstairs a room was set aside for dancing cotillions, with its own special band. And to cool the thirsty dancers there were ices, and syrupy drinks flavoured with almond and orange flower, and delectable foods and wine for all. "Among other ornaments, which were altogether superb, there were exact representations of Messrs. Hartshorne and Tremaine's new *Flour mill*, and of the *Wind mill* on the Common. The model of the new *Light house* at *Shelburne* was incomparable, and the tract of the *new road* from *Pictou* was delineated in the most ingenious and surprizing manner, as was the representation of our *Fisheries*, that great source of wealth of this country." Emphasizing the high social tone of the assemblage, that "*this* was only for the friends of the government and Mrs. Wentworth," the writer ends his description on a note of ecstatic praise:

That ease, elegance and superiority of manners, which must ever gain Mrs. Wentworth the admiration of the whole community; and that hospitality, perfect good breeding and infinite liberality which so distinguished the character and conduct of our beloved and adored governor, never shone with more lustre than on this occasion, when every care of his and Mrs. Wentworth's mind seemed to be to give one universal satisfaction. Everything tended to promote one sympathizing joy, and never was there a night passed with more perfect harmony and luxurious festivity.[20]

Social pages in the newspapers have changed little down through the years.

This ball summed up for Wentworth what he would attempt to do during his years in office. Other balls, plays, and festivities would follow. But more important would be the governor's shrewd handling of the province's business. In his first autumn as governor, he had made an official visit to Pictou where the majority of the settlers were pre-Loyalist Scots, and had seen the beginnings of their new road that was so cleverly modelled at his ball, showing the inhabitants that he was not just a Loyalist governor but a governor for all the people in the province.

In the years to come he would see to the building of a handsome new Government House, and initiate the plans for a neoclassical building to house the Legislature and its offices, which remains one of the jewels of Canadian architecture. Thanks to numerous fires, he would have a guiding hand in many other improvements in the city of Halifax which still exist. In a very few years he would change the province's heavy debt to a surplus. His address at his opening of the House of Assembly in June 1792 had emphasized the need to improve agriculture, commerce, fisheries, and revenues. He had praised the already-tested loyalty of the population and promised the protection of their rights by the Crown.

The Wentworths' ball ended the year on a high note. Wentworth took office at the peak of the first boom in British North America after the Revolution. Though many Loyalists had left the province, those who remained felt the prosperity was the result of their own hard work and their initiatives to lay the economic and political base of the province. The appointment of Wentworth, one of their own, confirmed this belief. James's naming his ship the *Governor Wentworth* was his expression of the hope the colony now felt in its future.

Soon the wars with France and Britain's desire to institute close ties with the new United States of America would see that boom collapse in her still-loyal colonies to the north. During these years the Wentworths and the Moodys would become good friends.

NOTES

1. Rev. Roger Viets, Notitia Parochialis of Trinity Church, Digby, Nova Scotia. Beginning 12 July 1786, Marriages 1789.
2. Margaret Budd Moody, Moody Family Papers.
3. *Nova Scotia Magazine and Comprehensive Review of Literature, Politics, and News* 1 (Nov. 1789): 400, PANS.
4. See Brian Cuthbertson, *The First Bishop: A Biography of Charles Inglis* (Halifax: Waegwoltic Press, 1987).
5. *Letters and Papers on Agriculture: extracted from the correspondence of a Society instituted at Halifax, for Promoting Agriculture in the Province of Nova Scotia. To which is added A Selection of Papers on Various Branches of Husbandry, from some of the best publications on the subject in Europe and America* (Halifax: 1791), 14.
6. See W.W. Gardner, "The Impenitent Loyalist," *The Atlantic Advocate* 47, no. 11 (Aug. 1957): 65, and Wentworth to Moody, 17 Nov. 1803, Moody Papers.
7. Rebecca Thompson to Jane Moody, 11 Sept. 1789, Moody Papers.
8. Jinny Boucher to the Moodys, London, 3 Oct. 1789, Moody Papers.
9. *Halifax Gazette and City Advertiser* (12 June 1792): 2.
10. Bill of Lading to John Moody, Nassau, 1 Oct. 1793, for 8 Packets Cotton and 20 Bags Coffee, Moody Papers. The voyage of the *Jane* is in PRO, Home Office Naval Office Returns, 76, vol. 2. Microfilm in the possession of Dr. Charles Armour, Chief Archivist, Killam Library, Dalhousie University.
11. Isaiah W. Wilson, *A Geography and History of the County of Digby, Nova Scotia* (Halifax: Holloway Bros., 1900; Canadiana Reprint Series no. 39, Belleville, Ont.: Mika Publishing, 1985), 179.
12. Deed for conveyance of land from James Moody, 15 June 1790, Vestry Records, St. Peter's Church, Weymouth, made available through the kindness of Mrs. John McNeill and the vestry clerk. These records are now in the Anglican Diocese of Nova Scotia Archives, Halifax.
13. Vestry Records.
14. There were three Jones brothers, Stephen, Josiah, and Simeon, who came to Weymouth in 1783 with their families. They were accompanied by the wife of their uncle Elisha, and her adult son Cerano Upham Jones. Cerano Upham Jones was thus a first cousin-once-removed of the three brothers. They were among the first Loyalists to settle in the area. Wilson, *History of the County of Digby*, 54, 326-27.
15. Monday, August 29, 1791, Journal of Charles Inglis, Inglis Family Papers, NAC, MG23 C6, Ser.1, vol. 5.
16. Simeon Perkins until now has been credited with the first known figurehead on a vessel in Nova Scotia, carved for his brig, the *Minerva*,

also in 1792. Stanley T. Spicer, *Masters of Sail: The Era of Square-rigged Vessels in the Maritime Provinces* (Halifax, NS: Petheric Press, and the Nova Scotia Museum, 1924), 124. However *The Diary of Simeon Perkins, 1790-1796*, vol. 3, ed. Charles Bruce Ferguson (Toronto: Champlain Society, 1961), Tues. 18 Dec. 1792, 198-99, states that the figure for the *Minerva* arrived on that day, whereas the *Mary*, with its female figure as a head was already registered in Shelburne on 16 March 1792 (PRO, Home Office Naval Office Returns, 76, vol. 2). Perkins remarked that the figure head was "pretty well executed but we do not like the head dress. It is an old fashioned kind of Bonnet."

17. Philip Young, *Revolutionary Ladies: Being the surprising true histories of some forgotten American women — all beautiful, rich, and Loyalist — whose lives were shaped by scandal and turned upside down by the War for Independence* (New York: Alfred A. Knopf, 1977), 117. For a fuller treatment of the Wentworths, see Brian Cuthbertson, *The Loyalist Governor: Biography of Sir John Wentworth* (Halifax: Petheric Press, 1983).

18. The forests were a strategic resource in the form of pine masts for the British navy.

19. William Dyott, *Dyott's Diary, 1781-1845: A Selection from the Journal of William Dyott, Sometime General in the British Army and Aide-de-Camp to His Majesty King George III*, ed. Reginald W. Jeffery (London: Archibald Constable, 1907), vol. 1, 42-43.

20. Beamish Murdoch, *A History of Nova Scotia or Acadie* (Halifax: James Barnes, 1867), 103-04.

16

THE OFFICIAL YEARS:

THE HOUSE OF ASSEMBLY, 1793-99

IN JANUARY 1793, the new lieutenant-governor dissolved the House of Assembly and called an election in accordance with the new law that no Assembly should last for more than seven years. James presented himself as one of three contestants for the two seats allowed to Annapolis County. The other two candidates were Millidge and Robert Fitzrandolf, a well-to-do Quaker and Loyalist with public experience in New Jersey, now living in Wilmot Township. It was no surprise that Millidge won his seat with a high majority. He had made a name for himself representing Digby in the previous House, and had now moved to a farm in Granville Township, at the eastern end of the Annapolis Basin, across the river and a little upstream from the town of Annapolis Royal.

For James and Fitzrandolf the contest was closer. However, the fact that James had established himself locally as a benefactor to the community, not only in his own successful enterprises, but in the help he gave to other members of the settlement, made him a logical choice to represent the Digby-Weymouth end of the county. Fitzrandolf was later appointed one of the commissioners looking into land titles in Digby Township. Annapolis County stretched almost from Yarmouth to half-way up the Annapolis Valley. James's responsibility would be the western end of the county, particularly Clare Township, where the

Acadians lived, and the area west of Digby, mostly populated by Loyalists like himself.

For the township of Digby, Henry Rutherford, and for the township of Annapolis, Thomas Henry Barclay were returned. The four Loyalists, including James and Millidge, would work closely together while they were in the House of Assembly.

Before the coming of the Loyalists, the Nova Scotia House of Assembly had been dominated by the Halifax establishment. When the colonial structure for Nova Scotia was set up after the founding of the new capital at Halifax, certain reforms were instituted to strengthen British authority in the province. In appearance, the constitution seemed to be fashioned on the New England model, with an appointed governor and council and an elected assembly making up the legislature. But in Nova Scotia there was a significant difference: the salaries of the governor and most of the chief officials were paid by the British Parliament, rather than out of taxes voted by the assemblies for that specific purpose, as had been the practice in the New England colonies. This freedom from the Assembly's financial control gave the governor of Nova Scotia, and through him, the British government, an independence in running local affairs that was never the case in the old American colonies. The fact that a number of governors were also military men reinforced this control.

The colony was ruled by the governor and his council made up of senior office holders or men dependent on government patronage, appointed from London, with or without the governor's consent, and based in Halifax. There was little opposition from the House of Assembly. Although this body was elected, the members who made up its effective majority also lived in Halifax and came from the same circles as the Council. Outside Halifax the population was small, and travel to the capital was almost only by sea. Most of the country members often found it impossible to attend the whole of the assembly sessions because they could not leave their farms, or could not make the journey because of the weather, or were too poor to stay in Halifax for the full duration. Since their arrival, the New England planters had been struggling to make the Assembly more responsive to their concerns, but attempts at reform had so far been defeated by powerful interests in the capital.[1]

The coming of the Loyalists, another set of Americans, but a more politically sophisticated group, not only further opened up the province to more substantial development, but their election to seats in the House of Assembly changed the complexion of that previously rather docile institution.[2]

The new men regarded themselves, as Barclay so eloquently expressed in a speech in the House of Assembly, as representing "the aggregate of the community. They were the guardians of their rights and liberties ... they were there placed as a check upon the other two branches of the legislature, and ought religiously to watch that the liberties of the people should be inviolably preserved, and obstinately defended."[3] "He saw," he continued, "many members in the house wanting confidence of their own powers, and he wished to take them by the hand, and place them in the seat they ought, and had an undoubted right to fill.... They had an undoubted right to scan, not only the conduct of his Excellency's Privy Council, but even the governor's also.... The king could do no wrong, but it did not follow ... that his representatives were equally perfect."

Loyalists like Barclay and Millidge had just finished fighting for the "British constitution." Their loyalty could not be doubted. As Americans, they were accustomed to elected representation and community responsibility, and had not been cowed by a "royal" establishment. They were not about to settle for fewer Parliamentary rights than they had enjoyed in the old colonies, nor than their fellow Englishmen enjoyed in Great Britain. In this they were greatly helped by two recent acts of the British Parliament: the first in 1778 stated that no revenue taxes would be imposed on the colonies; and the second in 1785, required that an appropriation bill, that included every sum voted during the session, be passed at the end of each session of the House of Assembly.

The Loyalist members had more self confidence and more money than their predecessors, even if they did live in the country. As in pre-Revolutionary America, those elected to the House of Assembly were as important in their communities as the members of the Council. The struggle was now a constitutional one among equals. The Council, which held its meetings in secret, tried to invoke the governor's ancient royal prerogative to override the wishes of the House of Assembly. However, the sessions of the Nova Scotia House of Assembly were open to the public, allowing the constitutional issues aired in that body to gain in time more widespread discussion and support outside the House.

Elected to the Sixth Assembly in 1785, now enlarged to represent the sudden increase in settlement throughout the province, the newly arrived Loyalists took an active role in the House that was far out of proportion to their numbers. They worked with their pre-Loyalist colleagues to push through much needed administrative, economic, and social reforms. In constitutional matters they were even more assertive. These included setting a limit of seven years to each assembly, introducing the idea that a member should live or at least own property in the constituency he represented, and be paid for his time attending the sessions of the House of Assembly and, most important, reaffirming the Assembly's sole right to initiate and amend all money bills. The removal of the religious test as a requirement to vote gave Roman Catholics the franchise, and the attempt to impeach two supreme court judges accused of "improper and irregular administration in office,"[4] though unsuccessful, gained the colony a new chief justice. The British government ruled in the judges' favour, but acknowledged their possible incompetence — "the frailty of human nature"[5] — and sent out the highly qualified Andrew Strange. Barclay and Millidge had been particularly active[6] in the impeachment proceedings. James, always outspoken in his criticism of authority or anything else he disagreed with, now joined himself to these men in the Seventh Assembly.

Millidge we have met, but Barclay deserves a special mention. Born in 1753, he was the youngest of the three men. His father and his grandfather had both been ministers of the Church of England at St. Peter's in Albany and had worked with great dedication among the Mohawks in Upper New York. Indeed Barclay's father, the Reverend Henry Barclay, just after graduating from Yale had gone as a catechist among the Mohawks taking with him the young William Livingston, whose father was anxious for him to learn the language and the customs of these people under the tutelage of a reputable guardian.[7] By the time Henry Barclay died he had served 18 years as rector at Trinity Church in New York, and had been active in the founding of King's College, present-day Columbia University. The young Barclay graduated from that institution at the age of 19, and read for law in the prestigious office of John Jay, who later became ambassador to Spain for the American revolutionary government and, at the close of the war, one of the American peace negotiators.[8] In October 1775, Barclay married Susannah DeLancey, sister of Col. James DeLancey, now also living in Annapolis, and cousin of Col. Stephen DeLancey of James's battalion. Like Millidge, Barclay had served through most of the war as a major in a Loyalist regiment. He had seen action not only on the Hudson and in New Jersey but also in Virginia and the Carolinas. He had just missed the surrender at Yorktown.

At the close of the war, Barclay had not gone to England to further his claim, but at the request of Sir Guy Carleton and of Brooke Watson, then commissary general, he had come directly to Nova Scotia to help settle the provincial troops. He himself had established his family in Wilmot Township half way up the Annapolis Valley to Grand Pré, but was now back to his profession of law, in the town of Annapolis Royal. In 1796, he would be appointed as one of the commissioners to settle the boundary dispute between New Brunswick and the state of Maine. He had distinguished himself as a constitutional lawyer and orator[9] in the Sixth Assembly, where he had pushed for Assembly reforms and supported Millidge in the attempt to impeach the judges.

Rutherford, the fourth member from the county, was originally from Ireland where he had studied to be a Presbyterian minister. He was seven years younger than James. Just before the revolution, he had been living at White Plains, New York, like Margaret Budd Moody's family, and had carried on a successful mercantile business there with George Nash during the war. In October 1783, he and Nash arrived in Digby, with a boatload of fellow refugees in their own ship, the *Joseph*. They had immediately set up their business in Digby, trading again with many of their previous customers.[10] Rutherford was particularly interested in the lucrative curing and exporting of herring — Digby's small smoked herring fillets are still a local specialty — and, like James, in anything to do with the sea.

The new Assembly met in Halifax on Wednesday March 20, 1793, shortly after France declared war against England. Barclay, elected as speaker, ended his traditional address to Governor Wentworth in Council with the customary caution: "I am directed by the *House of Assembly*, to request of your Excellency, as the Privileges of this House, that the members thereof during their Sessions, may be freed from all Molestation, that they may have Freedom of Speech in their Debates, that they may have the Power of punishing their own Members, and have free and favourable Access to your Excellency as His Majesty's immediate Representative, on all Occasions."[11] The new governor was being notified that the Assembly knew its rights.

The Seventh Assembly continued the work of the previous one. Legal institutions and the social infrastructure of the province were woefully inadequate to meet the needs of the colony, now quickly expanding with the sudden influx of money and skills brought by the Loyalists. The judicial reforms begun in the earlier assembly were continued with

The old governor's house and Mather's meeting house, Halifax, by Richard Short, 1764. Both would have been familiar to James during his Assembly days. The Assembly met in the courthouse, the one-storey house next door to the governor's house. St. Paul's Church can be seen behind this complex. The sign of the Golden Ball Inn can be seen facing the courthouse corner. The Wolf Inn was across the street from the governor's house. Courtesy National Archives of Canada (41185)

the cooperation of the newly appointed Chief Justice Andrew Strange. Stricter regulating of judges and better access to courts in the new districts were promoted. In close partnership with the governor, the legislature managed to change the province's heavy debt to a healthy surplus. Laws concerning the organization of local government in such matters as tax assessment, schools, and fire protection were enacted. Laws regulating the fishing and lumber industry, so that export standards were adhered to; environmental laws protecting partridge and blue ducks on the one hand, and sadly, ridding the country, through bounties, of wolves and lynx on the other; laws allowing the legality of civil marriages and the right of married women to dispose of property; laws to build more roads and bridges; and laws to limit smuggling and to collect unpaid import duties, were only some of the many pieces of legislation that this body of 39 men worked on during five or more weeks of each year for the next seven years. They were determined to open up the colony but also to lay a sound institutional foundation to what they developed.

They were determined that the mistakes made in the old colonies would not be made in this one. Their previous political experience made them all the more alert to the consequences, both political and personal, of careless procedures. When the treasurer died suddenly and his money chest and papers were seized by the solicitor general, Richard John Uniacke, and several of his supporters, a joint committee of the House of Assembly and the Council was appointed to go through his accounts. The House of Assembly determined that henceforth the provincial treasurer must lay the accounts before the House on the first day of every session. Stephen Skinner, former treasurer for the Province of New Jersey when robbers had stolen the provincial money chest from his house, and now sitting in the House as member for Shelburne, must have applauded these orderly measures.[12] When the Council sent an amended money bill, the House sent it back, reminding the Council of its sole right to initiate and amend money bills.

The House was fortunate in having Barclay as speaker, through whom it could work in harmony with an experienced civilian governor.[13] During his six years as Speaker, there were only two attempts on the part of the Council to usurp the lower House's prerogative of money bills. Perhaps the greatest achievement of this harmony was putting fiscal reforms in place[14] and adding duties which not only enabled the crippling provincial debt to be paid off but by 1797 resulted in a surplus which quickly grew to huge proportions.[15]

James had no difficulty integrating himself into the House of Assembly. Wentworth wrote to England in 1793 that James was "a very popular member of the Assembly."[16] Through his shipbuilding and trading interests he was well acquainted with Stephen Skinner, who had arranged cargoes to the West Indies for him. He worked closely with Millidge and Rutherford. Indeed he and Rutherford stayed in the same boarding house, Mrs. Black's, as did Simeon Perkins, during the sessions.[17] He became friends with a reforming pre-Loyalist, William Cottnam Tonge from Hants County, whose wife's sister, Mary Ann Bonnell, was married to Margaret Budd Moody's brother.

One of James's assignments at the beginning of his second session was to entertain Prince Edward, later Duke of Kent, the fourth son of George III, and destined to be the father of Queen Victoria. Edward came to Nova Scotia in May 1794. He was 26, fresh from two months of successful campaigning in the French West Indies, where he had shown outstanding bravery in the conquest of Martinique and Guadeloupe. Before that he had spent nearly three years in Quebec City as colonel of the Royal Fusiliers, living not the life of a dissolute royal prince as his brother, Prince William Henry, had done during his brief stays in the colonies, but with "an elegant lovely" companion he had brought with him, to relieve "the tedium and those problems of a bachelor hard to endure at his age," as a French visitor to Quebec wrote.

She is French; Prince Edward made her acquaintance at Marseille. She lived formerly in Paris, where according to what I have been told, she was a kept woman: though she has a well-bred manner, her earlier state is a little apparent: they say a gentleman lent her his name on taking her up. She lives conjugally with the prince, under the same roof, doing the honours of his home and his table at those times when he invites only men. Although the proper ladies of Quebec do not accept her socially, it seems to me that this arrangement is in no way scandalous: this kind of union of convenience is among a prince's privileges, especially in England where the heir presumptive to the Crown lives openly with a well-born lady, Mrs. Fitzherbert. For Prince Edward it is an impropriety less licentious than those temporary liaisons a young man of his age tends to form, with all the stir and publicity attached to his rank, especially in such a small community as Quebec.[18]

Prince Edward (Duke of Kent), by James Gillray, ca. 1799. The prince is wearing the star voted to him by the Nova Scotia Assembly in 1798. Courtesy John Ross Robertson Collection, Metropolitan Toronto Reference Library (T 16063)

Seven years his senior, Julie de Saint Laurent — she called herself Alphonsine Julie Thérèse Bernadine de Mongenêt, Baronne de Fortisson, though her real name was Thérèse Bernadine Mongenêt — charmed everyone who knew her by her intelligence, modesty, and devotion to Prince Edward. When Wentworth first met her in Halifax in 1794, before Prince Edward's arrival, he wrote:

Julie de Saint Laurent or Madame Alphonsine Julie Thérèse Bernadine de Mongenêt, Baronne de Fortisson, as she styled herself. Courtesy Archives nationales du Québec (P600-6/GH-1072-140)

Madame de St. Laurent (with an hundred names and titles) has been with
us several weeks, waiting a passage to England.... She is an elegant, well
bred, pleasing sensible woman — far beyond most. During her residence
here, her deportment has been judicious and most perfectly correct indeed.
I find she has great influence over him, and that he is extremely attached
to her. It is happy, that she is so excellent a character. By her prudence &
cleverness, she has restored his deranged finances, and I believe impressed
his mind with the best sentiments. She seems faithfully attached to him. I
never yet saw a woman of such intrepid fortitude yet possessing the finest
temper and refined manners.[19]

The prince arrived in Halifax the day after Madame de Saint
Laurent's departure for England. He was waiting for permission from
his father to return to England or to take another assignment, and he
too charmed everyone he met. Very fair in hair and complexion with
deep blue eyes, the prince was, like James, a very tall man.[20] He was also
a gracious, happy person who liked to help people. Perhaps as a result
of his early German military training, he was sometimes too punctilious
in the discipline of his regiment, and severe in punishing his men — a
characteristic that brought him mutinies in every post he held. But he
loved beautiful things around him, neatness, and order, and these
included his regiment. He was also an intellectually curious man, always
looking for a better way to organize things, and always trying out the
latest gadgets and inventions. He loved music and the theatre and travelled with a large library and his own regimental band. With the
Wentworths he brought a new sophistication to Halifax.

Prince Edward landed only a few weeks before the second session
of the Seventh House of Assembly was gathering for its five weeks of
sittings. The governor went on board his frigate to meet him and all
Halifax turned out to welcome him ashore. There were days of cele-
brations, with royal salutes, an evening illumination of the town where
every inhabitant put a candle in the window, a levee at government
house where he was formally addressed by groups of distinguished
citizens. In a grand ceremony on Citadel Hill he reviewed the troops
of the garrison. When the Assembly met on June 6, there were several
more days of eulogies.

The ever-curious prince decided to explore the province and visit
New Brunswick. The *Zebra*, a sloop-at-war that had accompanied him
from the West Indies, was sent off ahead around the province to meet
him at Digby. He himself set off by land on June 14, perhaps accom-

panied by James.[21] The prince, who went in for fast travel delighting in doing nine miles an hour on his horse, reached the vicinity of Annapolis Royal the next evening, where he presumably stayed at the house of Colonel James DeLancey at Round Hill. The colonel gave a reception for him, where legend has the lonely prince kissing a pretty serving maid behind a door.[22] He must also have inspected the fortifications and the militia at Annapolis Royal.

The *Zebra* had not yet arrived, and it was probably during the next two and a half days of waiting for it that James took formal charge of the prince.[23] An execrable road like the one from Digby to Sissiboo was always a happy challenge to Edward, who enjoyed what another officer called "violent" journeying.[24] James would have shown him the new settlement, and perhaps taken him across Saint Mary's Bay to Sandy Cove to see the cod and haddock being unloaded and dried. He would certainly have taken his royal visitor down the "French Shore" to Sainte-Marie, today's Church Point, to meet the Acadian community. Prince Edward spoke excellent French. Another bonus on the tour was the warm family atmosphere that Jane Moody created and that the prince had been missing since he and Julie left Quebec at the beginning of the year. But above all, Edward must have enjoyed James himself, with his forthright way of speaking, his self-deprecating irony, and his wonderful stories of derring-do and escape during the Revolution. Certain it is that a friendship was born and lasted well beyond James's death. When the prince returned to England he continued to correspond with James.

On June 18, James would have escorted Prince Edward back to Digby, where the *Zebra* was now waiting for him. Here the townspeople gave their royal visitor a banquet and addressed him with more eulogies. Perhaps in the evening the citizens put lighted candles in their windows as did the people in Saint John and Fredericton in the next few days. In any case, Prince Edward boarded the *Zebra* that night, a royal salute was fired from the ship, and the sloop raised anchor at four in the morning to set sail to cross the Bay of Fundy. James hurried back to Halifax to resume his duties in the Assembly. We find him on Monday, June 23, appointed to a committee to request the bishop to direct divine service to be performed at St. Paul's Church on the following Wednesday.

As today, James, as member for his county, was expected to see to the interests of his constituents. In 1795, he wrote a letter for Captain Pierre Doucet, with whom he had a long business association, asking that the crew of his schooner be protected from impressment — the detested British custom of seizing men off the streets for service in the British navy — when she docked in Halifax.[25]

In 1796, Reverend Roger Viets was writing James and Rutherford about events in their part of Annapolis County, including the baptism in February of James's two grandchildren, James Moody Taylor and John Wentworth Moody. He praised Sissiboo's schoolmaster and urged James to get the bishop to recommend the man to the SPG for a schoolmaster's salary as "you can do more with half an hour's discourse than we can all do with half a year's writing."[26] Like others, he also urged that the flour shortage be alleviated by allowing the province to import wheat from Canada, a course up till then forbidden by the Trade and Navigation Acts. James did speak to the bishop about the schoolmaster's salary, and importation of wheat from Canada was subsequently allowed. Viets reflected the feelings of the Loyalist community when he wrote his disgust at the conduct of the war with France, now in its third year:

The News you have at Halifax much sooner than We at Digby. The last News seemed to be continuously against us. The infernal French Rebels seem by their own story at least to be conquering in Germany as fast as ever — The Reinforcements for the West Indies not yet sailed nor so much expected to sail as they were 6 Months ago — Great Numbers of our Shipping destroyed by Hurricanes and other Accidents — The French taking our Merchantmen without the least Interruption — Whilst We with a Sea-Force sufficient to keep the whole World in Awe keep our Ships crowded up in Harbours to keep each other warm, or to make a fine Appearance at Anchor — The British Lion betrayed by his Allies — insulted by his Enemies — and vilified by his own Subjects — A Seditious Mob suffered with Impunity to attempt the sacred Life of the best of Kings — Speeches permitted in both Houses of Parliament to recommend French Rebellion and slander British loyalty and the Speakers of one House unguillotined, of the other House unhanged — Britain cajoled and fooled by a Treaty which America has not the least Intention to execute, longer than 'till they have gotten their Western Posts, the Posts which were the only Indemnification We had for their Nonobservance of their Treaty of Peace with us 13 Years ago. These Things are all against us — However we have some good News. The Capture of the Cape of Goodhope is a valuable Acquisition if it can be kept.[27]

James was a good representative of his county. Though not a lawyer, he was interested in legal matters. At the beginning of his first session, he was nominated with Millidge and other members to be a grand Committee of Justice. He supported increased authority for justices of the peace. By 1799, much of the basic legislation had been passed and James was appointed to a select committee to work on revising old laws that now needed bringing up to date. He also served on a committee to look into relief for the Mi'Kmaq, many of whom lived in Annapolis County. Already recognized as "having their natural Means of Subsistence, in this Their native Country ... almost destroyed by progressive Occupancy, Culture and Improvement," most of them were ill-housed and half starving. As today, temporary help was given but no satisfactory long-term solution was found.[28]

Aware of the difference in interests between the full-scale farming in the eastern half of the county and the fishing and lumbering community in his part, he was early pushing for a division of Annapolis into two separate counties. In local affairs, sheep raising, the fisheries, the lumber exports, and the roads in Annapolis County were of prime concern to him. Lighthouses around the province were another interest. He worked with Tonge and, of course, Millidge and Rutherford, although unsuccessfully, to establish a local tax base for schools, and he also tried hard to put teeth into legislation against the wartime illicit trading with American ships around the south and west coasts that was undermining local industries and business.

The war with France was having a disastrous effect on the economy of coastal communities like Weymouth, while enriching the city of Halifax, and also the provincial treasury.[29] Shipping and, consequently, the export of local produce was severely curtailed. At the same time, the fishermen abandoned their lines for lucrative privateering, which in turn brought a flood of saleable looted foreign goods to Halifax markets. Meanwhile, the Americans, as neutrals, took over Nova Scotia's markets in the West Indies and off-loaded their goods in the coves of the Bay of Fundy and Saint Mary's Bay. As the situation worsened, members from the country, whether Loyalist or pre-Loyalist, worked together to protect their own and their constituents' concerns. This made for an alliance between a number of country members against the rest of the House, some from Halifax and some from the regions close to Halifax. It was an alliance that pitted the interests of the town of Halifax against those of the rest of the province, often becoming an alliance between a majority of the House of Assembly against the Council and the governor. It was a confrontation that would harden in the next Assembly. The surplus of provincial revenue was to be the catalyst for the constitutional quarrel that was about to erupt.

In spite of the good work of the Seventh Assembly, the last session ended on an ugly note, foretelling future legislative battles. At the beginning of the session Barclay resigned as Speaker, and was replaced by Richard John Uniacke. Barclay had been named British consul general for the eastern United States and would take up residence again in his native city of New York. The loss of his smooth handling of the House of Assembly probably only precipitated a crisis that was inevitable.

The first flare-up began half way through the last session in 1799, with a routine money bill to cover the year's voted expenses. It included money for items that had already been approved by both houses, particularly expenditures for new roads throughout the province. The Council returned the bill with amendments, the same old constitutional no-no that the House had thought settled in earlier sessions. The House passed yet another resolution stating its inherent and sole right to originate and amend all money bills, and ordering that the amended bill "be thrown under the table." It then returned the original bill and the angry resolution to the Council. The usual conferences between representatives of the House and the Council were held but without the usual satisfactory accommodation being reached. Then the Council sprang a bombshell on the House. It said: "His Majesty's Council although authorized by the Royal Instructions to frame Money Bills, equally with the House of Assembly, yet they are not disposed to insist on the Exercise of such Right, but will as they usually have done agree or disagree generally on such Bills, for imposing Taxes, as may be sent up from the House, Provided, Clauses are not therein inserted, which relate to foreign Subjects, or Matters or Regulations, not necessarily connected with the Rate or Duty intended to be imposed or levied." [30]

The Assembly was furious. It voted a three-page resolution expressing its outrage at the Council's attempt to abrogate to itself the constitutional prerogatives of the Lower House. It added, referring to the war with revolutionary France, that to squabble over privileges was unbecoming "at a time when all the Privileges of civilized Society are in the utmost Danger" and it is the "Duty of all British Subjects to rally round the King's Throne, and with their Lives and Fortunes to maintain and defend the British Constitution under which alone the Liberties of

British Subjects can be secure."[31] It insisted that should the House of Assembly be "base enough to surrender the Privileges transmitted them from their ancestors, the Exercise of such a Right could only embarrass his Majesty's Council, and bring his Majesty's Government into Disgrace and Dispute amongst his Subjects." It went on to "unanimously avow that it is the sole inherent and unalienable Right of the Representatives of the People to frame and originate all Money Bills, that it is by the Law and Constitution of Great-Britain, so established from Time immemorial, that such Right is one of the main Pillars of the British Constitution, and is a Right which British Subjects will never surrender, but with their Lives." The message, written on the 4th of July, could not have been clearer. The Council backed down, but only for the moment.

Buried in the constitutional issue was the tug of war between the elected Assembly and the appointed Council as to who would decide on how the provincial money was to be spent. Was it to be for roads and other services throughout the province, or on public buildings in Halifax itself? As the session progressed, the issue became more divisive, not only between the House and the Council, and by extension the governor, but also between members of the House themselves. Having approved £10,500 as a ceiling for public buildings, and voted that the site, materials, and money should go to the governor's residence (as a measure to curb Wentworth's never-ending bills for repairs to the old Government House), the House, at the end of the session, voted to spend another £10,000 for roads and bridges. This the Council cut by almost half.

More radical than Millidge, who initiated social, economic, and judicial reforms, but who tended to support the Council on many constitutional issues, James throughout the Seventh Assembly voted with Tonge who was emerging as a leader against the Council. He supported the resolution limiting the commission to be paid to the commissioners for erecting public buildings to 5 percent of the money disbursed, a measure that did not pass the House but was adopted for the commissioners of roads. When a last attempt to win over Council on road allocations was made, James was one of the managers for the House in the conference with the Council.

The question of how the new revenue surplus should be spent and who would benefit from it would not be settled so simply. It was a twofold struggle, for constitutional power, and for control over the province's money. New alignments had been forming in the House of Assembly. The tensions that had been developing between Assembly, Council, and governor, and that suddenly came to a crisis in the dying days of the Seventh Assembly, would not be resolved in a week. The pause for the elections would consolidate members' positions. By 1800, when the Eighth Assembly met, these would be well established.

NOTES

1. The history of the New England planters in Nova Scotia is as complex and rich as that of the Loyalists. For a fascinating account of this period see John Bartlet Brebner's *The Neutral Yankees of Nova Scotia: A Marginal Colony during the Revolutionary Years* (New York: Columbia University Press, 1937; repr. New York: Russell & Russell, 1970). For more recent work on the period, see Margaret Conrad, ed., *They Planted Well: New England Planters in Maritime Canada* (Fredericton: Acadiensis Press, 1988), and Margaret Conrad, ed., *Making Adjustments: Change and Continuity in Planter Nova Scotia* (Fredericton: Acadiensis Press, 1991).

2. Margaret Ells, "The Development of Nova Scotia, 1782-1812," draft PhD thesis, University of London, 1949, 95, PANS, MG1. This work is an exhaustive and well written examination of the period, with chapters on the sessions of the Legislature, trade, industries, and so on.

3. These and the following remarks by Barclay are quoted in Beamish Murdoch, *A History of Nova Scotia or Acadie* (Halifax: James Barnes, 1867), vol. 3, 67-70.

4. For a full treatment of the affair of the judges, see Neil MacKinnon, *This Unfriendly Soil: The Loyalist Experience in Nova Scotia, 1783-1791* (Montreal and Kingston: McGill-Queen's University Press, 1986), 127-33. The problem was first brought to public notice by a report of Col. James DeLancey in 1786.

5. *Dictionary of Canadian Biography*, vol. 5, 109, s.v. Brenton, James.

6. Richard John Uniacke made a name for himself in the earlier sessions of the Sixth Assembly and, by 1789, he had been elected to replace Attorney General Blowers as speaker of the House when Blowers was appointed to the Council.

7. Milton Klein, "The American Whig: William Livingston of New York," PhD thesis, Columbia University, 1954, 87.

8. John Jay had a highly distinguished career in the United States government, during the Revolution and later. He was, among other things, secretary of foreign affairs in the U.S. government, its first chief justice, and the negotiator of the Jay Treaty.

9. Murdoch, *History of Nova Scotia*, vol. 3, 92. See *The Nova Scotia Magazine*, 1789, 1790, for a report of the debates in the House of Assembly for those years.

10. Isaiah W. Wilson, *A Geography and History of the County of Digby, Nova Scotia* (Halifax: Holloway Bros., 1900; Canadiana Reprint Series no. 39, Belleville, Ont.: Mika Publishing, 1985), 50, 53.

11. *Journals and Proceedings of the House of Assembly of Nova Scotia*, 1793, 3.
12. See William A. Whitehead, "The Robbery of the Treasury of East Jersey in 1768, and Contemporary Events," *Proceedings of the New Jersey Historical Society*, vol. 5, 49-65, for a full account of the robbery, and its consequences, to both Skinner and Governor Franklin.
13. Ells, "Development of Nova Scotia," 40.
14. *Dictionary of Canadian Biography*, vol. 6, s.v. Barclay, Thomas Henry, 35.
15. Ells, "Development of Nova Scotia," 161.
16. Wentworth to John King, 10 Oct. 1793, PRO, CO 217/36, no. 184.
17. *The Diary of Simeon Perkins, 1790-1796*, ed. Charles Bruce Fergusson, vol. 3 (Toronto: Champlain Society, 1961), 23 March, 1793, 218.
18. Diary of Bénigne Charles Fevret de Saint-Mesmin, a French visitor to Quebec in 1793, quoted from Mollie Gillen, *The Prince and His Lady: The Love Story of the Duke of Kent and Madame de St. Laurent* (Toronto: Sidgwick and Jackson, 1970; Halifax: Goodread Biographies, Formac Publishing, 1985), 76. I am most grateful to this author for her charming, well-researched book and, above all, the accuracy of her footnotes, which led me to the fascinating correspondence during these years between Governor Wentworth and John King, undersecretary of state in the Home Department, in the Public Record Office, CO 217, vols. 36 and 37.
19. Wentworth to John King, 8 May 1794, PRO, CO 217/36, no. 253.
20. Gillen, *The Prince and His Lady*, 75, 259, and McKenzie Porter, *Overture to Victoria* (Toronto: Longmans Green, 1961), 14. Porter is describing a portrait. Gillen's research is more thorough.
21. See "Journal of the Proceedings of His Majesty's Sloop Zebra, 24 April-14 Dec. 1794," kept by George Vaugham, PRO, and Nova Scotia House of Assembly Papers, vol. 4, PANS, RG 5. That Prince Edward visited James on this journey is attested to by Margaret Budd Moody, Moody Papers.
22. Legend also has the reception being held at the house of Thomas Barclay in Annapolis Royal, but as Barclay was Speaker of the House of Assembly which was then sitting in Halifax, this seems highly unlikely. The prince certainly dined and may well have stayed at the Barclay house on other visits to Annapolis Royal. Certainly he would have been entertained by the Speaker in Halifax. Legend also insists that the occupant of the Barclay house at this time was Col. James DeLancey's cousin Col. Stephen DeLancey, who by this time was living in the West Indies as chief justice of the Bahamas. The other Stephen DeLancey, brother of James, who moved to Annapolis County around 1791, did not live in Annapolis Royal. Col. James DeLancey is his most likely host on this occasion.

23. James's attendance during the session of the Assembly this year was eight days short, which would be the time he required to make this journey with the prince, receive him in Weymouth, and return to Halifax for his next order of business in the House of Assembly.

24. Daniel Lyman to Edward Winslow, Windsor, 6 Nov. 1797, in Rev. W.O. Raymond, ed., *The Winslow Papers, A.D. 1776-1826* (Saint John, NB: The Sun Printing Co., 1901), 426.

25. *The Halifax Herald*, Wed., 10 Nov. 1897, 5.

26. Roger Viets to Henry Rutherford and James Moody, Digby, 16 March 1796, Viets Family Private Papers, Ottawa.

27. *Ibid.*

28. On 4 July 1798, Wentworth sent the following message to the House of Assembly:

> It is a Duty incumbent on me to recommend to your Consideration, the indigent and distressed Situation of the Indians inhabiting this Province. Their natural Means of Subsistence, in this Their native Country, are almost destroyed by progressive Occupancy, Culture and Improvement. Their extreme Poverty, is too well known, to need Description, and I trust you will readily provide proper Relief to preserve them from perishing, the ensuing Winter, which otherwise is greatly to be apprehended.

> A committee of five members, of whom James was one, was appointed by the House to consider this message, and after deliberation reported that the principal cause of the Native People's distress "proceeds from their unwillingness to labour." Those who are "uncivilized" already have enough grounds for hunting and fishing, and those who are "civilized" are able to cultivate land for their subsistence. "Granting Money for their Relief, would be an Encouragement to that indolence, and supiness, they are too much addicted to, and Burthen the Province, with a heavy Expense, without answering any Salutary purpose." But "some Provision ought to be made," so the committee recommend, "A Tract of good land, well watered in such part of the Province, as to his Excellency shall appear best calculated for their Support ... granted in Trust to such Persons, as his Excellency may think fit."

> The governor replied that he had already caused lands to be laid out for the benefit of the Native People, but liked the idea of the trustees and would see to that aspect. However the Native People needed more immediate help else their condition "would not answer the salutary Views of the House." Immediate temporary relief was granted. *Journals and Proceedings of the House of Assembly of the Province of Nova Scotia*, 1798, 303-08.

29. Ells, "Development of Nova Scotia," 117.

30. *House of Assembly of Nova Scotia*, 1799, 344.

31. *Ibid.*, 345.

17

A SECOND MILITARY CAREER, 1793-99

THE MOST URGENT CONCERN for all of Nova Scotia during these years when James was a member of the House of Assembly was the war with France. For James, it changed the pattern of his life. It put an end to his shipbuilding and ruined him financially but it brought him once more into the military defence of his country against a republican threat.

Wentworth was in England in 1792 when he was appointed lieutenant-governor of Nova Scotia and already the signs of war were apparent. He certainly discussed the military situation there. In his first September as governor he wrote from Halifax to his old friend, John King, then permanent undersecretary for the Home Department, about the possibility of his raising a provincial regiment. When war was declared on February 3, 1793, authorization for the new regiment was given five days later. The terms were rather minimal. The regiment was to be under the control of the British commander in chief. Wentworth was to be its colonel, but to receive no pay. The officers were to be chosen from officers already on half-pay so that when the regiment was disbanded no extra pensions would be paid. Service was to be only within the province. The goal was to raise six hundred men and officers, these to be divided into six companies. Within days of the official notice, Wentworth had appointed an adjutant and begun to recruit men. He had 350 enlisted by the end of May.

The half-pay officers were mainly recruited from among Loyalists who had served in provincial corps during the American Revolutionary

War. These men felt genuinely concerned that the Americans might join forces with the republican French to seize the rest of British North America. In 1793, Halifax seemed the first target.

Wentworth was at pains to have his regimental choices approved. He wrote long letters on the subject to the undersecretary that he might lobby for him with Henry Dundas, the government minister who would confirm the appointments. James was to be the senior captain. Wentworth explained that James "did duty as a Captain in one of the provincial Corps, but on the reduction at peace, his promotion to a Capt. was casually omitted, whereupon Govt. added a pension to make it up equal to a Captain's halfpay." He then enclosed the narrative of James's "perilous Services, last war ... which will amuse you to read and convince you how exceedingly useful such an Officer must be to the King's Service."[1] On his own authority Wentworth back-dated James's commission to 1783. There was no hesitation about James in London, though some of Wentworth's other choices for officers were at first refused.

Finding a suitable commanding officer was difficult. First it was to be Thomas Barclay but he quickly persuaded the governor that his services would be better employed in raising, at his own expense, a special corps of defence militia for the province.[2] Wentworth's second choice was Samuel Vetch Bayard, a Loyalist from New York where his father had had a prosperous export business. Bayard had been a major in the Orange County Rangers and was now settled in Wilmot Township. In the end, the command was given to the much-liked Francis Kearney, a Loyalist officer descended from a proprietary family in Perth-Amboy, New Jersey, who was plucked out of Ireland where he had settled after the peace. As consolation, Bayard was made an honourary lieutenant-colonel, without pay.

Throughout the summer there was a military alert across the province. Everyone feared an imminent invasion. A Nova Scotia expedition conquered St. Pierre and Miquelon and brought back a large number of prisoners. French and Nova Scotian privateers did a brisk business, while the Americans maintained a strict neutrality that befriended whichever side suited their immediate interest. There were complaints about American fishing boats creating havoc in the Bay of Fundy and Saint Mary's Bay, over-fishing and polluting the water by throwing their fish offal overboard, illegally trading on the side, and showing contempt for the local authorities. They had a freer hand than usual because so many of the Nova Scotia fishermen were at sea plundering the enemy. In April 1794, cannon were brought to Digby for the defence of the settlements on the Annapolis Basin, four to the fort and others around the basin. Several still exist in their original positions, now hidden in the tangled underbrush. Block houses were set up at either side of the entrance to Digby Gut.

In addition, local companies of militia were ready to be called out at a moment's notice. Halifax had three such companies, Wentworth explained, where "the gravest wealthy citizens appear in the Ranks, giving, and maintaining good example, with the firmness, and obedience, of roman citizens assembled pro aris, & focis"[3] — for hearth and home. Annapolis County also had three: two English-speaking ones headed by Barclay and Millidge, and one mixed English and French for Clare, commanded by James's neighbour, John Taylor. Barclay put his group to repairing the old fortification at Annapolis so as to make "a small, snug, compleat redoubt, on the most commanding situation."[4]

To protect the deserted coast and isolated settlements, Barclay's corps of fencibles, the Nova Scotia Legion, specially equipped for rapid deployment throughout the province, was ready for quick muster in the case of a sudden emergency. It included a company each of infantry, cavalry, and artillery, to a total of one thousand volunteers, to be detached from the three Annapolis County militia formations when needed. Wentworth proudly wrote in July 1793, that they were:

distributed in different towns, and provided with Horses to carry them with celerity to any part of the Province. They are commanded by half pay officers who distinguished themselves last war, and most of the privates have been in Service. They are selected with great care and are at no expense to Govt. unless when called into actual Service upon an invasion, when they are to be paid & subsisted according to the Law. Each Man to bring ten days provision to Head Quarters, to prevent delay or other casualty, for which he is to be paid. This legion must have their field pieces and Arms & ammunition from the King's ordnance Stores. Every thing else they provide at their own expense; Their loyalty and usefulness may be as safely relied upon as any Corps in the Kings Service.[5]

In a departure from their traditional stance of refusing to bear arms, the Acadians had recruited four hundred men and agreed that they be commanded by English-speaking half-pay officers. However, a third of their officers were Acadian. James's son, John, was a lieutenant and the adjutant of their regiment. In addition, to Wentworth's emotional satisfaction, James's Acadian constituents, for the first time since their expulsion in 1755, actively opted to swear allegiance to the British Crown as part of their militia service, instead of merely subscribing to an oath of neutrality.[6] They offered the governor any security he pleased as a guarantee of their fidelity.

The governor had been wooing the Acadians. He wrote John King in the same July letter:

The Acadians of whom you may have read in the Abbé Reynal's work,[7] have had my careful attention. I have settled them on their lands, remitting the heavy fees formerly demanded, assured them, that it was my duty to the King, to afford them the same protection and justice, as to any other of His subjects, and that I sincerely compassionate all their sufferings, would relieve their troubles, when made known to me, and that they should at all times have personal access to me to meet their patriarchal habits, I have appointed Magistrates from those, they confided in, and referred their own private affairs to. No other Magistrates to interfere, where the case was entirely Acadian, where Acadian & English, then to be decided by one of each description. These and other Attentions have perfectly healed their old wounds. They are now satisfied, happy, and say that for the first time since their dispersion, they are again established.

Movingly he continues, "I confess I have real pleasure in being His Majesty's humble instrument, in administering his gracious Government to dry up the tears of these people, who have long excited the compassion of Europe, and America."[8]

In early October, the French fleet, hovering off New York since August with the tacit support of the Americans, was now rumoured to be preparing an attack on Halifax, a threat that persisted for most of the decade. The French were reported to have gathered an invasion force made up of a "motley crew — miserably dressed — their uniforms like Joseph's coat of many colours, and in every particular resembling the late Rebel Army."[9] To Loyalists, these republican associations were frightening. They saw themselves forced back into the republican America they had left, facing yet another dispossession of all their worldly goods. Nor were the devout Acadians of Clare tempted by atheistic French revolutionary rhetoric. They sent 75 of their young men to join the other militia of Annapolis County to march to the defence of Halifax in this moment of crisis.

Nevertheless, the French did try to subvert the Acadians. In early December, an extract from a proclamation and invitation in French sent to the people of Canada was passed to the governor by a loyal French-speaking Nova Scotian. Originally composed by Edmond Gênet, the document had been read in Halifax by a French emissary, memorized by the informer, and destroyed by the Frenchman. Genêt was a French diplomat of the ancien régime, now minister of the French republic to the United States, seeking support for the revolution in the United States. His invitation to the Acadians to rebel echoed the ringing tones of the Marseillaise. The unique orthography reflects the local scribe's ignorance of written French:

Savoir

freres et concitoyen, nous avons sécoue le joug de la tirannie, et nous sommes défait de notre tiran. suivé notre exemple, nos freres les americains nous ont ouvert le chemin, nous avons suivis leur exemple. le chemin en est tracé, c'est á vous maintenant citoyen á suivre la trace de nos peres, souvinér vous que vous etiez et que vous etes ... francais, rien de plus glorieux pour vous que de suivre leurs exemples. défaite vous freres et citoyen du joug de george avec sa petite armée qui croit nous faire peur. tirés vous des chaines d'un gouvernement tirannique, vos frere sont pret á vous recevoir dans leur sein ... magnifestés nous vos sentiment et nous irons vous secourir et vous eclairer sur le bonheur d'une constitution qui ne connoit que la liberté et légalité.[10]

Later in the 1790s, the government of the Directoire continued this French expansionist policy in America as well as in Europe. As one agent in America stated, "France must acquire Louisiana and the Floridas by negotiation, and Canada by force as the only means to contain the United States within peaceful bounds, ... to preserve our colonies exclusively to ourselves by feeding them with the products of our own soil, and, *finally, to recover in both hemispheres that preponderance to which nature entitles us.*"[11]

In 1797, a plot in Quebec, also instigated by the French government, was uncovered. Wentworth wrote to King that an American, Captain Daniel McLean, or McLane, "in the French service had enrolled 500 Canadians — were to give the Sentrys & as many Soldiers as they could, rum mixed with opium — at a certain time then to kill all the principal Officers, & friends of Govt., & declare for the French convention. Capt. M and his Servant were apprehended on suspicion and the latter discovered the plot." [12] As protection against French agents, both the American Congress and the Nova Scotia Legislature passed an Alien Act in 1798. This allowed for instant deportation of a non-citizen should he be considered seditious.

Meanwhile, the Acadians of Saint Mary's Bay were not impressed by the French appeal. Peaceably resettled in what they considered their ancient land, these people were not tempted to risk another expulsion in the name of what they saw as a godless revolution. Instead, they continued to sign up for the Clare militia and served loyally whenever needed throughout the war side by side with their English-speaking neighbours.

Wentworth was anxious that his regiment have the appellation "Royal." He pleaded that the word would give so much pleasure, would make recruiting easier, and — a telling bureaucratic argument down through the ages — would cost the government absolutely nothing. At first his request was refused but perhaps due to the good offices of John King, the governor was soon accorded his wish.

"It is impossible to describe the happiness 'royal' has given us all," he wrote ecstatically. "The Royal Nov. Sc. Rgt are delighted with the honour done them and equally grateful to Mr. Dundas for it, they feel his patronage from the Col. to every individual man nor will they ever quit their attachment." [13] The "Royal" allowed the regiment to have royal blue facings on their red jackets; their trousers were grey. They "are remarkable well looking, & for doing duty with spirit, and exactness," Wentworth wrote in May 1794. [14] "It would not be safe," he insisted, to call them "Sans Culottes" in Halifax, as the playwright Richard Sheridan had recently done in the British House of Commons in his attack against Dundas's supposed unpreparedness against the French.

James was also enhancing the regiment. During this first year he was organizing in Halifax a Masonic Lodge for its members. Being a "royal" regiment could only have helped. The warrant for the Lodge's formation was granted January 9, 1794. Meetings were to be held the second Thursday of every month at their mess room in Halifax, or wherever else they chose for as long as the regiment should exist. Though all the members who signed the original petition for its inception already belonged to lodges in their own communities throughout the province, stationed in Halifax they must have felt, as veterans in a new war, the need for a regular meeting place of their own in the city. James was chosen senior warden, a post he occupied again two years later when he returned to Halifax. With so few members in Sissiboo,

James had returned to the Digby Lodge. For the next four years he continued to belong to both lodges. Prince Edward was always an active Mason and his arrival in May 1794 in a military capacity must have added glamour to all the Halifax lodges.

For James, these activities in 1794 were perhaps a welcome distraction from the sad state of his own private concerns. In March, his only granddaughter died at the age of two. Another blow was the collapse of his shipbuilding. On the high seas the weakness of British naval forces made it impossible for them to protect commercial shipping. Although merchants in Halifax made large sums from captured booty, people in the coastal settlements, like James, in shipbuilding and the West Indian trade, saw their businesses come to a standstill. By the end of 1796, James's London partner, Thomas Yorke, was bankrupt and in debtor's prison. He was forced to sell his *Yorke*. John Moody's *Jane* went to the same buyer. Most of the ships that James had built, including *The Loyalist*, were sunk during these first years of the war with France.

For the governor, the appellation "Royal" in the regiment's name was a salve to the troubles he was having with the British garrison commander, Major General James Ogilvie. This last chose to snub the governor and refused to acknowledge the new regiment. Not only would he not speak to Wentworth but he denied the regiment provisions or arms from his stores, though he was more than happy to use the men for garrison and guard duty. The situation was all too familiar to most Loyalist veterans. Fortunately, the appointment in the summer of 1794 of Prince Edward as commander in chief of the forces in Nova Scotia and New Brunswick, put an end to this ill usage.

Prince Edward threw himself into his new command with fervour. At Halifax, he rebuilt large sections of Citadel Hill and fortified George's Island at the mouth of the harbour. Bringing the latest military technology, he had his men build three Martello towers — thick round constructions on a conical Corsican design whose shape tended to deflect contemporary cannon balls. He also instituted over the next few years a system of telegraphs using flags and large black wickerwork balls by day, and lanterns and drums at night or when the visibility was bad. He hoped to connect Halifax to Quebec City in this way, going through Saint John and Fredericton. Unfortunately the fog across the Bay of Fundy was too impenetrable even for him. However, he did institute a system between Annapolis Royal and Halifax by which a short message could be transmitted over a distance of 50 miles in 20 minutes.[15]

View of Halifax from George's Island, by George Isham Parkyns, 1801. The gun emplacements are part of Prince Edward's refortification of Halifax harbour. Courtesy John Ross Robertson Collection, Metropolitan Toronto Reference Library (T 15794)

Unlike General Ogilvie, Prince Edward very much acknowledged the officers of the Royal Nova Scotia Regiment. In October 1794, James was despatched to command the fort at Annapolis, and to recruit for the corps in that part of the country. The paymaster, Christopher Aldridge, another of Wentworth's choices, in a letter detailing accounting practices, wrote:

I have such an Opinion of you, that I shall always be perfectly at my Ease with regard to your Intentions and striving to do every Thing for the best. Oh! the grenadiers! but oh! the pleasant Country of Annapolis — Commanding Officer, close by your Farm, and no Person to tell you that you shall not go there, whenever you take the Matter in your Head, I think you are a lucky Fellow, I am sure your Change is not to your Disadvantage.[16]

Thinking in large terms, Prince Edward dreamed of manning the fort with 400 soldiers. He was sending James to Annapolis for the winter with the weakest company in order to begin the process.[17] But even James's prestige could not achieve the impossible and he left Annapolis the following spring with about the same complement of 37 men and non-commissioned officers that he had brought there. In the countryside, where men were needed to tend the farms and do other seasonal work, the militia, being part-time and only for emergencies, was a more attractive form of service than the regular army. In Annapolis County, as we have seen, there were three such companies of militia. In the extensive repairs that Prince Edward ordered in 1795, the militia were again employed, as in Halifax, to repair that fort.

In April 1795, with another invasion scare, the prince ordered the immediate return of James's company of the Royal Nova Scotia Regiment to Halifax. James's friend, Jesse Hoyt, was to bring them on the sloop *Betsey*, "together with the Stores, baggage, and Women and Children belonging to it." The provisions were to be shipped separately.[18] James was in Halifax when this order was drafted, attending the third session of the Seventh Assembly, a session called early because, wrote the governor, "summer sessions afford too much leisure for politics."[19] The members were loyal but, even in wartime, jealous of their Parliamentary rights. Soon afterward the companies in the Royal Nova Scotia Regiment were redistributed so that each one consisted of approximately 65 men. The garrison at Annapolis remained at around 30, including officers and men, right up to August 1797.

Although James was granted two weeks leave, he must have been back in Halifax the end of May to celebrate Wentworth's elevation to a knighthood. Some writers have suggested that this honour came to the governor as a reward for his wife's favours to Prince William Henry, now Duke of Clarence, in 1787 and 1788. But Wentworth had his own connections and he deserved the title in his own right. He had applied for a baronetcy two years earlier in June 1793, explaining that he would have been "received" by Lord North and Lord Sackville when he was appointed governor had not a new ministry suddenly taken office. In a letter to King in January 1795, he mentioned his 27 years of service to the Crown, and pointed out that his title would merely continue an earlier Wentworth baronetcy that had lapsed and, again, that the honour would cost the state not a penny.[20] Like the word "Royal" in the name of his regiment, the knighthood, he felt, added to the prestige of the Crown in the colony, and the honour could only strengthen the loyalty of the Nova Scotians.

In the autumn, Wentworth made a kind of "royal" progress through western Nova Scotia, reinforcing his policy of showing that he was governor for all Nova Scotians and accessible to their concerns. He took Lady Wentworth with him and travelled in style in a carriage, braving the primitive roads and stopping with friends to inspect parts of the country. When he visited the Acadians in Clare Township, he and his wife very probably stayed with the Moodys in Weymouth.

Restless and fussy, Prince Edward took Wentworth's provincials under his protection, and undertook to design their uniforms, along with those of his own Royal Fusiliers. He even gave instructions for recycling old army jackets into vests. Indeed he was soon taking too much interest in Wentworth's men. "He has fallen in love with about 400 men of my Regiment," the governor complained, "which he wants & given him the best & taken as many of the worst & oldest of his." The men were alarmed since they had agreed to serve only in Nova Scotia; the officers were so distressed they now wanted to resign their commissions and take up civil appointments. Recruiting was falling off to such an extent, Wentworth wrote, that people were predicting that 15, instead of 5 guineas would be needed per man as recruiting bounty.[21] This may also have affected James's recruiting. Tactfully, the British ministry succeeded in restraining the prince's military poaching, and Wentworth retained both his men and his good relations with the commander in chief.

Once Prince Edward had been given the command in Nova Scotia, Julie joined him immediately. Wentworth lent them the lodge he owned six miles outside Halifax overlooking Bedford Basin. He also provided rooms in Government House for the prince's business when in town. At Bedford, the prince expended some of his energies and a fair amount of money in altering and adding to the little country house, giving it wings and a large ballroom. At the front across the drive, he built for his regimental band the Rotunda, a circular gazebo consisting of Greek columns surmounted by a gilded cupola, in the fashionable neo-classical style in vogue in England. Below the Lodge, a little lake with its own tiny ornamental island was reshaped to take the form of a heart, and in the woods behind, miles of looping paths were cut through the trees, spelling out, the rumour said, the name of Julie. As in the Swiss Alps, small clearings were carved out of the forest and provided with wooden benches where walkers could rest and admire the magnificent view over the Basin. Other delights to amuse the stroller in this English park were little exotic buildings where he could find shelter, such as a Chinese pagoda with hanging bells tinkling in the wind or a latticed summer house in which to take tea.

The Wentworths made no scruples about receiving Julie, nor about accepting her invitations. The prince had small dinner parties of eight or ten people where Julie would act as his hostess. The guests would include several other wives as well as unattached men, officers, or people whose wives were not in Halifax. An abstemious man, the prince allowed his male guests three glasses of port after dinner and then led them to join the ladies for coffee and tea, and perhaps a little music provided by the hosts and guests, much as one reads about in the novels of Jane Austen. The prince never accepted invitations with ladies unless Julie was invited. A few people were shocked by the Wentworths. Chief Justice Strange, for one, complained to John King that "the Habits" of Wentworth's family "are so foreign to what it is possible for mine to be consistently with the Office I hold." King has added a little note on the letter, "I am afraid Mrs. W. is a little gay," meaning of course, naughtily flirtatious.[22] Bishop Inglis also felt more comfortable out of Halifax society during these years.

James felt no such qualms. When he was in Halifax in 1796 and 1797 on military duty he accepted the prince's dinner invitations with pleasure. Perhaps some of the Loyalists were a little old fashioned and still living in the freer eighteenth century, or perhaps their women, having themselves experienced the disruption of war and exile, were more understanding of sexual peccadillos. In any case until very recently, royalty has always had special privileges in this respect. James no doubt agreed with Wentworth when he wrote:

It is highly necessary, in these democratic times, that every possible distinguishing respect should be paid to the Royal family. For if it is once suffered for the people to think any part of the R family to be within the circumstances of any other Man, be he what he will, either Govr. Admiral or Genl., they will soon think it unnecessary to have any R. family. I therefore sedulously endeavour to surround him with the impenetrability due to his high Rank, which is sufficiently tempered by his gracious condescension, flowing from the finest temper any Man ever possessed.[23]

By the autumn of 1797, the immediate threat of a French invasion of Halifax had passed. Probably also James had had enough of Halifax military life. The gaiety of Halifax was fine, but his family were at Weymouth, and a man of 52 can only stand so many balls and levees, and amateur theatricals, or even fishing picnics and card parties. He sold his commission to a fellow officer for 400 guineas and went back to Weymouth.

James maintained his membership in the regiment's Masonic Lodge until 1800. In 1799, Governor Wentworth and his brother-in-law Benning Wentworth, now a member of the Council and treasurer of the province, took over the lodge and used it for their own social purposes. One suspects that the regiment itself had become more social.

But James had not entirely given up his military career. In 1798, he embarked on a third stage of it. In Weymouth, he replaced John Taylor as lieutenant-colonel of the Clare Division of the militia in southwestern Nova Scotia, the regiment that included the Acadians. The Seventh Assembly had passed several acts regularizing the militia so that rules for its embodiment and pay had been formally laid down. James must have felt he could be as useful guarding the coasts of Saint Mary's Bay as drilling in Halifax.

James also had much private business to attend to. He and his son John were working in partnership with their neighbour, James Cosman, to build a mud and brushwood dam in the Acadian manner, across the entrance to the pond where Cosman's Creek joined the Sissiboo. The energy from the twice-daily four-metre high tides was to be harnessed to drive a grist and sawmill. Such tidal mills were common in the eighteenth century not only on the Bay of Fundy and the Minas Basin where the Acadians had used them for cutting lumber, but also on the coasts of the English Channel where high tides are also common, and along the New England seaboard. The more confined Annapolis Basin has normal tides of over six metres, which are currently being harnessed for electric power at the mouth of the Annapolis River. James's mills at the Sissiboo Mill Pond were still in operation in 1824. He also owned the lots on either side of the Sissiboo Falls, farther up the river, where he was in partnership for another sawmill with William Taylor of Shelburne and John McConnell of Sissiboo.

James possessed, in addition, land across Saint Mary's Bay at Sandy Cove and further along Digby Neck, the peninsula that forms the north side of that bay, as well as a farm lot on Long Island. It was probably on this land that he raised more of the sheep, for which he was so well-known among his contemporaries. He also had a fish lot at Grand Passage where he could build a dock for unloading fish and stowing gear. This rather treacherous strait separates Long Island from Brier Island, the islands that are the continuation of Digby Neck.

We know very little about James's son John. He was involved in these enterprises and probably did most of the leg work for his father. We see his neat, clear handwriting for the first vestry records while he served as vestry clerk. He was also adjutant in the Acadian Militia in Clare Township well before his father replaced John Taylor as lieutenant-colonel. He belonged to the Digby Lodge of Masons from 1794 till 1798. He supervised the building of the dam across Cosman's Creek and must have been involved in the construction of the tidal mill there for both grain and lumber. From his sister's letters we know he made at least one trip to the Caribbean, and probably more, from the business he did with the West Indies. In addition to his trading with the brig *Jane*, he may well have done the buying for his father's coasting schooner, the *Yorke*, which ran up a bill in Saint John with John Ward in 1793 for £184 7d. By 1798, his wife Margaret had borne him two sons, James Budd and John Wentworth. A third son, Elisha William Budd, would be born in 1799, and a fourth, Charles Coulbourne, in 1802.

But by 1798 John was not well. In that year his father drew up his will and was "enduced to entail his landed property from a Consideration of the infirmities of his only son John Moody."[24] This meant that John could not sell any land that his father bequeathed to him. The will stated in addititon that after his own death this land would go to his sons. Moreover, at James's death any cash that might be left, after James's effects and chattels had been sold and his debts cleared (provided his wife had not opted to claim her dower and was neither remarried nor dead), was to be invested and the interest paid annually, not to John, but two-thirds to his "dear daughter-in-law, Margaret

Moody" and one third to his "dear daughter Maria Taylor." In other words, John was to have no control over any land nor was he to handle any cash. On the other hand, he continued to function as an adult in the family. One can only speculate on what his infirmity might have been, a mental illness like manic depression, or alcoholism, or who knows? This handicap would certainly not have helped the family's business affairs.

John's sister, Maria Jane, has left a deeper impression. Through her letters one sees a cultivated and gracious woman, but also one who is a little lonely. In 1800, she and her family left Weymouth for London. Their departure must have been a further cause for sadness.

Prince Edward too was chafing at life in Nova Scotia. Having drilled and disciplined his troops within an inch of their lives, rebuilt the fortifications at Annapolis and Halifax, and revamped the Lodge and its park at Bedford Basin, in 1798 he pleaded to be allowed back to England into the mainstream of English political events. Even the House of Assembly's resolution to allocate 500 guineas to buy him a diamond star, could not reconcile him to "this dreary and remote spot."[25] His chance came in August when the horse he was riding, mercifully, put its hoof through a wooden drain covering on a Halifax street, and fell over on the prince's left thigh against some rocks in the ditch. Though the damage to the prince was inconsequential, it gave him a pretext to return to England for medical treatment. When he came back to Nova Scotia late in 1799, as Duke of Kent and commander in chief of all the forces in British North America, including Upper and Lower Canada as well as the Maritime Provinces, he stayed no longer than another eleven months.

Despite his frustrations in Nova Scotia, he and Julie must have looked back with pleasure on the warmth and acceptance with which they were received in that colony. Their earlier time in Lower Canada with Sir Guy Carleton, now Lord Dorchester, had been a good deal frostier. Fascinated by mechanical gadgets and especially clocks, it was Edward who gave the city of Halifax its clock tower on Citadel Hill. He also initiated the building of the circular St. George's Church, that young arsonists set fire to in 1994. Always interested in raising standards, he left in the province three prize stallions, an Arabian, a Hanoverian, and a hunter, in order, as he wrote to James

to benefit the breed of horses, which appeared to me to be dwindling fast into a very inferior kind. If the people would only be advised to use the

Irish and Arabian, *solely*, when they wish to have horses for the Saddle, and always employ the black Hanoverian, and the black English horse when cattle are required for draught, they will in the course of five or six years, derive essential benefit from this mode of proceeding, but I fear they are so partial to the slighter sort of horses, that the two first named ones will be universally preferred; by which the country will still continue to have that narrow chested breed which is so ill calculated for draught up the heavy hills or through sand.[26]

The stallions were to be available at set fees for stud in different parts of the province at different times of the year so that each county would have the benefit of their strain.

Being a kind and decent man, the prince maintained his contact with his Nova Scotia friends, receiving them cordially when they came to England, and supporting their petitions although he knew he wielded little personal influence at court. He did this for James, and James's widow, successfully in their cases. He even sent James a cow and a calf, again with the hope that "the breed may spread in the country."[27] It was a fitting present for James returning to his own country seat.

NOTES

1. Wentworth to John King, 10 July 1793, PRO, CO 217/36, 183v-184.
2. George Lockart Rives, *Selections from the Correspondence of Thomas Barclay* (New York: 1894), 30.
3. Wentworth to John King, 10 July 1793, PRO, CO 217/36, 187v. "Pro aris & focis pugnare." To fight for house and hearth.
4. Quoted in Beamish Murdoch, *A History of Nova Scotia, or Acadie* (Halifax: James Barnes, 1867), vol. 3, 116.
5. Wentworth to John King, 10 July 1793, PRO, CO 217/36, 187v-88v.
6. *Ibid.*, 189v.
7. Wentworth is referring to Abbé Guillaume Raynal's *Histoire philoso-phique et politique des établissements et du commerce des Européens dans les deux Indes.* First published in 1770, and promptly banned in France, it had gone through 30 editions by 1789 and had been widely translated into many languages, including English. Among much else, it recounted the story of the deportation of the Acadians.
8. Wentworth to King, 10 July 1793, PRO, CO 217/36, 188v.
9. Extract of letter from Thomas Barclay, sent to John King by Wentworth, 11 Oct. 1793, PRO, CO 217/36, 218.
10. PRO, CO 217/36, 16254, 226, sent 7 Dec. 1793. The spelling and accents are as written in the document, perhaps reflecting the limited

education of the Acadian who took it down. A rough translation without the spelling mistakes gives: "Know ye, brothers and fellow citizens, we have shaken off the yoke of tyranny, and we have freed ourselves from the tyrant, follow our example, our American brothers have opened the way for us, we have followed their example, the road is laid out, to you now cititzens to follow in the footsteps of our fathers, remember that you were and are ... Frenchmen, nothing more glorious for you than to follow their example. Shake off, brothers and citizens, the yoke of George with his little army which thinks it can frighten us. Unshackle yourselves from a tyrannical government, your brothers are ready to receive you to their bosoms ... let your sentiments be made known to us and we will come to your help and enlighten you on the joy of a constitution which knows only liberty and equality."

11. Samuel Eliot Morison and Henry Steele Commager, *Growth of the American Republic* (New York, Toronto: Oxford University Press, 1942), vol. 1, 372, emphasis added.

12. Wentworth to John King, 4 June 1797, PRO, CO 217/37, 124.

13. Wentworth to John King, 7 Dec. 1793, PRO, CO 217/36, 232v.

14. Wentworth to John King, 8 May 1794, PRO, CO 217/36, 250.

15. McKenzie Porter, *Overture to Victoria* (Toronto: Longmans Green, 1961), 84-85.

16. Christopher Aldridge to James Moody, Halifax, 18 Oct. 1794, Moody Papers.

17. Prince Edward to Lord Dorchester, Halifax, 12 Jan. 1795, Royal Archives (RA) Add 7/75, Windsor Castle.

18. Frederick Augustus Wetherall, ADC, to Capt. Moody Commanding at Annapolis, Halifax, 13 April 1795, RA Add 7/89.

19. Wentworth to King, 23 Jan. 1795, PRO, CO 217/36, 309.

20. Wentworth to John King, 20 June 1793, PRO, CO 217/36.

21. Wentworth to King, 23 Jan. 1795, PRO, CO 217/36, 310v.

22. Chief Justice Thomas Andrew Strange to John King, 24 Aug. 1794, PRO, CO 217/36, 287v. *The Oxford English Dictionary* gives an eighteenth-century fashionable meaning for the word "gay": "Addicted to social pleasures and dissipations. Often *euphemistically*: Of loose or immoral life."

23. Wentworth to John King, 16 Sept. 1794, PRO, CO 217/36, 294.

24. Proceedings of the Executors of the Will of Col. James Moody, 12 Feb. 1810, Moody Papers.

25. From a letter from Prince Edward to the Prince of Wales in June 1798, Aspinall 6, *The Correspondence of George Prince of Wales*, vol. 3, 439, quoted in Mollie Gillen, *The Prince and his Lady: The Love Story of the Duke of Kent and Madame de St. Laurent* (Toronto: Sidgwick and

Jackson, 1970; Halifax: Goodread Biographies, Formac Publishing, 1985), 116. The House passed the resolution in June 1798, *Proceedings and Journals of the House of Assembly*, 1798, 300, and informed him of their intention a few days later, 305. It was presented to him in England in January, 1799. Murdoch, *A History of Nova Scotia or Acadie*, 177.

26. Edward, Duke of Kent to James Moody, 11 Sept. 1801, Moody Papers.
27. *Ibid.*

18

A SECOND SESSION IN THE
HOUSE OF ASSEMBLY, 1800-06

IN 1799, A NEW ELECTION was called and James was again returned with Millidge for the County of Annapolis. In this election, James was opposed by a rival in his own neighbourhood, John Taylor, the Sissiboo mill owner and land surveyor he had just replaced as lieutenant-colonel of the Clare militia. The vote, even with a second poll at Sissiboo, was 345 for James and 292 for Taylor.[1]

The new House of Assembly would have a different atmosphere. The clashes between the governor and his council and the House of Assembly would be both regional and constitutional. As Speaker, Attorney General Uniacke followed Barclay in maintaining that the House of Assembly must be governed by the rules and privileges current in the British House of Commons, rather than out-dated royal prerogatives vested in each new governor from an earlier period. In the end, the success of these arguments enhanced the prestige of the House of Assembly and served to strengthen representative government. However, the struggle to achieve this success was not easily won.

Barclay's departure was regretted by many people, from the governor, who had recommended him for the Council, to his colleagues in the House. Not least of these was James who wrote to congratulate him on his new appointment. Barclay's answer is worth quoting:

The Congratulations of a friend are doubly acceptable from a conviction of their being sincere; as such I receive and value yours.... I have ever considered you amongst the number of those who had an affection for me, and my heart assures me you hold at least an equal place in my warmest affection. Neither time or change of place will I trust ever lessen the attachment.... The Idea of leaving a number of near and valuable friends to whom I am connected by the tenderest ties of honour and affection; friends whose assistance I would ever rely on, and who they knew might at all times command mine distresses me beyond conception, it is like the separation of soul and body. I am sensible on the Score of friendship I leave treasures behind me whose equivalent cannot elsewhere be found.[2]

Without Barclay's presence in the House of Assembly, the tension between Council and House became more acute. We have seen the flare-up at the end of the Seventh Assembly. The governor now exerted power through his appointed Council rather than working in conjunction with the elected House. From 1800, when the new House met, Wentworth, a master in the art of patronage, was stacking the Council with his relatives and friends, most of whom were Haligonians on whom he showered a multiplicity of offices. These were men who, for the most part, were non-mercantile, to use historian Margaret Ells's expression,[3] and who seemed oblivious to many of the urgent needs of the developing colony. Wentworth hoped to control the Legislature through them, and above all the allocation of the financial surplus now accruing from import duties and a better collection system. He wanted a new, much grander Government House as his official residence. He reasoned that these men who would receive the contracts for its construction would support his project.

The two most offensive of the governor's supporters, though not related to him, were the Loyalist Michael Wallace who represented Halifax in the Assembly until he was appointed to the Council in April 1803, and the Englishman, Dr. Alexander Croke, sent out as judge of the Vice-Admiralty Court in Halifax and appointed to the Council in October, 1802. Wallace, a vindictive man and thoroughly disliked, was never accused of dishonesty. As treasurer of the province he had control over the province's expenditures. As auditor of public accounts and chief acting commissioner of public buildings, he oversaw his own public accounts as well as those for Government House. Alexander Croke was not only grasping and rude in and out of his court, but arbitrary in his dealings with the House of Assembly and contemptuous of almost all Nova Scotians. It was he who, over the objections of Bishop Inglis, insisted that entering as well as graduating students must subscribe in writing to the Thirty Nine Articles of the Anglican Church, and so managed for 18 years to bar non-Anglican students from attending the College at Windsor.[4]

The constitutional issue which was to preoccupy James's second term as a member of the House of Assembly was clearly evident when the House met in February 1800. William Cottnam Tonge led the movement. James supported him strongly on the constitutional issue, especially during the early years of the Eighth Assembly. When Tonge's opposition to the Council became so strident that it began to seem obstructive to the resolution of the conflict, James opted with Millidge for a more conciliatory approach, until this too failed against the Council's intransigence. In 1800, as chairman of the committee to look into 1799 contracts and accounts for expenditures on roads and bridges, James took a vigorous part in the struggle from the beginning. He continued to do so as he served on financial committees looking into both road and Government House expenditures throughout this Assembly. Often designated as one of the Assembly managers, he negotiated with the Council many of the bills that were in dispute between the two houses.

Tonge was a flamboyant man, charming and outspoken. His family on his mother's side were pre-Loyalist Nova Scotian. His grandmother, Deborah How Cottnam, was exceptional. Not only was she an admired poetess — a gift she passed on to Tonge's mother and particularly his daughter Grizelda — but in the course of her lifetime she had founded three startlingly progressive girls schools, in Salem, Halifax, and Saint John. Tonge himself was a brilliant orator in the House of Assembly. He was well educated and had studied some law, though he was never a member of the Nova Scotia bar. He was keenly interested in and well informed about contemporary British politics. He was the naval officer for Nova Scotia, locally responsible for overseeing the regulations of the Trade and Navigation Acts, and collecting the attendant shipping fees. He also represented Hants County. He was succeeding his father in both capacities. In the new assembly, James nominated him as speaker, and while Uniacke won the position, Tonge was Barclay's successor in the constitutional debate begun in the Sixth Assembly. Unfortunately, he never shared Wentworth's friendship or trust as Barclay had done. Instead, his Yankee roots, suggesting republicanism, and his family's own rival English connections to power, earned him the governor's assiduous hatred. However, it is easy to see why he and James enjoyed working together in the House of Assembly.

In the election of December 1799, Tonge had the bad taste to run in Halifax County, with two country candidates, against a slate of the Halifax establishment, as well as in Newport in Hants County, and, worse, to win the most votes in Halifax County. In the election returns, the trailing provincial treasurer, Michael Wallace, was eliminated from the Assembly. When Wallace protested that Tonge owned no property in Halifax, the latter was disqualified, and the former elected in the now vacant seat. But Tonge had shown that even Halifax County strongly supported his ideas. Tonge of course kept his seat for Newport. Wallace's defeat hardly endeared Tonge to the group.

The constitutional debate focussed on the appropriation of money raised by the House of Assembly. As we have seen, both the revenue to be raised and the appropriation of how it was to be spent was considered the exclusive right of the House of Assembly, a constitutional point that had long been accepted in England, and that the American colonial assemblies had been insisting on since their earliest founding.[5] It was a principle that the New England planters had also on occasion vainly attempted to establish. To become law, bills embodying these money measures must be passed by the Council and signed by the governor, though neither could change them. They could of course discuss changes in conference with members designated by the House. The House was at liberty to change its bill or disregard the Council's suggestions.

The new element in the Assembly was concerned with measures that affected the welfare of the settlements outside the capital. The opposition was not so much between Halifax and the country, as a member for Truro wrote in 1799, "as between Court party measures and what would be for the interest of the province at large."[6] This country party could also have been called an Assembly party in opposition to a Council and governor party. It was hardly a party in the modern political sense; rather it was a shifting alliance of like-minded Assembly representatives that coalesced differently over each issue. It was made up of men of property and substance mostly from outside Halifax, like James and Millidge and the pre-Loyalist, Tonge. They voted for roads and subsidies to help industries like fishing, mining, and agriculture to develop enough strength to hold their own against American competition, particularly in the trade with the West Indies.

These members, therefore, favoured import duties on non-competitive items, and embargoes on the import of competitive items, and subsidies for agriculture and shipbuilding. They were particularly concerned about the undermining effect of smuggling and American fishing concessions along the coast. In this they were supported by Halifax exporters who could see the benefits of greater trade in Nova Scotia products. The court party, the Halifax establishment, represented in the Council and to a lesser extent by Halifax members in the House, for the most part stood to gain by cheap imports, and spending on public buildings they could contract for. The lieutenant-governor wanted a grand elegant residence. There was bound to be a clash of interest.

The dispute narrowed itself to how much money should go into roads and how much into this residence. The provincial surplus was in the nature of £23,000. The Assembly in 1799 had voted a limit of £10,500 for the governor's official residence, and an allocation of £10,000 for roads. The Council tried to limit the money spent on roads. In 1800, the dispute between town and country took the constitutional form of the Council insisting that revenue bills be passed separately from appropriation bills.

The House, however, was not to be so easily bested in its control over the provincial finances. In 1801, it passed a resolution that forbade the provincial treasurer, under penalty of a £500 fine, to pay any sum not directly authorized by a provincial act. This measure was to maintain some control over both the money raised by provincial taxes, voted in the Revenue Bill, and the £5,000-odd paid directly by the British government for the civil establishment of the province.[7] In 1802, the House, led by Tonge and much to the indignation of the governor and his Council, passed a resolution to examine the Government House accounts, now well beyond their legislated limit. In 1803, the House, still battling over the Government House accounts, claimed the right to search the journals of the Council, who were refusing to pass the appropriation bills, until the House passed the revenue bills. The House replied that it:

is ready and willing to raise a revenue as soon as the purposes to which such revenue is to be applied are settled and agreed upon, by previous communication between the two branches of the legislature, which communication the house is and has ever been ready to hold; but that the house, conceiving it unconstitutional and derogatory to the rights of the subject to raise a revenue until the purposes to which such revenue is to be applied are ascertained, cannot give effect to the bills before the house until they have assurance of the assent of H.M. council to such appropriations as were in contemplation of the house whenever those acts were passed.[8]

This particular wrangle caused the governor to complain to the colonial secretary that the members of the House of Assembly "are endeavouring to create dissentions, with a view to obtain an *elective* legislative council, which would make two popular assemblies, instead of three distinct branches in the legislature."[9] In the end, the House reluctantly gave in to the Council, with the Speaker summing up the House's disappointment:

If the House of Assembly has encountered difficulties in appropriating the Supplies of the present Session to purposes of the first importance to the Province it has, at least, manifested its prudence and moderation, in making its feeling a sacrifice to its wishes to preserve harmony in the several departments of his Majesty's Government ... people of this Province will patiently wait a more favourable opportunity, to accomplish the numerous objects that yet remain unattained.... It is not safe, in the present times, to indulge speculative opinions.[10]

Not so in 1804. War or no war, the House was no longer willing to be bullied and the confrontation became even more direct. The governor stated his case:

My object is merely to reserve to the executive government the general superintendence and direction of all appropriations of monies granted to the crown for public service, and the control of such persons as should be appointed to expend the same; and these powers being prerogative rights, although they may have been in some instances left to the management of the assembly, may be constitutionally resumed by his majesty's representative whenever he thinks the general interest requires it.[11]

In his suggestion that rights "left to the management of the assembly" could be "constitutionally resumed by his majesty's representative," Wentworth was forgetting his English history — the English civil war that had ended with the decapitation of Charles I.

The House of Assembly was adamant on the issue. That year it passed no appropriations bill. In 1805, Uniacke was in England on private and public business. Sir John found Tonge, the man he held responsible for these disputes, elected to replace him as Speaker. James had seconded his nomination. The Legislature sat from the end of November until January 18, 1806, a longer session than usual. It insisted that the treasurer present a proper account of the money spent the previous year when no appropriations had been passed, and disputed the Council's right to change the House's money bills. A compromise was finally reached whereby the expenditures the treasurer had made, despite the absence of an appropriations bill, were accepted, and £6,000 were voted for roads and bridges. The Council at the end accepted the money bills of the House intact.

Sir John's answer to the Assembly's fractiousness was to dissolve the House in May, and to call an election for August, a year earlier than needed. James did not run again for the House of Assembly.

Although during the Eighth Assembly the House was often frustrated in its attempts to strengthen, with sustained bounties, local industries like agriculture and the fisheries, it did manage to lay a good infrastructure of roads and local government. Land grants were reinstated and holdings in such communities as the Acadians were confirmed. James's grant of 1,000 acres behind Sissiboo and his water lots on either side of the Sissiboo River were among these. There was also an attempt to encourage a bog-iron mining industry on the Nictaux River and James had part of a grant of land in this concern.[12] Old statutes were brought up to date and published; the need for a more equitable allocation of roadwork was considered. A committee was set up to recommend a judicious system of paper credit, another pre-Revolutionary American problem, as a solution to the crippling shortage of "a circulating medium"— cash money in the form of coins — caused by the war, and early thoughts on an incorporated bank of Nova Scotia were discussed.

In addition to his involvement in the fight over money and roads with the Council, James was also busy throughout these years on a number of other issues, serving on committees and helping with reports, often with Tonge. The problem of the Mi'Kmaq was further explored through a lengthy questionnaire which hoped to find ways of encouraging their viable settlement. The committee's report concluded that a beginning could be made with proper lands chosen and surveyed for them, and a few families settled as an example, but that any solution would entail more money and consistent perseverance in a long-term plan. The advice is still not outdated.

Another of James's concerns was reform to the militia law so that proper rules for payment and for clothing were laid down. He worked hard to have a substantial set sum of money laid aside for the improvement of the fisheries industry, he supported payments for the provincial health officers who were constantly being short-changed by the Council, and he helped lay out a plan for subsidizing and settling the new Scottish immigrants on new roads where their houses could also act as stopping places for travellers. He supported agricultural subsidies. His clear mind can be seen at work in comments on the 1804 report of the Committee on Sable Island which he found inadequate. He moved that it be returned and include the number of persons saved from shipwreck, the value of the saved property, the allowance for making the salvage, and how money and property so received as compensation had been disposed of — a cost-benefit analysis, in today's jargon.[13]

On the question of slavery he fudged, like others. There had been colonial attempts to ban the trade before the Revolution, but these had usually been overruled by the royal governors with the approval of the British government and the king. After the Declaration of Independence, various states began to legislate against the commercial importation of slaves. New Jersey did so in 1786, largely through the efforts of Governor William Livingston. At this time in England, Thomas Clarkson and William Wilberforce joined forces to fight the practice through the Society for the Abolition of the Slave Trade, enduring insults and death threats. At last a bill was passed in the British House of Commons abolishing slave-trading vessels in any British possession after March 1, 1808.

In Nova Scotia, opposition to slavery had also been growing. Through the anti-slavery preaching and writing of the Presbyterian minister, Dr. James MacGregor, who arrived in Pictou from Scotland about the same time that James arrived in Nova Scotia, many people were questioning the practice. Among those in the Nova Scotia establishment adamantly opposed to the system were Chief Justice Andrew Strange and Sampson Salter Blowers who succeeded him in 1797, and the attorney general and Speaker of the House of Assembly, Richard John Uniacke.[14]

James, as a slave owner, obviously felt differently: slaves were property that had been bought with money, like other property. If the system was to be abolished then slave owners should be compensated by government for their financial loss. The issue was debated in the House of Assembly in the first years of the new century.

In 1801, the House discussed the possibility of appointing commissioners "to look into the rights which individuals have to the Service of Negroes and People of Colour as slaves and the value of such slaves and the sum of money appropriated to pay such individuals for their Property in such slaves."[15] Tonge suggested that instead of paying off the owners, the commissioners be authorized to try such rights in court and appeal to the king and the Council and the province to pay the attendant expenses. James voted with the majority to defer the issue to a future session, which in effect left the whole question of owning slaves to the courts, at the owner's expense. Legislation on the subject was again deferred in 1802 and 1803.

At the same time, Colonel James DeLancey brought a law suit to the supreme court which turned out to be a test case against slave ownership. He was attempting to retrieve a runaway slave's wages, from the man's new employer, in lieu of his loss of the man himself. In the end, DeLancey received no compensation and the man remained free.

In 1807, James signed a petition presented by 27 residents of Annapolis County, "who are far from advocating Slavery as a system," but nevertheless were asking that a legal ruling on the ownership of slaves should be made, and if "the true interests of Humanity, may require, in this Colony, the abolition of that particular species of property claimed by your petitioners," that compensation should be made to the slave owners.[16] The bill that resulted from this petition did not get past second reading. The issue was seen as a personal moral one that the House did not wish to legislate.

The petition describes the slaves as "Negro Servants brought from His Majesty's late Colonies, now called the United States." James is shown as owning eight slaves: two men, one woman, and five children. The petitioners also included such pre-Loyalists as William Winniett, a scion of one of Annapolis's oldest families, who owned two men, one woman, and one child, and several Acadian families. In James's case, the adults probably did come from New Jersey. They remained part of his household as long as he lived. Earlier in the year, he had sold the 10-year-old Sylva, daughter of one of these, to his son's widow, Margaret, for £5. This is very late for such a transaction in Nova Scotia, but perhaps it was a way of keeping the girl in the family. She had been baptized by Viets in 1798, in Sissiboo, with the family's obvious blessing.[17] Slavery was officially abolished in the British Empire in 1833.

Of personal interest to James was the building of lighthouses in his area. In June 1801, he was associated with a petition to the House for a lighthouse at the entrance to the Annapolis Basin, stating that "the entrance from the Bay of Fundy into the harbour of Digby is so contracted & winding that in Dark, Hazey & Stormy Weather, the most skilful Mariners well acquainted with this Harbour are obliged to Beat in the Bay of Fundy, till the Storm ceases & the weather clears." It argued that "when Peace take [sic] place which from appearances is not far distant the Navigation trade of this place will so increase that the Light Duties will it is hoped soon be adequate to defray the Annual expense of said Lighthouse." Appended was a proposal from the carpenter in Saint John who had erected the lighthouse there. His estimate was for a building that would be 40 feet, 4 inches high, with an octagon frame measuring 23 feet in diameter. It would have four stories, with a parapet on the top measuring 5 feet 8 inches high and having a diameter of 6 feet 4 inches to receive the lantern. For £220 the carpenter would find the timber, plank, boards, nails, and shingles and do all the carpentry work but would need to be assisted with tackles, rope, and "some hands in the time of raising."[18]

This project received the immediate backing of the House. It voted £250 toward the lighthouse, provided that the local inhabitants could raise another hundred. As 14 people, including James, had already subscribed £70 the previous April, it did not take long to gather the rest of the money. In 1803, James, Rutherford, and Isaac Bonnell were appointed commissioners to procure the necessary land and to oversee the construction of the building at Rogers Point, today called Point Prim. Unfortunately the bills for the work done were presented in 1804 in the middle of the crisis over the appropriations with the Council and this body chose not to pass the payment of £77 19s 8d which had been advanced by the commissioners to pay for the construction of the lighthouse keeper's house. Even more unfortunately, the lighthouse burned down in 1806 leaving the commissioners and their heirs scrambling to collect their money. In the spring of 1808, the sum of £300 was voted for rebuilding the lighthouse and tenders were again invited for the work and finding a keeper, but it was another nine years before the Point Prim lighthouse, now twice as high, was in full operation.[19] According to a contemporary map, the light was displayed in the window of a house during this intervening period.[20]

Another nearby navigational hazard that received the House's attention was the high cliff at the western end of Brier Island, the outer tip of the continuation of the Digby peninsula that forms the north side of Saint Mary's Bay. Since a light here is so crucial to navigation in the Bay of Fundy, in 1802, at Tonge's suggestion, a committee of himself and James and one other member was formed to discuss with Wentworth negotiations on the possibility of Nova Scotia and New Brunswick cooperating on its building and maintenance. Although it was not until 1807, after James was no longer a member, that tenders went out for a lighthouse on Brier Island, he must have been pleased to see the beginnings of these much needed navigational aids. This lighthouse, completed in 1809, was to be smaller than the one at Point Prim and made of stone.[21] His fish lot was not far away, on the east shore at Grand Passage.

In spite of his independent stance in the House of Assembly, we can see the trust reposed in James by Wentworth in the letters that the two exchanged about county and personal affairs. The topics discussed ranged from sheep for the governor and others in Halifax, Father Sigogne and his Acadian parishioners, English agricultural pamphlets, new Scottish emigrants to be settled between Digby and Weymouth, and the possibility of procuring a bottle or two of fir or balsam sap from the Acadians to assuage the soreness in the pit of Lady Wentworth's stomach.[22] There is a coy invitation from 1802: "Lady Wentworth requests the favor of Capt. Moody's company to dinner to day at Govt. House at 4 o'clock, she was sorry not seeing him this morning when he called on Sir John, if she had known he was in the House, Lady Wentworth would have seen him."[23] There was no question of James refusing Lady Wentworth's friendship. She and her husband also visited the Moodys in Weymouth on three separate occasions.[24]

The Wentworths were not James's only important visitors. During these years, James entertained the bishop and his family ten times in his "very hospitable mansion,"[25] his daughter-in-law recalled, as well as friends of the governor's and visiting clergymen. Much of this was also due to Jane who always felt concern for people far from home.[26]

The constitutional struggle continued into the next Assembly. The governor had become so arbitrary that when Tonge was again elected speaker, Sir John, with the backing of his Council, invoking an old disused prerogative, refused to accept him. He also refused to issue the necessary writ for a new election in Annapolis Township when the sitting member was shown to have used "undue influence" in persuading a voter to support him. This became another constitutional battle in the House of Assembly that was only settled again by recourse to current practice in the British House of Commons; there the elected House determined who, within the law, could sit as a member.

Wentworth, in 1807, dismissed Tonge from his post as provincial naval officer, giving no just public cause for his removal. This evoked public meetings in Hants County where Tonge lived and in Annapolis County where his wife's family lived, to write a petition supporting Tonge to the king. Wentworth retorted by threatening to suspend the magistrates of the counties who countenanced these meetings, including the brother of James's daughter-in-law, Elisha Budd. Although James was no longer representing the county, he must have watched these events with mixed emotions, torn between friendship and disillusionment with both men: Wentworth for his ever more arbitrary governance, and Tonge for his often open aggression against the governor in the House of Assembly. In private he must also have been torn between family feeling and sympathy for the recently widowed Tonge, and distaste for some of Tonge's Chaucerian escapades. In the end, further meetings were not held.

In 1808, Sir John was replaced as lieutenant governor by Sir George Prevost. A "tiny, light, gossamer man," [27] fluent in French thanks to his French-Swiss father, Sir George was a respected British professional soldier, and a governor skilled at reconciling personalities and points of view. He would soon be appointed governor in chief and commander of British forces in North American, and would use all his abilities to defend British North America against American invasion throughout the War of 1812.

Almost immediately after his arrival as the new governor in Nova Scotia, Sir George was called away to lead a military force in the West Indies. During his absence, Croke's arrogant unconstitutional behaviour thoroughly roused the House. As acting lieutenant-governor, he refused to give assent to the Appropriations Bill that had been passed by the House and the Council. He insisted that the government would spend the money in a better way than the Assembly had appropriated. He even refused to allow the King's Printer to publish the House resolutions condemning his action, and urged the British government to discontinue the members' pay. They were, he said,

principally farmers, who have a little leaven of American democracy amongst them ... suspicious of government — jealous of their rights, and strongly retentive of the public purse.[28]

...Whatever outward appearances there may be of loyalty and affection to Great Britain, the relations — the family and commercial connexions, and the property of a great part of its inhabitants, centre in the United

States. Is it, then, to be wondered at that they should be attached to American principles and democratic forms of government?[29]

With the exception of Michael Wallace, even the Council refused to allow him to draw warrants on the treasury, and certainly an appeal to the British attorney general would have shown his behaviour as unconstitutional. Fortunately, Sir George returned a few months later, in time to cut the constitutional Gordian knot. He immediately called a special session of the Legislature, and gave his assent to the represented money bills passed by both houses in the previous session, wisely insisting on current 1808 British practice. At last, after four assemblies, in two of which James had played a key role, a decisive victory for representative government had been won. This victory laid the foundation on which later responsible government could be built.

NOTES

1. Brian Cuthbertson, *Johnny Bluenose at the Polls: Epic Nova Scotian Election Battles, 1758-1848* (Halifax: Formac Publishing, 1994), 138.
2. Col. Thomas Barclay to Lt. Col. James Moody, 3 May 1799, Moody Papers.
3. Margaret Ells, "The Development of Nova Scotia 1782-1812," PhD draft, University of London, 1949, 127.
4. For Croke's sabotaging of Inglis's attempts to have the subscription to the Thirty Nine Articles revoked or at least deferred until graduation by the students of King's College, see Brian Cuthbertson, *The First Bishop: A Biography of Charles Inglis* (Halifax, NS: Waegwoltic Press, 1987), 162-63. Although the Archbishop of Canterbury did defer the entrance subscription to the Thirty Nine Articles until graduation, Croke's earlier version of the statutes of the college remained in circulation, and in force, until 1821.
5. Theodore Draper, *A Struggle for Power: The American Revolution* (New York: Times Books, Random House, 1996), 36-37.
6. James Fulton to Edward Mortimer, 18 October 1799, printed in the *Colonial Patriot*, Nov. 6, 1830, quoted in Ells, "Development of Nova Scotia," 349.
7. Beamish Murdoch, *History of Nova Scotia or Acadie* (Halifax: James Barnes, 1807), vol. 3, 237, 193.
8. *Journals and Proceedings of the House of Assembly of Nova Scotia*, 1803, 78, 235. James was one of the managers in presenting this message to the Council.
9. Wentworth to Hobart, 24 December 1803, PRO, CO 217/78, 189.

10. *House of Assembly*, 1803, 97.
11. *Ibid.*, 1804, 35.
12. Will of James Moody, dated 24 Sept. 1798. He leaves to his son John 320 acres, being half of his grant of 640 acres on the northern side of the road leading from Nictaux in the County of Annapolis to Halifax.
13. *House of Assembly*, 1804, 29.
14. See Robin W. Winks, "The Attack on Slavery in British North America," in *The Blacks in Canada* (Montreal: McGill-Queen's University Press, 1971), 102-07.
15. *House of Assembly*, 1801, 72.
16. Petition of John Taylor and others, "Slave Proprietors in Annapolis County," 3 Dec. 1807, PANS, RG5, Ser. A, vol. 14, no. 49.
17. Rev. Roger Viets, Notitia Parochialis of Trinity Parish, Digby, Nova Scotia, Beginning July 12, 1786, 42, "Baptism, 1 April 1798, in Sissiboo, of Sylvia, a black child of Captain Moody's Bristol." Her bill of sale in the Moody Papers calls her Sylva.
18. Petition on Behalf of the Inhabitants of Annapolis County for building a lighthouse at the entrance to Annapolis Gut, 10 June 1801, PANS RG 5, Ser. A, vol. 8, no. 19.
19. *Nova Scotia Royal Gazette*, Tuesday, 12 April 1808, NAC.
20. "Updated map of the Coast of Nova Scotia, including the Bay of Fundy, by Messers Des Barres, Holland, and others" (London: 1823), in the possession of Kelsey Raymond of Smith's Cove, NS.
21. *Saint John Gazette*, 8 June 1807, 3, NAC.
22. Sir John Wentworth to James Moody, 17 Nov. 1803, Moody Papers.
23. Visiting card dated Saturday, March 6, Moody Papers.
24. Margaret Budd Moody to James Budd Moody, no date, Sir John Wentworth to James Moody, 16 Sept., 1806, Moody Papers.
25. Eliza Inglis to Mrs. Moody, 31 Aug. 1803, Moody Papers. Eliza Inglis was the wife of the bishop's son, John, who later became third bishop of Nova Scotia. She states in the letter that August 31 is her wedding day, and also "I hope you have not forgotten the promise you made of indulging us with a visit at Clermont. I am desired of the Bishop and Mr. Inglis who desire their best compliments, to say how happy they will be to have the pleasure of your company next month, to which I heartily join." She is stated to be Elizabeth Cochran, daughter of Thomas Cochrane, but she signs this letter Eliza.
26. Jane Moody to James Budd Moody, 26 Jan. 1819, Moody Papers.
26. Chief Justice Sampson Salter Blowers, quoted in the *Dictionary of Canadian Biography* (Toronto: University of Toronto Press, 1983), vol. 5, 698.
27. Alexander Croke to the colonial secretary, 23 Dec. 1808, quoted in Murdoch, *History of Nova Scotia*, vol. 3, 289.
28. *Ibid.*, March 1809, 294.

19

THE WEYMOUTH CHURCH
AND THE ACADIANS, 1797-1809

WHEN JAMES RESIGNED from his regiment in 1797, and came home again to Weymouth, he had much work waiting for him. The chief task was to get on with building the Anglican church and the formation of a parish in Sissiboo with its own minister. Weymouth's struggle in this gives an insight into the complexities of such an endeavour in a small Nova Scotia community at the beginning of the nineteenth century.

During the years that James had been preoccupied with military service, the bishop had evidently considered that the occasional care of the "very worthy and diligent" Reverend Viets and the lay readings in James's house were sufficient for the congregation of Sissiboo. "Every attention that is practicable is paid to the spiritual wants of the people; the interests of the Church do not suffer, and the place will be better prepared to receive a Missionary some time hence than it is at present," he had written in a letter to the SPG secretary in November 1792. During these years, both Viets and James extended religious help as far as Yarmouth at the southwestern tip of the peninsula. In 1796, we find Viets offering the communion wine there from a handsome silver flagon "brought from London by Captain Moody." [1]

Nevertheless, Alline's New Light successors had not gone away. After a period of antinominian excesses — believing that their "New Life" conversion dispensed them from the obligations of the moral law under the "law of grace"— by the end of the 1790s they were coalescing into a Baptist Association to achieve both doctrinal discipline among themselves and credibility with regard to other denominations. In the process, these men revitalized their teaching to bring about the Second Great Awakening in Nova Scotia. During the first decade of the 1800s, there would be at least three great revivals in the Digby area that would challenge the religious affiliation of the Anglican community in Weymouth.

Moreover, the cruelty of the "atheistic" French Revolution reinforced the notion in Loyalist minds that the Church of England in Nova Scotia could form a political as well as a religious bulwark against the wicked republicanism that had spread across the Atlantic. No doubt James fully agreed with the bishop's analysis that "in an age distinguished by extraordinary revolutions like the present one" it was important to build and expand the Church.[2] France's imperial ambitions added to the argument.

It was not surprising therefore, that in September 1798, the bishop could write to James:

It is with much pleasure I inform you that there is a prospect of my being able to accomplish what has long been the object of my wish as it probably was Yours — viz the settlement of a Clergyman at Weymouth, formerly Sissiboo.... They have at last authorised me to appoint if I judge it right, Mr. Charles Weeks to be their Missionary at Weymouth, when he is admitted to Holy Orders. Mr. Weeks (youngest son of the Rev. Mr. Weeks) is a young man of irreproachable moral character, studious and of good abilities; and of whom I have great expectations. If the Inhabitants of Weymouth will comply with the Society's requisitions, he may be fixed there this Fall, as I hold an Ordination the 21st of October, when Mr. Weeks can be admitted to Holy Orders.[3]

James had written on August 8 that the church was now fit for use, that there was a good tract of reserved glebe land, and that the people of Weymouth had raised the required subscription of £30 a year for the missionary. These financial arrangements were vital, the bishop explained, as Weeks would only have, in addition, his SPG salary. In his case, no government allowance was to be provided. Inglis was concerned about the building of the parsonage. Was the church land conveniently situated, as well as good in quality? "The Glebe is probably in a State of nature," he continued, "and the best method to accomplish Your design will be for the Inhabitants to unite and clear a certain number of acres; and when about 40 acres are cleared, then to set about building a house."[4] If these conditions were met the new clergyman would be officially confirmed to the community by the bishop.[5] It did seem at last that the parish would be born.

In February 1800, James formally registered the deed to the land, donated ten years before, on which the church now stood almost completed. The church measured close to 30 feet by 45 feet.[6] It had a chancel and a steeple. It must have been like most of the Anglican churches built in Nova Scotia and New Brunswick during Inglis's term as bishop, very much influenced if not actually drawn by Inglis himself. Not only was his aesthetic judgement respected by his colleagues — his old Connecticut friend, the Loyalist Reverend Doctor Samuel Seabury on being named first Episcopal bishop in the new United States had him design his bishop's mitre — but he also had decided ideas about the interior layout and furnishings of these buildings. The original model was the late-seventeenth century St. Martin-in-the-Fields in London, by James Gibbs, with its elegant gothic steeple and palladian east window. This had been copied well before the Revolution in Christ Church, Philadelphia, and St. Paul's Chapel in New York, two churches which were familiar to Inglis. Moreover Gibbs's *Book of Architecture*, in wide circulation, had become a design manual for eighteenth century colonial churches.

Inglis wanted his churches to be distinctive from Dissenter meeting houses. They should be clearly discerned as houses of worship and be located at the centre of the community they were serving in a traditional east-west orientation. He insisted that the width of the nave be two-thirds of its length, and he encouraged a rounded chancel on the east end to emphasize the importance of Holy Communion. St. Peter's had a rounded pulpit at the left, and a reading desk at the right, flanking the chancel. To have as much natural light as possible, Inglis favoured tall round-arched windows in a single tier along the sides, and where his favourite Palladium window was not possible at the chancel end, as seems very likely in Sissiboo, another tall round-arched window. The steeple tower, set in a square base with rondel windows, should be an integral part of the west front, following the style of Sir Christopher Wren's churches. It should taper to a concave-shaped spire on which sat a weather vane, rather than a Popish cross. The proportions in these wooden churches are particularly harmonious, while the beautiful woodwork of the interiors, like the seventeenth century Catholic churches along the St. Lawrence River, gives them their New World originality.

St. Mary's Church, Auburn, NS, where Bishop Inglis officiated, displays many of the features that were typical of Anglican churches throughout the province under Inglis's guidance. Author photo

The church that James was associated with has been replaced by a nineteenth century building, but one can still see a superb example of some of its features in St. Mary's Auburn, where Inglis himself officiated. James's church was probably meant to hold, with the gallery, 150 to 200 worshippers on feast days, though the congregation could dwindle to less than 50 on normal Sundays. This church, which would be called St. Peter's, was set on a hill looking down over the water of Cosman's Creek and James's shipyard.[7]

At first, Weeks seemed to be settling in as the new missionary. He married Susanna Jenkins in Digby, on February 12, 1801, and bought a plot of land the following June. By September the frame of the parsonage house was up, and the roof would be on shortly. In another summer the missionary and his family, which would then be three, could hope to move into it.

Yet trouble lay ahead. In 1802, James sent a memorial to the bishop to have Weymouth erected into a parish, the petition to be forwarded to Governor Wentworth with the bishop's endorsement. But Inglis stalled, worrying about the new parish glebe, which he saw as essential for its support. Delicately he insisted: "If my Memorial concerning the Glebe is thus delayed, the Governor will naturally think, either that the friends of the Church at Weymouth are luke warm and indolent in the business, or that nothing of any weight can be offered to prevent an alienation of the Glebe, neither of which, I trust is the case."[8] The bishop was all too close to the mark, in both suggestions. The new clergyman found ministering to his scattered flock difficult; perhaps unlike the robust Viets, he suffered from seasickness. Nor was he a match for the New Light Baptist enthusiasm that was "infecting" the county and the neighbourhood of Sissiboo, through the preaching of the inspirational Enoch Towner.

Towner was seen as an immediate threat to Sissiboo Anglicans. A New England Loyalist who had served as a sergeant in one of the provincial regiments during the American Revolution, he was, by 1790, settled in Granville Township. He had been a devout Anglican, even elected a church warden. His conversion came after attending a New Light service where Joseph Dimock was preaching, the same Dimock who would visit Sissiboo a year later. Like many people, including James, Towner went to the meeting to hear for himself the "strange things"[9] that were being pronounced. Within a few years, he too was spreading the New Light message as an itinerant Baptist clergyman.

In 1799, Towner was ordained pastor of the newly organized Sissiboo Baptist Church, the first in old Digby Township. It was a church in the sense of an institution or a parish, not in the sense of a building. Avoiding the towns, it took in as its territory the rural communities of present-day Digby County. Towner's followers were largely "nominal Episcopalians" living in the countryside. Among his converts in the Sissiboo area was the wife of Reuben Hankinson, James's

Sissiboo neighbour and fellow officer in the First Battalion of the New Jersey Volunteers, and the wife of Benjamin McConnell, another Loyalist friend, to whom James gave his sword. The husbands continued to contribute to the Anglican Church although Baptist meetings were often held at their houses.[10] Other adherents were the old Congregationalists like the Sabean family, that Dimock had converted.

Towner particularly infuriated Weeks and Viets, by marrying two members of the Titus family, Loyalist Anglican converts to his church, living on Digby Neck, in their very own parish. As in England at the time, licences to marry Protestants were issued only to Justices of the Peace and ministers of the Church of England. This privilege gave a much needed supplement to the incomes of Anglican clergymen. The bishop saw Towner's action as an encroachment by religious "enthusiasts" on the prerogatives of the Anglican Church. All three Anglican clergymen saw the New Lights as "democrats," bent on overthrowing established government in yet another horrific revolution. Actually, as James had found, the New Lights were anything but revolutionaries.

Viets lodged a complaint with the Court of Marriage and Divorce, a court made up of the governor and the Council. The trial, held in Halifax in 1800, was prosecuted by Attorney General Richard John Uniacke, with the equally distinguished Simon Bradstreet Robie defending Towner. The judgement came down in favour of Towner for a number of sensible reasons, as well as the two legalistic ones that the Church of England had not been formally established in Nova Scotia by a special act of the provincial legislature and that the officiating clergyman was a regularly ordained pastor, loyal and teaching the essential tenets of the Established Catechism. Of course this raised Towner's stature even further.

Worse still, Weeks was having disagreements within his own congregation. He had tangled unpleasantly with the large Jones family. James was writing soothing letters to the bishop, being "clearly of the opinion that the matter would drop and all differences be amicably adjusted."[11] But subscriptions were falling off. The parishioners were showing a reluctance either to pay Weeks his salary or to get on with the building of his house. The strong support for the Church of England evident when the Loyalists first arrived had by now weakened. Weeks's appointment had come too late.

Equally important, the quarrel over the titles to the glebe land brought the new church into direct confrontation with the Catholic, French-speaking Acadians. The land reserved for the glebe lay on the west side of the Sissiboo River in the district of Clare, while the church and most parishioners were situated on the east side of the river. The river formed a natural limit to this French settlement where the returning Acadians had begun to establish themselves after the close of the Seven Years War. After an initial hesitation, they had preferred to regroup as a larger Acadian community along the south shore of Saint Mary's Bay, rather than live scattered among the Protestant English-speaking communities. In 1803, they would petition the governor against the erection of any Anglican parish in Clare, "or the taking of any part of it into the new Parish because we are of the Religion of Rome."[12]

Quite apart from the religious aspect, the physical possession of the land was in dispute. The Acadians had cleared part of this land, built their houses on it, and begun to farm it as early as 1764. In 1768, Clare had been officially designated an Acadian area, as was Argyle to the south. Grants along the south shore of Saint Mary's Bay were made to Acadians from 1771 onward as the population expanded. By 1803, a third generation of returnees was pressing for land in the area. It was explained to the new surveyor-general, Charles Morris, that although they did not all have registered deeds — the licences and certificates they had been issued before the Loyalist survey allowed them only the privileges of tenants — the fact that they had occupied the land peaceably for more than 21 years gave them rights of possession.[13] Moreover, if evicted, these people would be destitute. In a letter to James, the bishop described these representations as "artful methods" taken "to impose upon" Morris "in this business in which he was not well acquainted."[14] It was further contended that these Acadians had appropriated to their own use church land adjoining their own.

Defending the Acadians against much of the rest of the parish were three prominent Anglican Loyalists who owned land on the New Edinburgh or western side of the river. These were Colonel John Taylor who had commanded the Acadian militia from 1793 until James succeeded him and whom James had defeated in the election of 1799, and Judge Josiah Jones and his cousin Cerano Upham Jones, originally from Massachusetts.

Glebe lands were a continual problem in the British colonies, where the surveying seems to have been slipshod, deliberately or otherwise. As we have seen, these reserved lands were to be a capital base for income for the clergyman of the parish, bound to accrue in value as ever more settlers arrived.

However, as the settlers themselves were equally hopeful of land-value appreciations, and often highly skilled in land speculation, the best tracts in a settlement quickly tended to become the property of resident individuals rather than institutions. Both Taylor and the Joneses had bought up vacant lots on the New Edinburgh side during the final decades of the old century. Leasing land was unprofitable over the long term because in the New World almost anyone could quite quickly raise enough money to own land. Besides, much of the land was, and still is, infertile, rocky, or covered with dense forest. James himself had a "wilderness grant" in Clare, though not on reserved land, that the Acadians laid claim to.

In New Jersey, where the multiplicity of religious and national groups made any public support of one church unthinkable, lands for church use had been donated by private individuals. No doubt it was following this practice that James had given his own land for the church at Sissiboo. However, everywhere in Nova Scotia the official glebe and school lands were coveted by lay inhabitants, especially if they gave promise of producing revenue. Reverend Jacob Bailey in Annapolis had fought hard and expensively to hold his glebe.[15] Even in Digby, with its large Loyalist Anglican congregation, the original glebe allotment had to be redesignated. The growing strength of the Baptists was also eroding public support for the privileged position of the Anglican Church.

In Weymouth, the situation was further complicated by the war with France and the latent fear that the Acadians might sympathize with their mother country. James, as militia colonel, and Wentworth, as governor, were obviously working together to avert such a threat. In correspondence conducted between the two during the autumn of 1803, Sir John gave politic praise to "the wise and loyal conduct of the Rev. Mr. Sogogne [sic] and his Acadian parishioners," which he said gave him "sincere pleasure and does them great honour." He went on to discuss a recent sermon by the Catholic priest:

I esteem his sermon highly, as a sensible pious and excellently well timed discourse, and a good example to all Denominations of Protestants who are unfeignedly attached to their Religion, which they enjoy in Safety thro' the protection of the British Government, of which we are the happiest part. Christians therefore, of all Men on Earth, have the most serious cause of loyalty and zealous fidelity to our most excellent King and Constitution.... I beg you to present my regards and best thanks to Mr. Sogogne, and assure him and his people of my friendship and protection.[16]

Wentworth then enclosed several copies of the Alien Act, passed in 1798, to be locally distributed and enforced, "as we have reason to believe french Emissaries are every where employed to corrupt and destroy."[17]

Father Jean-Mandé Sigogne was a 40-year-old French royalist priest who had come out from England to serve the Acadians of Clare and Argyle only four years earlier. He was as antipathetic to French republican ideas as any British governor could have wished. The year of the letter just quoted, he was preaching to his parishioners civil submission to the civil authority, even threatening damnation and excommunication to would-be recalcitrants. Wentworth had asked him to receive the oath of allegiance from Acadians in his region.[18]

As for the enforcement of the Alien Act, with the renewal of hostilities with France in 1803, Wentworth was concerned that French government agents were again trying to encourage a French-supported republic among the Acadians. He may have also been worried about provocateurs among escaped French prisoners of war who could easily and quickly assimilate with the French-speaking colonists. Most of them, at least under Father Sigogne's tutelage, were not urging subversion, but rather happily burying themselves in the community. Indeed Father Sigogne was delighted to have them, and made use of their skills.

Sigogne was an exceptional man and a lasting force for good in the area. Born in the Loire Valley, not far from Tours where he studied for the priesthood, he was a well-educated, cultivated man. As "loyal" as his English-speaking colleagues, he had, when the French Revolution broke out, refused to sign the new oath to the state and had, as a result, not only been expelled from his own family but also forced to flee to England in the summer of 1792. Here, over the next seven years, supported by a committee for refugee clergy, he taught French, Latin, Greek, and geography, and learned English. Meanwhile, with Wentworth's support, the Acadian community had been petitioning since 1796 for a priest from among the French royalist émigrés. Finally, a fellow émigré priest in Boston sent over the 20 guineas necessary for the transatlantic passage. In April 1799, Sigogne sailed to Halifax. By mid-July he was established in Clare.

Sigogne's first description of his long-neglected flock reminds one of Chandler's earlier shock at the state of irreligion of the inhabitants of Sussex County in 1769. Sigogne wrote that the Acadians were "un peuple ignorant et d'une ignorance crasse ... entachés des idées d'égalité et de liberté ou plutôt de license et de libertinage." Indeed, his Halifax Catholic superior, the Irish Father James Jones, had warned him that he would be dealing with people who were difficult to manage, "true Americans in regard to their ecclesiastical regulations."[19]

Sigogne was a frail man, small in stature, and seemingly modest to timidity, but was nevertheless as determined as he was devout. He quickly set about getting his community back on track, baptising, confirming, and marrying hundreds of people who had been living without these sacraments, and setting up councils of elders to help lead the young and the fractious back to grace. As a last resort, he had no compunction in using the weapon of excommunication. Rather harshly, he absolutely forbade dancing.

As courageous and indefatigable as Viets in his pastoral duties, Sigogne travelled through the bush over forest trails on horseback between Sainte-Marie, today's Church Point, and Sainte-Anne-du-Ruisseau in the Argyle district, a distance of 90 kilometres. He also ministered in the other direction to isolated Roman Catholics along the upper half of Saint Mary's Bay from Sissiboo to Digby. He interested himself in the Mi'Kmaq, learning their language, soliciting government help for them, and founding, much later in the 1830s, a mission for them at Bear River where many still live today.

In addition, he managed to raise money and oversee the building of new churches at Sainte-Anne and Sainte-Marie, and others later, as the Acadian population increased. He set up schools to teach reading and catechism, using some of the better-educated, escaped French prisoners as teachers. "Ignorance is a vice," he used to say, "a vice which places you in an inferior position with regard to educated people."[20] But, like Weeks, he had continual trouble collecting his own salary from his parishioners.

Sigogne maintained good relations with the English-speaking Protestant leaders in the county and the province. He liked to exchange presents of apples and wine, and books, which he loved, with his Protestant neighbours, and he enjoyed an evening of intellectual discussion over these and other matters of burning concern, such as education and roads. In 1819, when the new Digby Agricultural Society was formed, he was chosen vice-president to Viets's president.[21] He acted as the private spokesman for members of his community, and also as their public champion, learning how to draw up registers and deeds and petitions with the help of his English-speaking friends.[22] In 1806, at the height of the glebe struggle, he was sworn in by James as justice of the peace for Clare Township. From the very beginning, Sigogne had Wentworth's support as priest and leader of the Acadians.

In Weymouth in 1802, Bishop Inglis had no intention of giving up his church's glebe. He insisted that the case revolved around whether the Acadians had been warned that they were occupying lands already granted. This James attested to. Inglis considered the whole attempt to "alienate" church property as "sacrilegious," "dictated by malevolence or low self-interest,"[23] and saw it as a test of glebe grants throughout the province. Although the governor approved the formation of the parish that summer and passed James's memorial on to the surveyor-general, the SPG, reading the bishop's reservations, resolved otherwise: "as there appears to be so little probability of the people fulfilling their engagements after so many years vain expectation of it, the Society cannot ... establish the mission of Weymouth."[24]

In August, the bishop, after his visitation in Annapolis, brought his son and new daughter-in-law to stay with the Moodys in Weymouth. Soon afterwards, it became official that Weeks would leave Weymouth to take up the mission of his dead father, the Reverend Charles Weeks, in Guysborough. It should have been a gracious retreat.

Unfortunately, the clergyman's departure was tempestuous. As he presided over his last meeting of the vestry, things got completely out of hand. There was a tie over the election of the church wardens and rowdy members tried to seize control of the proceedings. In an angry hand, Weeks recorded that, "a difference arising as to the appointment and the Persons who met being equally divided I found it necessary, agreeable to what I understand to be the practice in such cases, to appoint one of the Wardens my self, and I do hereby appoint James Moody Esq. to act in that Capacity."[25] And equally angrily, with seven big fat ink splotches, Simeon Jones recorded his side of the story:

At the Meting above mentioned, Mr. Weeks took Upon himself the office of Clerk, and After Nominating James Moody Esq. and Capt. Grigg as Church Wardens — not being able to carry his plan into Execution, took upon himself furthermore the privilege of appointing James Moody Esq. as Warden in direct opposition to the Members — Afterwards Mr. John Cosman says;, as we cannot agree in the choice of Mr. Grigg, let us appoint Mr. Simeon Jones as Church Warden and Mr. James Cosman says yea.[26]

The backing of the bishop was no longer enough.

Weeks was soon away and Viets took up where he had left off in 1799, ministering to all of Saint Mary's Bay as well as the area around Digby. There is no further mention of Simeon Jones or James Moody as churchwardens. Inglis, nevertheless, continued to enlist James's support over the church's control of the glebe lands. By the end of 1805, the glebe grant was officially confirmed. The bishop was now determined to get it producing revenue as speedily as possible. He urged "improvements — so that the land could be divided into farm lots and leased out." [27]

Alas, the bishop was too late. "Improvements" were already taking place, illegally. "Trespassers," probably Acadians who felt they owned the land, had been removing timber, no doubt with the connivance and to the profit of some of their vociferous English-speaking supporters. The alarmed bishop ordered the immediate posting of "advertisements, forbidding all such trespass ... in several places, the most frequented and public, at Weymouth" including "the cutting down all Timber on the Glebe, and declaring that All persons who shall so offend, and are legally convicted of such Trespass shall be prosecuted according to law." By March 22 the notices were posted. One faithful adherent of the church, Samuel Doty, was expressly allowed "to remain in peaceable possession of the lot he now lives on." [28] By now the community was in an uproar, truly split by more than the river. Shockingly, the "No Trespassing" notices "were treated with indecency, torn down and scattered in the Highway and some of them interlined with scurrilous words not fit to be mentioned." [29]

But worse was soon to follow. If the bishop could get tough, so could others. With the more moderate weather of June, the churchwardens called upon a commissioned surveyor, Major Robert Timpany, to run out the lines and partition off the glebe and school lands. Word of their purpose had preceded them. When they arrived on the New Edinburgh common, they found an angry group of Acadians already assembled there, with Taylor, who had been negotiating for them in Halifax, and the two Joneses, all set to forcibly prevent their carrying out the survey. "Judge Jones told us in the face of the public that he was going to fence in that Land tomorrow and we should find him there," the churchwardens later reported. Before actual bodily harm was effected, Taylor produced the clincher: "a grant with the Seal of the Province to 18 people of 10 Acres each which Lands are within the lines of the Glebe, but in the grant sent to us there is no mention or description made."

There is no doubt that the original surveying in 1783 had been sloppy and had ignored, in the town plan of New Edinburgh, land already occupied. The opposition carried the day, declaring sternly, "that they would not allow any entry to be made on those lands until the matter was decided by a regular course of Law which they were ready to submit." [30]

The bishop had lost the battle, though he was not yet willing to concede defeat. In 1808, he suggested that at least the land not claimed could be leased for the benefit of the church. James received a last letter on the subject in January 1809, three months before his death. The bishop had persuaded the new governor to his side. This last had declared that the title of the church was clear, and insisted that people illegally on glebe land would have to be made to leave, through a court of law if necessary. But the Acadians remained in possession of their land.

In this dispute James was clearly in an awkward position. He favoured an established Anglican parish and clergyman for Weymouth, but at the same time he was constantly working with the Acadians as commander of the Clare militia and as their representative in the House of Assembly. The bishop was pressing him hard. It is also evident that Taylor and the Joneses would not lose financially by a decision that opened up the church land for private gain. James seems to have believed negotiation could have brought about a settlement had both sides not forced the issue. Moreover, he was quickly losing his energy. When the final push came he supported the church's claim. The longer the delay the more entrenched the Acadians became. Perhaps because of Weeks's shortcomings, or lack of numbers, or sympathy for the Acadians, support, even Anglican, for the church's demands against them was not strong enough to win out.

When James was no longer there, the issue of the glebe was dropped, and with it the possibility of a permanent clergyman for Weymouth for almost another two decades. The proposed parish at Weymouth was too remote and too scattered in population. On the east lay Digby, and on the west lay the Acadian settlements, stretching as far as Yarmouth, cutting off expansion in that direction. Neither the bishop nor the governor would support wholeheartedly the formation of a separate parish from among these quarrelling Anglicans, while the bishop's rigidity over the glebe promoted dissension within the church's adherents. James wanted an Anglican parish, but neither he nor the governor nor most of the community were willing to evict the

Acadians from their land. In the end, the Anglican Church lost the glebe land. In 1835, the Acadians finally received unequivocal title to their holdings.

As for the establishment of a clergyman, once New England Loyalists, like the Jones family, were at odds with New Jersey Loyalists, like James and Grigg, this tiny community had no hope of supporting an Anglican mission in the face of competition from vigorous evangelical sects. By contrast, the Anglican community at more populous Digby had largely transplanted itself whole from Charles Inglis's congregation of Trinity Church, New York. It seemed to have a cohesive strength that Weymouth still lacked.

Nevertheless, in spite of its difficulties, the Anglican church in Weymouth did survive. With no resident minister, it kept its community and its organization intact for the next 23 years. It was the Baptist, Enoch Towner, who moved on in 1806. Perhaps it was the sound foundation that James had laid in those early years of lay reading and the example he had set that made this possible.

In 1826, a minister was at last sent to Weymouth. By this time the Archbishop of Canterbury had agreed to a more generous stipend for the church's Nova Scotia missionaries, accepting the fact that other religious denominations were now too strong to allow the government to favour an officially established Anglican Church.

Jane Moody would be among the first to welcome the new minister.

NOTES

1. Rupert B. Blauveldt, *Holy Trinity — Anglican Church, Yarmouth, N.S.* (Yarmouth, NS: 1972), illustration, 21.
2. Charles Inglis to Dr. Morice, 25 Nov. 1792, Inglis Family Papers, MG23 C6 Ser. 1, vol. 2, p. 40, NAC.
3. Charles Inglis to James Moody, 19 Sept. 1798, Moody Papers.
4. *Ibid.*, 12 Nov. 1798.
5. *Ibid.*
6. These dimensions are extrapolated from the measurements of the pews laid out in 1823 when the church was being restored, in readiness at last for a permanent minister and separate parish.
7. See Brian Cuthbertson, *The First Bishop: A Biography of Charles Inglis* (Halifax, NS: Waegwoltic Press, 1987). I am indebted for this material on church construction to his chapter, "Churches and Worship," 122-35.
8. Charles Inglis to James Moody, 28 July 1802, Moody Papers.

9. Isaiah W. Wilson, *A Geography and History of the County of Digby, Nova Scotia* (Halifax, NS: Holloway Bros., 1900; Canadiana Reprint Series no. 39, Belleville, Ont.: Mika Publishing, 1985), 313.

10. *Ibid.*, 314. A next generation of McConnells, Hankinsons, and Marrs emigrated to Elgin County in present-day Ontario, and formed there in Malahide Township a vigorous Baptist community. The McConnells took with them James's sword, which was paraded as a symbol of loyalty to the Crown in the rebellion of 1837. Newton McConnell, "'Malahide' School Section no. 3 Gravesend, Ontario," *A Pioneer History of Elgin County*, prize-winning school essays published by James S. Brierley in *Southern Counties Journal* (St. Thomas, Ont.: 1896; repr. Pretoria, Ont.: 1971), 91.

11. Inglis to Moody, 28 July 1802, Moody Papers.

12. Charles Inglis to the Archbishop of Canterbury, 16 Feb. 1804, Inglis Family Papers, MG23 C6, Ser. 1, vol. 3, p. 131, NAC.

13. The issue of confirming Acadian land holdings is very complex. The Acadian community tended to work out among themselves who would occupy what and how much land in a given location. For a fuller account of these practices, see the informative chapter "Identity Established," in N.E.S. Griffiths, *The Contexts of Acadian History, 1686-1784*, published for the Centre for Canadian Studies, Mount Allison University (Kingston and Montreal: McGill-Queen's University Press, 1992).

14. Wilson, *History of the County of Digby*, 134. Charles Inglis to James Moody, 28 July 1802, Moody Papers.

15. Jacob Bailey to SPG 29 May, 1788. SPG Journal MG17 B1, vol. 25, p. 94, Reel A-157 NAC. For a broader treatment of the glebes and other issues see Judith Fingard, *The Anglican Design in Loyalist Nova Scotia, 1783-1816* (London: Church Historical Society, 1972).

16. Sir John Wentworth to James Moody, 17 Nov. 1803, Moody Papers.

17. *Ibid.*

18. Gerald C. Boudreau, "Doléances et indolence cléricales envers un peuple délaissé," *Les cahiers de la société historique acadienne* 23, nos. 3, 4 (1992): 132.

19. *Dictionary of Canadian Biography*, vol. 7, 1836 to 1850, s.v. "Sigogne, Jean-Mandé," 802. Mr. Bernard Pothier, the author of this article, gave me Father Sigogne's original French. He translated as follows: "A benighted people (steeped) in crass ignorance ... infected with ideas of equality (and) liberty, or rather licence and libertinism."

20. Sally Ross and J. Alphonse Deveau, *The Acadians of Nova Scotia Past and Present* (Halifax, NS: Nimbus Publishing, 1992), 96.

21. Wilson, *History of the County of Digby*, 277.

22. Sigogne drew up an Acadian land petition for Argyle in 1808 and for Clare in 1817. He also much later collaborated with Thomas

Haliburton to bring about the abolition of the Test Oath for political office, an oath that in effect had barred Roman Catholics from office since the reign of Queen Anne. Ross and Deveau, *The Acadians*, 84.

23. Charles Inglis to James Moody, 11 Aug. 1802, Moody Papers. *Ibid.*, 4 Jan. 1809.

24. General Meeting SPG, 18 March 1803, SPG Journal, MG17 B1, vol. 28, p. 346, Reel A-158 NAC.

25. Vestry Records.

26. *Ibid.*

27. Charles Inglis to Churchwardens, St. Peter's Church, 21 Jan. 1806, Vestry Records.

28. John Grigg and John Cosman, 1 May 1806; Charles Inglis to Churchwardens, Jan. 21, 1806, Vestry Records.

29. John Grigg and John Cosman to Charles Inglis, 23 June 1806, Vestry Records.

30. *Ibid.*

20

FADING OUT, 1806-09

JAMES DID NOT RUN for a third term in the Nova Scotia House of Assembly. A progressive and paralyzing illness was sapping his strength. For the next three years, as his executors' petition said, "he would continue in a weak and languishing way from thence forward to the day of his death."[1] His illness became acute in the summer of 1806, which perhaps explains how matters over the glebe were allowed to deteriorate so dramatically. In fact, his whole world was crashing around him.

In April 1806, there was a judgement against James's son, John, in favour of William and Robert Pagan, merchants in Saint John, New Brunswick for £200 1s 6d, including costs.[2] Loyalists from Penobscot, Maine, the Pagans were highly successful merchants, shipbuilders, and county representatives in St. Andrew's, New Brunswick. The bill may have been for the work done earlier for the schooner *Yorke*, which amounted to just over £184.[3] The court execution was stayed until October 1808, when the debt had to be paid. In the court order John is described as an "absconding debtor," which means that he was not present at the trial. He could have run off or merely been out of the country. Presumably the court believed he could pay the debt within the next two years.[4]

In September 1806, there was a hurricane in the West Indies which wrecked a number of ships both at sea and in harbour. In the 18 November 1806 issue of the *Nova-Scotia Royal Gazette*, an item appeared mentioning the arrival of Mr. John Moody, supercargo of the brig *Aurora*, owned by Messrs Prescott and Lawson of Halifax, wrecked off Dominica, on September 9, in a violent storm.[5] The supercargo was the man who handled the selling of the cargo, and earned a percentage as remuneration. Did John, with his West Indies connections, go off to recoup the family fortunes? Or is this the John Moody, merchant and auctioneer, of Halifax? (There were at least four unrelated James-John Moody families in Nova Scotia at this time.)

During the summer, James took to his bed, too weak to hold a pen and deeply depressed. His friends worried for his life. In early September, Inglis wrote from Halifax to express his concern. Thomas Millidge had brought the news. Was it a continuance of his old complaint, the bishop asked, or was it something new? "I lament the distance that is between us, which puts it out of my power to pay You a visit.... For I am sensible how chearing the face & conversation of a friend are when we are laid on a bed of sickness," his old friend continued, no doubt remembering the hours of vigil James had sat by his bed in London.

Then he attempted to administer the spiritual comfort that had helped him through difficult periods in his own life:

We live in a world where everything is uncertain & transient — where trials & disappointments constantly await us — & where our earthly comforts are of a brittle texture, & often fail to bring relief. This is our state, nor should we repine at it, since it is the will of our heavenly Father, who consults our truest happiness; & knows what is best for us.... Redeeming love is the cordial of life, the anchor of the Soul, which supports it, when every thing else fails. — May it prove such to You, my good friend. May it, under the influence of divine Grace, animate & chear You under any dispensation which your heavenly father may be pleased to send.[6]

A friend who did come to visit him that September was the governor. He wrote from Digby on the 16th, that he and Lady Wentworth were on their way to take him by the hand. "We propose to be with you as soon as the roads permit our Chair wheels to pass, to morrow." They brought with them two army friends. Jane as well as James must have welcomed this diversion.

In October, his own business affairs in a tangle, and perhaps spurred by the realization that his son would never be able to pay off his debts in time, James took out a huge mortgage with the firm of Goodall and Turner. This was a London merchant and banking house used by many Loyalists in which Brooke Watson had been the head and whose representatives in Halifax were James Foreman and George Grassie. To be paid in a year's time, the bond was for £2,159 12s 1d, three farthings, plus interest, and penalties for late payment which would soon have doubled that amount. It had as collateral all the land of any value that James owned, except his water lots and his shipyard, and his half interest in the mill pond dam and mill. It even included his house and the three lots he used as farm land, which alone amounted to 1000 acres.[7]

We do not know exactly how he became so indebted. In 1798 when he made out his will, he was still a very prosperous man. In 1809 the probate inventory valued his estate at £3,544 10s, but later revalued it at not quite half that amount. This did not include his shorefront property. He also received £88 19s 4 1/2 d sterling per annum, from his two pensions. He had been paid £634 4s of the £1,608 awarded on an original claim of £1,719 10s by the Loyalist Claims Commission, and had been left £5,000 from an English admirer. This he had invested heavily in his shipbuilding.

After his death, his executors wrote that "owing to unfortunate mercantile concerns," he "became involved in Debt to an extent far beyond the value of his personal effects and in consequence was induced to mortgage the whole of his said landed property in fee to Messrs. Foreman Grassie & Co. for the securing a large Sum of money due to them."[8] In another petition, Jane mentions that "in consequence of a generous Act rendered by him toward a fellow creature she is now left without means to supply herself through the short remaining period of her Life."[9]

The Weymouth registry records show that James lent out a great deal of money. Some of these loans were never repaid, and others were discounted. Perhaps as the principal man of the neighbourhood he felt compelled to do this. Perhaps there were more loans that were not even secured. A month before he took out his own loan, James gave a mortgage to William Muir of Digby, for £500, which he then reduced in early October to £400. This alone would have strapped him for cash.[10] Was this his kindness? This mortgage was also part of the collateral to Foreman and Grassie. It was repaid in 1809 at less than face value.

However, the overall problem was deeper and beyond his control. It was due to two basic factors: the war with France and the poverty of his region. During his first seven years in the province, his shipbuilding had taken advantage of a postwar shortage of British bottoms, a surplus of easily obtainable lumber, and British government commercial protection against the Americans in the West Indian trade, with the added bonus of a bounty on the tonnage of his first ship. These had made his shipbuilding business highly profitable. It had provided employment in the neighbourhood and capital he was able to lend out for other projects. During this time, he also built docks and warehouses, and shortly afterwards, his dam and its two mills, grist and lumber. He also invested in another lumber mill upstream at the Sissiboo Falls. At the same time, he laid the foundation for his sheep farm.

The war with France, beginning in 1793, put an end to the shipbuilding. The risk to his English partners became too great. Indeed most of his vessels were sunk in the next few years and Thomas Yorke in London spent a year in debtor's prison. With the lack of roads and large rivers, the lumber supply in Nova Scotia and in his area was no longer so accessible to the sea or the mills, raising costs to a less competitive margin. Privateering lured the fishermen away from their traditional calling, so that the area's exportable product was not bringing trade into the neighbourhood. Moreover, with the Jay Treaty negotiated in 1794, the British government became more tolerant of American ships trading in the British West Indies, giving up the commercial protection it had afforded to Nova Scotia shipping just after the American Revolutionary War.

The "unfriendly soil" around Weymouth is not particularly good for farming. Although James, unlike many Loyalists of his class, was an experienced farmer, even he could not produce enough hay on his land in 1806, to tide over the winter the cow Prince Edward had sent him.

All of this meant that the local employment James's industry had created was now lost and there was nothing to replace it. No new money was being generated. The people were too poor to pay back the loans he had made, and he was too generous to foreclose. Besides it was cash, not land, that he needed, and cash — specie — was in very short supply because of the war. As a consequence, by 1805 property values had dropped by three-quarters of their previous worth.[11] Selling off bits of his considerable land holdings was no solution: there were no buyers. The area was too poor to sustain his vision.

On the personal side, as he devoted more time after 1793 to public concerns he was perhaps not aware of his financial decline, and probably continued to live more expansively than was prudent, until he was stretched beyond his resources. His son's infirmity and his own failing health further prevented him from working out of the debt.

A side effect of this economic depression was the closing of the little school in Weymouth in 1806. The schoolmaster moved to Saint

John in search of a better livelihood, and the schoolmistress, Anna Towner, followed her husband to Argyle.

And to end this ghastly year of 1806, there was yet another setback, one that must have rankled the sick man. It was more a humiliation than a disaster. It was a libel suit brought against James by Josiah Jones, a judge of the court of common pleas in Weymouth, and member of the extensive Jones family that had been at odds over the glebe with the recent Anglican minister, the Reverend Charles Weeks. The case concerned the church collection money, and must have caused a certain amusement, and perhaps sadness too, in the county and in Saint John where the story was published. Again the facts are tantalizingly fragmentary. They suggest a long-standing rivalry between the Moodys and the Joneses.

James had accused Jones of stealing money from the collection plate while he was churchwarden between 1794 and 1801. The amount was trifling, 10 shillings and 6 pence, out of a total of £7 or £8 over several years. But James insisted when Jones went out of office that Jones had wickedly embezzled the money. When Jones called upon him in 1806 to avow or disclaim the scandal, James, always a man to speak his mind and stand by his judgement, had publicly repeated the charge. At the trial Jones's lawyer observed,

that the slanderous words avowed by the Defendant were such as struck at the very root of the Plaintiff's religious and moral character, and if believed by the public or acquiesced in by his client, must establish an opinion greatly to his disadvantage, as being at once wicked and hypocritical in the most base and pitiful degree. That such an opinion, once established, would attach in some degree to his whole family. That being in a public station, the scandal would have the greater spread; for, already, the eyes and attention of the whole community were in some measure turned upon a Judge against whom there appeared so strange an accusation. That the Defendant moreover holding a respectable rank in society; having been a member of the General Assembly, and in other important offices, was frequently in the way of conferring with people of all stations. That possessing an extensive acquaintance, and having a plausible turn in conversation, he had the means of spreading his slander so generally, so confidentially, and so ingeniously, as not only greatly to injure the Plaintiff by it, but also to put it out of his power by any private efforts to refute it. On all these accounts the Counsel contended that, the Defendant was such a person as is in a high degree answerable for whatever he should venture to say of his neighbour; and the Plaintiff being shewn to be such an one as is intitled to the peculiar protection of the public, and being under something like a necessity of bringing this action.[12]

James's lawyer insisted that James was of such a generous, candid, and manly character that he was "incapable of uttering anything he did not *believe* to be true," that he could only have reaccused the plaintiff through "a love of truth, and a love of making that truth public."

However, the trial soon revealed that no one had actually counted the money between the time it was collected from the congregation, to the time it was handed over to the clergyman, and that, consequently, there was no way to prove that Jones or anyone else had actually stolen any money. The judge in addressing the jury concluded that:

Nothing had appeared in evidence sufficient in any degree to hurt the Plaintiff's reputation with a thinking mind. That the Plaintiff having now gained the purpose of his action, namely, that of clearing up his character, ought not to want to enrich himself by draining the Defendant's pocket. True however it was, that persons standing high in society were particularly bound to be cautious of what they said of their neighbours, and such kind of persons were entitled to be cautiously spoken of. In the present case, neither trifling nor severe damages were to be given. *Something* to mark the displeasure of the Country at the Defendant's imprudence, but not so much as to bear unreasonably heavy upon his circumstances; yet *something* to vindicate the character of the Plaintiff from trifling estimation.[13]

James was made to pay damages of £25. Had he made the charge only in 1806 one would be tempted to accuse him of deteriorating brain power. That he first brought his charge of embezzlement when Weeks was in office suggests a deeper cause in the quarrel, and that the "trifling" disagreement between Weeks and Jones, never really buried, perhaps concerned him too. It was brought out at the trial that James was not a communicant. Was he perhaps a Deist like Washington and Jefferson, and many others in the eighteenth century? As he obviously attended the services and contributed generously to the church, the fact that he did not take holy communion hardly seems relevant to the case. James must have thoroughly detested Josiah Jones. The libel was an act of foolish obstinacy and a bitter end to James's devoted attempt to create a parish in Weymouth. Strangely, the trial does not seem to have diminished James's stature within the Anglican community.

Worse was to follow. In 1807, probably in the spring, according to Moody family accounts, John went to visit friends in Elizabeth Town in New Jersey. While crossing the North River from New York, the ferry he was travelling on collided with another boat. The boat foundered and John was drowned. When the family received the news is not clear, though a series of property transfers suggest sometime in June.

In early July, James made over to John's eldest son, James Budd Moody, a lad of 17, the land that he considered likely to produce the most revenue. This was his shipping property which consisted of: the shipyard; wharves; storehouses; two water lots, totalling 58 acres, which included the mill pond situated at the mouth of Cosman's Creek and the entrance to the mill pond on his side of the Sissiboo River; his half of the mill plot itself, containing the dam and the grist and sawmill; and, on the New Edinburgh side across the river from his house, his third water lot of seven and a half acres, with its adjoining wharf and parcel of land. These properties were not mortgaged to Foreman and Grassie. None of these assets are included in any probate evaluation. James also gave this eldest grandson another key holding which was part of the mortgage. This was a lot upstream on the south side of the Sissiboo Falls which James had rented out two years earlier for the rebuilding of a new dam. It seems likely this action was taken as the result of the tragedy that must have befallen the young man's father. This whole property transference did, in fact, save the family from financial ruin.

In the summer of 1808, James gained enough strength to write to the bishop about the glebe and again in October. In January 1809, Inglis wrote back and ended by saying: "I sincerely sympathise with You & deeply regret, that You still remain in Your languid state; & pray God to support You by his Grace, & sanctify this affliction to Your best & eternal interests. Mrs. Moody, I hope, will show her usual fortitude under this trial, & God grant her the aid which she stands in need of." [14] For James the rest of the winter of 1809 brought more illness. In February, his grandson James was sick too. Father Sigogne was negotiating with Margaret Moody over the winter pasture for Prince Edward's cow, and sent his "humble respects to Col. Moody and Mrs. Moody," and best wishes for the lad's recovery. Whatever his "Infirmity," the loss of James's son must have been devastating and could only have furthered weakened his condition.

The end came on April 6. The cause of death is registered as a "numb palsy," [15] that is paralysis, perhaps the end of multiple sclerosis.

He was 64. He was buried in the churchyard of St. Peter's, the church he had struggled so hard to see built and functioning. Since his illness all construction had stopped. Its steeple had never been closed in and, like his own fences, was falling into decay. The Reverend Roger Viets came from Digby to read the burial service and one wonders what aspect the building presented on that chilly April Monday. Loyal hearts tried to give it warmth in a grand military funeral, with detachments of the Digby and Clare regiments of militia doing the honours, and friends and comrades from Digby and the surrounding country present to pay their last respects to this man who had given so much during his life.[16]

On his tombstone of red sandstone, now unreadable, was carved the moving verse:

> Here lies the Man who once of tranquil mind
> Felt friendly sympathy to all Mankind
> His Country valued and his Sovereign loved
> While honest zeal his patient valor moved
> His Soul has fled above on Angels wings
> And lives triumphant with the King of Kings.

Not a pompous word about his exploits or his achievements, just a celebration of his devotion.

A man of great physical and mental energy, with an ironic self-deprecating sense of humour, James had been loved and respected by his contemporaries. His flair for the dramatic had made him a good storyteller. It had also saved his life on several occasions during the Revolution. Though boldly outspoken, he had been able to express his criticisms of authority gracefully, upholding his point of view in a conciliatory manner. Quick to judge people and circumstances, once he had made up his mind, he had never wavered in his course of action. His imagination had seen both sides of a situation so that his sometimes violent sense of outrage had, in a crisis, been held in check by his sense of compassion for the circumstances of his opponent. Enjoying people, he had been unstinting in his generosity and his loyalty, perhaps too much so, failing in the end to take proper care of his own interests. During the American Revolution he had set an example of courage and probity. His narrative of his experience during the war had brought home to sceptical people in England the true nature of the passion and the sacrifice of the Loyalists for the British constitution.

The same characteristics that had carried him through this struggle had helped him to prosper in his new life in Nova Scotia. Here, as with many other Loyalists, the goals he had set were beyond his circumstances. The province and the community at Weymouth were as yet too underpopulated, too scattered, and in the end too poor, to support these projects. They would be for future generations to accomplish. He had laid the basis that would allow them to prosper.

NOTES

1. Proceedings of the Executors of the Will of Col. James Moody, Digby, 12 Feb. 1810, Moody Papers, PANS, MG 1, vol. 2684, no. 115.
2. Described in the Sheriff's sale of property of John Moody to Elijah McConnell, 16 Nov. 1808, Weymouth Registry Office, Bk. 6, p. 98.
3. Account Book of John Ward, General Merchant, Saint John, NB, Archives of NB, A 141, 3-4, and following.
4. Unfortunately all the records for this period for Digby Township were destroyed when the courthouse burned in the nineteenth century.
5. *The Royal Nova-Scotia Gazette*, vol. 6, no. 310, 18 Nov. 1806, 2, 3.
6. Charles Inglis to James Moody, 2 Sept. 1806, Moody Papers.
7. Mortgage to Foreman and Grassie, 7 Oct. 1806, Weymouth Registry, Bk. A 1, pp. 222-26.
8. Proceedings of the Executors of the Will of Col. James Moody. The will is no. 106 in the Moody Papers.
9. Petition for continuation of James Moody's pension by his widow Jane Moody, PANS, RG1, vol. 225, Doc. 80.
10. *Ibid.*, Bk. 5, p. 167.
11. Petition of Halifax Merchants, William Sabatier, James Fraser and others, *House of Assembly Journals*, 1805, 27.
12. *Saint John Gazette*, 29 Dec. 1806, 3, NAC.
13. *Ibid.*
14. Charles Inglis to James Moody, 4 Jan. 1809, Moody Papers.
15. Roger Viets, Notitia Parochialis of Trinity Parish, Digby, Nova Scotia, beginning July 12th, 1786.
16. *Nova Scotia Royal Gazette*, 16 May 1809.

IV

EPILOGUE

21

FAMILY

JAMES HAD LEFT A DEVOTED FAMILY, but also a vulnerable one. Jane did indeed need all the aid that God could give her. Not only had she lost "an affectionate husband"[1] but she and her daughter-in-law, Margaret, must take on alone the raising of her husband's four Nova Scotia grandsons, who were as dear to her as if they had been her own. Fortunately, she had good friends and wise heads to help her. Needless to say Inglis, Wentworth, and Prince Edward, now the Duke of Kent, supported her petition to receive her husband's military pension. After two tries she was successful in being paid £81 yearly, Nova Scotia currency, £50 sterling. The financial tangle of her husband's affairs was sorted out over the next few years by obtaining an annulment of the entail on James's property. In this way, the land could be sold in fee simple and most of the debts paid off. Debts owed to James were collected usually for considerably less than the original sum.

In spite of these difficulties, Jane continued a kindly, warm person, very much the centre of her family. She and Margaret remained in Weymouth and worked closely together to bring up James's grandchildren and great grandchildren. Jane's deep love for all of them comes through in her letters. Of John Wentworth Moody, her husband's second grandson, she wrote just after his death, "I have viewd his growing virtues from early life with very great pleasure and satisfaction — and promised my self more than I ought and am now sensable that I placed my affections two much on him, he was two great a treasure for

Elisha William Budd Moody, grandson of James Moody, later Yarmouth shipowner and philanthropist. Miniature in the possession of John Wentworth Moody, Ottawa

us to possess." [2] There is every indication that she was equally devoted to the other children.

She was also kind to those outside her family. There is a letter written in 1819 concerning a new clergyman going to Yarmouth, urging her grandson, James Budd Moody, to pay what attention he can to him. "He is a stranger in a strange land and attention in that case is very greatfull," she wrote.[3] She and Margaret gave strong support to the Anglican community as it struggled on without a minister. In 1823, when the Weymouth church members reactivated the church in readiness for the establishment of a permanent minister, both ladies were quick to buy pews, and make further financial contributions. The next year, Jane was thanked for "her liberal donation to the Church in the Hangings for the Pulpit, reading desk and Communion."[4] In 1832, she "sold" for one pound two acres of shore front property beside the church to the newly arrived Reverend Alfred Gilpin, seeing at last the establishment of Weymouth as an Anglican parish. One hopes that the slave "wench" that James had left her did indeed stay with her till the end of her life.[5]

A little family flurry was caused in late November 1817. A letter arrived addressed to Colonel James Moody of Nova Scotia, from a John Moody of Licking County, Ohio. The writer claimed to be the son of William Moody, the supposed third child of James and Elizabeth Moody of New Jersey. Charles Moody had forwarded this to William Brittain, one of James's first wife's Loyalist brothers settled in New Brunswick, presumably for clarification or perhaps to alert him. Then, 11 years later the same man appeared in New Brunswick stating that his grandmother, Elizabeth Moody (that is James's first wife), was living in New York. The man also wanted information about other members of the family.[6]

On looking into the records, this author discovered that there were Moodys in Licking and Knox counties in Ohio. They were descended from William Moody, the only son of a James William Moody who died in Newfoundland. William Moody had gone to Ohio from Northumberland County, Pennsylvania about 1805. He had a son John, but this last was born about 1810, making him too young to be the letter writer. Another John Moody from Licking County, of the right age, fought for the Americans in the War of 1812.[7] There seems, however, to be no connection with the James Moody of Sissiboo. One would like to have seen William Brittain's comments.

The four Nova Scotia grandsons would have made James proud. James Budd Moody and John Wentworth Moody went into business together with a store on Brier Island and also worked for another John Moody, the merchant and auctioneer in Halifax who had, despite the name, no family connection. When John Wentworth suddenly died of typhus, at the age of 22 in Yarmouth, James Budd took on his younger brother Elisha William Budd, as a business partner. The two became very successful in the shipping business in Yarmouth. They married sisters within a few years of each other. James Budd was elected to the House of Assembly, and represented Lloyds for the western end of the province. He was a founding member and treasurer of the Yarmouth Book Society, the first public library in Nova Scotia. When he died in 1828 he left five very young children. His mother gathered in three of them until they were old enough to go to school. The older two stayed with Elisha William Budd in Yarmouth.

Elisha succeeded his brother as Lloyd's agent. He was active in the Yarmouth Education Society, which through private subscription and public money built the Yarmouth Academy, after the demise of the Yarmouth Grammar School. One can understand his interest in education since he now had two families of children to provide for. He was soon the largest shipping magnate in Yarmouth. In 1838, he launched the first barquentine in Nova Scotia and fittingly christened her *The Loyalist.* He alone of the four grandsons lived out his full life and only died in 1863 at the age of 65, two years older than his grandfather. At the time he was justice of the peace and "custos rotulorum" (president of the bench of magistrates) of Yarmouth County.

Charles Coulbourne Moody, the youngest of the grandsons, stayed in Weymouth where he supported the Anglican Church like the rest of his family, serving as vestry clerk and churchwarden. He was a merchant farmer, in business with a son of Thomas Millidge in a store situated on Shipyard Point. He died in 1851, aged 49.

In the end it was Elisha who took in the widows in his family. Jane moved to Yarmouth in 1820 and lived there with Elisha at "Buena Vista," a handsome three-storey bow-fronted house that still stands, until she died in 1837. His mother, Margaret Moody, remained in Weymouth running the farm and overseeing her mother-in-law's land. In 1820, she wrote Elisha, "At ten at night I sit down to write you for fear I will not have time in the Morning. We are in our Hey and a number of work people to wait on that I have not one Moment to sit down till dark so I can be very Fashionable too with my Tea without putting myself out the least bit."[8] Earlier in the week she had been picking fruit in the pouring rain to send to him. In 1837, Elisha wrote "My mother is very much broken from hard work and looks very old for her years."[9] One is hardly surprised since the kind lady had been raising children most of her adult life. She too died at "Buena Vista," in 1848.

James's daughter Maria also died in 1848. After moving to London, she had given birth to two daughters, Jane Maria and Mary Ann. The family had then taken up residence in Boulogne where their money could go farther than in London. Maria's husband, James Taylor, continued as agent for Lloyds and had during the years some business contact with Elisha. Maria's eldest child and only son, James Moody Taylor, was a moderately successful solicitor in London. He sired ten children, nine of whom grew to adulthood. He acted as the family's government liaison, collecting and forwarding documents for various petitions. Maria's second daughter, Mary Ann, married a Mr. Brown, a Scotsman, who held a position in the office of the Signet, and went with him to live near Liberty, Missouri, where she and their new baby died in 1838. Maria kept in contact with her Weymouth relations. In 1845, she and Elisha met in Boulogne, where her only surviving daughter, Jane Maria, lived with her and had earlier taken on the education of her brother's eldest daughter. If the women were as charming as their letters, the young girl had been in good hands.

The family continues to produce engineers, business men and scientists, artists and writers, men and women quick to spring to their country's defence in time of war. They still devote much kindness in helping those in need, and above all the stranger in a strange land. James left them a good legacy.

NOTES

1. Petition of Jane Moody, 6 Nov. 1810, PANS, RG1, vol. 225, no. 80.
2. Jane Moody to Mr. John Moody, Auctioneer, Halifax, Weymouth, 1 May 1817, Moody Papers.
3. Jane Moody to James Budd Moody, Yarmouth, 26 Jan. 1819.
4. Vestry Records, St. Peter's Church, 1824, Anglican Diocese of Nova Scotia Archives, Halifax.
5. The first codicil to the will of James Moody states: "For the Good liking and tender Regard I have For my wife Jane I further Bequeath her in addition to what is already mentioned, one Bead and Bedding with furniture for a Room the same to be of her own Choosing, and I further give her the Choice of the Wenches to Serve her during her life." The will itself is dated 1798. The codicil is undated. Moody Papers.
6. Moody Papers.
7. The information about the Ohio Moodys comes from Norman Howell Hill's *History of Licking County, Ohio* (Newark, OH: A.A. Graham, 1881), 393, 775, and his *History of Knox County, Ohio* (Mt. Vernon, OH: A.A. Graham, 1881), 745, through the courtesy of John Wentworth Moody, Ottawa.
8. Margaret Budd Moody to Elisha William Budd Moody, Weymouth, 27 July 1820, Moody Papers.
9. Elisha William Budd Moody to Maria Moody Taylor, Yarmouth, 17 Aug. 1837, Moody Papers.

22

LEGEND AND LEGACY

JAMES MOODY HAS BEEN DEAD for nearly two hundred years. In Canada, he is forgotten. But not in America. There his legend lives on in local histories, fireside tales, and even children's books. That he is seen as an obnoxious villain, a traitor, "an atrocious monster of wickedness," a "cannibal," a "turk," goes without saying. Nevertheless, as with some of the other "egregious villains" who dared to fight against the Revolutionary cause, there was also from the very beginning a grudging admiration for his enterprise and his daring. These legends are amusing to look at.

Just after the Revolution, it was unacceptable to have been anything but an ardent Patriot. For the first hundred years, it was not admitted that James had been part of Sussex County at all, and he and his descendants were sworn undying enmity. A noted New Jersey historian of the nineteenth century, Thomas Edsall, in a Centennial Address in 1853 castigates such people as Moody, as "fiends incarnate" and then with Biblical thunder visits the sins of the fathers unto succeeding generations: "He who violates the laws of health, transmits to his posterity a physical curse; and so he who sets at naught all social obligation and stabs with traitorous hand the community which nurtures him, by every principle of political justice, bequeaths a portion of his infamy to the luckless issue of his detested body."[1] Edsall then proceeds to disclaim Moody for Sussex County, passing him on to nearby Hunterdon, and calling him Bonnell Moody. He grudgingly admits that Moody did open the jail in Newton, but insists that this happened a year later.

Edsall goes on to add various accounts collected by one Nelson Robinson, Esq., which have a slight basis of truth. One cold winter night Moody is supposed to have robbed the elderly Robert Ogden, a Patriot of Sparta, Sussex County, of his valuable household silver, and then to have taken him outside and forced him to swear not to call for help until the robber had had time to escape. But someone not bound by oath had given the alarm and the neighbours had followed the Tories' tracks in the snow all the way to Goshen, across the border into New York State. Here they had found the plunderers' camp fires still burning and some of the booty left on the ground. Such an incident may have occurred and the robbery committed by what Moody called "a less conscientious Loyalist," like the two who later confessed to the crime that Robert Maxwell had been hanged for. But the culprit was not James. James was not out on partisan expeditions during the winter. In the summer of 1778 he did, however, force two elderly justices of the peace to take the oath of allegiance to the king.

Another of Robinson's stories is that the Whigs of Newton heard that Moody was hiding in a Tory house. The Whigs descended upon the house and searched it from top to bottom, in every nook and cranny, but could find him nowhere. He was there, though, according to the story, packed in straw under the floor boards, and emerged to escape after his hunters had gone. Perhaps this originates in a similar story recounted by Isaac Swayze about himself in later years. In the Swayze version, his brother Benjamin was killed in lieu of him. Isaac emerged from under the house, alive, very bloody from the bayonets that had been stuck through the floor by searching Patriots, who suspected that he might, indeed, have been lurking there.[2] Other Loyalists were not always so lucky. Such incidents must have happened to many of them.

Yet another story may well have occurred on any of Moody's forays into Sussex County. The story goes that just as the Whigs — one assumes the Patriot militia is meant — "were on the point of springing on him and his band, a Negro conveyed intelligence of their designs, and Moody, with his men, narrowly escaped; the bread which was baking for him, and the other provisions which were prepared, falling into their hands." We do know that the Buchners and Swayzes all claimed to have supplied him rather generously with food in 1780. The fresh bread is particularly appealing.

Less convincing though tantalizing is the account of Moody spying on the American army near Morristown. He is portrayed as being shabbily dressed "on an old broken-down nag ... riding carelessly along before the lines, like a simple-hearted rather soft-headed rustic, not over well supplied with either worldly sense or substance." Someone became suspicious of his odd inquisitiveness, someone else thought he had seen him before, and a horseman was despatched to bring him back. Unfortunately for the horseman, Moody recognized his danger and shot his pursuer dead. Moody then dragged the body into the woods so that no one would be alerted, and himself hid in a nearby swamp. One does wonder how James spied on the army, but he seems to have been much too prudent a man to go about in civilian clothes without a good military alibi as to what he was doing. However, when in May 1781 his group captured the express rider with enemy despatches, they did drag the rider's dead horse into the bushes. Moreover, they had been hiding in a nearby swamp. The captured courier rider they brought back alive to New York with the despatches.

Robinson's final summing up of James's activities in Sussex County is accurate:

Moody is believed to have been employed by the English to obtain recruits in this section of such as might be found favorable to Great Britain. He likewise was to act as a spy upon the movements of the Whigs, and to check and overawe them by a show of opposition in their midst; by making divisions and difficulties close at hand, and thereby "drawing off" their attention and assistance from the Colonial army. For a short period he concealed himself in a cavernous retreat among the rocks at the lower extremity of the Muckshaw Pond, about two miles south of the village of Newton. Two or three miles south-west of this spot, on the Pequest river, resided some disaffected persons, who are suspected of having furnished Moody with supplies while he was hidden in the ravines near the Muckshaw.[3]

Robinson may have collected these stories from people who had been alive at the time of the Revolution. The robbery at Sparta and the shooting of the Whig horseman are repeated in James Snell's *History of Sussex and Warren Counties.*

Moody's Rock in the Muckshaw Pond has particularly fascinated the myth makers. From a damp and snake-infested rock surrounded by swamp it has become a glorious cave, worthy of Ali Baba and the forty thieves, with Turkish rugs and Persian hangings and champagne, a chandelier and the not-yet-invented grand piano. Here he was said to have entertained an Iroquois princess, who liked to roller skate, but who turned down his advances and hanged herself for her own true Iroquois love; and another of whom he tired, the daughter of a Hessian, named Pauline, who, when he failed to return from an expedition, threw herself in despair into the nearby stream, which from then on was called Paulinskill. These are obviously told with tongue in cheek, though the supposed rock is still shown to sightseers.

But the one about the Tory's daughter who died in true highwayman's lover's fashion is equally dramatic. It was written up by a resident of Newton, Augustus C. Schooley — obviously a would-be Longfellow — and printed in the *Sussex Register* of 1885.

> In the hollow west of Newton ...
> When the mantle of the evening
> From all prying eyes concealed them,
> Here they whispered brimful nothings ...
> Here they both high treason plotted.

According to the poem, for some months the course of true love ran smoothly, but eventually the Patriots got wind of the affair. They made a plan to capture Moody at the meeting place. Hearing of the plot, our Tory maiden rode off to warn her lover, but failed to intercept him and so rode back to the tryst. As he approached on his horse, she called out the alarm from hers. The Patriot soldiers, hiding in the bushes, ordered the Loyalist to surrender. Instead, Moody fired, the Patriots returned the salvo, and Moody rode off to the safety of his rock, his "castle on the Muckshaw."

> But the brave girl, so devoted,
> Paid most dearly for his rescue,
> For her horse, now wild with terror,
> Madly reared, and over backward,
> Fell and crushed the helpless maiden,
> Crushed to death the Tory damsel.
> On the very spot a tree grows,
> By the blood of this girl nurtured,
> And the turtle-dove's sad cooing
> You may hear there any day now.

This story would make a wonderful scenario for the death of the first Mrs. Moody. Her father was a staunch Tory and family tradition says she died of a fall from her horse. Did James attempt a quick visit to Sussex County in late February 1782?

On the other hand, an American great-granddaughter had claimed that Elizabeth Brittain Moody was not in favour of her husband's Loyalism. Her three older brothers served in the rebel militia, though how ardently is unknown. However, three other brothers, her husband, and her father were documented Loyalists. Her objection, if it did exist, may well have been a fear for their safety rather than one of a political nature. It could also be an instance of the same no-Loyalist-in-our-family syndrome from which another Brittain descendant has just recently been found to be suffering. The story may also have orig-inated with the letters of 1817 and 1828, from the would-be John Moody descendant. Or she may, indeed, have been a Patriot. We will never know.

The poet Schooley, introducing a little historical verisimilitude, recounts how his own Quaker grandfather, living outside Newton, "between two hostile parties" and "foraged on by either," was visited by Moody:

> There to levy on a filly.
> Which the Quaker prized quite highly.
> Stealthily the Tories gather
> 'Round the barn, but my grandsire
> Got there first and with a pitchfork
> Took his stand within the stable
> And alone repulsed King George's army,
> Saved the filly from the clutches
> Of this bold, bad Ensign Moody.

But the poem goes on to say that the next night "Moody came and got her." The devout old Quaker was so angry that he

> Hired an able-bodied swearer
> To express his indignation
> At the British and the Tories.

The story about the robbery of the Ogden silver at Sparta is further embellished by the supposed existence of an underground passage connecting a cavern known as Devil's Hole, near the Newton town line, to Moody's Rock some miles away. On this occasion, the robbers are said to have disappeared into the cavern, while Patriot troops posted at the entrance, confidently waited to catch them when they re-emerged. The Loyalists never did re-emerge. Five days later, they were spotted in another county, impersonating Yankee soldiers.

Moody is said to have financed his operations in Sussex County with British gold, which is exactly what he did. Actually, as we have seen, the gold, perhaps British-minted, was his own. Tradition has it that he would do his recruiting in Hairlocker's tavern in Newton, buying liquor and tobacco for all comers. We know he paid the recruits their bounty for enlisting out of his own pocket. The local tavern, as a highly public place, seems a risky location for such a traitorous activity. But who knows? He must have met his recruits somewhere. The legend has grown, of course, that there is a lot of Moody's gold still buried in his cave.

Another tribute to his memory is in the story of the burning of the Mount Pleasant Presbyterian church in Middleton, Monmouth County, New Jersey, in June 1777. On this occasion, Moody is said to have descended on the church with a party of Hessians while the congregation was attending a prayer meeting. In the story, he took everyone prisoner and set fire to the church. Moody was not in that part of New Jersey in June 1777, nor would the British have given an untried "gentleman volunteer" the command over a raiding party of their own foreign mercenaries. In June 1777, James was recruiting men in Sussex County and keeping them in a holding pattern in the hope that General Howe would march through that part of New Jersey. In any case, the people he is said to have seized are the very ones that he later captured in his expedition against Tinton Falls in June 1779. This incident is reported in *The Royal Gazette* of June 24, 1779 and corresponds with James's own account. There is no mention of any church being burnt. One assumes that the two incidents have been confused and the first has taken on more glamour by having Moody the perpetrator.

People in Newton will still tell you that as small children they were threatened by their grandmothers, "If you don't behave, Moody will get you!" They may not have read his *Narrative*, but the memory of his raids and his Scarlet Pimpernel personality lives on.

Another scenario, from another source, this time about the second Mrs. Moody, is that on his way back from escaping from Washington's camp, sick and exhausted, Moody was passed from safe house to safe house, finally to be hidden by the newly widowed Jane Lynson. This kind beautiful lady nursed him back to health and in the process the two bereaved people fell in love. When Moody got back to New York, he sent for her, and the two were married. One would like this one to be true.

When this author visited Newton, she saw a new Moody legend taking shape. In a recent story printed in a local newspaper, it was said that Moody had first been a Patriot militia captain, and then had switched sides, pointing up just what kind of a renegade he was. The story was repeated on a local television interview celebrating the bicentennial of the American Revolution, and then in yet another newspaper article. When the last writer was asked for the source of this information, she referred the author to the first article and said, "The writer is very reliable. He must have a good reason for saying that."

The idea that James Moody had first been a Patriot, let alone commanded a company of rebel militia, seemed so preposterous that the present author hunted all over again through all the records she could find. Of course, nothing of the sort emerged. Then the truth dawned. The story had taken shape from a misreading of a passage in Snell's rather disjointed *History of Sussex and Warren Counties*. Here under a section headed, "Toryism — Lieut. James Moody," the historian gives an account of another man, a militia captain indeed turned Loyalist. Only three paragraphs later does Snell begin to discuss Moody. The twentieth century writer had leapt to the conclusion that the captain in the first paragraph was Moody. How easily legends are born, and stories spread.

Then there is Bonnell Moody, who never existed at all. He is at first Edsall's version of James. Eleven years later, in 1864, Lorenzo Sabine in his *Loyalists of the American Revolution*, gives him a separate entry. There were now two notorious Moodys: Bonnell of Sussex County, leader of a band of Tory marauders and James of Sussex County, author of the *Narrative*. Bonnell's exploits are cribbed from Edsall's account of the man who is really James, and James's from his own *Narrative*. Sabine attributes to each Moody the exploit of opening the Sussex County jail and freeing the prisoners — in almost identical circumstances — but adds that Bonnell and a companion were eventually captured by Whigs as they attempted to cross the Hudson to join the British, and then hung as traitors and spies. This ending sounds like a garbling of the account of the death of James's brother, John, in Philadelphia. Indeed James is often called John, even in contemporary accounts. One might almost say that he had by now become three entities.

There is no evidence that James Moody ever stole horses or robbed his neighbours or murdered. If there had been the slightest shred of evidence to support such charges, it would have been used against him in the trial that Washington and Livingston were planning for him.

But what of those, like Joe Mulliner, who were tried as felons and spies and did not escape? For them there is the dubious newspaper account of how hated they were and how at the end they repented. Or others who died on the battlefield? Men as well as officers? Who remembers their tenacity throughout the bitter war, who extols their bravery? Who has even heard of the Siege of Ninety Six or the Battle of Cowpens, or the holdout at the block house at Bull's Ferry? The fighters' names remain in tales of villainous acts and confused identity. Or perhaps not at all.

*

The Loyalists were a cross section of American colonial society. They were not a sinless aristocratic élite as some of their Canadian descendants like to imagine. Nor were they demented rogues and villains as many Americans wanted to believe. Many were poor and ill educated. A few were very rich. James was in between. He belonged to the upper-middle group in his society, a man who derived a comfortable living from the land he owned and supervised himself. When such a man made a substantial profit, he would invest his extra income in either more land or new projects, like mills, iron mines, or whatever, as the Ellisons and Bartons and Ogdens had done, laying the basis for the industrial development that was gathering momentum in the colonies.

However, it was the ownership of land that was the most important holding in a man's economic and social portfolio. In the eighteenth century, it above all else determined a man's status. The lure that brought people to America was the possibility of owning one's own land, a dream beyond most people's reach in England and Europe. As a consequence, in America there was never what the Europeans called a peasantry, despite James's use of that word. Nevertheless, between the small farmer who worked his own land as we think of the small farmer today, and a larger enterprise, such as James's, with servants or slaves to do the hard physical labour, the difference in social standing and education was wide. In prerevolutionary America, James had neither the university education of a lawyer that might lead to public office, like the Skinners, nor a lucrative business that would make him very rich, and therefore powerful, like the DeLanceys, nor the established land and connections that would give him status, like Washington. He was, however, a gentleman, a member of the lesser landed gentry as the English would phrase it, perfectly acceptable in any upper strata of society. When the war threw all these people together, he was an officer among them. Indeed, because so many people owned land and could therefore raise themselves socially in a generation, there was on both sides in the Revolution, an overabundance of officers and a dearth of rank and file. Some members of the officer class in the militias accepted to fight as simple soldiers during an emergency, as they did in the Halifax militia later, and in World War I much later.

A man in James's position in society received respect for his station from those in his community, and in turn was expected to provide leadership in times of trouble. When the Revolution broke out, people like James, on both sides of the controversy, rushed out to defend the cause they believed in — the Moodys, the Millidges, on one side, the Hoops, the Dickinsons, on the other, along with the Skinners, the DeLanceys, and the Washingtons. It was unthinkable that they would not have done so. All of them, no doubt, were convinced that it would be only for a short duration but, once committed, the conscientious people gave their all. James's story during the Revolution is particularly exciting because of the man himself, but Millidge and Barclay, for example, also had heroic war experiences. There are many moving accounts on both sides of tremendous courage and clever outmanoeuvering. There were cruelties on both sides, and betrayals, but also feats of great bravery and sacrifice and compassion. Indeed, the steadfastness on either side, and the fact that it was brother against brother, contributed to the exaggeration of villainy passed down in tradition. As civil wars go, it was, for all its heartache, extraordinarily gentlemanly.

The Loyalists could not believe that in this prosperous land there were Americans who could be so foolish as to disrupt the social fabric and actually want, let alone scheme and fight for, separation from Great Britain. They also could not believe that the British government did not have their best interests at heart and that they would not make the necessary reforms once they knew the true situation in America. They were caught unprepared. By the time they had worked out their own ideas, the initiative was with the revolutionaries. It took most of the war before the arrogant indifference of British authority disillusioned them. By then it was too late.

After the war is a different story. Now the Loyalists were brought closer to Great Britain. Immediately the British redeemed themselves in their superb evacuation of New York and their assisted settlement of the Loyalists on new land. Their generous financial compensation for war losses provided a working capital that allowed the refugees to rebuild quickly. The Americans had won the war, they knew they were in the right, and they continued in the ideals that had carried through the Revolution in their own land. The Loyalists in Nova Scotia, and the other parts of what is now Canada where they took refuge, had to start all over again from almost nothing, as they had in America several generations earlier, and this time on much meaner soil. They would do so with evolving British institutions. For James, it was repeating the labour he had already begun as a young man.

For the Loyalist refugees sheltering in New York, especially those who had seen actual fighting, the war had been a great melder, within the educated groups. People whose paths might not have crossed, like Franklin and Moody, were thrown into each other's company through their devotion to the common cause. The war had drawn together men from all thirteen colonies with a common set of values. They emerged with a vision of the kind of society they wanted to achieve, a society that would be just and equitable and orderly, so that no one would be tempted to rebel, a society based on British rights and freedoms. Resettling in familiar conditions where they could draw on past experience made it possible for them to carry out, in great measure, this vision.

James's contribution to this effort was remarkable. His energy and the vigour of his mind were used in the service of his new country. His exploits during the war, coupled with his decency, won him great respect, and as a consequence, not only the return of the full value of his prewar assets, but also a large unexpected legacy. This capital he invested locally in Nova Scotia. Within a year, in a small, isolated community, he established a shipbuilding industry that not only launched the second full-rigged ship to be built in Nova Scotia, but that over a period of six years produced seven ocean-going vessels, four of them full-rigged ships, totalling 1,420 tons. At the same time, he used the meagre soil to best advantage by establishing a sheep farm that supplied ewes to notables across the province. He also built a dam for a tidal grist and sawmill, and was partner in another sawmill.

Within the community from the very first he was a leader. He gave a tract of land as a site for an Anglican church, and oversaw its construction, believing that this institution would develop a stable, moderate, and law-abiding society. He worked tirelessly to bring about the formation of a parish, giving generously from his own pocket and lobbying with the religious and civil authorities on behalf of the community. Although he failed in his final objective, the church and the parish were all the easier to organize later because of the work he had done. In the same vein, he lent money to help others get established. He was a director of the new Agricultural Society, and a founder of two masonic lodges.

He sat in the Legislature for two Assemblies, where he joined forces with those fighting for the continued right of the House of Assembly to control money bills — both appropriation and revenue — against the attempts of the Council and the governor to take back this prerogative. In this, both he and the majority of the House were as determined as any American revolutionaries could have been to maintain the same rights and privileges for the lower House that were current in Great Britain. In so doing they laid the foundation of representative government.

With these colleagues, James pushed for judicial and militia reforms, for the organization of a needed infrastructure in new roads and bridges, lighthouses, and other protection against navigational hazards, and supported funds for fisheries, agriculture, and industries, to name but a few of his concerns. Measures for the betterment of the Aboriginals were attempted. The band of men sitting in the Legislature who laid the economic and civic base for the province at this crucial period were Loyalists from the same background as James, or pre-Loyalists like Tonge, stimulated by the new vigour that they brought. Under Loyalist leadership, Loyalist, pre-Loyalist, and Acadian united to defend their colony in what threatened to be another North American war.

This group of Loyalists, knit together through war and defeat, brought to their new land a rush of energy and talent, not unlike the Huguenots who left France after the Revocation of the Edict of Nantes, or the Hungarians who came to Canada in 1956. For the American refugees, their prewar lives had given them many of the skills they needed to succeed in Nova Scotia and Canada. For those who survived the brutalities of the war, as soldiers or civilians, even the harsh ordeal of Nova Scarcity was not insurmountable. Working together, they brought new ideas and determination. They brought to their new land their knowledge, their initiative, and their imagination. They had indeed been "obstinately loyal," but their misfortune soon transformed itself into the building of a new country. In the end, the American Revolution was a gift to Canada. James Moody and his fellow Loyalists have left us a rich legacy, a heritage that is too valuable to forget.

NOTES

1. Benjamin B. Edsall, "Centennial Address," *The First Sussex Centenary*, ed. Benjamin B. Edsall and Joseph F. Tuttle (Newark, NJ: 1853), 54.
2. Benjamin Franklin Swasey, *Genealogy of the Swasey Family which includes The Descendants of the Swezey Families of Southold, Long Island New York and The Descendants of the Swayze Families of Roxbury, now Chester New Jersey*, privately printed for Ambrose Swaysey (Cleveland, OH: 1910), 235.
3. All the accounts quoted above are given in a long footnote in Edsall's "Centennial Address," 55.

BIBLIOGRAPHY

Armour, Charles A., and Lackey, Thomas. *Sailing Ships of the Maritimes: An Illustrated History of Shipping and Shipbuilding in the Maritime Provinces of Canada, 1750-1925.* Toronto: McGraw-Hill Ryerson, 1975.

Atlas of Early American History: The Revolutionary Era, 1760-1790. Princeton, NJ: Princeton University Press, 1976.

Bailyn, Bernard P. *Ideological Origins of the American Revolution.* Cambridge, MA: Belknap Press, 1967.

———. *The Ordeal of Thomas Hutchinson.* Cambridge, MA: Belknap Press, 1974.

Bakeless, John. *Turncoats, Traitors and Heroes.* New York: J.B. Lippincott, 1959.

Baldwin, Ernest H. "Joseph Galloway, The Loyalist Politician," *The Pennsylvania Magazine of History and Biography* 26, no. 2 (1902): 161-91; no. 3, 289-321; no. 4, 417-42.

Barck, Oscar T. *New York City During the War for Independence.* New York: 1931.

Bell, D.G., ed. *The Newlight Baptist Journals of James Manning and James Innis.* Saint John, NB: Acadia Divinity College and the Baptist Historical Committee of the United Baptist Convention of the Atlantic Provinces, 1984.

Bell, Winthrop Pickard. *The "Foreign Protestants" and the Settlement of Nova Scotia: The History of a Piece of Arrested British Colonial Policy in the Eighteenth Century.* Toronto: University of Toronto Press, 1961; repr. for the Centre for Canadian Studies, Mount Allison University, 1992.

Binks, Robin W. *The Blacks in Canada: A History.* Montreal: McGill-Queen's University Press, 1971.

Blackman, Leah. *History of Little Egg Harbour Township, Burlington County, NJ from Its First Settlement to the Present Time.* Tuckerton, NJ: Great John Mathis Foundation, 1880; repr. 1963.

Blauveldt, Rupert B. *Holy Trinity-Anglican Church, Yarmouth, N.S.* Yarmouth, NS: 1972.

Boucher, Jonathan. *Reminiscences of an American Loyalist, 1738-1789.* Boston: Houghton Mifflin, 1925.

———. *A View of the Causes and Consequences of the American Revolution.* London: G.G. & J. Robinson, 1797.

———. *Letters of Jonathan Boucher to George Washington.* Ed. Worthington Chauncey Ford. New York: Repr. from the New England Historical Genealogical Register, Historical Printing Club, 1899.

Boudreau, Gerald C. "Doléances et indolence cléricales envers un peuple délaisssé," *Les cahiers de la société historique acadienne* 23, nos. 3, 4 (1992).

Brown, Wallace. *The Good Americans: Loyalists in the American Revolution*. New York: William Morrow, 1969.

———. *The King's Friends: The Composition and Motives of the American Loyalist Claimants*. Providence, RI: Brown University Press, 1966.

Brierley, James S. "A Pioneer History of Elgin County." Prize-winning School Essays published in the *Southern Counties Journal*. Saint Thomas, Ont.: 1896; repr. Pretoria, Ont.: 1971.

Brush, Theodore. "The Most Distinguished Partizan," *The North Jersey Highlander* 14, nos. 3, 4 (1979); 15, nos. 1, 2 (1980) (issues 52-55), Newfoundland, NJ.

Burnaby, Andrew. *Travels Through the Middle Settlements in North America, 1759-1760*. London: T. Payne, 1775.

Burr, Nelson R. *The Anglican Church in New Jersey*. Philadelphia: Church Historical Society, 1954.

Calhoon, R.M. *The Loyalists in Revolutionary America, 1760-1781*. New York: Harcourt Brace Jovanovich, 1973.

Callahan, North. *Flight from the Republic: The Tories of the American Revolution*. New York: Bobbs-Merrill, 1967.

Calnek, W.A. *History of the County of Annapolis*. Toronto: William Briggs, 1897; Canadian Reprint Series no. 30, Belleville, Ont.: Mika Publishing, 1980.

Chambers, Theodore Frelinghuysen. *The Early Germans of New Jersey: Their History, Churches, and Genealogies*. Baltimore: Genealogical Publishing, 1969.

Charlier, R.H. *Tidal Energy*. New York: Van Nostrand Reinhold, 1982.

Clinton, Sir Henry. *The American Rebellion: Sir Henry Clinton's Narrative of His Campaigns, 1775-1782*. Ed. William B. Wilcox. New York: Alfred A. Knopf, 1964.

———. Henry Clinton Papers, William L. Clements Library, Ann Arbor, Michigan.

Coldham, Peter Wilson, ed. *American Loyalist Claims*. Washington, DC: National Geneological Society, 1980.

Commager, Henry Steele, and Morris, Richard B., eds. *The Spirit of 'Seventy-Six: The Story of the American Revolution as Told by Participants*. New York: Harper & Row, 1975.

Condon, Ann. *The Envy of the American States: The Loyalist Dream for New Brunswick*. Fredericton, NB, 1984.

Conrad, Margaret, ed. *They Planted Well: New England Planters in Maritime Canada*. Fredericton, NB: Acadiensis Press, 1988.

———. *Making Adjustments: Change and Continuity in Planter Nova Scotia 1759-1800*. Fredericton, NB: Acadiensis Press, 1991.

Cook, Don. *The Long Fuse: How England Lost the American Colonies, 1760-1785*. New York: Atlantic Monthly Press, 1995.

Crary, Catherine S. *The Price of Loyalty: Tory Writings from the Revolutionary Era*. New York: McGraw-Hill, 1973.

Cresswell, Nicholas. *The Journal of Nicholas Cresswell, 1774-1777*. London: Jonathan Cape, 1925.

Cruikshank, E.A. *The Story of Butler's Rangers*. Welland: Lundy's Lane Historical Society, 1893.

Curwen, Samuel. *The Journal of Samuel Curwen*. Ed. Andrew Oliver. Cambridge, MA: Harvard University Press, 1972.

Cuthbertson, Brian. *The Old Attorney General: A Biography of Richard John Uniacke, 1753-1830*. Halifax: Nimbus Publishing, 1980.

———. *The Loyalist Governor: Biography of Sir John Wentworth*. Halifax: Petheric Press, 1983.

———. *The First Bishop: A Biography of Charles Inglis*. Halifax: Waegwoltic Press, 1987.

———. *Johnny Bluenose at the Polls: Epic Nova Scotia Election Battles, 1758-1848*. Halifax: Formac Publishing, 1994.

Davies, K.G., ed. *Documents of the American Revolution, 1770-1783*, Colonial Office Series, vol. 15, Transcripts, 1778. Dublin: Irish University Press, 1976.

Deveau, J. Alphonse. *Along the Shores of Saint Mary's Bay: The Story of a Unique Community*, vol. 1, *The First Hundred Years*. Church Point, NS: Imprimerie de l'Université Sainte Anne, 1977.

Dictionary of Canadian Biography, vols. 4, 5, 6, 7. Toronto: University of Toronto Press, 1979, 1983, 1987, 1988.

Dunlap, William. *History of the American Theatre, and Anecdotes of the Principal Actors*. Burt Franklin Research and Source Works Series, no. 36. New York: Burt Franklin, 1963.

Draper, Theodore. *A Struggle for Power: The American Revolution*. New York: Times Books, Random House, 1996.

Dyott, William. *Dyott's Diary, 1781-1845: A Selection from the Journal of William Dyott, Sometime General in the British Army and Aide-de-Camp to His Majesty King George III*. Edited by Reginald W. Jeffery. London: 1907.

Eardley-Wilmot, John. *Historical View of the Commission Enquiring into the Losses, Services and Claims of the American Loyalists, At the Close of the War Between Great Britain, and her Colonies, in 1783*. London: 1815; repr. Boston: The American Revolutionary Series, The Loyalist Library, Gregg Press, 1972.

Eddis, William. *Letters from America, Historical and Descriptive, Comprising Occurences from 1769-1777*. London: 1792; repr. New York: Eyewitness Accounts of the American Revolution, New York Times and Arno Press, 1969.

Edelberg, Cynthia Dubin. *Jonathan Odell: Loyalist Poet of the American Revolution*. Durham, NC: Duke University Press, 1987.

Edsall, Benjamin B. "Centennial Address." In *The First Sussex Centenary*, ed. Benjamin B. Edsall and Joseph F. Tuttle. Newark, NJ: 1853.

Einstein, Lewis. *Divided Loyalties: Americans in England during the War of Independence*. Freeport, NY: Books for Libraries Press, 1969.

Ells, Margaret. "The Development of Nova Scotia, 1782-1812," PhD draft, University of London, 1949.

Fingard, Judith. *The Anglican Design in Loyalist Nova Scotia, 1783-1816*. London: Church Historical Society, 1972.

Fitzpatrick, John C., ed. *The Writings of George Washington from the Original Manuscript Sources, 1745-1799*. 39 vols. Washington, DC: 1931-44.

Fleming, Thomas. *The Forgotten Victory: The Battle for New Jersey, 1780*. New York: Reader's Digest Press, 1901.

———. *New Jersey: A History*. New York: W.W. Norton, 1977.

Flick, Alexander C. *Loyalism in New York during the American Revolution*. New York: Columbia University Press, 1901.

Ford, Corey. *A Peculiar Service*. Toronto: Little, Brown, 1965.

Fowler, David J. "Egregious Villains, Wood Rangers, and London Traders: The Pine Robber Phenomenon in New Jersey during the Revolutionary War," PhD thesis, Rutgers University, 1987.

Gaine, Hugh. *The Journals of Hugh Gaine, Printer*. Ed. Paul Leicester Ford, vol. 2. New York: Dodd, Mead, 1901.

Galloway, Grace Crowden. *Diary of Grace Growden Galloway*. Ed. R.C. Werner. New York: Eyewitness Accounts of the American Revolution, Series III, New York Times and Arno Press, 1971.

Gardiner, W.W. "The Impertinent Loyalist," *The Atlantic Advocate* 47 (Aug. 1957): 61-65.

Gerlach, Larry R. *Prologue to Independence: New Jersey in the Coming of the American Revolution*. New Brunswick, NJ: Rutgers University Press, 1976.

———, ed. *New Jersey in the American Revolution: A Documentary History*. New Brunswick, NJ: New Jersey Historical Commission, 1976.

Gillen, Mollie. *The Prince and His Lady: The Love Story of the Duke of Kent and Madame de Saint Laurent*. Halifax: Sidgwick & Jackson, 1970; Goodread Biographies, 1985.

Gilroy, Marion. *Loyalists and Land Settlement in Nova Scotia*. Halifax: Public Archives of Nova Scotia, 1937.

Goldenbert, Joseph A. "With Saw and Axe and Auger: Three Centuries of American Shipbuilding." In *Material Culture of the Wooden Age*, ed. Brooke Hindle. Tarrytown, NY: Sleepy Hollow Press, 1981.

Griffiths, N.E.S. *The Acadians: Creation of a People*. The Frontenac Library, ed. Geoffrey Melburn, Althouse College of Education, University of Western Ontario. Toronto: McGraw-Hill Ryerson, 1973.

———. *The Contexts of Acadian History, 1686-1784*. The 1988 Winthrop Pickard Bell Lectures in Maritime Studies, published for the Centre for Canadian Studies, Mount Allison University. Montreal and Kingston: McGill-Queen's University Press, 1992.

Haarman, Albert. "Some Notes on American Provincial Uniforms, 1776-
    1783," *Journal of the Society for Army Historical Research* 199 (1971):
    141-51.
Haliburton, Thomas C. *History of Nova Scotia*, 2 vols. Halifax: Joseph
    Howe, 1829; repr. Belleville: Ont.: Mika Publishing, 1973.
Harris, Reginald V. *The Beginnings of Freemasonry in Canada*. Halifax, NS: n.d.
Hart, Charles H. "Letters from William Franklin to William Strahan,"
    Pennsylvania Magazine of History and Biography 35 (1911): 415-62.
Hatch, Robert McConnell. *Major John André: A Gallant in Spy's Clothing*.
    Boston: Houghton Mifflin, 1986.
Hill, Norman Howell. *History of Knox County, Ohio*. Mt. Vernon, OH: A.A.
    Graham, 1881.
————. *History of Licking County, Ohio*. Newark, OH: A.A. Graham, 1881.
Hindle, Brooke, ed. *America's Wooden Age: Aspects of its Early Technology*.
    Tarrytown, NY: Sleepy Hollow Restorations, 1975.
Historical Atlas of Canada, vol. 1, *From the Beginning to 1800*. Toronto:
    University of Toronto Press, 1987.
Honeyman, A. Van Doren. "Concerning the New Jersey Loyalists in the
    Revolution," *Proceedings of the New Jersey Historical Society* 51, no. 2
    (April 1933).
Hutchinson, Thomas. *The Diary and Letters of His Excellency Thomas
    Hutchinson, Esq*. Ed. Peter Orlando Hutchinson, 2 vols. Boston:
    Houghton, Mifflin, 1884.
————. *The History of the Province of Massachusetts Bay*. London: 1828.
Inglis, Charles. Journals and Papers. Public Archives of Canada, Transcripts,
    MG23, C6, Ser. 1, vols. 1-6.
Jensen, Arthur L. *Maritime Commerce of Colonial Philadelphia*. Madison, WI:
    State Historical Society of Wisconsin for the Department of History,
    University of Wisconsin, 1963.
Jones, Alfred E. *The Loyalists of New Jersey*. Newark, NJ: New Jersey
    Historical Society, 1927; collections of the New Jersey Society, vol. 10.
Jones, Thomas. *History of New York during the Revolutionary War*, 2 vols.
    New York: New York Historical Society, 1879.
Journals and Proceedings of the House of Assembly of Nova Scotia. Halifax:
    1785-1810.
*Journals of the Continental Congress: Edited from the original records in the
    Library of Congress*, vol. 21 (July 23-Dec. 31, 1781). Ed. Gaillard
    Hung. Washington, DC: U.S. Government Printing Office, 1912.
Klein, Milton M. "The American Whig: William Livingston of New York,"
    PhD thesis, Columbia University, 1954.
————. *The Politics of Diversity: Essays in the History of Colonial New York*.
    Port Washington, NY: Kennikat Press, 1974.
Lamb, John. Col. John Lamb's Papers, New York Historical Society.
Leake, Isaac Q. *Memoir of the Life and Times of General John Lamb, an*

Officer of the Revolution, who Commanded the Post at West Point at the Time of Arnold's Defection and his Correspondence with Washington, Clinton, Patrick Henry, and Other Distinguished Men of his Time. Albany: Joel Munsell, 1850.

Lee, Capt. Joseph. Letter to Lt. Edward Stelle, 3rd Battalion, New Jersey Volunteers, Ninety-Six, South Carolina, June 18, 1781. The Papers of the Continental Congress, compiled by John P. Butler, vol. 3, 1978, National Archives, Washington, DC.

———. Letter to Lt. Col. Isaac Allen, 3rd Battalion, New Jersey Volunteers, Ninety-Six, South Carolina, June 18, 1781. The Papers of the Continental Congress, compiled by John P. Butler, vol. 3, 1978, National Archives, Washington, DC.

Levitt, James H. *For Want of Trade: Shipping and the New Jersey Ports, 1680-1783.* Newark: New Jersey Historical Society, 1981.

Levy, George Edward. *The Baptists of the Maritime Provinces, 1753-1946.* Saint John: Barnes-Hopkins, 1946.

Livingston, William. *The Papers of William Livingston.* Ed. Carl E. Prince et al. 4 vols. Trenton, NJ: New Jersey Historical Commission, 1979, 1980, 1986, 1987.

Lossing, Benson F. *The Pictorial Field-Book of the Revolution, or illustrations by pen and pencil of the history, biography, scenery, relics, and traditions of the war of independence.* New York: Harper and Brothers, 1859; repr. Rutland, VT: Charles E. Tuttle, 1972. 2 vols.

Loyalist Claims. Public Record Office, AO/12 and 13. Microfilm, National Archives of Canada.

Lord, Eleanor Louisa. *Industrial Experiments in the British Colonies of North America.* New York: Burt Franklin, 1898; repr. 1969.

Lundin, Leonard. *Cockpit of the Revolution: The War for Independence in New Jersey.* Princeton: Princeton University Press, 1940.

MacFarland, Philip. *The Brave Bostonians: Hutchinson, Quincy, Franklin and the Coming of the American Revolution.* Boulder, CO; and Oxford, U.K.: Westview Press, 1998.

MacKenzie, Frederick. *Diary of Frederick MacKenzie: Giving a Daily Narrative of his Military Service as an Officer of the Regiment of Royal Welch Fusiliers during the Years 1775-1781 in Massachusetts, Rhode Island and New York,* vol. 2. Cambridge, MA: Harvard University Press, 1930.

MacKinnon, Neil. *This Unfriendly Soil: The Loyalist Experience in Nova Scotia, 1783-1791.* Montreal: McGill-Queen's University Press, 1986.

MacNutt, W. Stewart. *New Brunswick: A History, 1784-1867.* Toronto: Macmillan, 1963.

———. "Introduction to Lt. James Moody's Narrative," *Acadiensis* 1, no. 2 (1971-72): 72-90.

Mariboe, William H. "The Life of William Franklin, 1730-1813: 'Pro Rege et Patria,'" PhD thesis, University of Pennsylvania, 1962.

Mathews, Hazel C. *The Mark of Honour*. Toronto: University of Toronto Press, 1956.

Mellick, Andrew D., Jr. *Lesser Crossroads*. Ed. Hubert G. Schmidt, from *The Story of an Old Farm*. New Brunswick, NJ: Rutgers University Press, 1948.

Middlekauf, Robert. *The Glorious Cause: The American Revolution, 1763-1789*. New York: Oxford University Press, 1982.

Minchinton, W.E. "Early Tide Mills: Some Problems," *Technology and Culture* 20 (1979): 777-86.

Moody, James. *Lieut. James Moody's Narrative of His Exertions and Sufferings in the Cause of Government, Since the Year 1776; authenticated by proper certificates*. London: 1782, 1783; repr. New York: The New York Times and Arno Press, 1968.

———. Moody Family Papers, previously in the possession of John Wentworth Moody, Ottawa, now in the Public Archives of Nova Scotia, Halifax, NS.

———. Claim for losses and services. PRO, AO 12/13, AO 12/99, AO 12/109. AO 13/110. Microfilm, National Archives of Canada.

Moore, Frank. *Diary of the American Revolution from Newspapers and Original Documents*. New York: 1860.

Morison, Samuel Eliot, and Commager, Henry Steele. *The Growth of the American Republic*, vol. 1. New York; Toronto: Oxford University Press, 1942.

Murdoch, Beamish. *A History of Nova Scotia or Acadie*. Halifax: James Barnes, 1867.

Nash, Howard P. "James Moody, British Partisan of the Revolutionary War," *Transactions: The American Lodge of Research, Free and Accepted Masons* 2, no. 2 (1936): 338-51.

Nelson, William H. *The American Tory*. Oxford: Clarendon Press, 1961.

New Jersey, State of. *Archives of the State of New Jersey*. Ed. W.A. Whitehead et al. Series 1 and 2. Newark and elsewhere, 1880-1949.

———. *Minutes of the Council of Safety of the State of New Jersey*. Jersey City: John H. Lyon, 1872.

———. *Minutes of the Provincial Congress and the Council of Safety of the State of New Jersey, 1774-1777*. Trenton, NJ: Near, Day and Near, 1879.

———. *Documents Relating to the Colonial History of the Sate of New Jersey*. Ed. William Nelson, et al. *Extracts from American Newspapers, Relating to New Jersey*, 1766-67, 1768-69, 1770-71, 1772-73, 1776-77, 1778, 1779, Nov. 1, 1779-Sept. 30, 1780. Trenton, NJ: New Jersey Historical Society, 1901-14.

———. *The Minutes of the Governor's Council, 1779-1789, New Jersey Archives*. Ed. David A. Bernstein, Series 3, vol. 1. Trenton, NJ: 1974.

Norton, Mary Beth. *The British Americans: The Loyalist Exiles in England, 1774-1789.* Boston: Little, Brown, 1972.

Papers of the Continental Congress. The National Archives. Washington, DC.

Peckham, H.H., ed. *Sources of American Independence,* 2 vols. Chicago: University of Chicago Press, 1978.

Pennypacker, Morton. *General Washington's Spies.* Brooklyne, New York: Long Island Historical Society, 1939.

Perkins, Simeon. *The Diary of Simeon Perkins,* vol. 2 (1780-89), ed. D.C. Harvey. Toronto: Champlain Society, 1958; vol. 3 (1790-96), ed. Charles Bruce Fergsson. Toronto: Champlain Society, 1961.

Pierce, Arthur D. *Smugglers' Woods.* New Brunswick, NJ: Rutgers University Press, 1960.

Porter, McKenzie. *Overture to Victoria.* Toronto: Longmans Green, 1961.

Randall, Willard S. *A Little Revenge: Benjamin Franklin and His Son.* Boston: Little, Brown, 1984.

————. *Benedict Arnold: Patriot and Traitor.* New York: William Morrow, 1990.

————. *George Washington: A Life.* New York: Henry Holt (John MacRae Books), 1997.

Rawlyk, George A. *Champions of Truth: Fundamentalism, Modernism and the Maritime Baptist.* 1987-88 Winthrop Pickard Bell Lectures in Maritime Studies, published for the Centre of Canadian Studies, Mount Allison University. Montreal: McGill-Queen's University Press, 1990.

————. *Ravished by the Spirit: Religious Revivals, Baptists and Henry Alline.* Montreal: McGill-Queen's University Press, 1987.

Raymond, W.O. "Roll of Officers of the British American or Loyalist Corps," *Collections of the New Brunswick Historical Society* 5 (1909): 224-72.

————. *The United Empire Loyalists.* Saint John, NB, 1893.

————, ed. *The Winslow Papers.* Saint John, NB: The Sun Printing Co., 1901.

Reynolds, Paul R. *Guy Carleton: A Biography.* Toronto: Gage, 1980.

Rives, George Lockart. *Selections from the Correspondence of Thomas Barclay.* New York: 1894.

Robertson, Barbara R. "Tide Mills: A Past for the Present," *The Occasional* 4, no. 2 (1976-77): 25-32.

Ross, Sally, and Deveau, J. Alphonse. *The Acadians of Nova Scotia, Past and Present.* Halifax: Nimbus Publishing, 1992.

Ruttember, E.M. and Clark, L.H. *History of Orange County, New York.* Philadelphia: Everts and Peck, 1881.

Ryerson, Egerton. *The Loyalists of America and Their Times,* 2 vols. Toronto: W. Briggs, 1880.

Sabine, Lorenzo. *Biographical Sketches of the Loyalists of the American Revolution,* 2 vols. Boston: 1864; repr. Baltimore, MD: Genealogical Publishing, 1979.

Salter, Edwin. *History of Monmouth and Ocean Counties*. Bayonne, NJ: E. Gardner & Son, 1890.

————, and Beekman, George C., *Old Times in Old Monmouth: Historical Reminiscences of Old Monmouth County*. Freehold, NJ: 1887.

Serle, Ambrose. *The American Journal of Ambrose Serle, 1776-1778: Secretary to Lord Howe*. Ed. E.H. Tatum, Jr. San Marino, CA: 1940.

Shenstone, Susan Burgess. "Loyalist Squire, Loyalist Church," *Nova Scotia Historical Review* 3, no. 2 (1983): 71-88.

————. "*The Loyalist*: Genesis of a Ship," *Nova Scotia Historical Review* 11, no. 2 (1991): 65-74.

Shy, John. "A New Look at Colonial Militia," *William and Mary Quarterly*, 3d ser., 20 (1963): 175-85.

————. *A People Numerous and Armed*. New York: Oxford University Press, 1976.

Siebert, William Henry. *The Loyalists of Pennsylvania*. Boston: Gregg Press, 1972.

Skinner, Stephen. Letter Book, 1780-1793. New York Historical Society.

————. Diary of Stephen Skinner, 1783-1787. *Public Archives of Nova Scotia Reports*, 1968.

————. Ledger, Jan. 1786-Dec. 1791. Public Archives of Nova Scotia.

Smith, Joshua Hett. *An Authentic Narrative of the Causes which led to the death of Major André, Adjutant-General of his Majesty's Forces in North America*. New York: 1809.

Smith, Paul H. "The American Loyalists: Notes on Their Organization and Numerical Strength," *William and Mary Quarterly*, 3d ser., 25 (1968): 259-77.

————. *Loyalists and Redcoats: A Study in British Revolutionary Policy*. Chapel Hill, NC: University of North Carolina Press, 1964.

————. "New Jersey Loyalists and the British 'Provincial' Corps in the War for Independence," *New Jersey History* 87 (1969): 69-78.

Smith, William. *Historical Memoirs from 26 August 1778 to 12 November 1783 of William Smith*. Ed. William H.W. Sabine. New York: Eyewitness Accounts of the American Revolution, Series III, The New York Times and Arno Press, 1971.

————. *The Diary and Selected Papers of Chief Justice William Smith, 1784-1793*. Toronto: Champlain Society, 1965.

Snell, James P. *History of Sussex and Warren Counties, New Jersey*, 2 vols. Philadelphia: Everts and Peck, 1881; repr. Washington, NJ: Centennial Edition, Genealogical Researchers, 1981.

————. *History of Hunterdon and Somerset Counties, New Jersey*. Philadelphia: Everts and Peck, 1881.

Society for the Propagation of the Gospel. Original Letters from New Jersey, vol. 24, Library of Congress microfilm 10,020.

Society for the Propagation of the Gospel. Journals, vols. 24, 25, 28. National Archives of Canada. MG17 B1, reels 156, 157, 158.

Spicer, Stanley T. *Masters of Sail: The Era of Square-rigged Vessels in the Maritime Provinces.* Toronto: McGraw-Hill Ryerson, 1968.

Stewart, Gordon, and Rawlyk, George. *A People Highly Favoured of God.* Toronto: Macmillan, 1972.

Stokesbury, James L. *A Short History of the American Revolution.* New York: Quill, William Morrow, 1991.

Stryker, William S. *The New Jersey Volunteers: Loyalists in the Revolutionary War.* Trenton, NJ: 1887.

Sutherland, Stuart R.J. "Moody, James." *Dictionary of Canadian Biography, 1801-1820,* vol. 5. Ed. Frances G. Halpenny. Toronto: University of Toronto Press, 1983: 604-05.

Swasey, Benjamin Franklin. *Genealogy of the Swasey Family, which includes The Descendants of the Swezey Families of Southold, Long Island, New York, and The Descendants of the Swayze Families of Roxbury, now Chester, New Jersey.* Cleveland, OH: Ambrose Swaysey, 1910.

Swiggett, Howard. *War Out of Niagara: Walter Butler and the Tory Rangers.* Port Washington, NY: Empire State Historical Publications, Ira Friedman, 1963.

Trebbenhoff, Edward H. "The Associated Loyalists: An Aspect of Militant Loyalism," *New York Historical Society Quarterly* 63 (1979): 115-44.

Valentine, Alan. *Lord Stirling.* New York: Oxford University Press, 1969.

Van Doren, Carl. *Secret History of the American Revolution.* New York: Viking Press, 1941.

Van Name, Elmer Garfield. *Britton Genealogy: Early Generations from Somersetshire, England to Staten Island, New York.* Gloucester County Historical Society Publications, Oct. 1970.

Van Tyne, Claude H. *The Loyalists in the American Revolution.* New York: 1902.

Viets, Rev. Roger. Notitia Parochialis of Trinity Parish, Digby, Nova Scotia, Beginning July 12, 1786. Transcript. Public Archives of Nova Scotia.

———. Annapolis Royal: A Poem, 1788. Halifax: A. Henry, 1788; repr. Kingston: Loyal Colonies Press, 1979.

Walker, James W. *The Black Loyalists.* Halifax: 1976.

Wand, Clarence. "The Story of Brooke Watson," *The New Brunswick Magazine* 1, no. 2 (Aug. 1898): 96-103.

Washington, George. *Writings.* See Fitzpatrick.

———. The George Washington Papers. Manuscript Division, Library of Congress.

Whitehead, William A. *Contributions to the Early History of Perth Amboy.* New York: 1856.

Whitehead, William A. "A Biographical Sketch of William Franklin, Governor from 1763 to 1776," *Proceedings of the New Jersey Historical Society* 3 (1848-49): 137-59.

————. "The Robbery of the Treasury of East Jersey in 1768, and Contemporary Events," *Proceedings of the New Jersey Historical Society* 5 (presented Sept. 12, 1850): 49-65.

Who Was Who in America, 1607-1896. Chicago: 1963.

Wilcox, William B. *Portrait of a General: Sir Henry Clinton in the War of Independence.* New York: Alfred A. Knopf, 1964.

Wilson, Isaiah W. *A Geography and History of the County of Digby, Nova Scotia.* Halifax: Holloway Bros., 1900; Canadiana Reprint Series no. 39, Belleville, Ont.: Mika Publishing, 1985.

Wilson, Thomas B. *Notices from New Jersey Newspapers, 1781-1790*, vol. 1, *Records of New Jersey.* Lambertville, NJ: Hunterdon House, 1988.

Wright, Esther C. *The Loyalists of New Brunswick.* Hantsport, NS: Lancelot Press, 1981.

Young, Philip. *Revolutionary Ladies.* New York: Alfred A. Knopf, 1977.

Zimmer, Anne Y. *Jonathan Boucher: Loyalist in Exile.* Detroit: Wayne State University Press, 1978.

INDEX